MODEL RAILWAY PROJECTS MANUAL

ANDREW DUCKWORTH

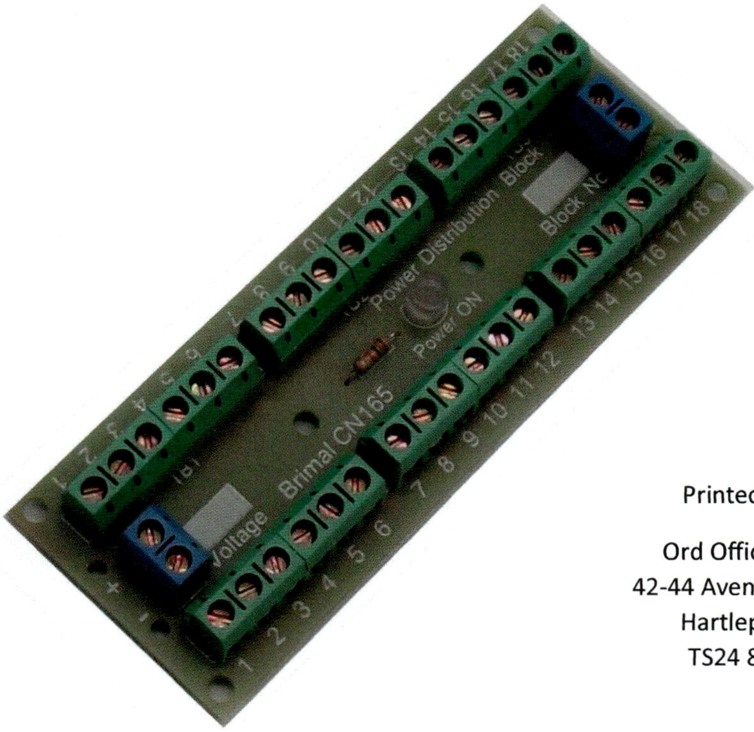

Printed by

Ord Office Ltd
42-44 Avenue Road
Hartlepool
TS24 8AT

Printed August 2021

2nd Print November 2021

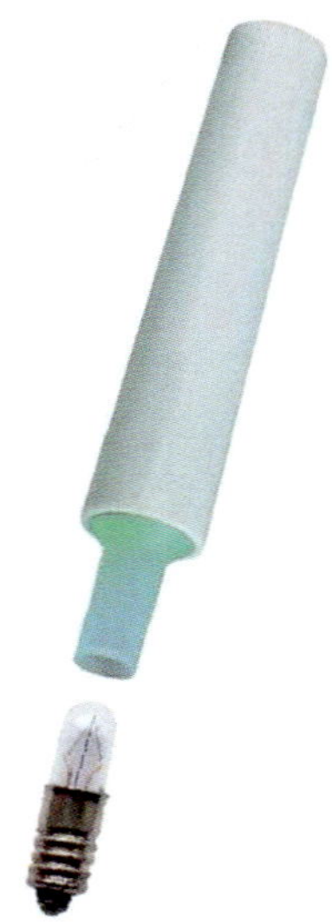

Published by

Brimal Consultants Ltd

MODEL RAILWAY PROJECTS

PROJECTS

Wiring a Layout

Equipment Wire

Introduction.

Equipment wire comes in two forms, Solid wire is composed of a single piece of copper wire, also known as a strand. Stranded wire is composed of many pieces of solid copper wire all bundled into one group. Stranded wire is much more flexible than solid wire of equal size. Conversely, solid wire is used when little or no movement is needed.

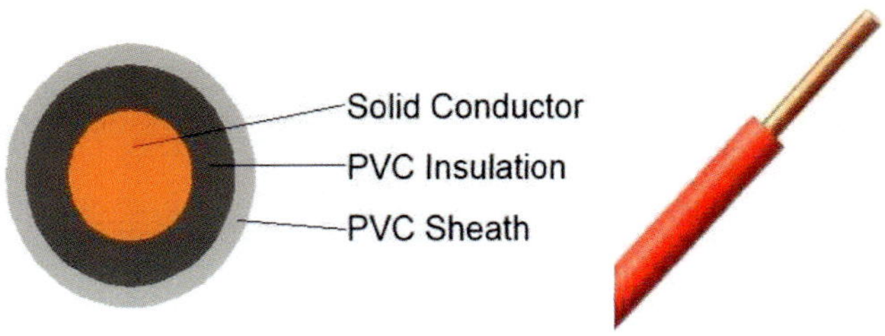

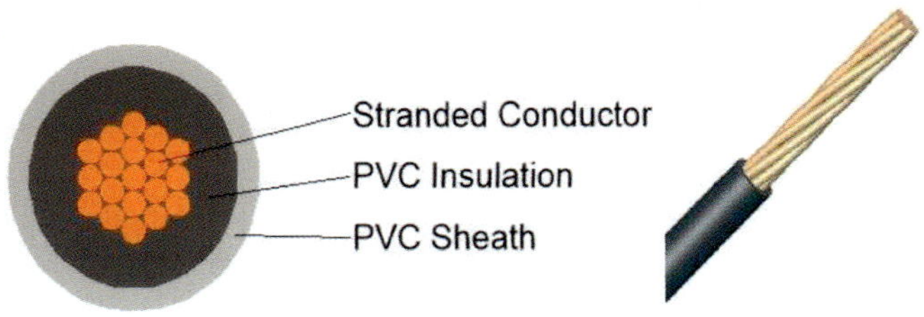

The method of describing wire appears at first complicated, but in fact is very simple once you know. The first number refers to the number of strands, the second number refers to the diameter of each strand in millimetres. For example, 16/0.2mm is 16 strands of 0.2mm wire, or 1/0.6mm is 1 strand of 0.6mm wire. In general, the more strands the wire has, the higher the current carrying capability.

In a Model Rail system your individual pieces of equipment may all use the same voltage but will probably all have different current requirements. Therefore we concentrate on the current rating of the wire, and not so much the voltage. When you run 2 or more pieces of equipment you must add the current used by each piece together and then check that the wire you will use can carry that amount of current.
Here is a list of the most commonly used wires in Model Railway with their current rating.

1/0.254(0.02mm sq) **500mA**

Single strand wire it stays in its formed shape without cable ties.
Rating: 0.5 A @ 1,000V RMS max
O/D: 0.55 mm nominal
Wall cover: PVC 0.15 mm to MIL- 81822/13;
Rolls: CB700-CB709
Spools: CB720-CB729

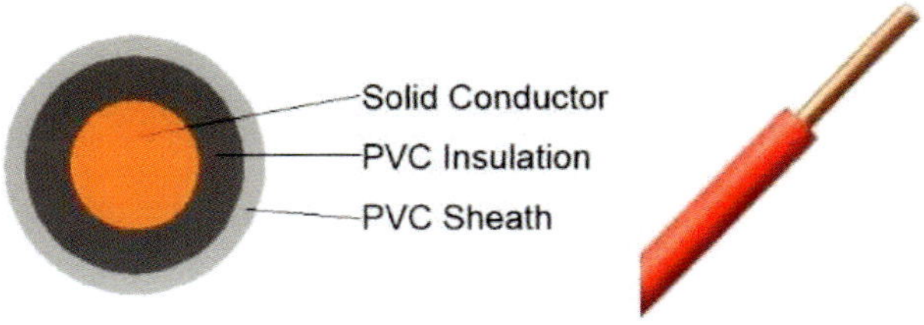

Primary use: Inside signals and Locomotive, anywhere space is at a premium. This wire is very thin and as you can see has only 0.5A (500mA) current rating. It therefore can only be used to power low current equipment such as LED's, and data transfer within the Locomotive body.

1/0.6(0.02mm sq) **1.8A**

Single strand wire it stays in its formed shape without cable ties
Rating: 1.8 A @ 1,000V RMS max
O/D: 1.2 mm nominal
Wall cover: PVC 0.3 mm to DEF61-12 Type2
Rolls: CB058-CB065
Spools: CB070-CB079

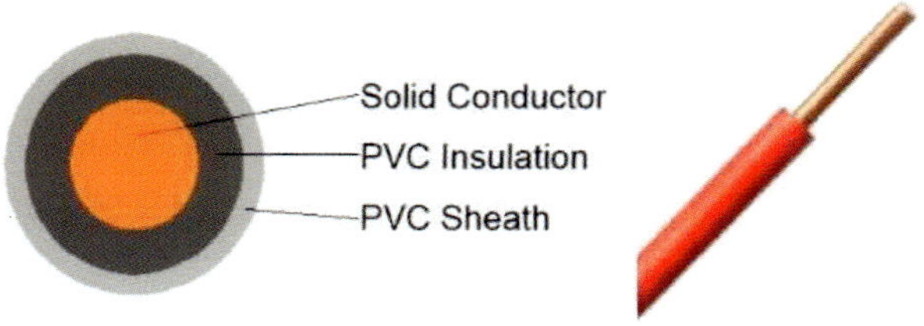

Primary use: Individual points and signals

7/0.2(0.02mm sq)

1.4A

Multistrand wire, it requires cable ties to hold in Place
Rating: 1.4 A @ 1,000V RMS max
O/D 1.2 mm nominal
Wall cover: PVC 0.3 mm to DEF61-12 Type2
Rolls: CB101-CB109
Spools: CB020-CB029
Primary use: Individual points and signals

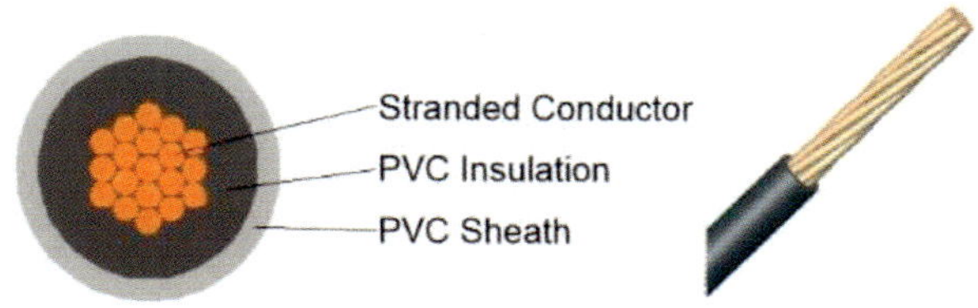

16/0.2(0.05mm sq)

3.0A

Multistrand wire, it requires cable ties to hold in place
Rating: 3.0 A @ 1,000V RMS max
O/D: 1.6 mm nominal
Wall cover: PVC 0.3 mm to DEF61-12 Type 2
Rolls: CB120-CB131
Spools: CB132-CB143
Primary use: Individual points and signals

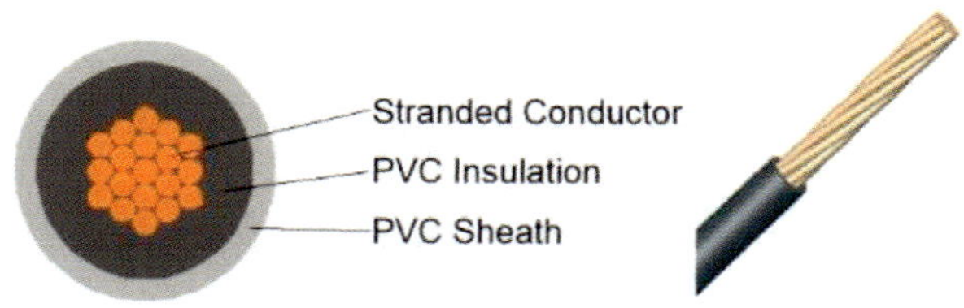

25/0.2(0.75mm sq)

4.5A

Multistrand wire, it requires cable ties to hold in place
Rating: 4.5 A @ 1,000V RMS max
O/D: 2.3 mm nominal
Wall cover: PVC 0.6 mm to DEF61-12 Type 2
Rolls: CB144-CB154
Spools: CB155-CB165
Primary use: Individual points and signals

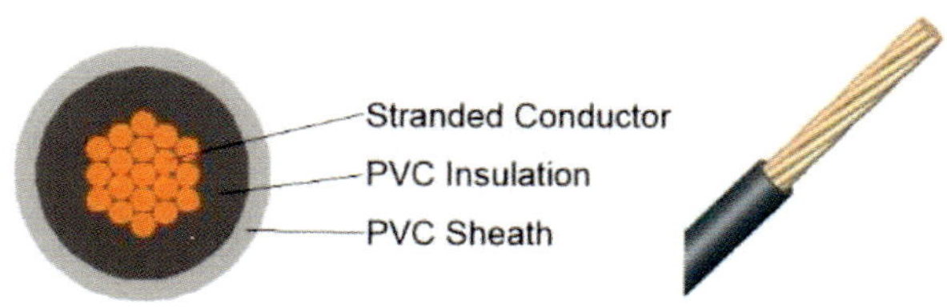

32/0.2(1.00mm sq)

6.0A

Multistrand wire, it requires cable ties to hold in place
Rating: 6.0 A @ 1,000V RMS max
O/D: 2.6 mm nominal
Wall cover: PVC 0.3 mm to DEF61-12 Type 2
Rolls: CB180-CB189
Spools: CB191-CB199b
Primary use: Individual points and signals

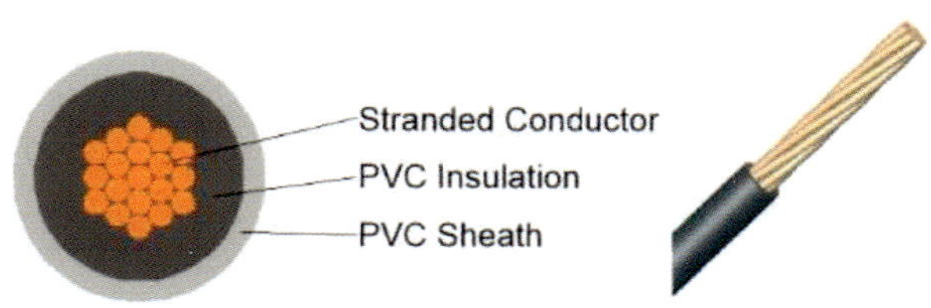

	BLACK	RED	GREY	BLUE	BROWN	YELLOW	GREEN	WHITE	ORANGE	GREEN/ YELLOW	VIOLET	PINK
1/0.6mm Single Core Wire (1.8 Amps)												
10m	CB072	CB076	CB071	CB073	CB070	CB077	CB074	CB078	CB075			
100M	CB060	CB064	CB059	CB061	CB058	CB066	CB062	CB065	CB063			
7/0.2mm Stranded Wire (1.4 Amps)												
10m	CB021	CB020	CB026	CB027	CB023	CB025	CB022	CB024	CB028		CB029	
100M	CB102	CB104	CB106	CB105	CB101	CB107	CB103	CB109	CB108		CB099	
16/0.2mm Stranded Wire (3.0 Amps)												
10m	CB132	CB133	CB134	CB135	CB136	CB137	CB138	CB139	CB142	CB140	CB141	CB143
100M	CB120	CB121	CB122	CB123	CB124	CB125	CB126	CB127	CB130	CB128	CB129	CB131
24/0.2mm Stranded Wire (4.5 Amps)												
10m	CB156	CB155	CB164	CB157	CB161	CB159	CB158	CB160	CB163		CB162	CB165
100M	CB145	CB144	CB153	CB146	CB150	CB148	CB147	CB149	CB152		CB151	CB154
32/0.2mm Stranded Wire (10 Amps)												
10m	CB192	CB191	CB199	CB195	CB194	CB198	CB193	CB197	CB196		CB199B	CB199A

100M	CB181	CB180	CB188	CB184	CB183	CB187	CB182	CB186	CB185		CB190	CB189

Multicore Cables

7/0.2(0.02mm sq) Multicore Cable

1.4 Amps per Core

This cable is available in 4, 6, 8 core, 12 core, 18 core, 25 core

Rating: 1.4 A @ 1,000V RMS max per core

O/D: 4c = 3.5mm, 6c =4.1mm,
8c = 4.6mm, 12c = 6.0mm,
18c = 7.3mm, 25c=8.7mm

Wall cover: PVC 0.3 mm to DEF61-12 Type 2

Rolls: CB599-CB641

Spools: CB598-CB640

Primary use: Individual points and signals

16/0.2(0.5mm sq) Multicore Cable

1.6 Amps per Core

This cable is available in 3 core, 6 core,

Rating: 1.6 A @ 1,000V RMS max per core

O/D: 3c = 5.3mm, 6c =6.4mm

Wall cover: PVC 0.3 mm to DEF61-12 Type 2

Rolls: CB650-CB651

Primary use: Individual points and signals

Where there are 2 colours on the strand the base colour is the first colour and the strip is the second colour

Colour	3 Core	4 Core	6 Core	8 Core	12 Core	18 Core	25 Core
Red	X	X	X	X	X	X	X
Black	X	X	X	X	X	X	X
Yellow		X	X	X	X	X	X
Blue	X	X	X	X	X	X	X
White			X	X	X	X	X
Green			X	X	X	X	X
Brown				X	X	X	X
Orange				X	X	X	X
Grey					X	X	X
Pink					X	X	X
Purple					X	X	X
Turquoise					X	X	X
White/Red						X	X
Yellow/Red						X	X
Green/Red						X	X
Red/Blue						X	X
Red/Brown						X	X
Red/Black						X	X
Grey/Blue							X
Yellow/Green							X
Green/Blue							X
White/Blue							X
Orange /Blue							X
Blue/Black							X
Yellow/Blue							X

Screened Equipment Wire

Why would you want to use Screened Wire.

All electrical wire and equipment create noise either radiated or conducted as EMI (electromagnetic Interference), this can seriously disrupt the proper operation of equipment near the wire. This is not the place to go into the science behind this, It is important to state that the average Model Rail Layout will not suffer from the effects of EMI, but if you are using sensitive electronic modules, as used in DCC systems, there is a greater possibility.
The effects of EMI are that things happen that you don't expect, or you have not initiated, or things don't work when they should.

How do we solve this:

We must mention at this point that some people say that twisting the cable together solves the problem, there is some truth in this, but can be very difficult to achieve. In straight cable, all noise current is flowing in the same direction. When the cable is twisted, in some parts of the signal lines the direction of the noise current is the opposite from the current in other parts of the cable. Because of this, the resulting noise current is many factors lower than with an ordinary straight cable.

The alternative is to use Screened cable. The shield can act on the EMI in two ways. First it can reflect the energy. Second it can pick up the noise and conduct it to ground. (This is important 'to ground', if you use Screened cable you must Earth one end, otherwise it has nowhere to put the noise.)
Screened Cable normally has a foil sleeve and then wire braid and finally the plastic outer protective covering. The braid is a woven mesh of bare or tinned copper wires. The braid provides a low-resistance path to Earth. The effectiveness of the braid depends on the tightness of the weave, EMI will get through the holes in the weave, so the tighter the weave the better.

A shield system is only as good as its weakest component. If you do not tie the braid to earth then it will not work. Placing shielded cable between point A and B without earthing it, is a waste of time.

Termination of Wires

The equipment you have purchased will normally have short wires (100 to 200mm long) which will need to be terminated in a terminal block under the baseboard. From this terminal block extension wires are run to the control panel, these wires must be selected correctly. If they are just powering the one piece then the extension wire can be run in 7/0.2 or 16/0.2, if they are common wires they may need to be larger 24/0.2 or 32/0.2, or a Bus Bar can be used.

There are many types of Terminal blocks it comes down to a personal choice, do you want screw type or solder type here we are showing just a few. The basic terminal block (some people call it a chocolate block), these normally come in a length of 12 terminals, and various current ratings, but can be cut to any length required. (CN171)

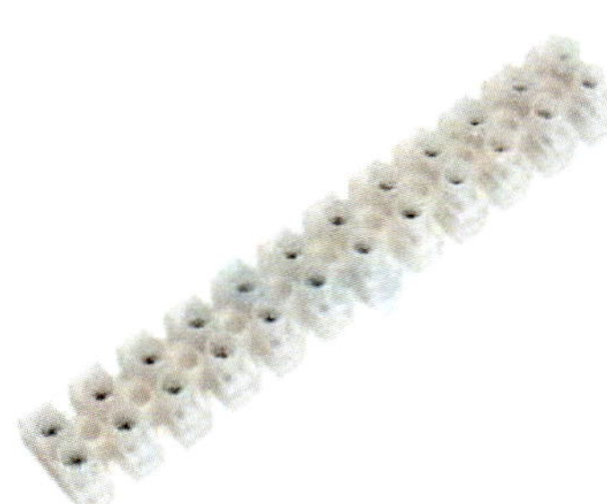

The pluggable terminal block, again comes in 12 terminals & various current ratings and are easy to cut into desired lengths. These are ideal for places where you have removable sections of layout, or your whole layout is demountable. (CN179)

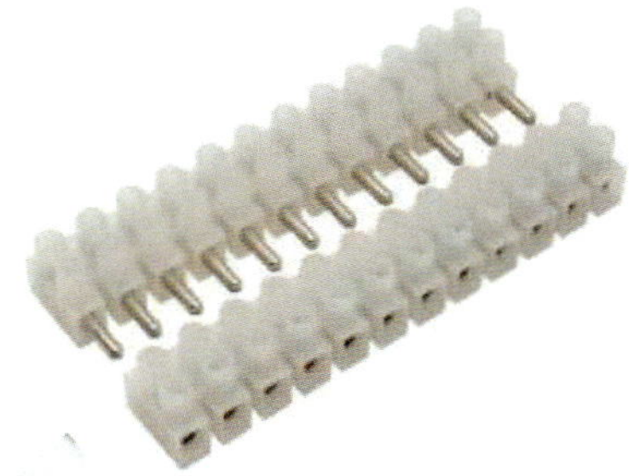

3 Way Termination block is easily fitted near points and signals to take the wires From the equipment and then extend them to where ever you need them. They are supplied in a 6 way unit but each 3 way section can be snapped off. (MR230 / MR235)

Common Voltage Junction Block are solid brass and are available in 4 or 8 way. Ideal for termination all your Negatives, without having to make loops or overloading a Single terminal with too many Wires (NS)

Wire Clips are great for adding a spur to an existing wire without cutting the existing wire. You place the existing wire in the back grooves, place the new wire in the front groove, then press the 2 halves together. No need to strip the wire. They come in 2 sizes (CT101 / CT102)

The CN164 is a wire termination board 106mm x 46mm with 5 fixing holes. It can accept all size of cable to 32/0.2mm, 2.5mm miniature 2 way and 3 way plugs, and 2way to 6 way rising clamp terminals – all at the same time. Common terminals can be increased from 2way to 8 way

The CN164 has 14 twin 6 Amp terminals for joining wires from different points on the layout. A 3way terminal block connected to 1.3mm pins on a 5mm grid for plugging rising clamp terminals. A 3way terminal block connected to 0.8mm pins on a 2.5mm grid for miniature 1, 2 or 3 way plugs

A DC Power Distribution Board . There is a set of Input Terminals and a set of extension terminals for the next Distribution Board. The output consists of 18 Positive terminals and 18 negative terminals. The board has a Power ON indicator, which is also a polatity indicator - Green is the correct polarity, Red is incorrect, & Orange is DCC. There are 6 fixing positions. Each board has a position to record the voltage, and the board No. The boards can be used for any voltage up to 48vDC, and upto 15 Amps per terminal. Length 140mm, Width 40mm, Height 15mm

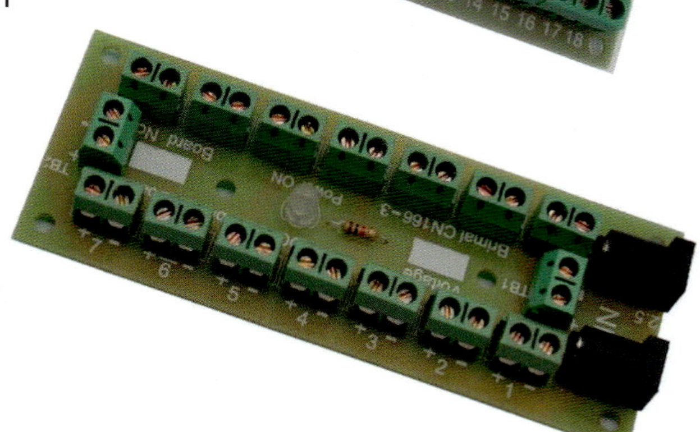

The CN166 basic unit has 14 Positive and Negative Terminals. The input power can be connected either by wires, a 2.1mm DC plug or a 2.5mm DC plug, the input terminal will handle up to 15 Amps, the board can be used for DC voltages up to 24vDC & DCC. (The board can be used with higher voltages; however the resister should be removed to disable the LED) The LED will show Green if the

Polarity is correct, Red if the Polarity is reversed by mistake or Orange if you are running a DCC system.
The Input is via a 2.5mm DC socket or screw terminal block and can be any DC voltage up to 48v or a DCC voltage. There is a Main ON/OFF switch behind the Input terminal Block which isolates both the Positive and Negative Input feeds. The Input then passes through a 5 Amp fuse to feed the outputs and light the 'ON' LED. The ON Led is Tricolour so will indicate that the input is +- DC (Green), if connected the wrong way around -+ (Red) or DCC (Orange). This LED is after the fuse so will go out if the fuse blows.
The CN169 has 6 individually switched outputs, each output can accept a load of up to 3 Amps and has an ON LED indicator.

This Distribution Board can be used for controlling individual lighting circuits on your layout, controlling sections of Points or Signals, or controlling power to sections of the layout. There are 3 input to the Distribution Board, AC up to 24volts via a green terminal block, DC up to 24 volts via a 2.1mm socket, and DCC via a black terminal block. Each board can only be used for one type of supply at a time. Each output is double switched as DC or DCC this means that both the Positive and the negative are switched ON or OFF, and with DCC both lines are switched. Each output has an ON LED which is Green for DC or Orange for DCC. Each of the 8 outputs can switch a load of up to 6 Amps..

/';'/Some people will tell you the correct wire for your layout should be based on the maximum current being emitted by your controller with a safety margin of around 15%. This however would mean that the whole layout be run in very large cable, such as 24/0.2mm or 32/0.2mm (see below) (CN165)

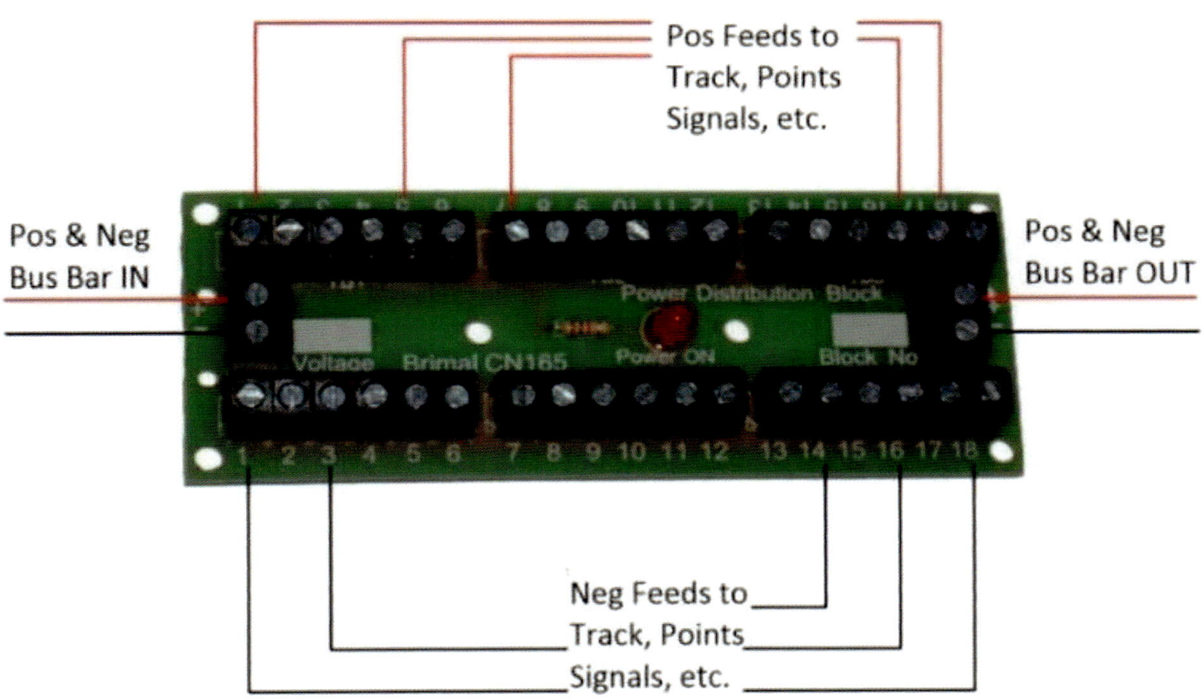

I prefer the other approach – run the larger cable to a distribution point (like the one above) Brimal CN165 Distribution Board on the baseboard, and then run smaller cables to each piece of equipment, as long as the smaller cables are capable of carrying the required current for that piece of equipment

MODEL RAILWAY PROJECTS

Keeping Wires & Cables Tidy.

It is essential you start from day one to keep all cables and wires as neat as possible. Decide on four or five main routes around your layout. Remember if anything goes wrong you will be working upside down. There are several products that can help with this.

The Cable Clip, the most well-known cable clamp. Ideal for the multicore Cables but not so good for individual wires. They come in a range of sizes, usually with a nail to fix them in place. Nailing things to the underside of a base board is not a good idea. OK on struts or legs. (NS)

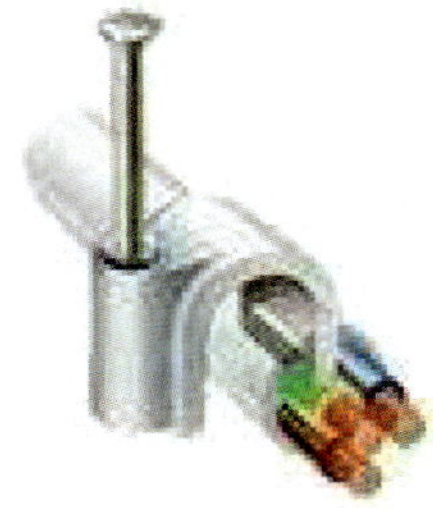

The Cable Tie and Base. This is probably the best to use as you can fit them around the baseboard and leave them fully open until you have finished. Just thread the wires through until you need to terminate. (Base CB890/891 Tie CB869 – 873)

Aluminium Clip. Great idea but will not hold the cables while you are Assembling the layout. They need to be closed as you put the cable or wire in place, they can be opened and closed a few times, but being aluminium they will eventually break (CB420 / CB421)

The P Clip. This is another great idea as long as you pick a large diameter hole From the start and then you can add cables and wires as you expand.
(CT400 – CT408)

Miniature Cable Trunking. This is also very useful but has one disadvantage. As you are working upside down, each time you take the cover off to fit a new cable all the existing wire and cables are going to fall out. Best used on Legs or areas you know you will not be adding to. (NS)

Cable – Wire Markers 0 to 9 made from soft PVC and will fit wires from 1mm to 3mm diameter. Each number is a separate colour.

You will find that as your layout progresses a combination of all the above will wind up on your layout.

Protection:

As most of the wiring is under the baseboard it is advisable to wear protective glasses when working under the board because of off cuts of wire and even solder could fall on you causing a damage to your eyes and face. A good light source is also a great help.

Why Colour Code Wires

As your layout grows you are going to have more and more wires running around the underside of your baseboard. The best thing to do is decide before you start a colour code system, for example. DC main feeds Positive RED, Negative BLACK. DCC main feeds BROWN & BLUE. These would normally be in either 24/0.2mm or 32/0.2mm depending on the size of your layout.

Always best to start with the bigger cable so your layout can grow into the cable capacity. The last thing you want to be doing is re-wiring the layout in 6 months.

Now decide what colours to use for other equipment. Most equipment will need a negative feed so you could keep these as BLACK, or if they are DCC then BLUE.

Solenoid points require two other wires, one for each solenoid, let's say YELLOW and PURPLE.

Some Signals also require two extra wires so they could be WHITE and GREEN. Then other equipment could be a combination of other colours.

You could create your own table for future reference

Code No	From	To	Size	Colour	Description
SW12C1	Control Panel 12	Points No 12	16/0.2mm	Blue	Up wire for Points 12
SW12C2	Control Panel 12	Points No 12	16/0.2mm	Yellow	Down wire for Points 12
SN10C1	Signal Switch 10	Signal 10	7/0.2mm	Brown	Green for Signal 10
SN10C2	Signal Switch 10	Signal 10	7/0.2mm	Orange	Red for Signal 10
		AND SO ON			

Now let's have a look at the above wires in detail.

As far as your layout is concerned you should try to select the correct size wire to power the equipment without exceeding the current limitations of the wire. Each piece of equipment, motor, light, animatronics or LED will draw a certain amount of current to make it work. This means you will need to have a rough idea of the current consumption of all the electrical products you are going to use. Luckily, most manufacturers print this information either on the equipment or in the instructions.

An example would be the Hornby Point Motor R8014. With a 12v DC supply you will need a minimum of 3 Amps to switch over the coil – this now gives you a fairly good idea what size cable you should use. Looking at the table above the minimum size of cable will be 16/0.2mm, to switch just one-point set. If you are going to switch 2 points simultaneously then you are going to need a bigger wire. There are a few points you need to bear in mind. The Point motor only requires that 12vDC at 3 Amps for a fraction of a second. This gives you a little leeway as the cable will not have time to heat up and break down in the time it is being used, so you should be able to run 2 or 3 point sets from the

Bus Bars

A Bus Bar is a set of wires (one Positive, and one Negative) that run around your layout, at a larger current carrying capability. The most commonly used is 32/0.2 which will carry up to 8.5 Amps. From this Bus Bar spurs are run at appropriate points to terminal blocks to run equipment in that area. Remember control wires will have to be run back to the control panel, and 1/0.6 or 7/0.2 wires can be used.

The drawing below shows how a Bus Bar with spurs is laid out. (See the Separate Datasheet on Bus bars)

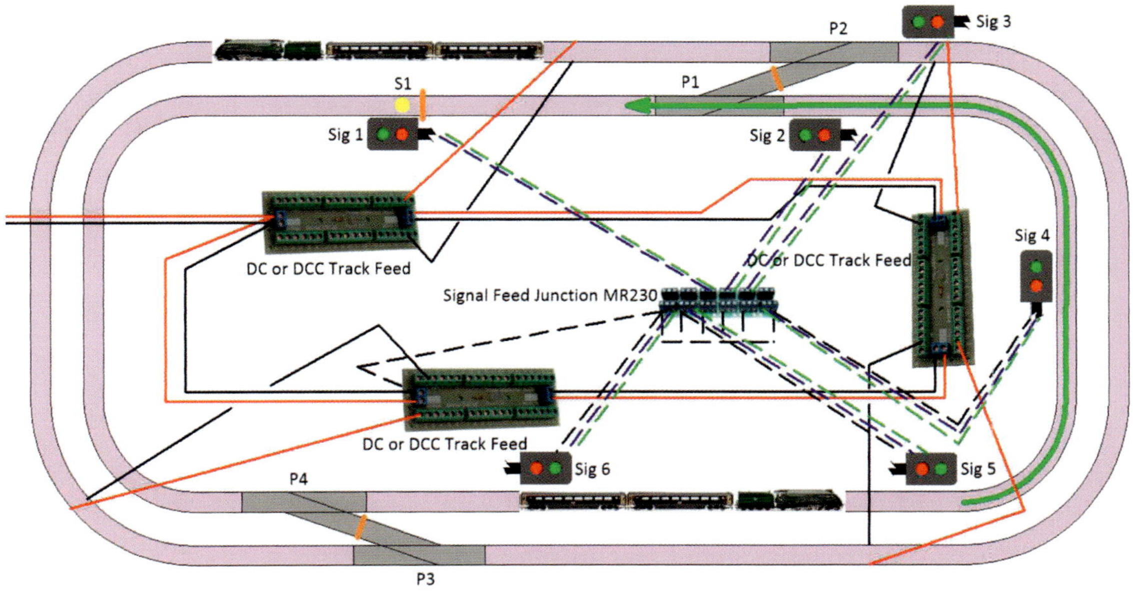

Connecting to the Track.

The first task is to power the track from the controller. It is recommended that you use a minimum of 16/0.2mm Black and Red wire, the larger the layout the bigger the wire, so 24/0.2mm or 32/0.2mm for larger layouts. All proprietary manufactures have their special connectors to supply power to the track

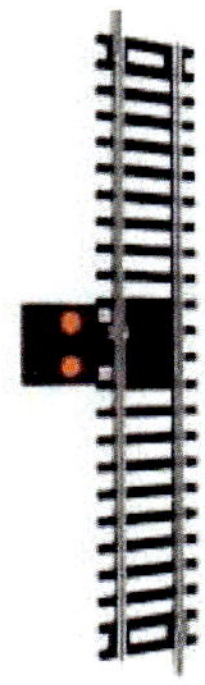

Peco ST-273 | Hornby R8242 | Hornby R8241 | Bachmann

The following drawing shows the connection between the Power Source / Controller and the Track using one of the above. It is also recommended that you feed the track several times to reduce voltage drop along the rails. In this drawing TRACK 2 wire colours have been changed for clarity of the illustration.

Please Note: When using 2 controllers the polarity from each has to be controlled at points and crossovers. It is advisable to use isolating fishplates to separate the two power sources.

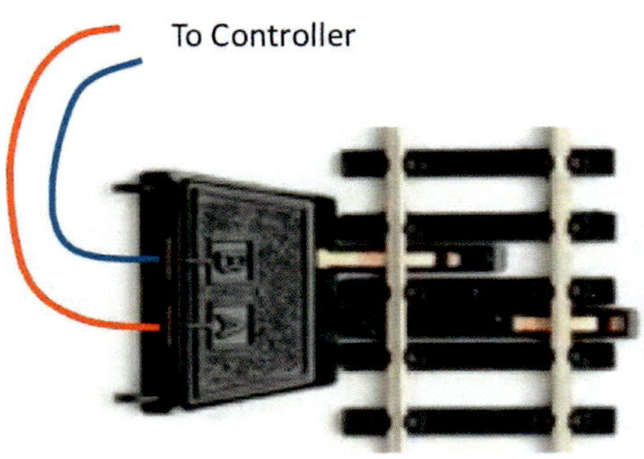

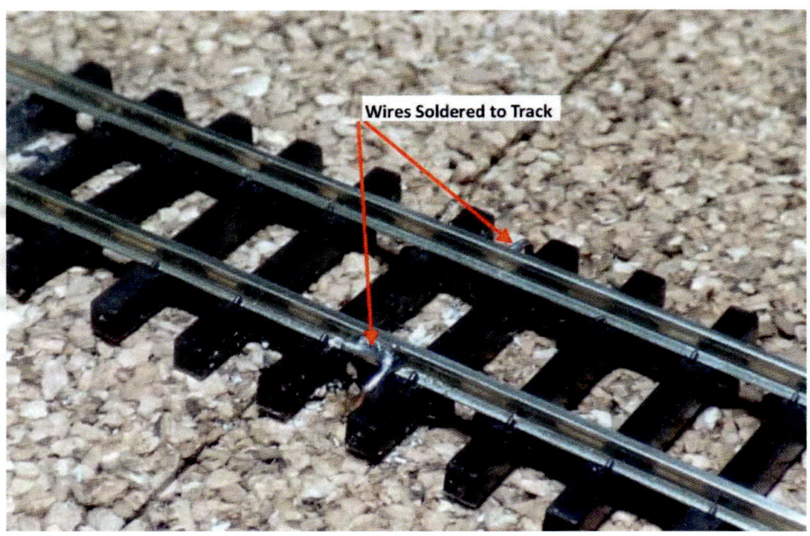

To summarise:

You will need

A variable voltage – Speed Controller

A fixed voltage of 12v DC and or 15vAC

(Remember check the current rating – the higher the better – build into your Power Source, rather than changing it every 5 minutes.

Create a Bus Bar if your layout is large.

Wire – again don't go for the minimum current rating, go at least one size up. So if the equipment comes with 7/0.2mm wire attached then connect to it with 16/0.2mm.

Keep the wires tidy and maintain a record of colour codes. If you get a fault so much easier tracing a wire if it's not in a birdsnest.

Use Multi-core cable to run back to the Control Panel, again less individual wires.

Use the correct connecter where possible

Connect the track to the controller several times to avoid voltage drop.

LED's & How to wire them

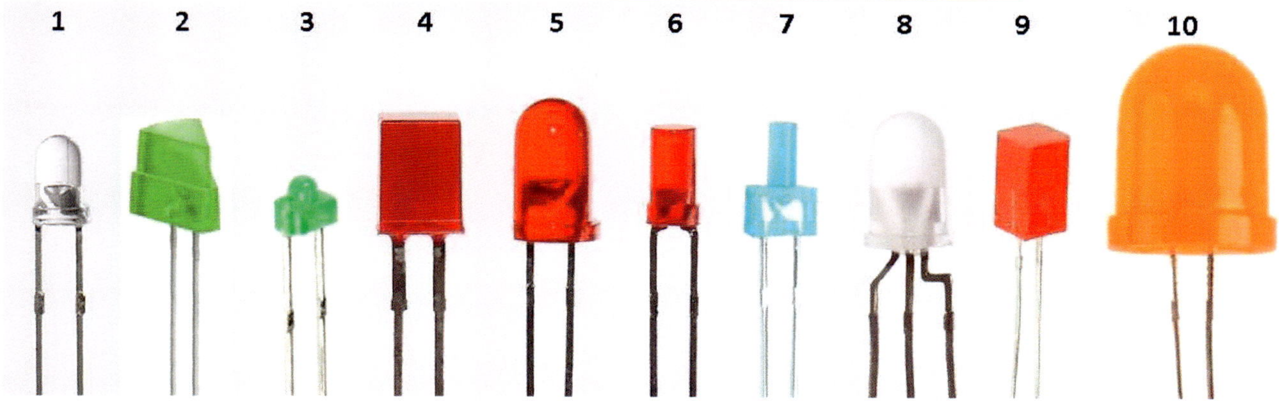

Fig: 1

The LED is a Light Emitting Diode so only allows voltage to flow in one direction. That is from the Anode to the Cathode. The Cathode is shown as the shorter lead and the base of the LED has a 'flat' on the Cathode side. Most LED's have a maximum working voltage of 2 to 3 volts DC, however some have a built-in resistor so can work from a voltage of 12volts. LED's come in many shapes and sizes, here are a few examples.

1) 10mm round, 2) 8mm round, 3) 5mm round, 4) 3mm round, 5) 3mm cylinder flat head, 6) 2mm tower flat head, 7) 1.8mm dome head, 8) 5x5mm Square, 9) 5x2mm rectangular.

Single Colour LED.

The diagram opposite shows the internal wiring of a standard LED. The positive voltage is connected to the ANODE and the Negative voltage is connected to the CATHODE.

As mentioned, the Cathode is always the shorter lead.

Most circuits work on 9v, 12v, or 24volts so a dropping resistor will be required to drop the voltage to 2 to 3 volts In most cases a 1K resistor will do the job.

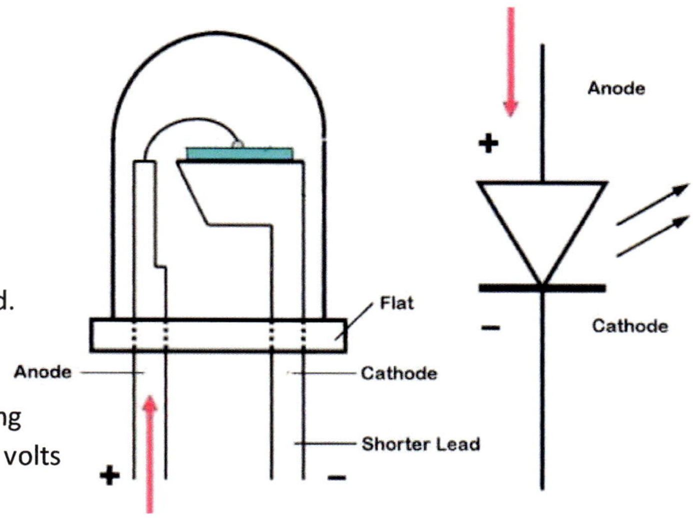

Fig: 2

The following are a few examples of wiring a 2 wire LED.

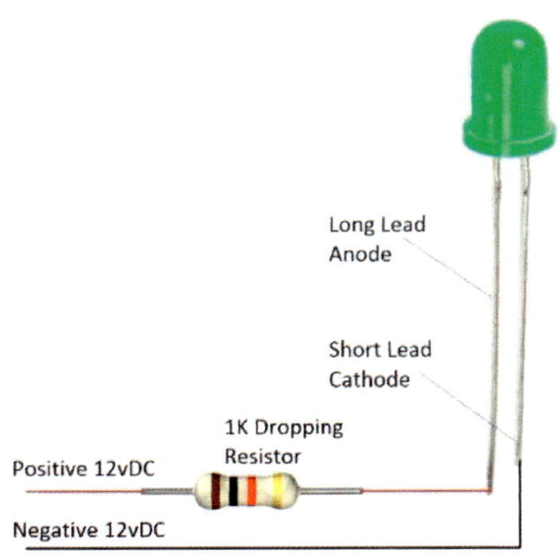

Fig: 3

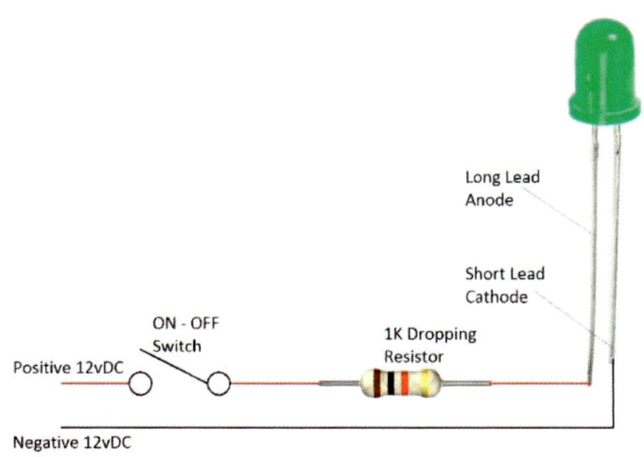

Fig: 4

Fig 3 shows the basic wiring of an LED, this could be the Power Supply ON Indicator.

Fig 4 shows the LED being switched ON & OFF through a switch, which could be a toggle switch, micro switch, magnetic switch, leaf switch, slide switch etc.

MODEL RAILWAY PROJECTS

5mm LED

High Efficiency Red diffused 5mm LED from the Kingbright L-53 Series, with luminosity of 50mcd. Made with gallium arsenide phosphide on a gallium phosphide orange light emitting diode

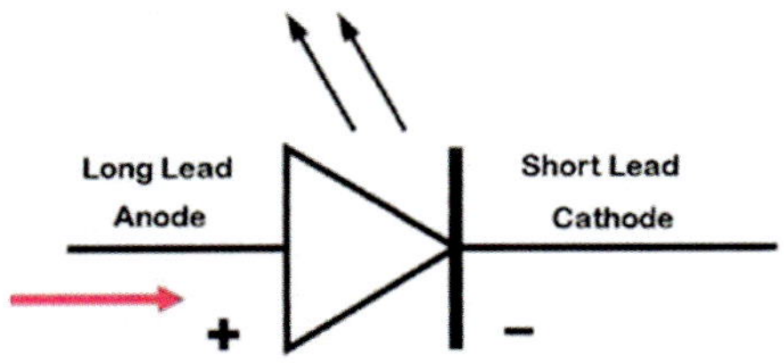

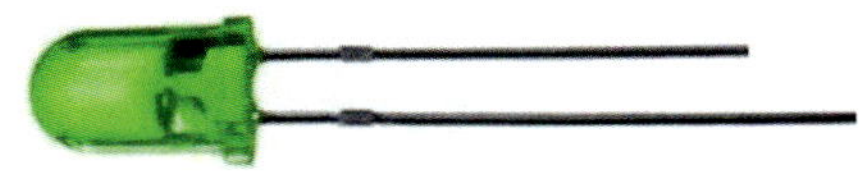

Red	JPRR6LU5B6DA	SL101
Green	JPRG8NU5B6DA	SL100
Yellow	JPRY5LU5B6DA	SL102
White	JPRW5YK5B62A	SL104
Blue	JPRB5YU5B64A	SL103

3mm LED

A 3mm red diffused solid state LED. Reliable and rugged, long life – solid state reliability with low power consumption. Made from GaAsP/GaP emitting colour material. Suitable for full colour LED displays. Viewing angle 40°

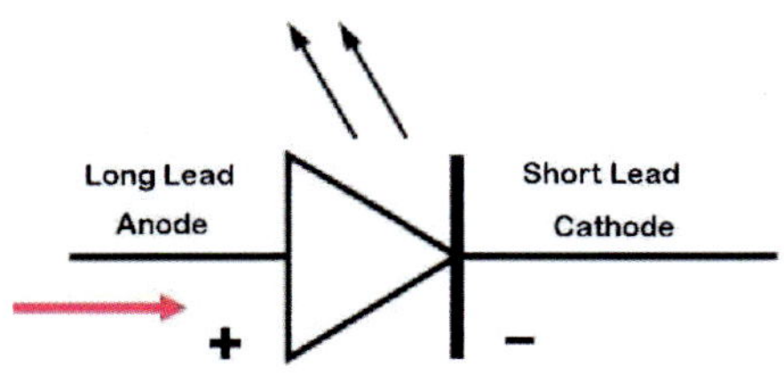

Red	Kingbright L-7104HD	SL250
Green	Kingbright L-7104GD	SL251
Yellow	Kingbright L-7104YD	SL254
Orange	Kingbright L-7104ED	SL252
Blue	Kingbright L-7104BD	SL253

2mm Tower LED

A 12V yellow 2mm tower LED is a TTL compatible solid state lamp with an integral current limiting resistor, so there is no requirement for external current limiting components, simplifying design and saving cost. The high luminosity and long lifetime of this tower LED makes it suitable for many applications in electronic signage, signalling, small

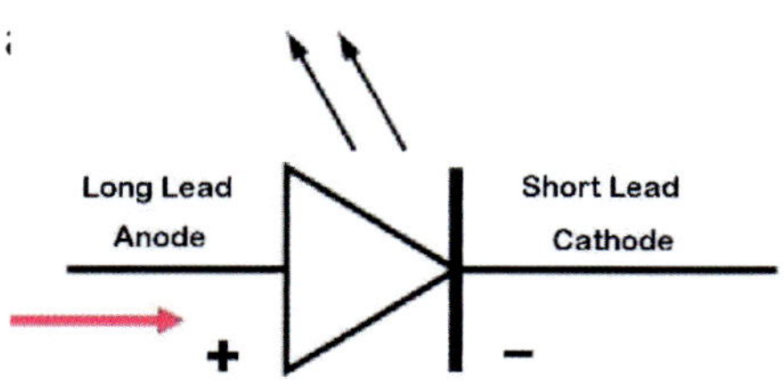

Red	OSR5JA7K94B -12V	SL260
Green	OSG8HA7K94B -12V	SL261
Yellow	OSY5JA7K94B -12V	SL262
White	OSW5DK7K92B -12V	SL265
Blue	OSB5SA7K94B -12V	SL263

Bi-Coloured LED 2 Pins.

There is a range of two-coloured LED's with 2 pins. These require the polarity to be reversed to switch from one colour to the other colour.

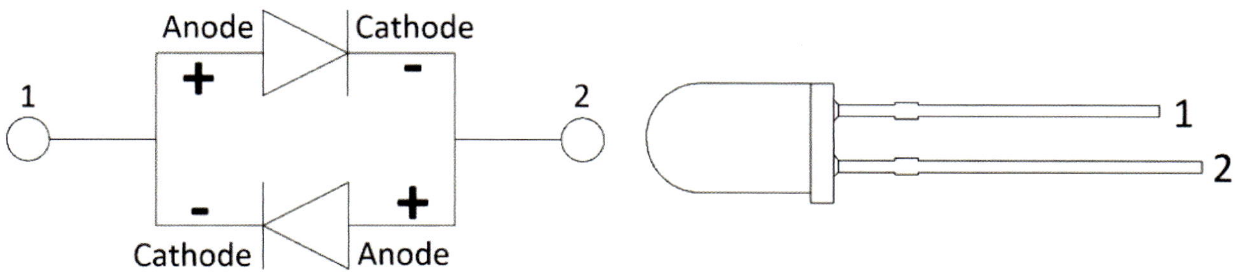

Fig: 5

In Fig 5 we have for example a Red / Green LED. When Positive is applied to pin 1 and Negative to pin 2 the LED will glow Green. If you then reverse the polarity to Negative on pin 1 and Positive on pin 2 the LED will glow Red. In most cases you will still need a dropping resistor on one of the pins. A 1K 0.25w resistor should be good enough.
You can get two colour LED's that do not require the polarity reversed. See below.

Red – Green	Kingbright L-57EGW 5mm	SL110
Green – Yellow	Kingbright L-57GYW 5mm	SL112
Red – Yellow	Kingbright L-57EYW 5mm	SL113

Here are two examples of Reverse Polarity switching for a two colour 2 wire LED.

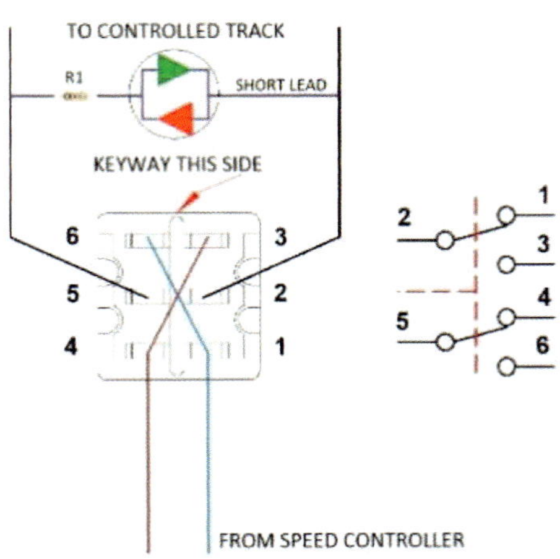

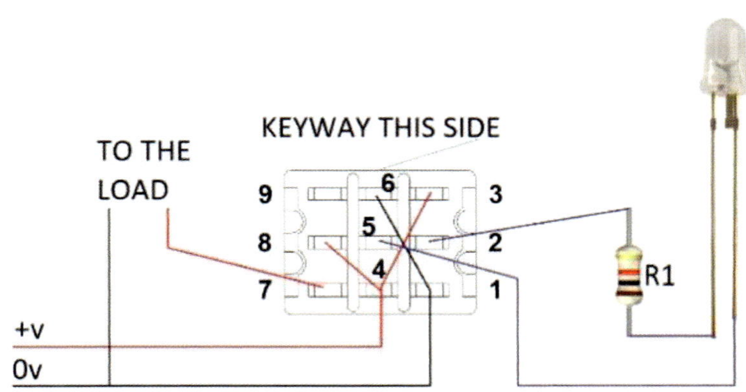

Fig: 6

When you have Positive on Terminal 5 and Negative on Terminal 2 then the LED is Green, when you have Negative on terminal 5 and Positive on terminal 2 then the LED is Red.

Fig 8 Here the bi-coloured LED is indicating when the LOAD is On or Off. With switch in the down position the Load is switched off and the LED shows Red, when the switch is in the up position the Load in On and the LED shows Green.

Bi-Colour (Tri-Colour) LED 3 Pins.

This is a range of 3 pin Bi-colour LED's, which in many situations have a distinct advantage over the two pin LED. The 3 Pin LED does not require the polarity to be changed and can create a third colour by switching both pins ON at the same time. It would be of little use in Figure 8, where we want an indication that the polarity has changed, however a lot easier to wire in Figure 8. The Bi-Colour Led is ideal in changeover situations as shown in Figure 6.

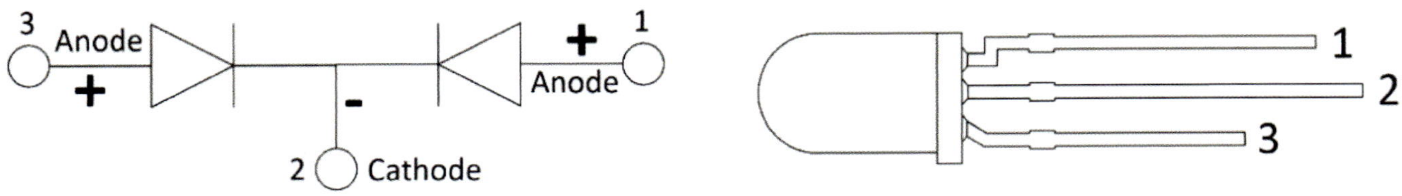

Fig: 7

Red – Green	Kingbright L-59EGW 5mm	
Green – Yellow	Kingbright L-59GYW 5mm	
Red – Yellow	Kingbright L-59EYW 5mm	

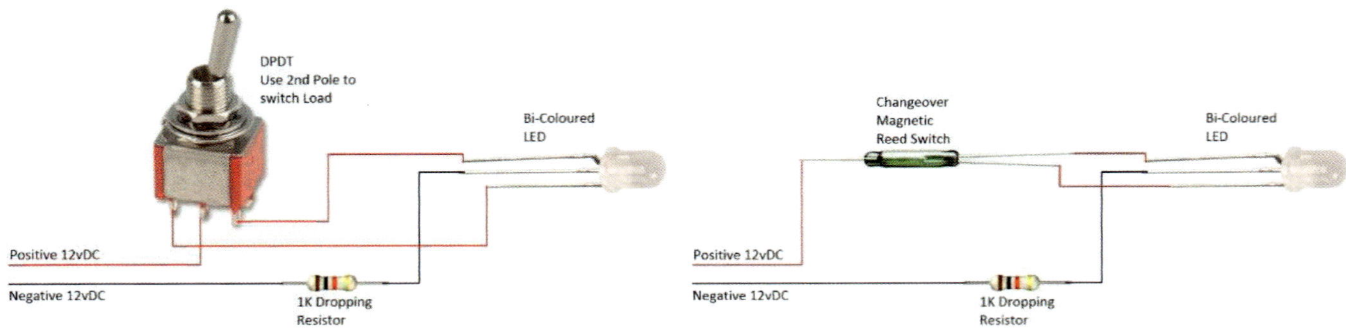

Fig: 8

Figure 8 the switch could be ON-OFF, ON-OFF-ON, or ON-ON DPDT switch. Here we can indicate either ON / OFF, Left / Right, Up / Down and so on. Figure 8 shows a Magnetic Reed switch being used to change the colour of the LED. When there is no magnetic influence on the reed switch the LED is Green. When a magnet is placed close to the reed switch the contacts will change and the LED will show Red.

In the brackets in the table above is the third colour which can be obtained if both LED's are switched On at the same time, e.g. If Positive power is placed on 1 & 3 and Negative on 2.

Tri-colour LED 4 Pin.

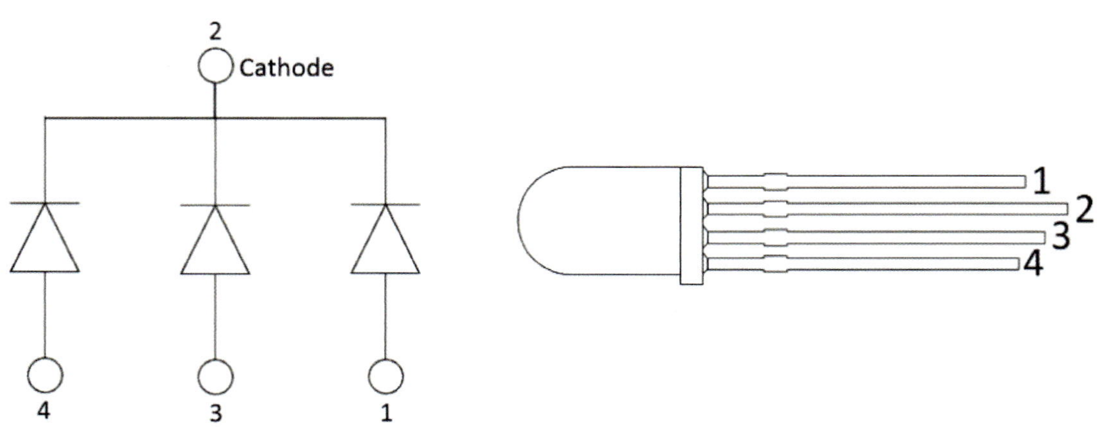

Fig: 9

Red(1) – Blue(3) –	Kingbright L- 154A4SUREQBFZGC 5mm	
Red(1) – Blue(3) –	Kingbright L- 154A4SUREQBFZGEW 5mm	

These LED's are normally common cathode, however they are also available with common Anode, and are in clear or diffused housings. Here we will concentrate on the common cathode type. You will notice that each of the 4 leads are at a different length so that you can easily identify the colour associated with the pin

Reverse Polarity Switches & Indicators.

There will be cases where you will want to reverse the polarity going to Point Motors or a section of track or to a piece of equipment. This could be to change the direction from Forward to Reverse of a Locomotive on a section of track, in a Fiddle Yard etc.

The following is a range of Basic switches that can be used to Reverse Polarity for either track or Motors. Later we show some examples of where they can be used.

Double Pole
Double Throw
ON – OFF or ON – ON
SW315
Salecom
T8011-SEBQ-H

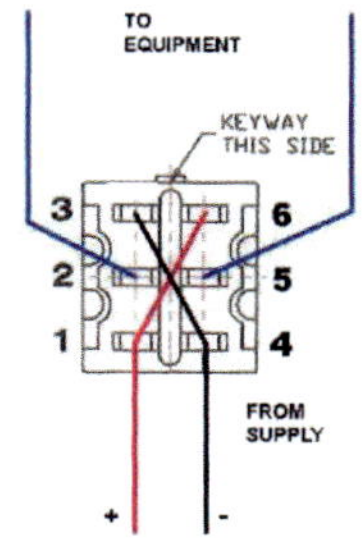

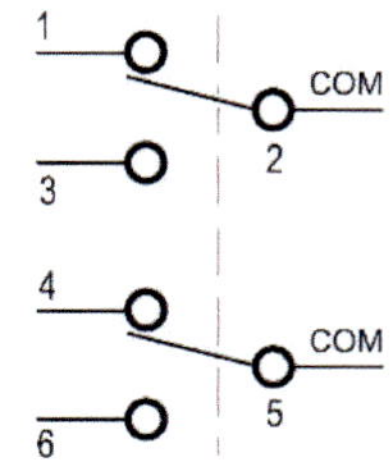

Double Pole
Double Throw
Centre OFF
ON – OFF – ON
Salecom
T8012-SEBQ-H

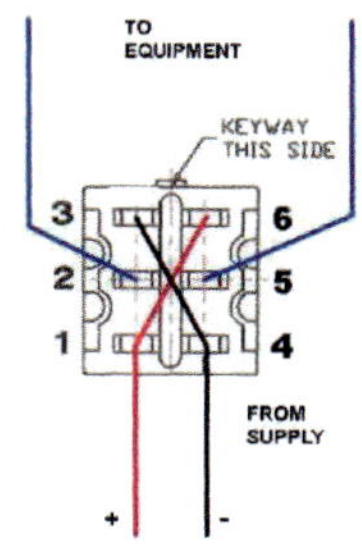

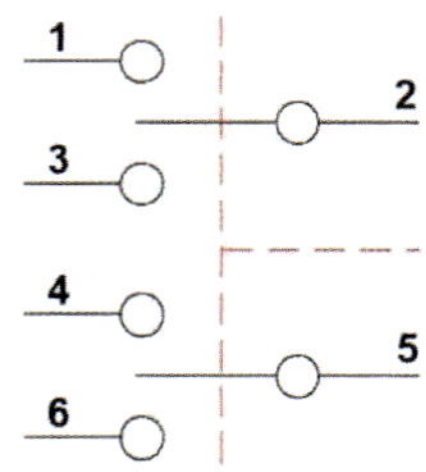

Triple Pole
Double Throw
ON – OFF or ON – ON
Salecom
T8301-SEBQ-H

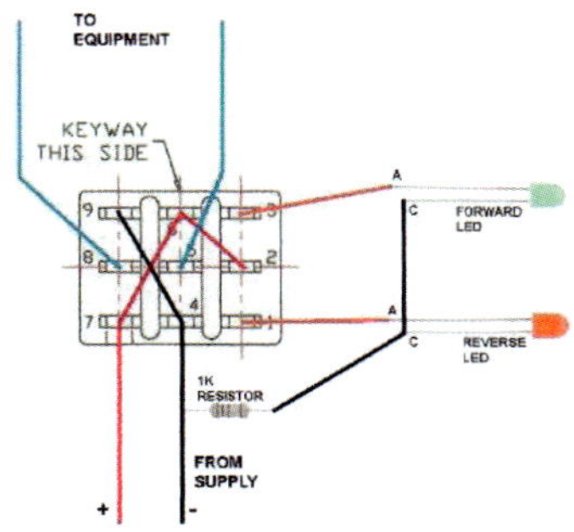

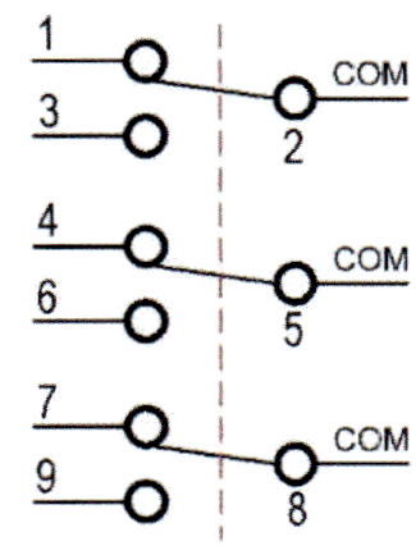

Double Pole
Double Throw
Slide Switch
ON – ON or ON – OFF
Pic
SS-22LO3-G9

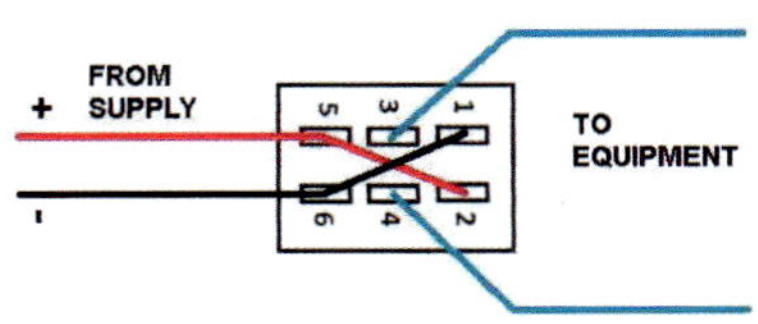

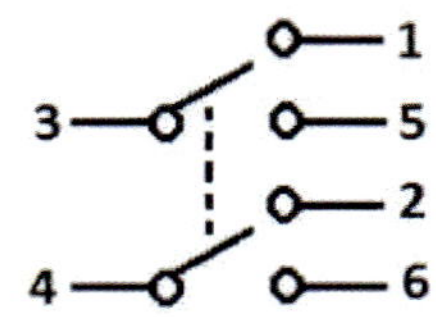

Double Pole
Double Throw
Centre OFF
ON – OFF – ON
Pic
SS-23F19-G9

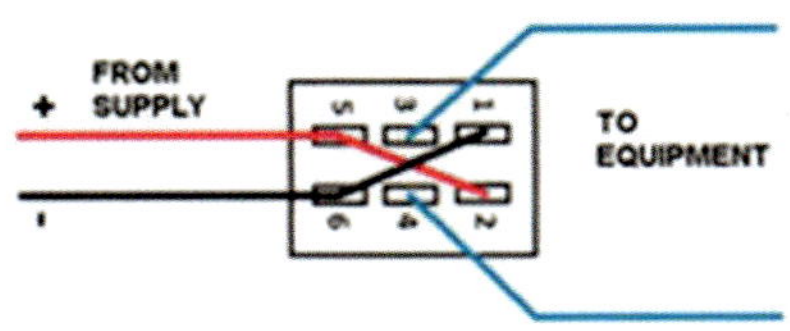

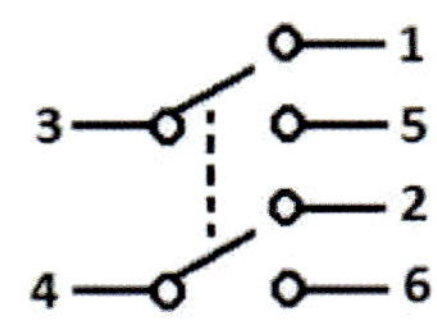

Miniature Double
Pole, Double
Throw
ON – ON or ON- OFF
Pic
SS-22F25-G7

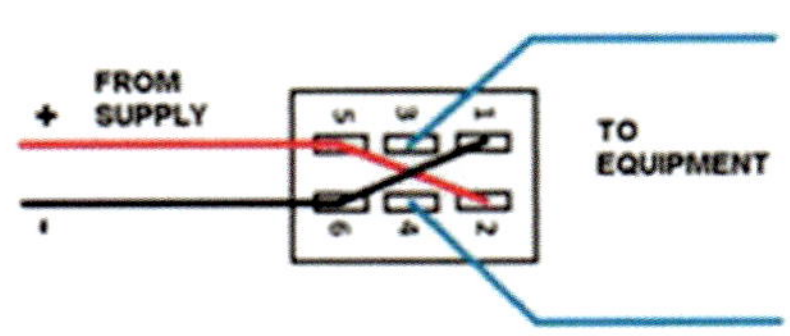

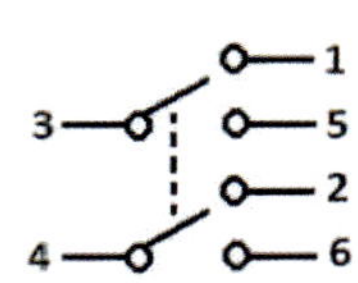

Double Pole
Double Throw
with centre OFF
with dual Indication
MR325

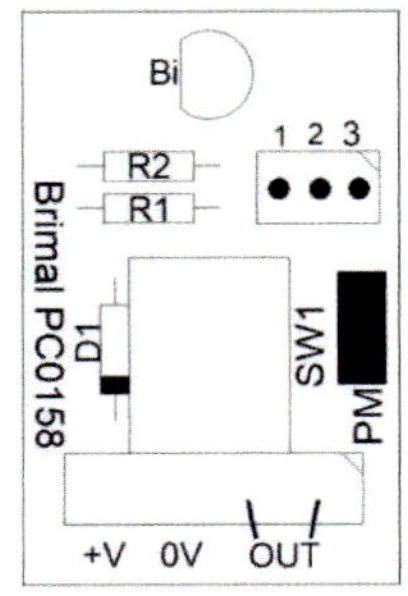

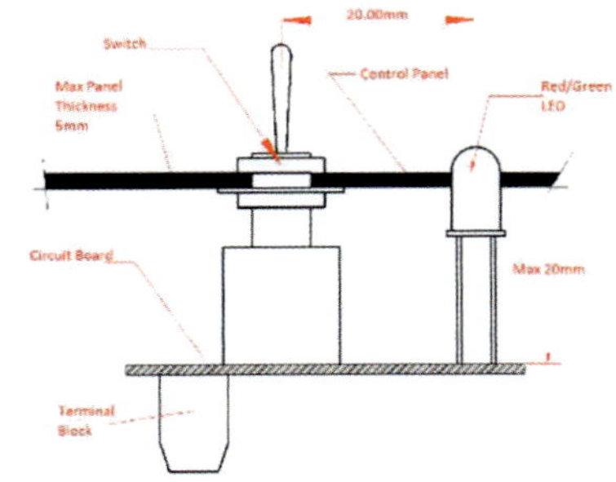

Double Pole
Double Throw
with dual Indication
MR326

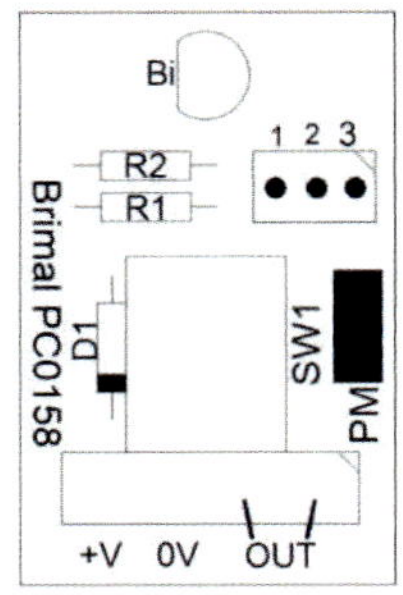

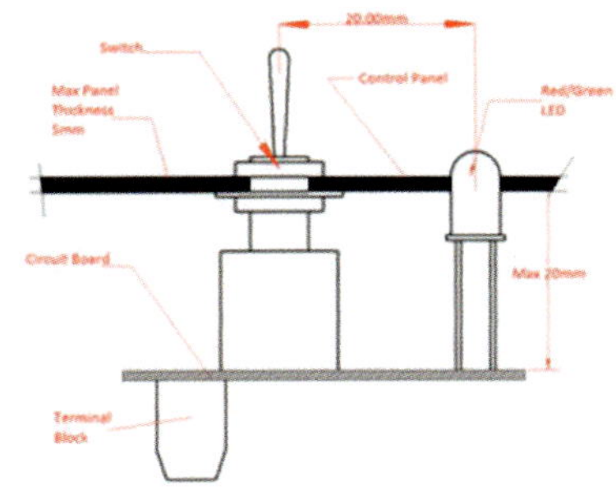

Double Pole
Double Throw with
Red & Green
Indications
MR601

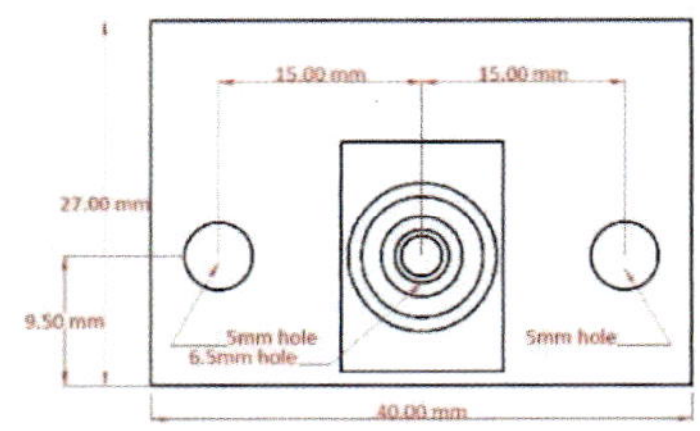

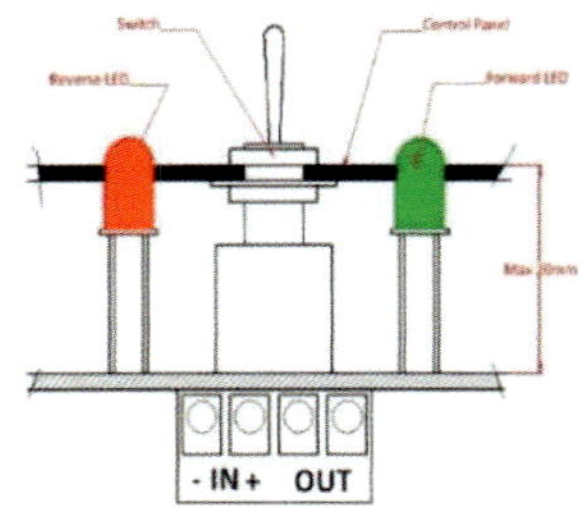

Dual Changeover
Latching Relay
MR204

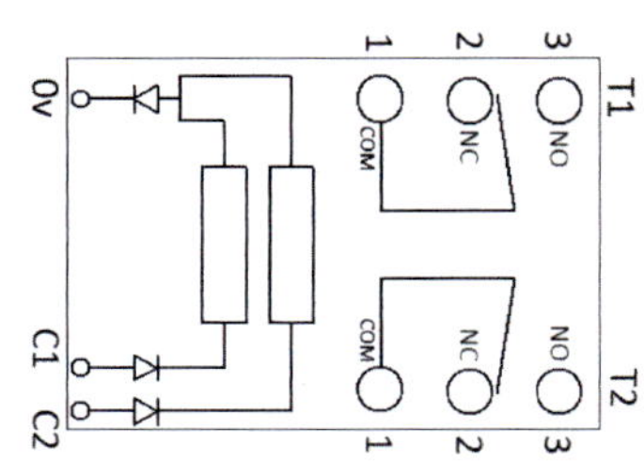

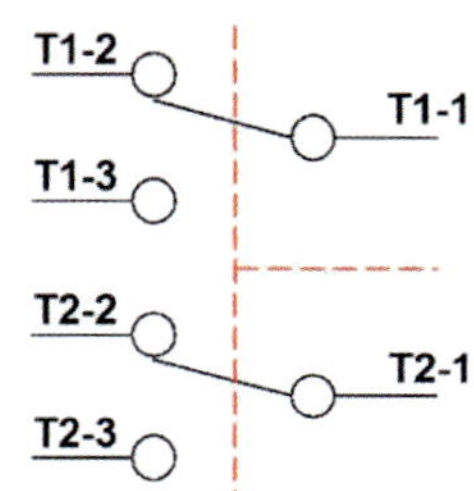

Now let's look at some practical circuits.

Basic Circuit

This circuit will be the same for Toggle switches or Slide Switches. If the switch is ON-ON then the feed coming from the uncontrolled section of track goes into the switch and depending on the position of the switch determines if the output has been reversed or not. Problem here is remembering the polarity of the Controlled section. If you want to you can add an Indicator to the circuit.

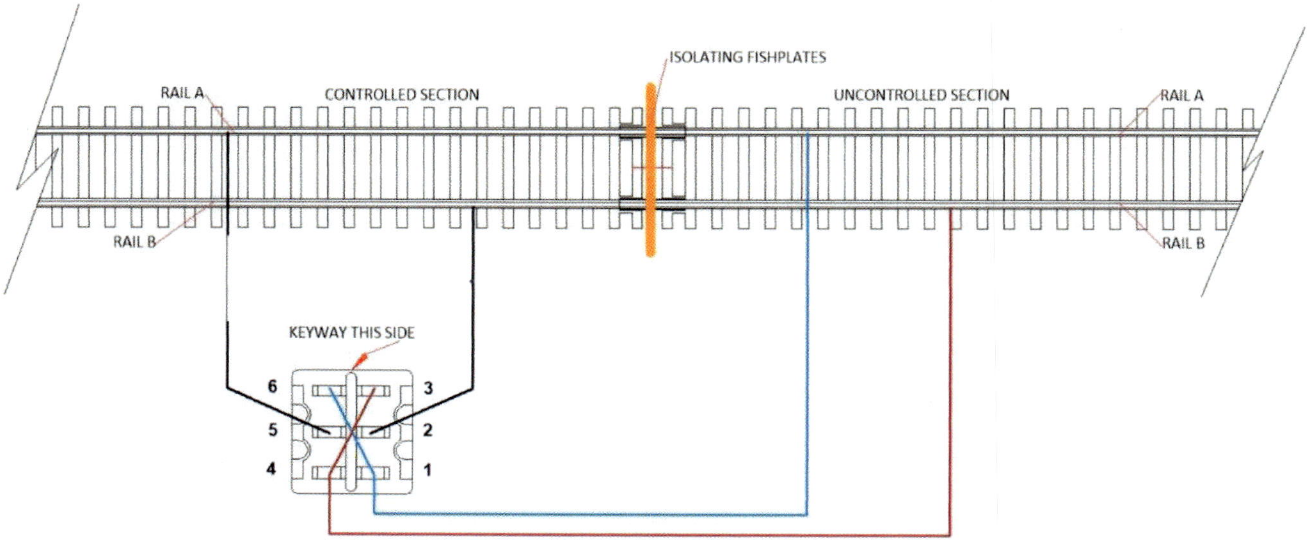

Fig 1

In this diagram we have added bi-coloured LED and a dropping resistor. The indicator will show Green if the polarity of both sections is the same, if the left-hand section has been reversed the LED will change to RED

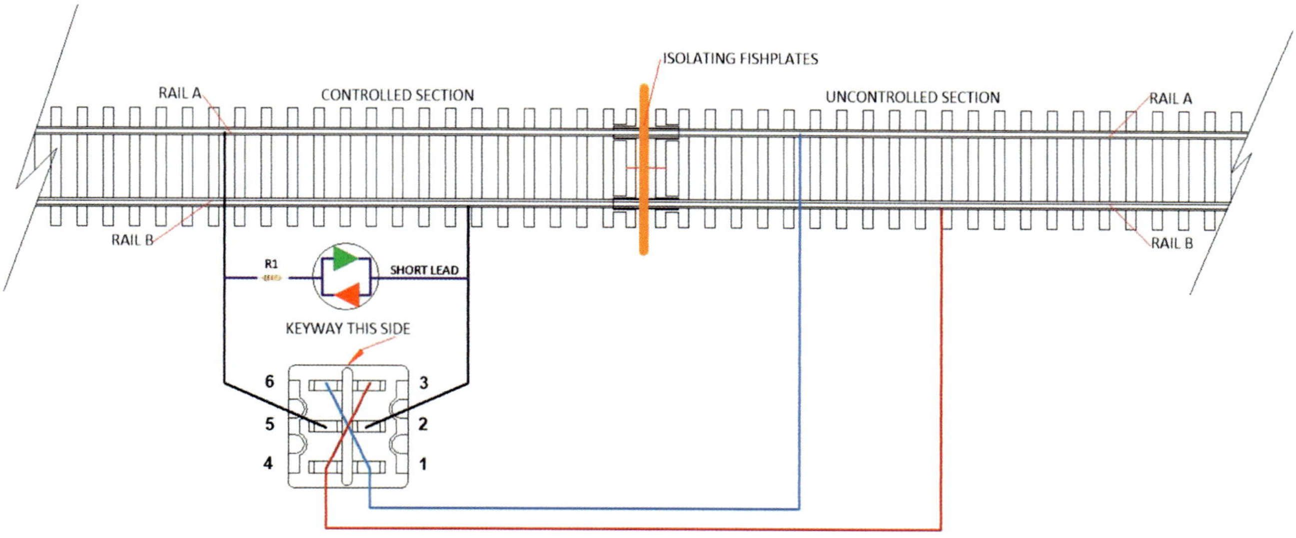

Fig 2

In this example we are using the MR325, however the MR326 will work just as well if you want centre OFF for the track you are controlling. The 2 poles are used to reverse the polarity of the incoming power so that when the switch is moved down the output polarity is reversed. Instead of complicated wiring on the back of the switch the PCB does all this for you. It also gives an LED Indication of the status of the points & an output for Mimic displays. The complete PCB with switch and indicators is only 41 x 27mm.

<u>The Bi-colour LED Indicator</u> is in the same line as the switch 20mm apart and at a predetermined height so that they just poke through a front panel without any bezels or holding mechanism. The switch requires a 6.5mm hole and the LED without bezel requires a 5mm hole.
Wiring is very simple 2 wires comming in from a Live Track. The OUT wires go to track you want to control.

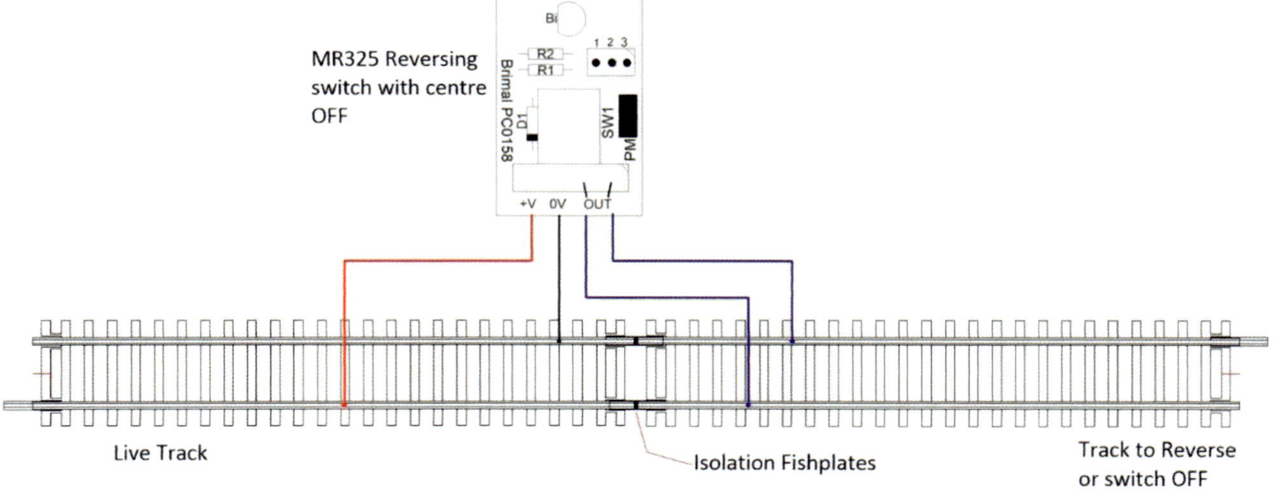

Fig 3

<u>NOTES</u>

Points, Signal & Control Panel Indication

In this application the MR204 is used to control a Point Motor, a Signal, and 2 LED's at the Control Panel. This circuit also has a CDU to help move the points, if required. The switch is a Momentary action Mini Toggle Switch, (this can be replaced by 2 mini Push Button switches). Ideally the MR204 should be fixed near the set of points it is controlling, as the Signal will also be in the same area. If you are using a Positive & Negative Bus Bar - the toggle switch and the LED's only require a 6 core back to the control panel. The relay has latching contacts, this means once energised and power is removed the contacts stay in that state until the second coil is energised. Once you have the system wired as above, you may find the indicators are back to front, this is due to the state of the relay when you first switch ON. In this case you may have to swap 2 & 3 around.
R1 is a 1K quarter or half watt resistor placed in the negative line to the LED's, to reduce the current drawn by the

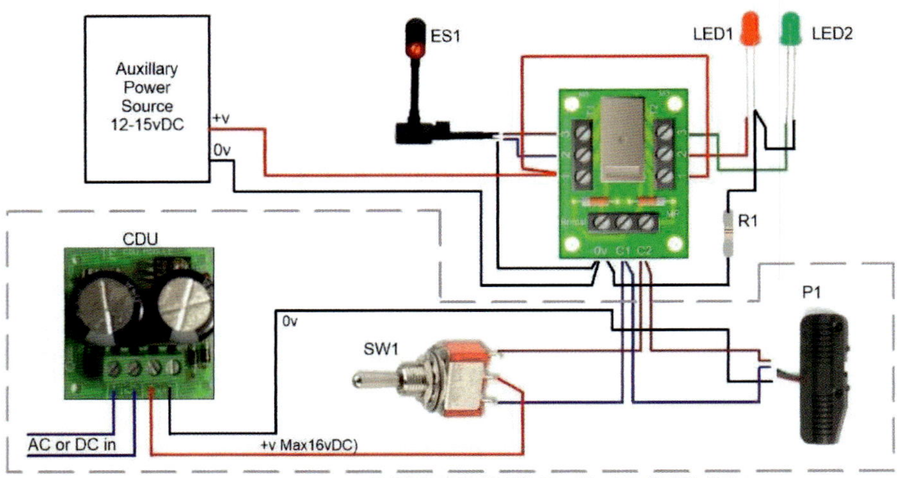

Points Control with CDU, Signal Control with CP Indicator

Automatic Forward / Reverse (Shuttle) (MR204)

In this application the Latching Relay is used as a Automatic Forward / Reverse (Shuttle) Control. Sensor 1 and Sensor 2 could be placed anywhere on a loop. The train will run from Sensor 2 to Sensor 1, when it passes sensor 1 the circuit will change the polarity of the tracks putting the train in reverse. The train will now travel in reverse until it passes over sensor 2, at which time the Latching Relay will again change the polarity of the track putting the Train into forward again. This will continue until power is removed from the system. By adding a toggle switch to the 0V line from the Auxiliary Power Source you can disable the Latching Relay so the polarity remains the same. Please note there is no slow down or slow start up facility in the Latching Relay, so the train will have it's power Reversed at whatever speed you have set the Train Speed Controller. Connecting power to the rails can be done in a number of ways, most proprietary manufacturers have their own rail connectors, or you can solder wires directly to the underside of the tracks.

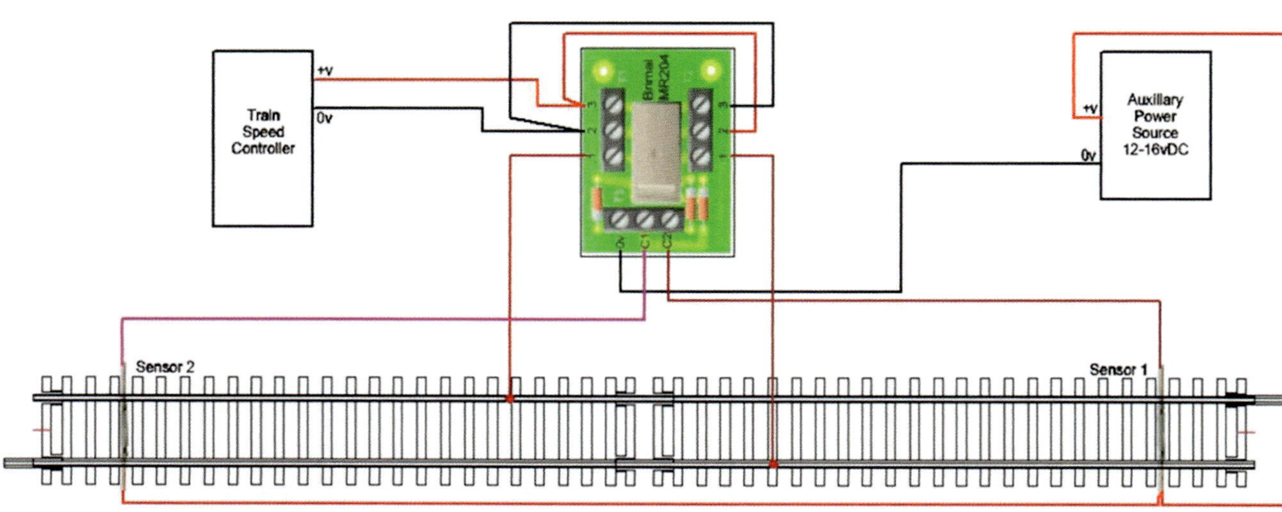

Reversing Loop

In the following application the Reversing switch is used to reverse the track in a Reversing Loop situation. As the Locomotive travels around the loop and arrives at 'G' you will need to reverse the polarity of the track between E1 and E so that the Locomotive can proceed along the main line. Please not the polarity of the Loop never changes, you are only changing the section between the loops.
The switch in this diagram is any of the toggle or slide switches mentioned earlier.

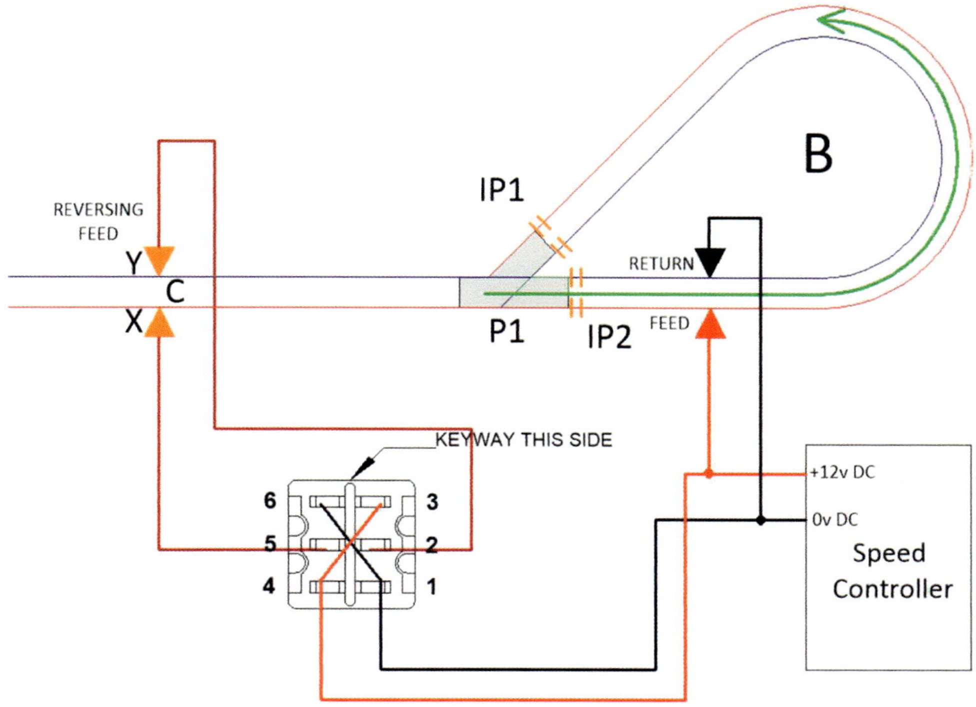

Fig: 1

In the following circuit we are using the MR326 to control the polarity of the 'C' section of track. In all these examples you still need to switch the points. By using certain types of point switches, you can switch the polarity automatically. This is covered in other sections.

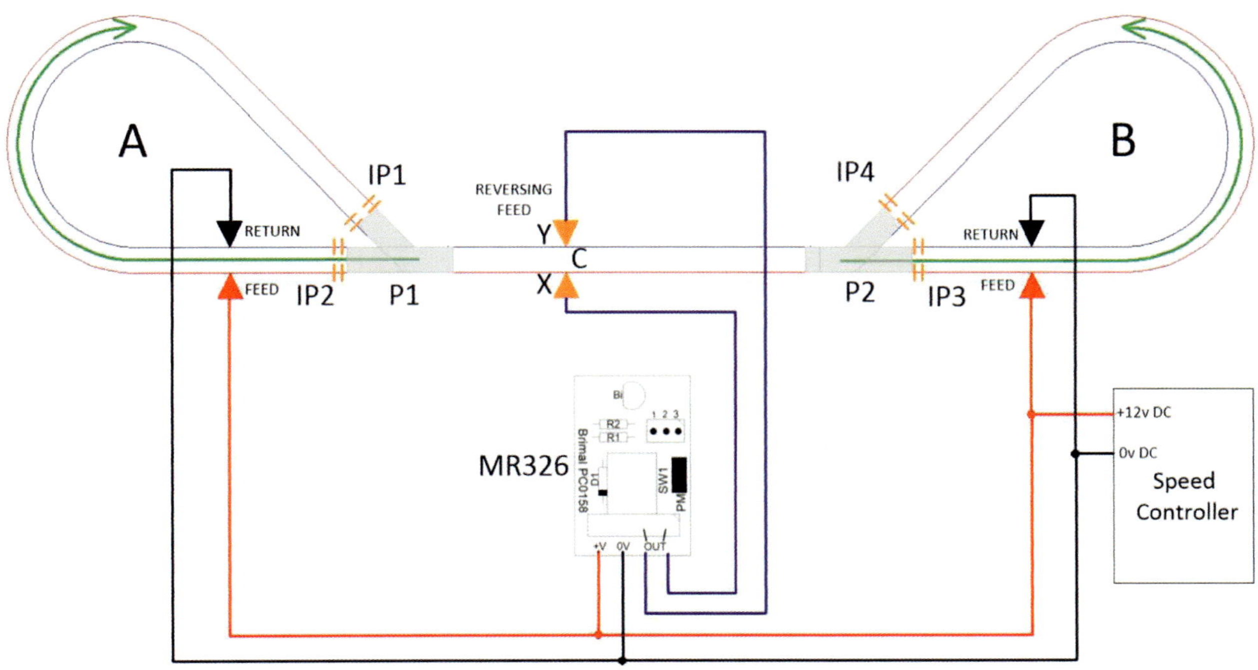

Fig: 2

You will have to change both the Positive and Negative feeds. You must remember to ensure that the section of track you are changing should be isolated from the rest of the Layout or you are going to create a dead short and blow something. You will also need to make sure the polarities are the same if you attempt to move the Locomotive out of this controlled area otherwise as it passes over the isolation fishplates it will try to go back.

Semi Automatic

Below is a complete Layout of a Reversing Loop, the distance between P1 and P2 can be any length to suit your layout. In the Semi-automatic layout, the changing of the points is done manually with a toggle switch, see diagram below, but the power reversing is done automatically via the MR204.

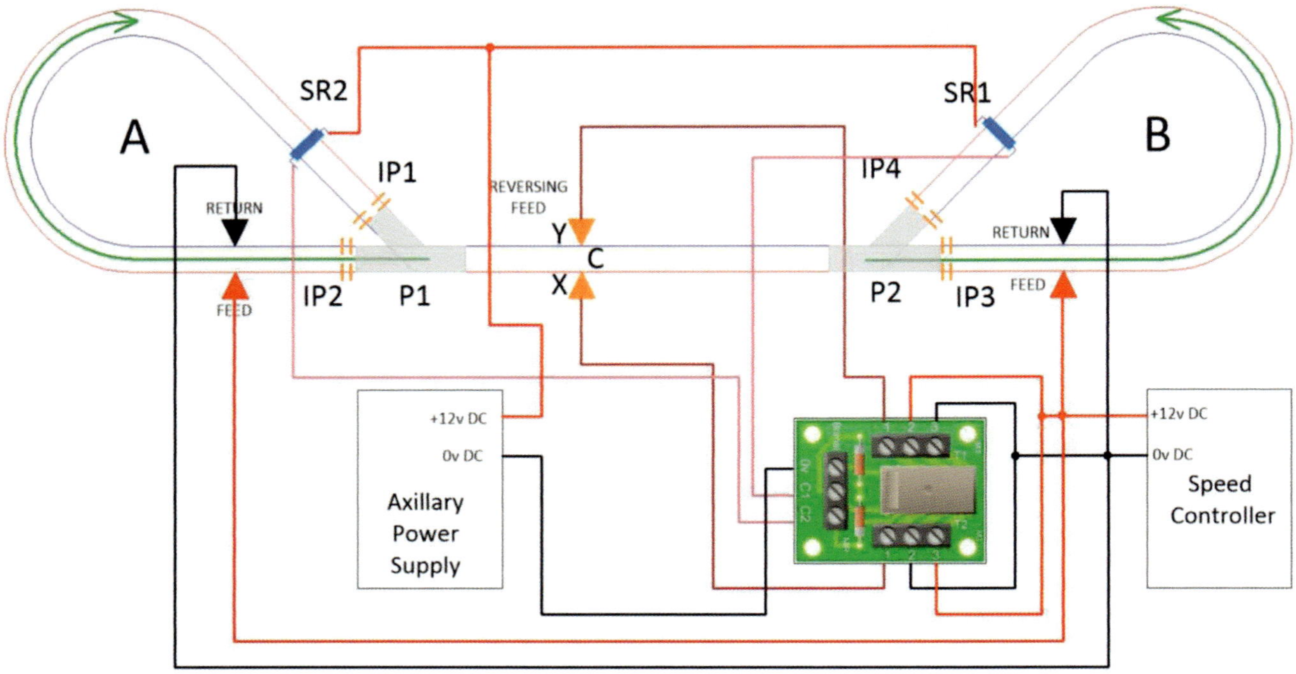

Fig:3

The sequence of operation is as follows: Fit Isolating Fishplates in positions IP1 to IP4. Connect the Speed Control Power to both loops in positions Return (ov) and Feed (+v). Fit magnetic sensors in positions SR1 & SR2. The position of SR1 and SR2 should be far enough away from the points to give you time to change the points. Both sets of points should be controlled by one double pole toggle switch, each set is wired the opposite to the other. In other words when P2 is in Turn Out position P1 will be in Straight Through position. The train travels along the straight from left to right, through P2 around the loop and then passes over SR1 the polarity of the track at X & Y reverses ready to allow the train to proceed onto the straight in the opposite direction. As the train passes over SR1 you will need to ensure the points are in the Turn Out position to allow the train to proceed, this will put P1 in the Straight Through position to allow the train to travel around Loop A

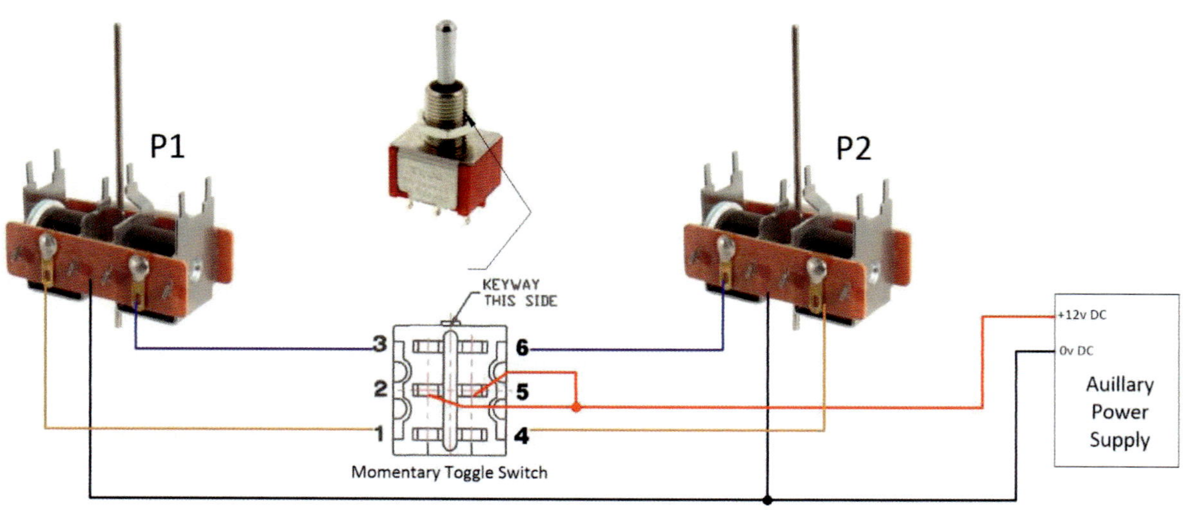

Fig:4

This diagram shows the two Point Motors Connected to a single Momentary Toggle Switch. The Negative (0v) power is connected directly to each point motor (Black). The positive (+12v) power is connected to both sides of the switch at terminals 2 & 5 (Red). The Blue wire, terminals 3 & 6 (up position) are connected to the right-hand coil on P1 and the left-hand coil on P2. The Brown wire, terminals 1 & 4 (down position) are connected to the left-hand coil on P1 and the right-hand coil on P2. *Note 1*: Check the position of the Keyway when wiring the switch is as per the drawing. *Note 2*: Check the orientation when fitted to your layout, as turning one motor through 180 degrees when fitting will make both motors work in the same direction.

Reversing Point Motors

There are a number of point motor that require the polarity to them to be reversed to change the state of the points. These are usually called stall motors or reverse polarity motors. They are in fact true motors rather than the motors that work with 2 coils, which are in fact solenoid motors.

The first one shown is the Tortoise Motor.

In this example the switch is the Brimal MR325, with the connection to the motor MR162.

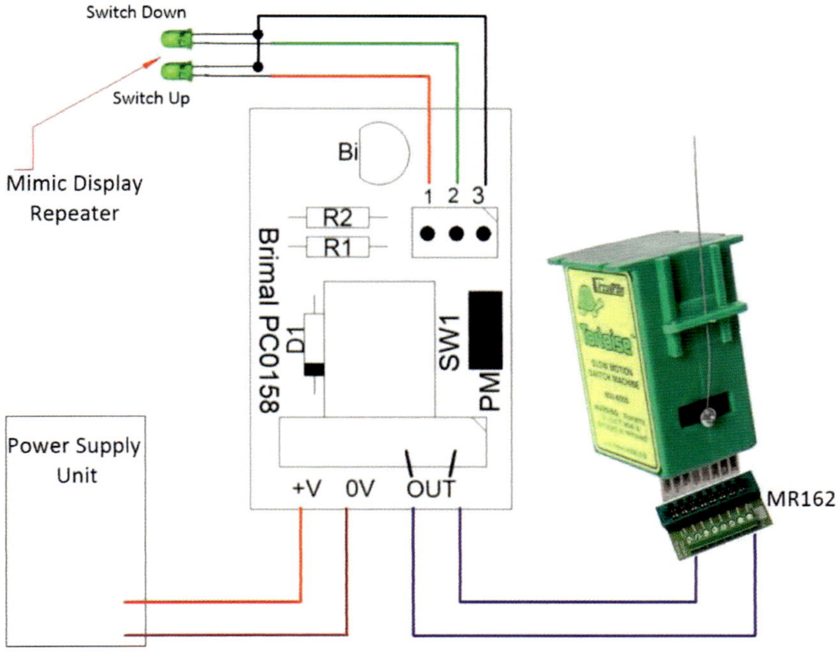

Fig: 1

In the following example the MR325 is switching a Cobolt Omega.

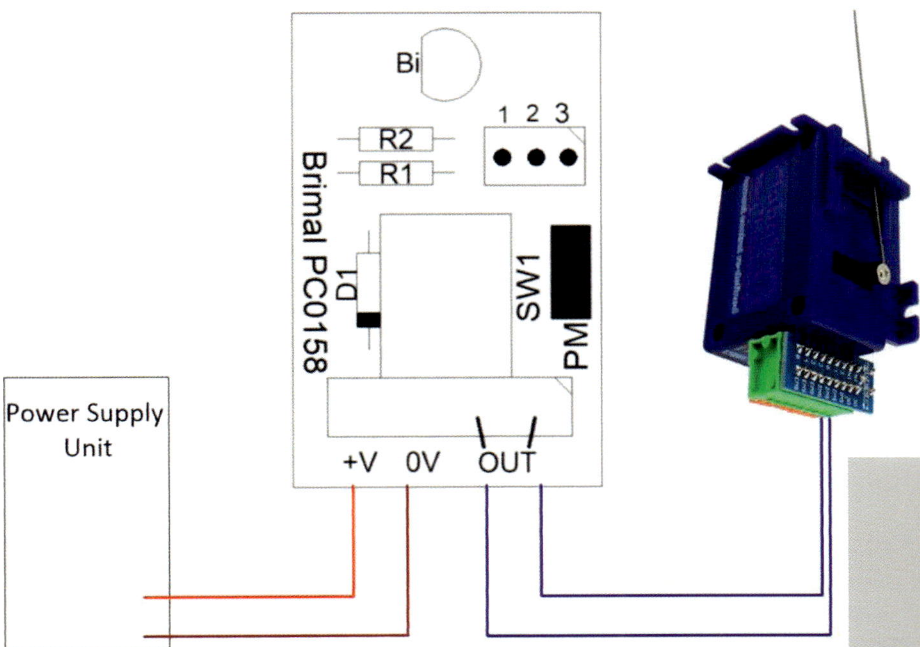

Fig:2

The Printed circuit board is held in place on the Control Panel by the Toggle Switch, this also holds the LED at the correct height. The terminal block is on the underside of the PCB so is easy to get at without removing the pcb from the panel.

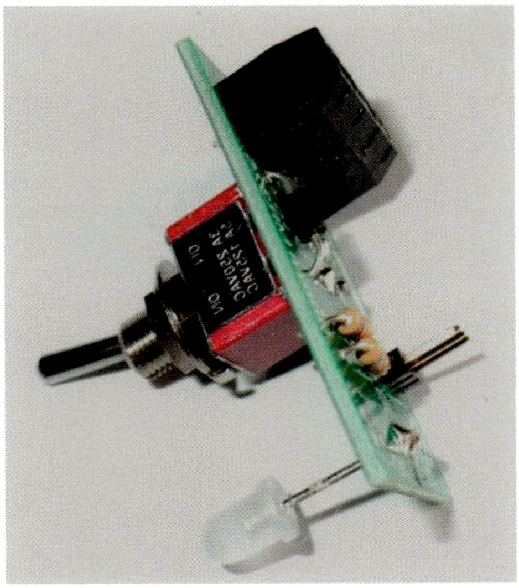

Fig:3

MODEL RAILWAY PROJECTS

You can use a range of toggle switches to do the same job, but there is a little more wiring and soldering.

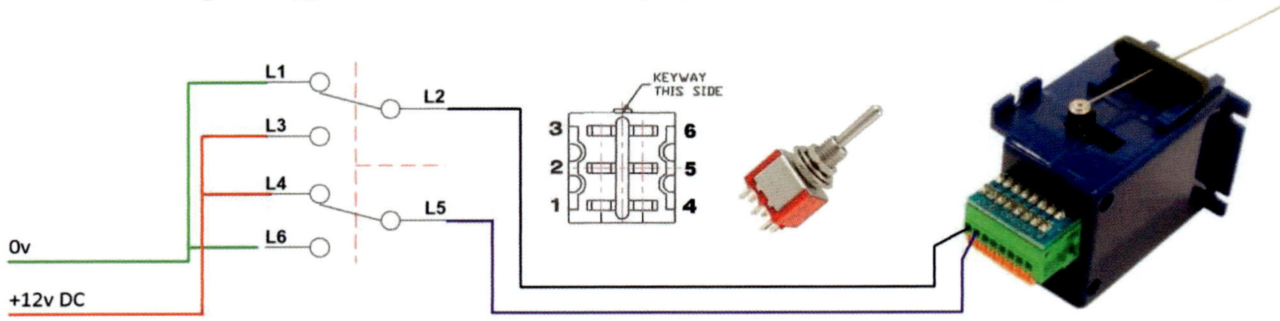

Fig: 4

The best switch is a DPDT (Double Pole Double Throw) ON / ON, Toggle switch (SW315). The wires to the controlled Track come from Terminals 2 & 5 on the switch. Terminals 6 & 1 are connected together and go to the Speed Controller. Terminals 3 & 4 are connected together and go to the Speed Controller. In one position the controller track is the same as the other track, in the other position the track Polarity is Reversed. You could also use a DPDT with centre OFF switch (SW312) if you want to Isolate the Track completely from the Speed Controller. In this situation in one position the Track Polarity is the same as the rest of the layout. In the centre position the power is OFF, and in the 3rd position the Polarity is reversed.

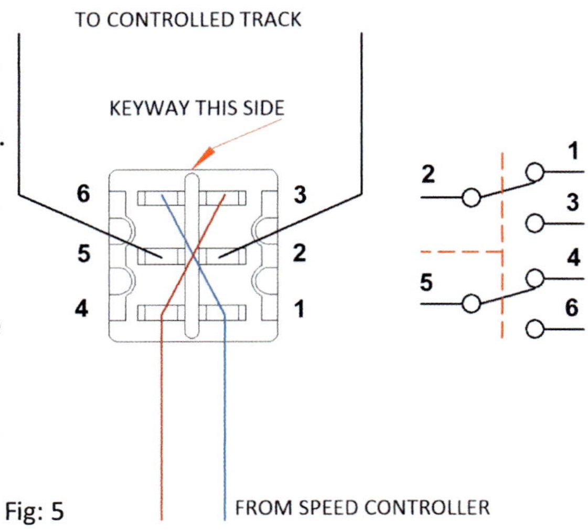

Fig: 5

In this circuit we have added a Bi-colour LED across the output of the switch to indicate the Polarity of the track. R1 is a dropping resistor of 1K. So when terminal 5 is Positive and terminal 2 is Negative the bi-coloured LED will show Green, and visa versa. This LED will repeat what the LED on the switch panel is showing. You could also use the 3 pin output on the switch board to do the same, to indicate which section of track is either isolated or reversed. The advantage of using the 3 pins on the board is that you can use 2 separate LED's one on each side of the isolation point so that when they are both Green you know the polarity is the same.

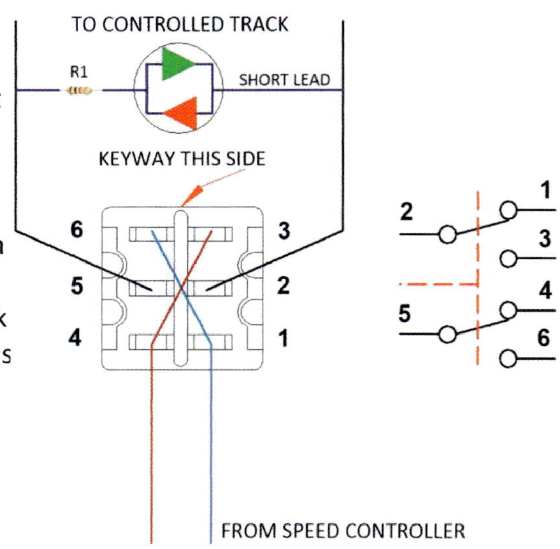

Fig: 6

The next drawing shows how you can position LED's either side of an Isolation point to indicate the polarity of the tracks. As long as the colours are the same the Locomotive will move over the junction without problem.

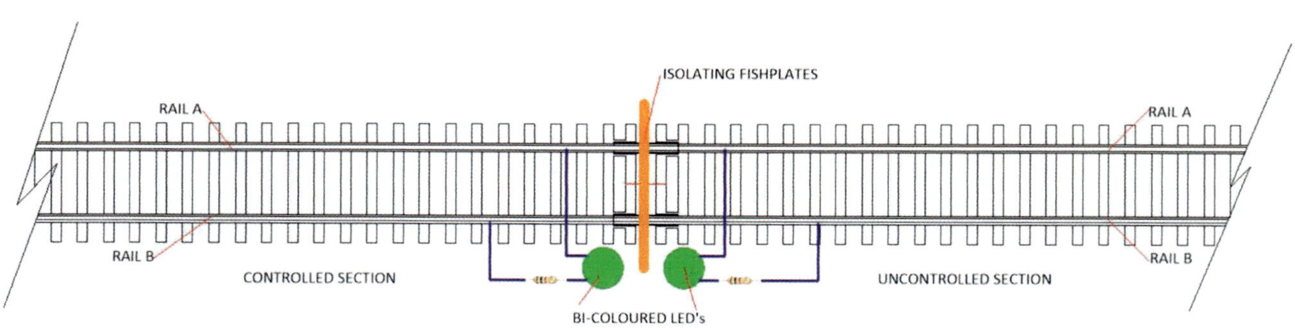

Fig: 7

Reversing Power Supply Output

It can be used to feed the whole system or local sidings or certain tracks. The Printed circuit board is held in place on the Control Panel by the Toggle Switch, this also holds the LED at the correct height. The terminal block is on the underside of the PCB so is easy to get at without removing the pcb from the panel.

In this circuit the Forward/Reverse switch is used to change the Polarity of Terminals 1& 2 also 3 &4. You could wire 3 & 4 directly from the speed controller, so you had one set 1 & 2 reversable and the other set 3 & 4 fixed.

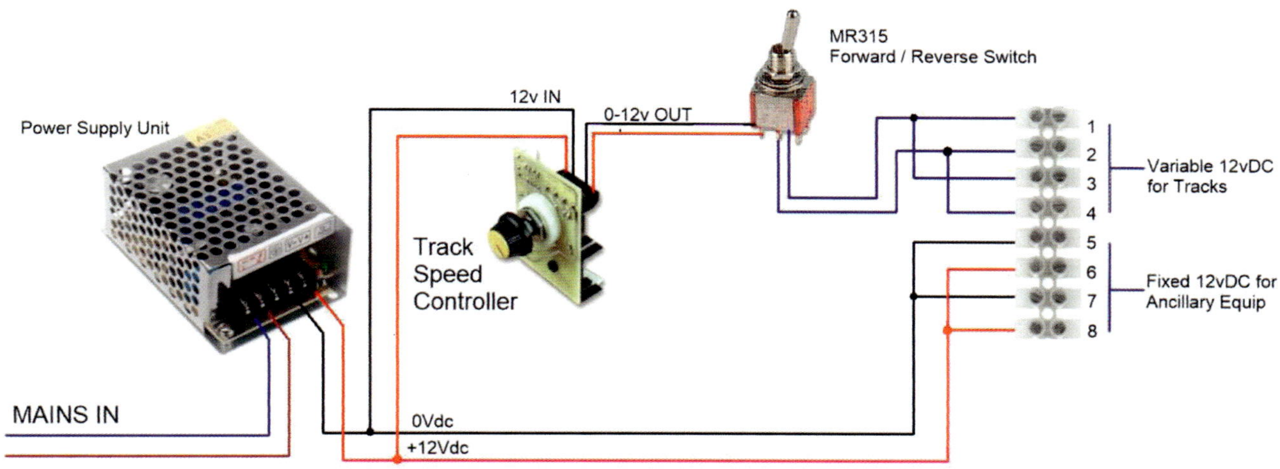

Fig: 1

In this circuit we are using the MR326 switch board. The advantage of this board is that it will also indicate the polarity status on the control panel. You can use the 2 LED's as remote indication on the layout if you require. It is very simple to add to a layout as there are only 4 wires to connect and no soldering.

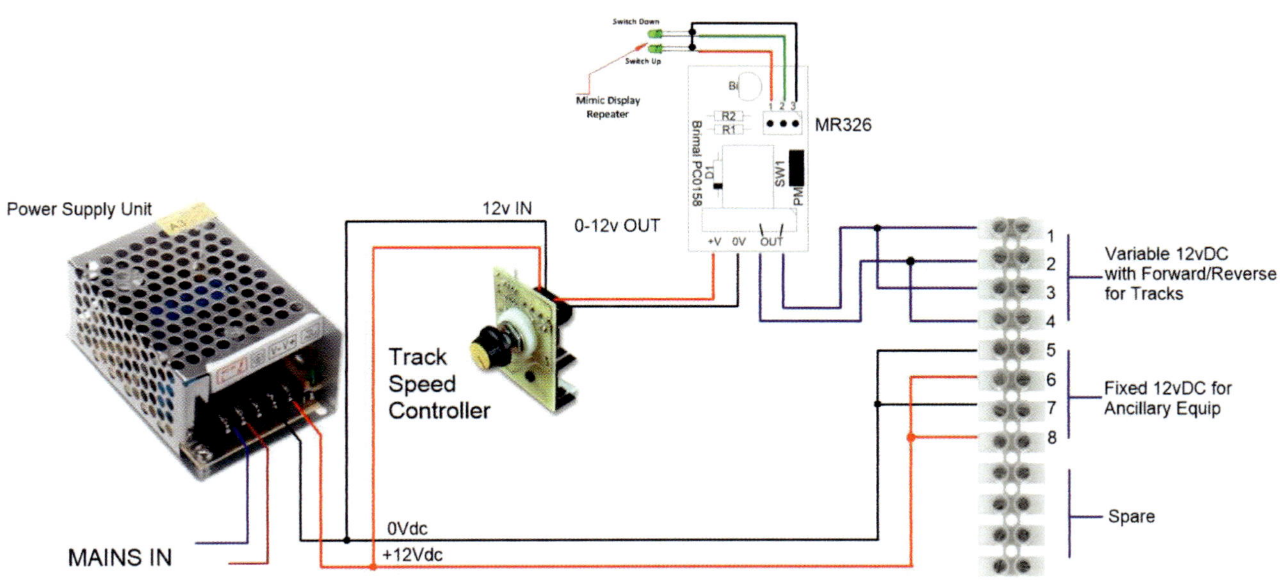

Fig: 2

Switches available from: Layouts4U, JPR Electronics, 2K Technologies
Printed Circuits available from: Layouts4U, 2K Technologies.
Point Motors available from: most Model Rail Stores.

Train Position Indicator

There will be times when you need some form of indication as to the position or movement of the train if in hidden areas of your layout, such as tunnels and underground areas, or parts of the layout you just cannot see from the control area.

Here we give some ideas for solving that problem.

A very basic sensor is shown below which consists of the Magnetic Reed Switch, a Magnet, a Capacitor and an LED.

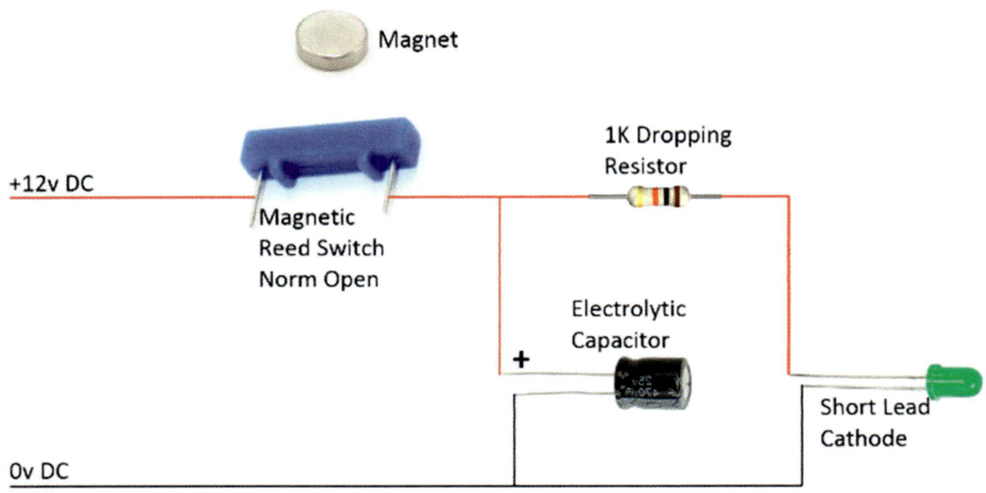

Fig: 1

The basic circuit for a simple panel indication is shown opposite. The higher the value of the capacitor the longer the LED will stay on – the value shown is 470uF this will keep the LED ON for 2 to 3 seconds. The magnet is fitted to the underside of the train/s, the reed switch is fitted in between the sleepers or across the sleepers (watch out for clearance with the magnet – the operating distance from reed to magnet can be up to 10mm apart). When the train passes over the reed, the reed switches ON which illuminates the LED on the control panel, and charges up the Capacitor. Once the train has passed the reed the LED will switch OFF, this could turn out to be just a flash depending on the speed of the train. The capacitor is there to hold the LED ON for 2 to 4 seconds

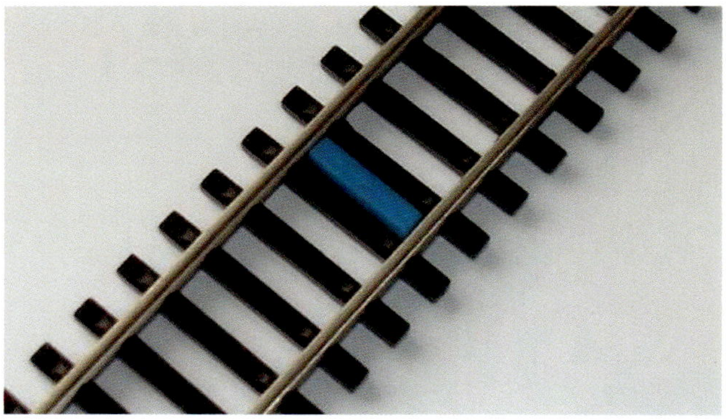

Fig: 2

Fig: 3

The magnet is fitted to the underside of the train/s, the reed switch is fitted in-between the sleepers or across the sleepers (watch out for clearance with the magnet – the operating distance from reed to magnet can be up to 5mm apart). When the train passes over the reed, the reed switches ON which illuminates the LED on the control panel, and charges the Capacitor. Once the train has passed the reed, the LED will switch OFF, this could turn out to be just a flash or a couple of seconds, depending on the size of Capacitor used. The Capacitor in the circuit above is 470uf and will hold the LED ON for approximately 2 to 3 seconds.

Sensors.

There are many ways to detect the train at any point on a track. The simplest is probably using the sensor and circuit as described above.

You can get Barrel sensors (Fig: 4) which only requires a 6 or 7mm hole drilled between the sleepers. This is the same as the sensor above only being used at its end, which will make the sensor less sensitive so the magnet will need to be a little closer.

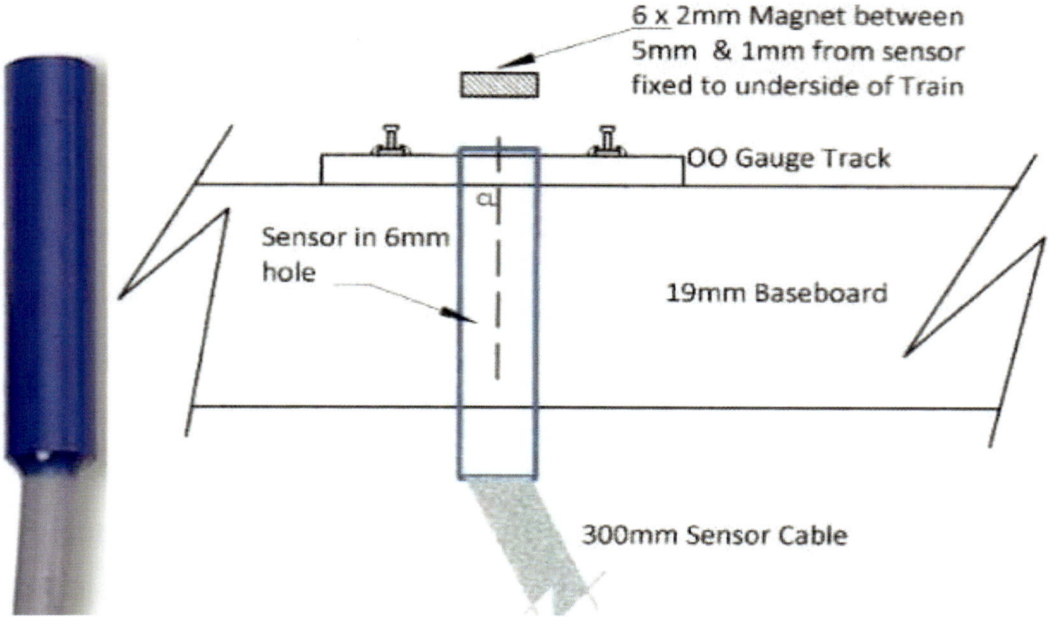

Fig: 4

Infrared Sensors

There is a range of Infrared sensors and circuits on the market which will do the job. Some come with the sensors fixed to the circuit board, so require the board to be fixed at the location, whereas some have remote sensors so the circuit board can be fitted near the Control Panel. The advantage of the remote sensors is that you can get the sensors into very small or tight positions, and then run the wires back to the circuit board.

Here are a few examples positioning remote sensors.

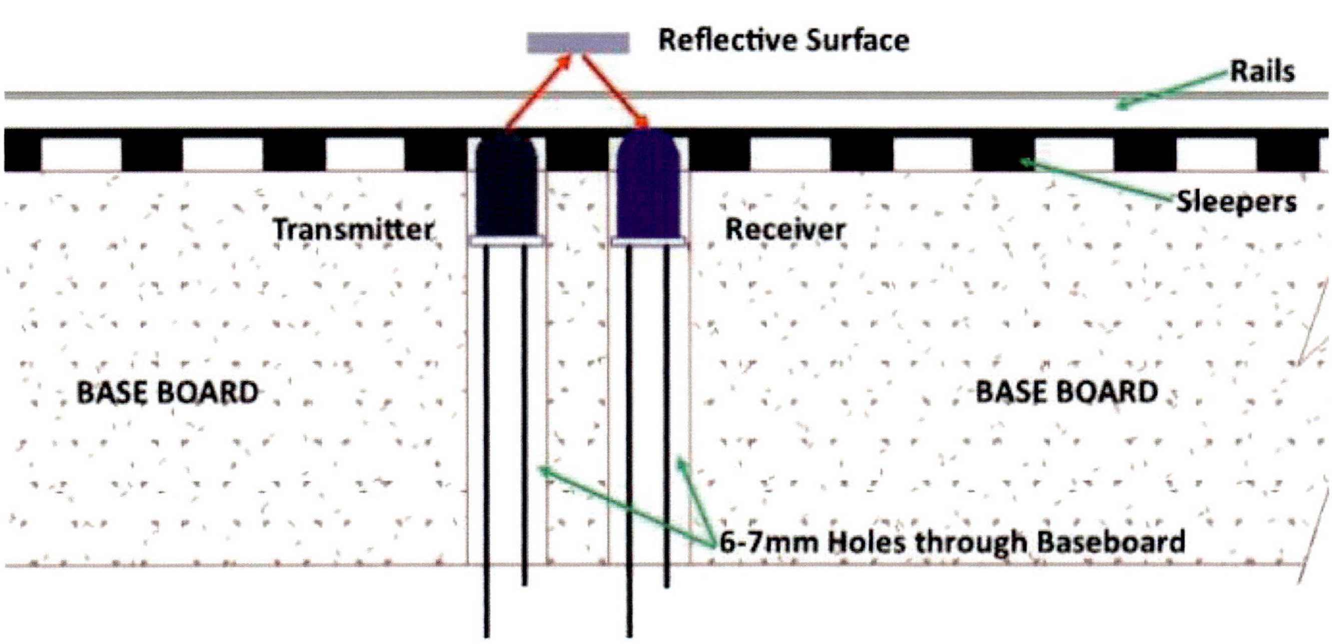

Fig:5

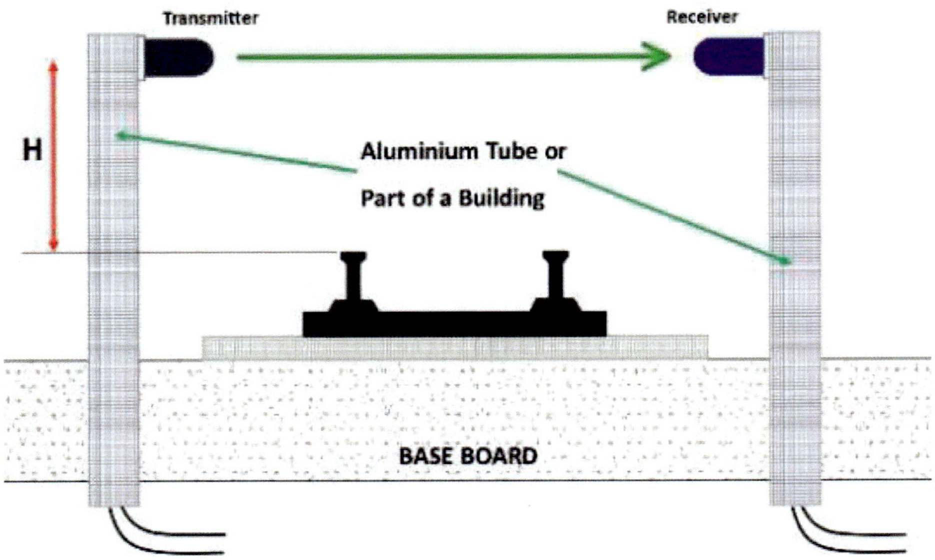

Fig: 6

With most Infrared circuits you will have a Normally Open Output, that closes when the sensor is activated. This NO contact can be used to drive other circuits or equipment as shown below.

Latching Indication.

There may be times when you want the Indication to stay on after the Train has passed and be switched off by some other event. An example of this is if you had the front of the train switch the Red LED ON and the rear of the train switch it back to Green.

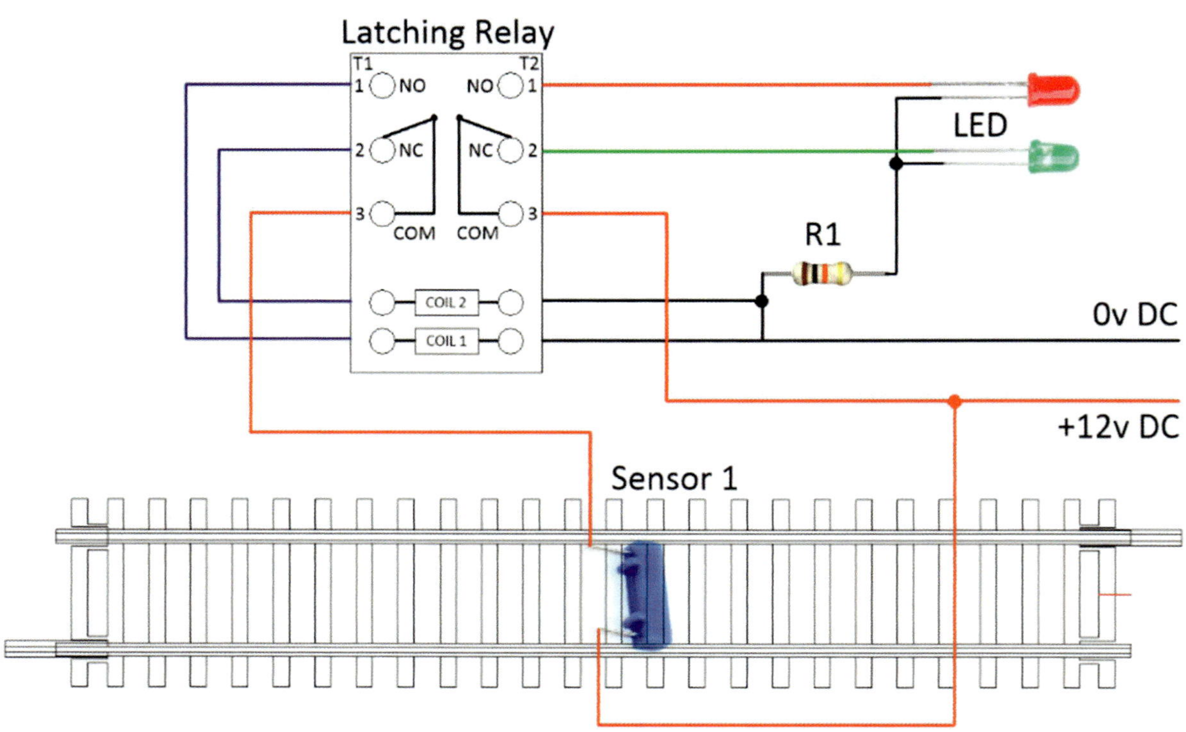

Fig: 7

In this circuit the train passes over the Sensor and switches the Latching Relay, which changes the Green LED to the Red LED (this could be a 2 Aspect Signal if you want). As the rear of the train passes over the sensor the relay switches back to the original state switching OFF the Red LED, and switches ON the Green LED. You will need a Magnet at both ends of the train. If you are using a signal, then you would wire the Red into T2 (1) and the Green into T2 (2) so that when there is no train the Green in the signal is showing.

AC to DC Converter

MR150 AC Voltage max 5v to 230v, Current max 4 Amp
MR151 AC Voltage Max 5v to 230v, Current max 8 Amp

These modules can be used to convert AC to DC. The most common AC supply voltages are 5, 12v, 15v, 16v, 18v and 24v, these modules will handle all these voltages, and convert them into DC. The output voltage will depend on the input voltage from the transformer. There is typically a voltage drop of 2 volts through the circuit.
There is a LED indicator to show there is output power. Due to the smoothing capacitor when AC power is removed DC power may take a few seconds to go to 0v.
The module can be used to drive all non voltage sensitive equipment, such as point motors, signals, and LED indicators. Do not use it to power sensitive electronic circuits as they require a regulated power source.

The Basic Circuit

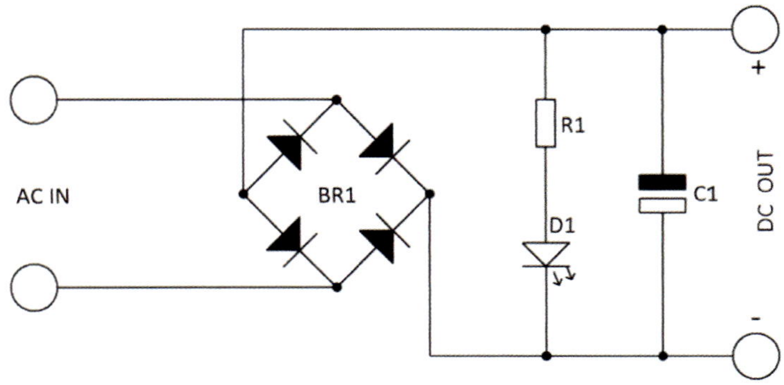

Connection Diagram

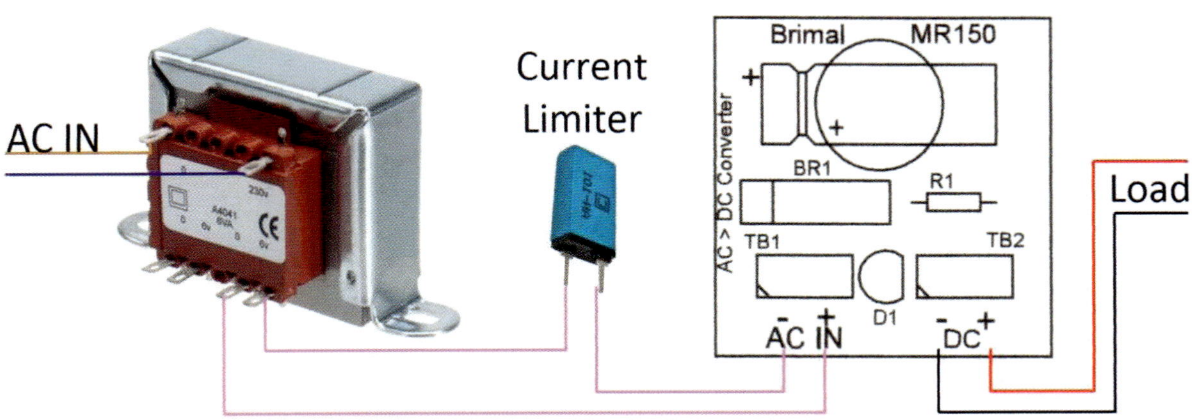

The Current Limiter is optional, however it is advisable just to protect your equipment.
Note: The Converter circuit has a maximum current output of MR150=4Amps or MR151=8Amps
A 6v transformer will give about 5v DC output.
A 12v transformer will give about 10v DC output.
A 15v transformer will give about 13v DC output.

Depending on the current capability of the transformer you may see a voltage drop when you add a load to the output. The higher the VA, the more likely the voltage will be steady.

To calculate the current capability of a transformer The output voltage divided by the VA example a 6 volt transformer at 12VA has an output current of 2 Amps
A= output volt/VA

PROJECT 11

Siding Occupied Indication

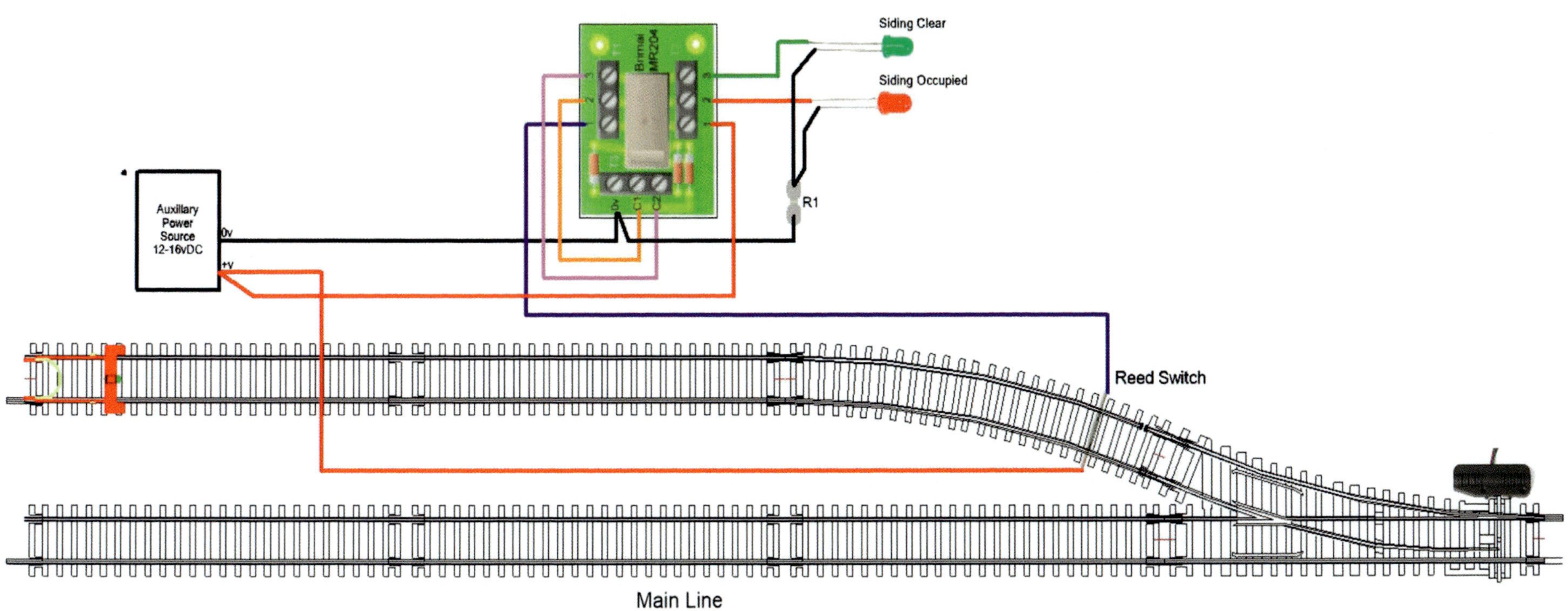

In this application the MR204 is used to indicate back at the Control Panel if a Siding is Occupied or not. As the train passes over the Reed Switch the indication changes from Green (Siding Clear) to Red (Siding Occupied). When the train leaves the siding it passes over the same Reed switch which will change the relay back to Green on (Siding Clear).

The second set of contacts on the relay are used to change the function of the Reed switch, in effect converting it into two separate switches.

A second circuit can be used in conjunction with this first circuit to Isolate the track (so the train enters the siding and then power is removed from the track stopping the train) and controlling the Points with an indication back at the Control Panel as to the status of the points.

Points Position Indicators

One of the biggest problems with an Analogue system is knowing what state the points are in, especially in those far corners, tunnels, and fiddle yards to name a few. Here we look at all the different types of position Indicators. Starting with the very basic.

Basic Kit

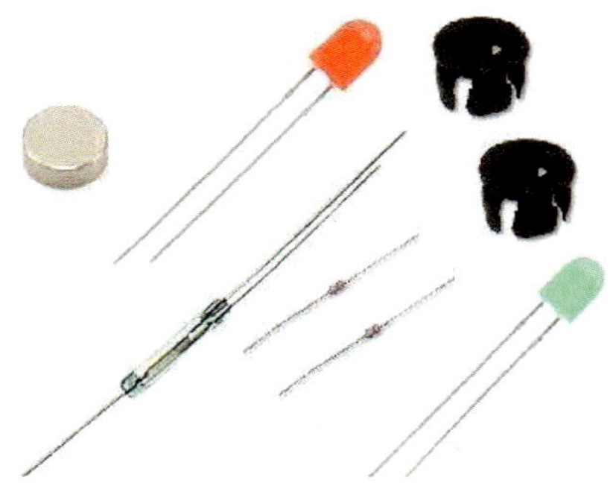

This Kit is designed to Indicate the state of a set of Points. The position of the Sensor and the magnet is shown in the drawing below. Set it up with the points set at straight through and the sensor about 10 to 15mm from the lever. Glue the magnet to the moving lever of the points. When the points are changed the magnet should move to within 10 to 5mm of the Reed, this will then change the state of the switch.

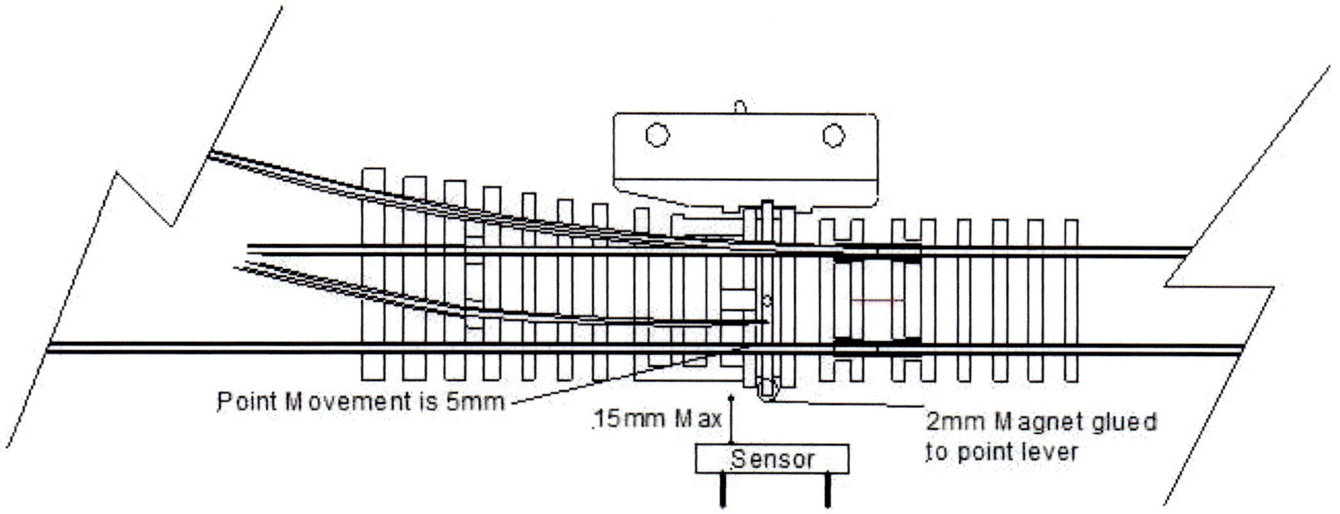

Connect the Green LED to the longer of the 2 wires on the Reed switch as shown in the drawing below. This indicates the points are straight through. Connect the Red LED to the shorter of the 2 wires on the reed switch as shown. Connect a Positive voltage to the other end of the Reed via a 1K resistor as shown. Connect the negative feed to the shorter leads on the LED's. When the magnet is brought close to the Reed the LED's should change.

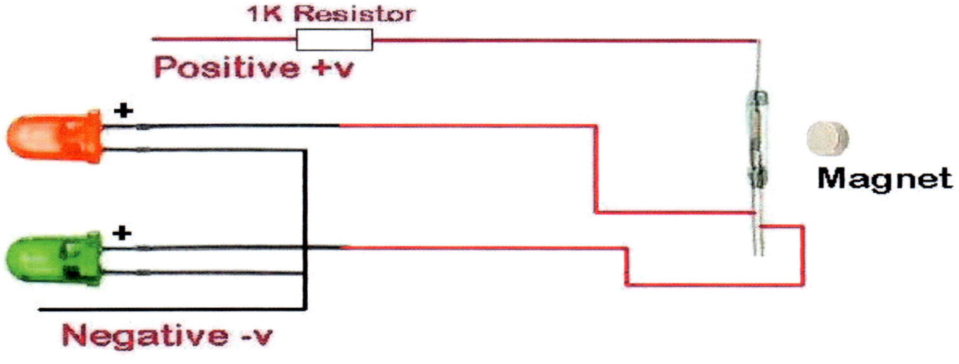

Microswitch

(SW052 to SW054)

This switch is a Microswitch in the state shown the Green LED is ON. When the switch is activated (pressed down) the Green LED switches OFF and the Red LED switches ON. This situation will remain until the lever is allowed to go back to the resting position.

Check the points are straight through. Fit the Roller switch as shown and screw down with a 2mm self tapping 16mm long screw in position 'A' only. Now wire the LED's as shown above with the green Wire going to the Green LED and the red wire going to the Red LED. Connect the power and check that the Green LED on ON, now move the points to turn out position, and the Green should go out and the Red come on. Make small adjustments of the

switch by rotating the switch around the screw 'A', when you are happy that all is working well fit the other screw to lock the switch in position.
In each case the wire from the switch is connected to the Anode of the LED (See below) and the Cathode is connected to the Negative voltage via a 1k dropping resistor.

This drawing shows the Switch SW054

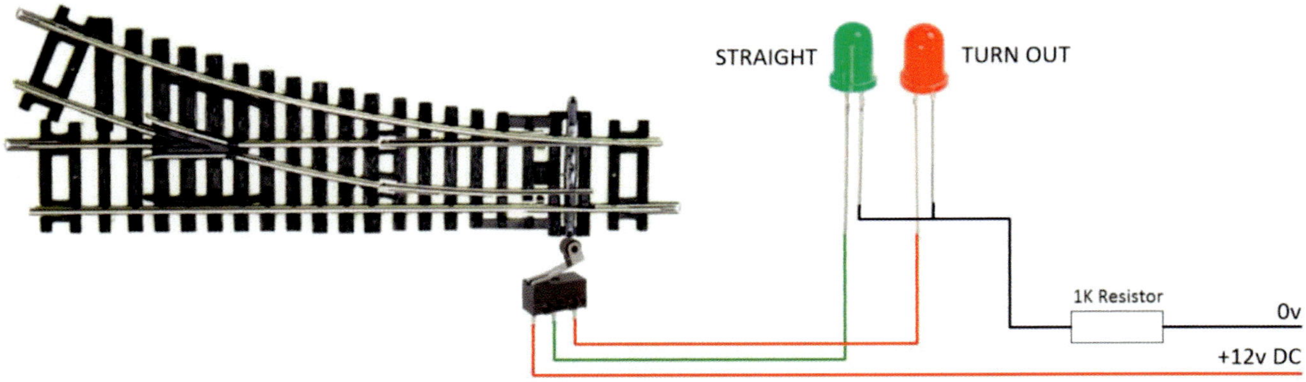

Reed Switch

This drawing shows the Switch SW929

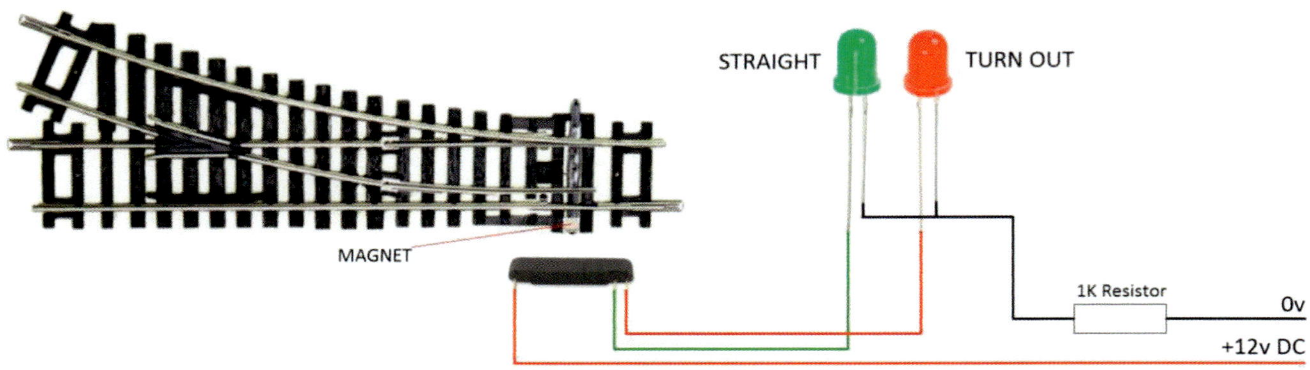

Leaf Switch

Circuit using the SWP100 Leaf Switch

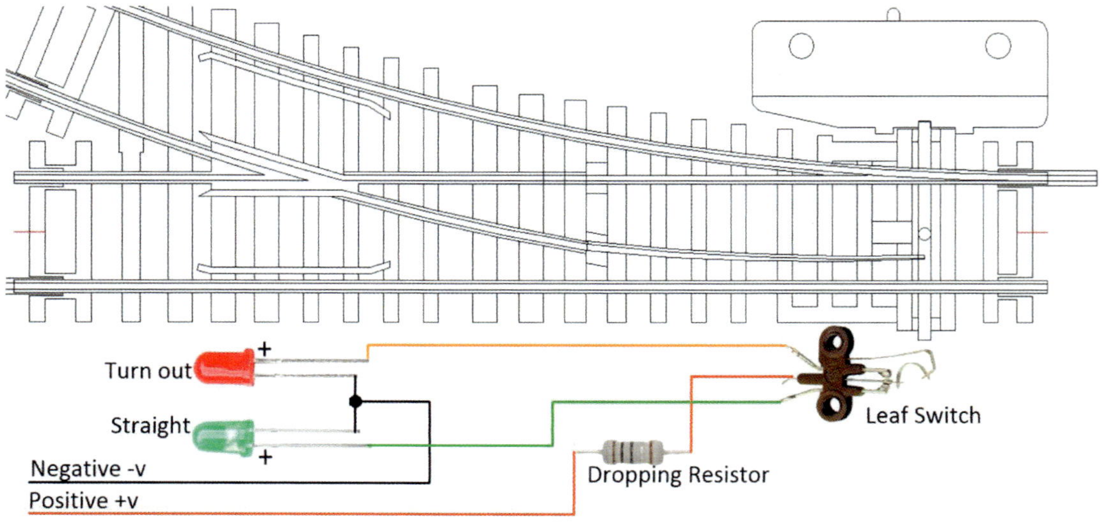

This switch is a Leaf Switch in the state shown the Green LED is ON. When the switch is activated (pressed down) the Green LED switches OFF and the Red LED switches ON. This situation will remain until the lever is allowed to go back to the resting position. Check the points are straight through. Fit the Leaf switch as shown and screw down with a 2mm self tapping 16mm long screw in position 'A' only. Now wire the LED's as shown above with the green Wire going to the Green LED and the red wire going to the Red LED. Connect the power and check that the Green LED on ON, now move the points to turn out position, and the Green should go out and the Red come on. Make small adjustments of the switch by rotating the switch around the screw 'A', when you are happy that all is working well fit the other screw to lock the switch in position.

Peco PL13

This circuit shows the Peco PL13 switch which will fit on the Peco PL-10, PL-10E, PL-10W , Gaugemaster GMC-PM10, Hornby R8014 and Hattons HAT-PM-01 point motors

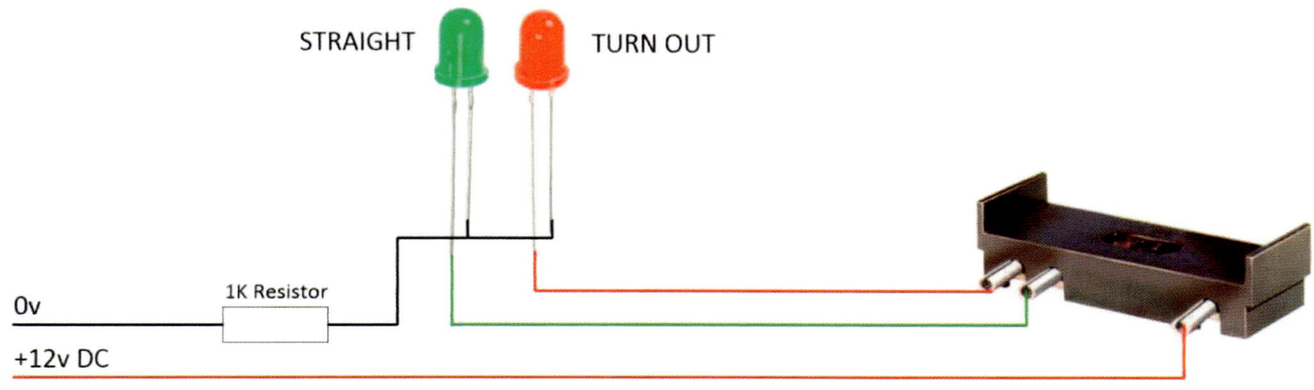

MR204

All solenoid type point motors require a short burst of power. When using a momentary toggle switch or push button switch, once energised there is no indication as to the status of the points.

In this circuit we are using the MR204 to give the indication. When the toggle switch is moved UP momentarily the circuit changes the state of the points and Green switches off and the red comes on, and visa versa.

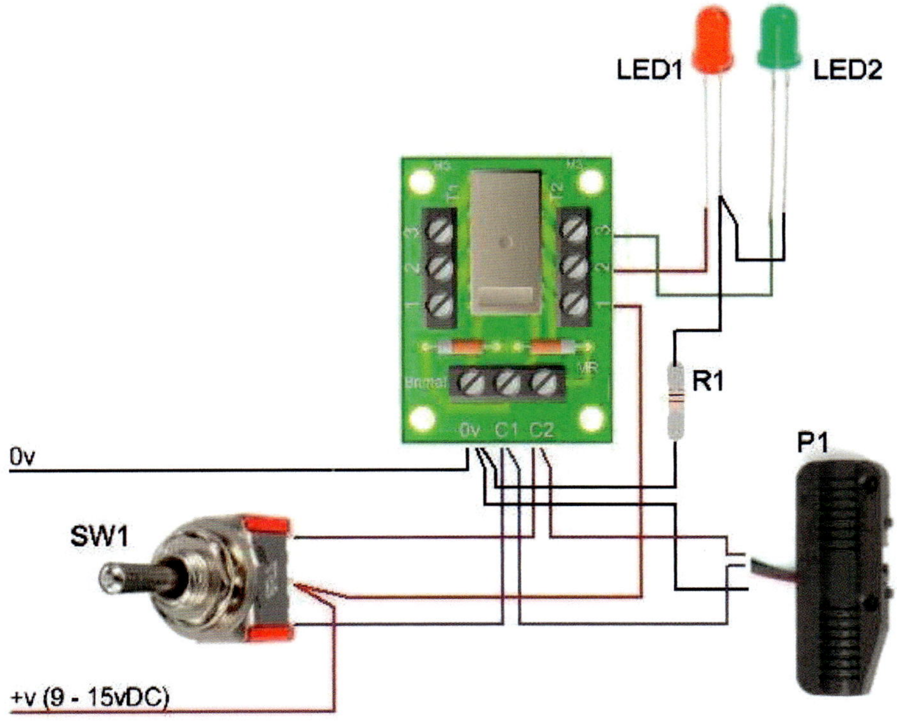

Peco PL15

MODEL RAILWAY PROJECTS

This circuit shows the Peco PL15 switch which will fit on the Peco PL-10, PL-10E, PL-10W , Gaugemaster GMC-PM10, Hornby R8014 and Hattons HAT-PM-01 point motors

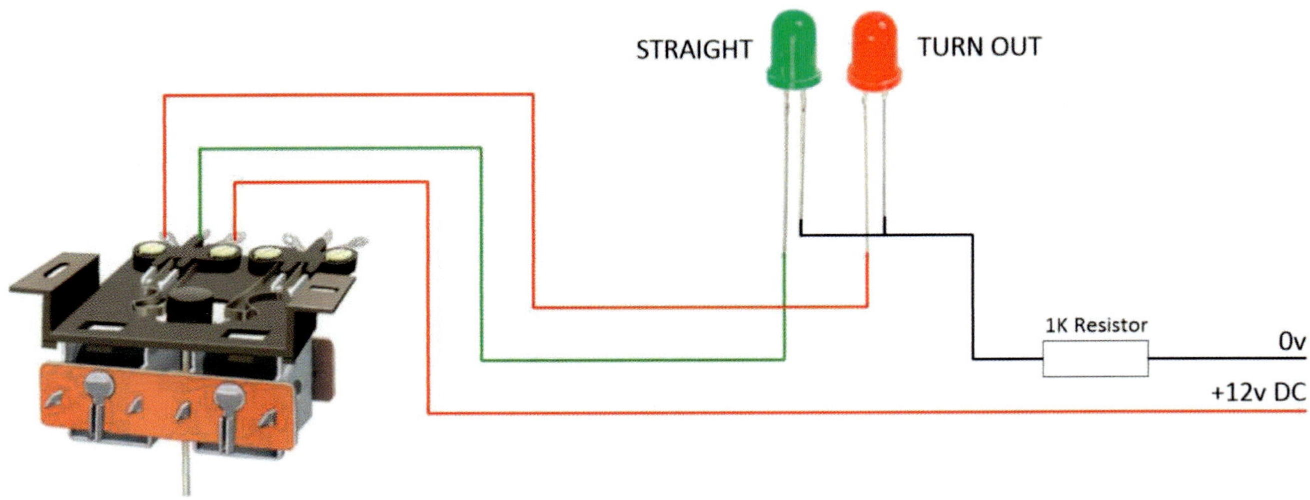

SEEP Point Motor

This circuit shows the indication using a SEEP point motor

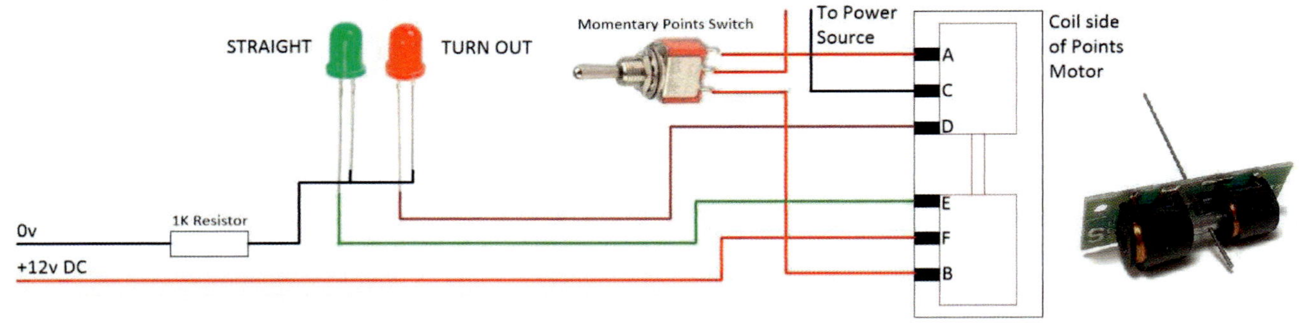

Colbalt Classic

Connection of indicator LED's to the Classic Cobalt Motor

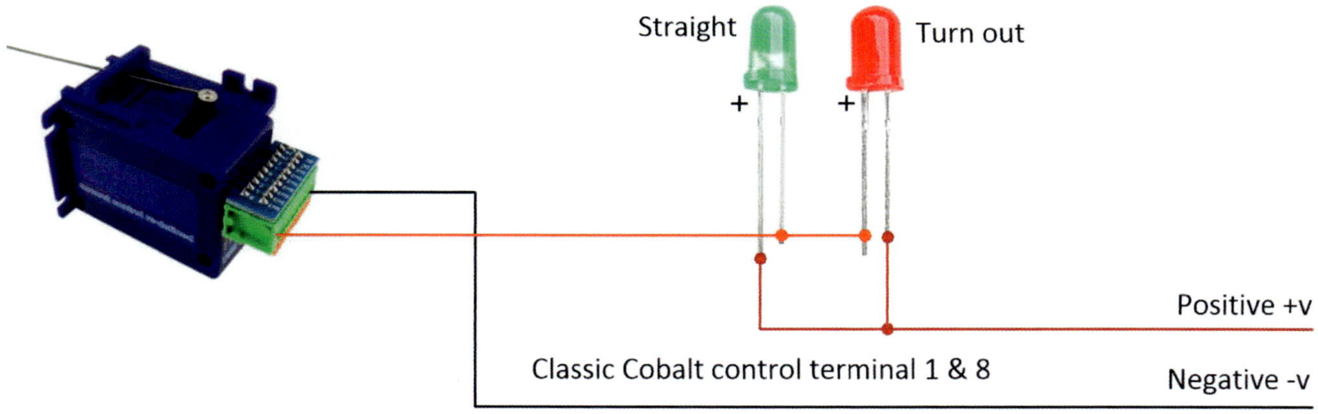

Cobalt Omega

Connection of indicator LED's to the Colbalt Omega Motor

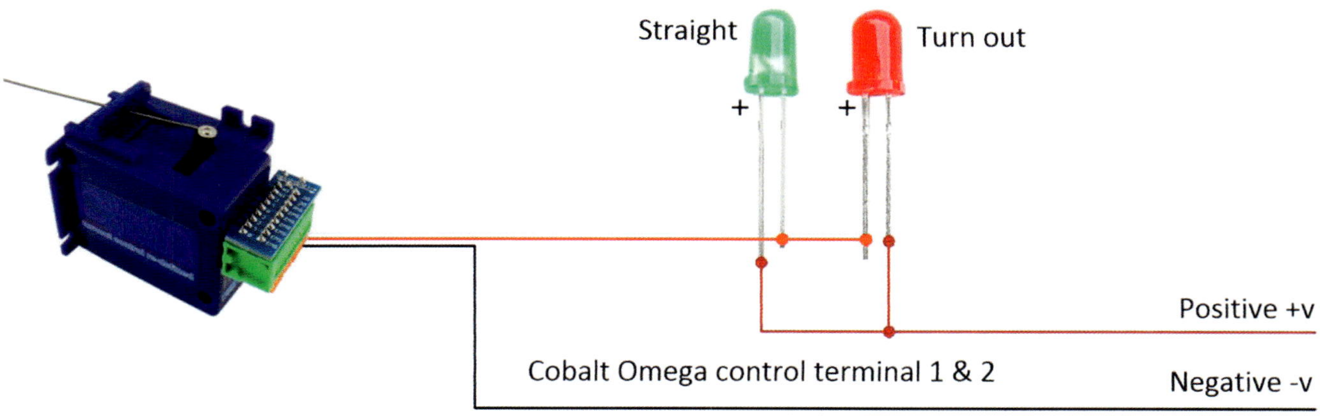

Brimal MR322

The MR322 is a momentary switch complete with panel indicator and mimic display indicator all on the one board. No extra wiring is required just the wires to the switch and then to the motor as you would normally do. The terminals are on the opposite side to the switch so very easy to connect once the switch is on the panel.

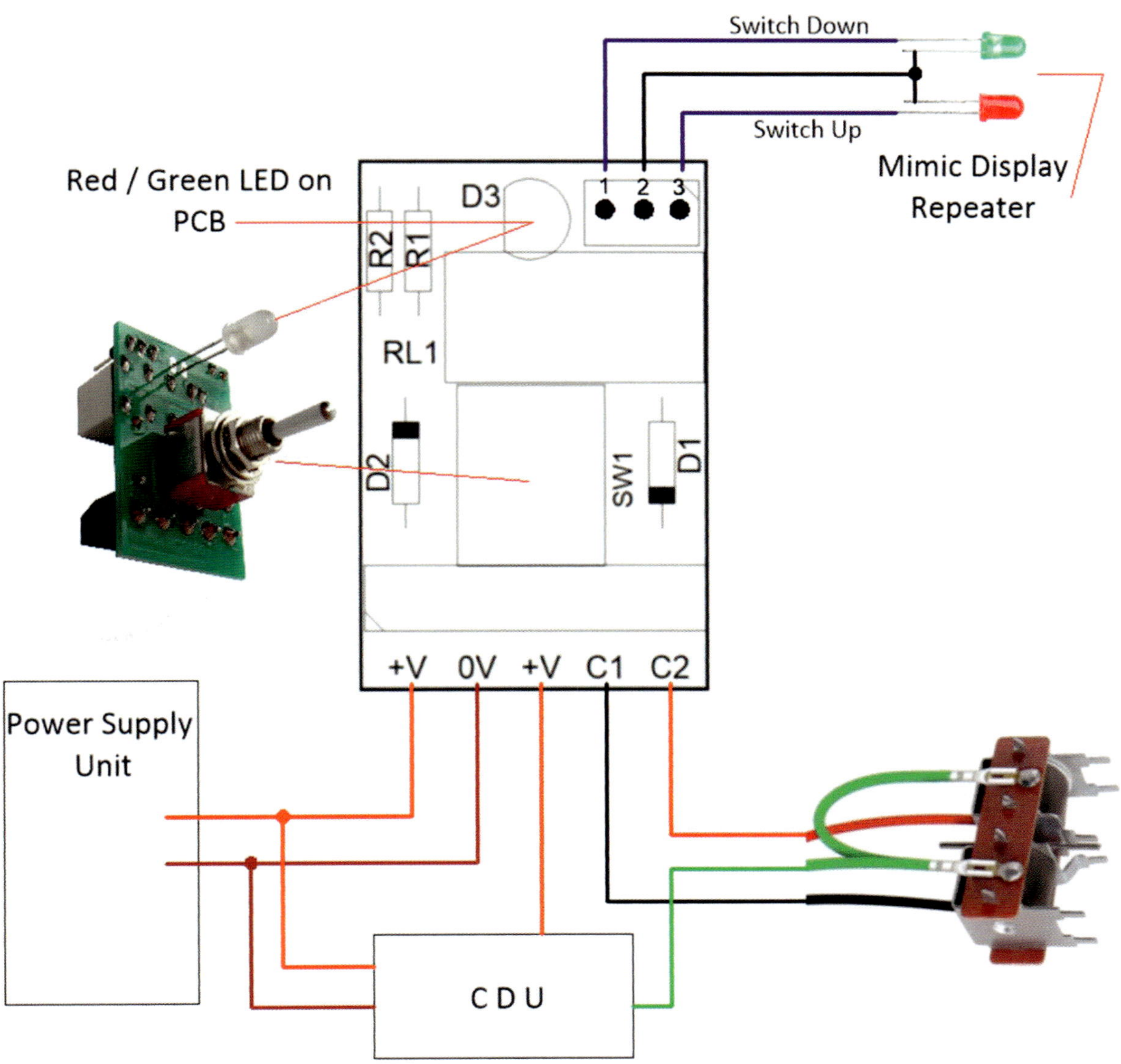

It is possible to use filament LES, or wheatgerm bulbs with all the above switches except for the MR322, you just need to leave out the dropping resistor in all cases.

Now let's look at LED's

This is the wiring diagram of a standard LED. The **shorter lead** on the LED is always the Negative. You will also need a dropping resistor in either the Positive or Negative lead.

Single Colour LED

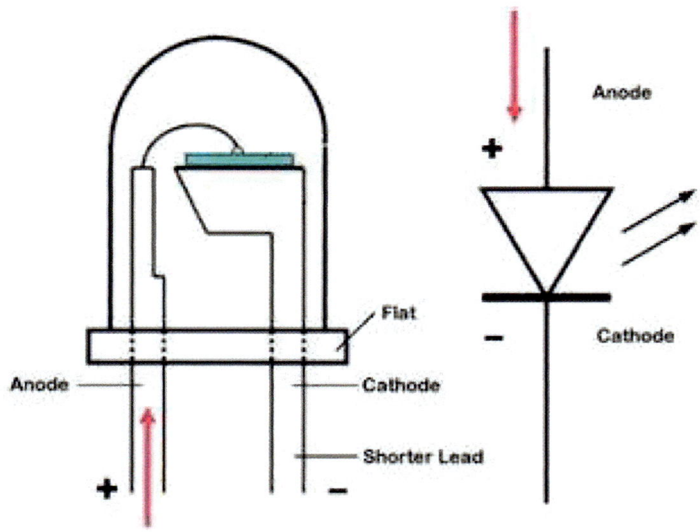

Bi-colour LED

In all cases except the MR322 you could use a single bi-coloured LED. Just wire it as though it's 2 LED's
Pin 1 is the positive for the Red.
Pin 2 is a common Negative where you would connect the dropping resistor.
Pin 3 is the positive for the Green.

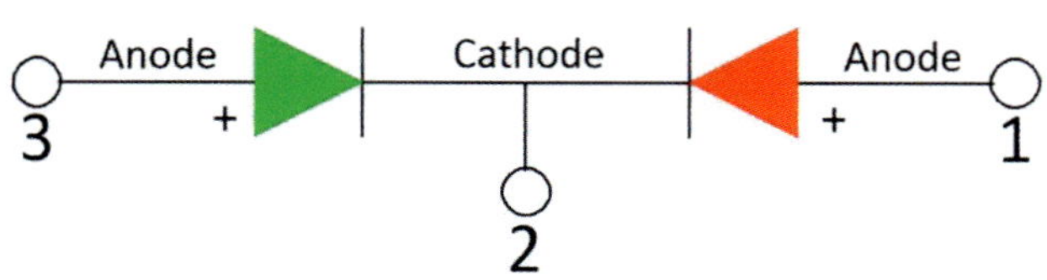

Dropping Resistor

An LED (Light Emitting Diode) emits light when an electric current passes through it. The simplest circuit to power an LED is a voltage source with a resistor and an LED in series. Such a resistor is often called a dropping resistor. If the voltage source is equal to the voltage drop of the LED, no resistor is required.

The resistor can go before – or after – the LED, and it will still protect it. the current that flows out of a power source is always equal to the current that flows back into the power source. The current through the resistor is the same as the current through the LED.

Use this formula to determine the resistor value: Resistor = (Power source Voltage – LED voltage) / desired LED current. For a typical white LED that requires 10mA, powered by 12V the values are: (12-3.4)/. 010=860 ohms. To use several LEDs in parallel, sum the current values.

PROJECT 13

Points Indicator using a Latching Relay

In this application the MR204 is used to control a Point Motor, and 2 LED's at the Control Panel. The switch is a Momentary action Mini Toggle Switch, (this can be replaced by 2 mini Push Button switches).
Ideally the MR204 should be fixed near the set of points it is controlling.
If you are using a Positive & Negative Bus Bar – the toggle switch and the LED's only require a 6 core back to the control panel.
If you are not using Bus Bars then you will require a 8 core cable back to the control panel
The colour code for the wiring is 0v Black, +v Red, please see the individual product instruction sheets to see the colour code they are using.
The relay has latching contacts, this means once energised and power is removed the contacts stay in that state until the second coil is energised.
Once you have the system wired as above, you may find the indicators are back to front, this is due to the state of the relay when you first switch ON. In this case you may have to swap 2 & 3 around.
R1 is a 1K quarter or half watt resistor placed in the negative line to the LED's, to reduce the current drawn by the LED's

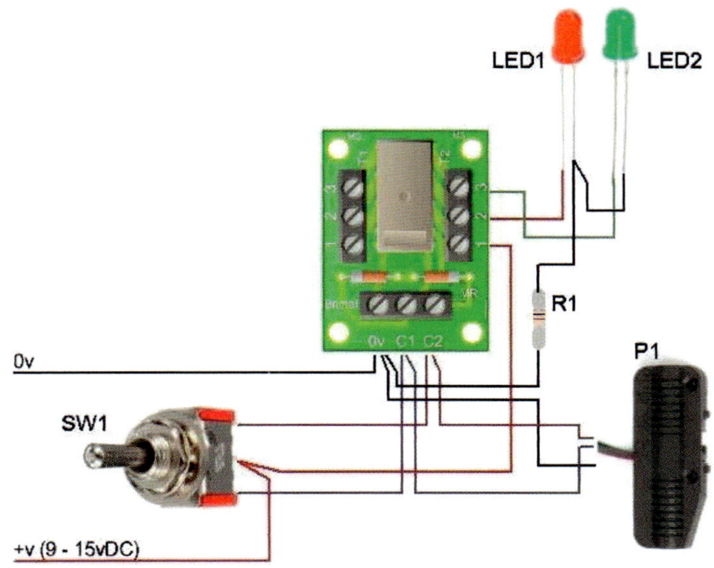

Points, Signal & Indicator

PROJECT 14

In this application the MR204 is used to control a Point Motor, a Signal, and 2 LED's at the Control Panel. The switch is a Momentary action Mini Toggle Switch, (this can be replaced by 2 mini Push Button switches).
Ideally the MR204 should be fixed near the set of points it is controlling, as the Signal will also be in the same area.

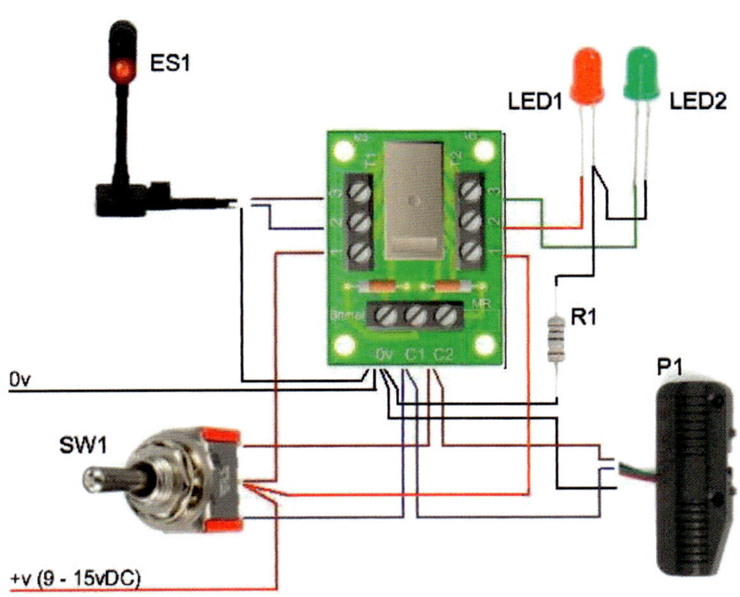

Wiring a 2 wire LED Signal

Some LED signals have only 2 wires to power both the RED & GREEN LED's. An LED is polarity sensitive so if the polarity is reversed the LED will not work, so if two LED's are joined together but with opposing polarities only one will be ON at any time.
There are a number of ways of switching these signals, the following are a few ideas to help.

SLIDE SWITCH

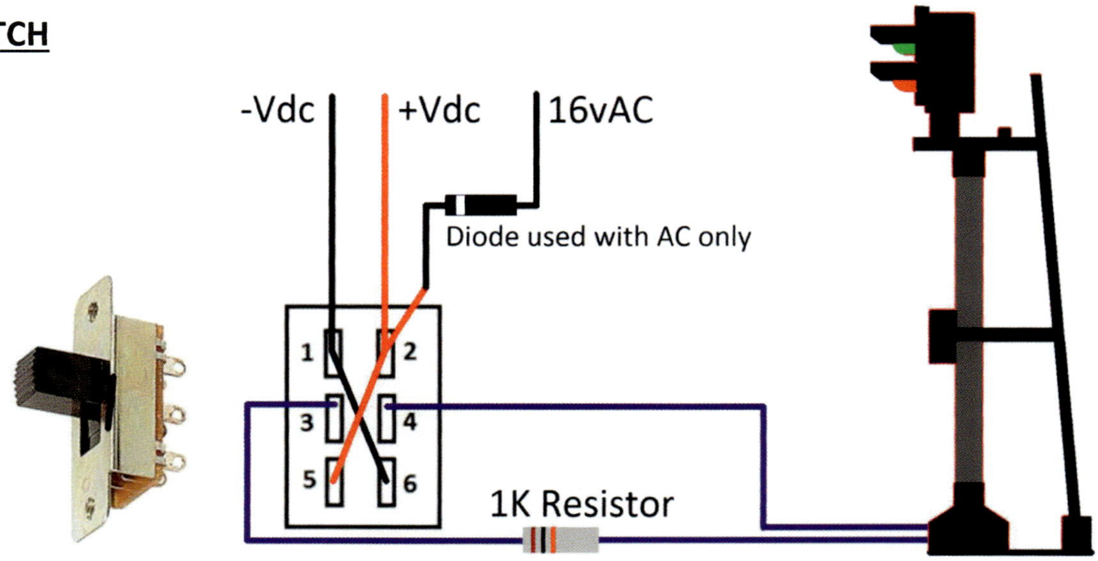

12VDC

First connect the Negative supply to pins 1 and 6 of your slide switch, then connect the Positive supply to 2 and 5. Now connect the two wires from the Signal to pins 3 & 4 of the slide switch. One wire must go through the Resistor as shown above.

16VAC

First connect the Negative supply to pins 1 and 6 of your slide switch, then connect the Positive supply through a Diode as shown to pins 2 and 5. Now connect the two wires from the Signal to pins 3 & 4 of the slide switch. One wire must go through the Resistor as shown above.

TOGGLE SWITCH

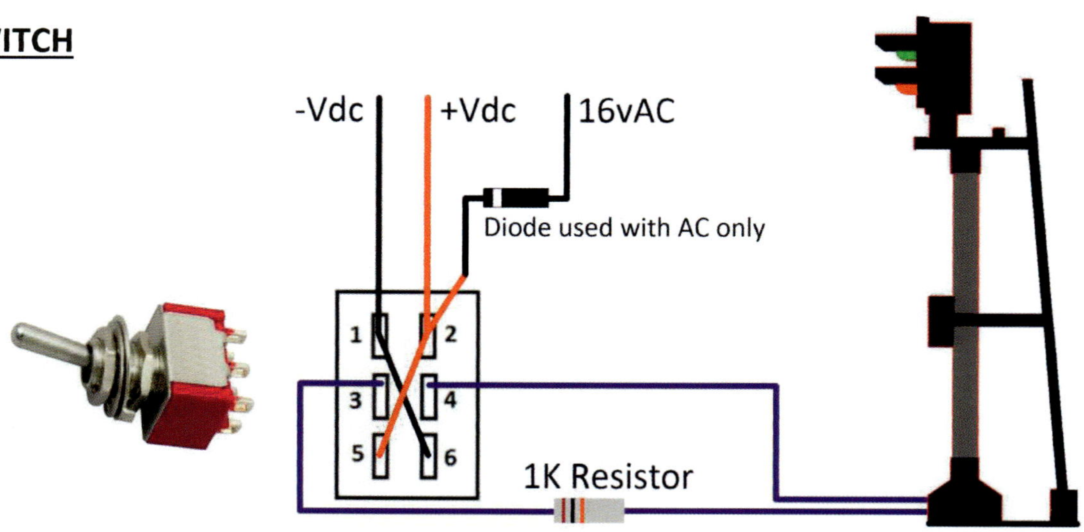

12VDC

First connect the Negative supply to pins 1 and 6 of your slide switch, then connect the Positive supply to 2 and 5. Now connect the two wires from the Signal to pins 3 & 4 of the slide switch. One wire must go through the Resistor as shown above.

16VAC

First connect the Negative supply to pins 1 and 6 of your slide switch, then connect the Positive supply through a Diode as shown to pins 2 and 5. Now connect the two wires from the Signal to pins 3 & 4 of the slide switch. One wire must go through the Resistor as shown above.

MR204 & Leaf Switch

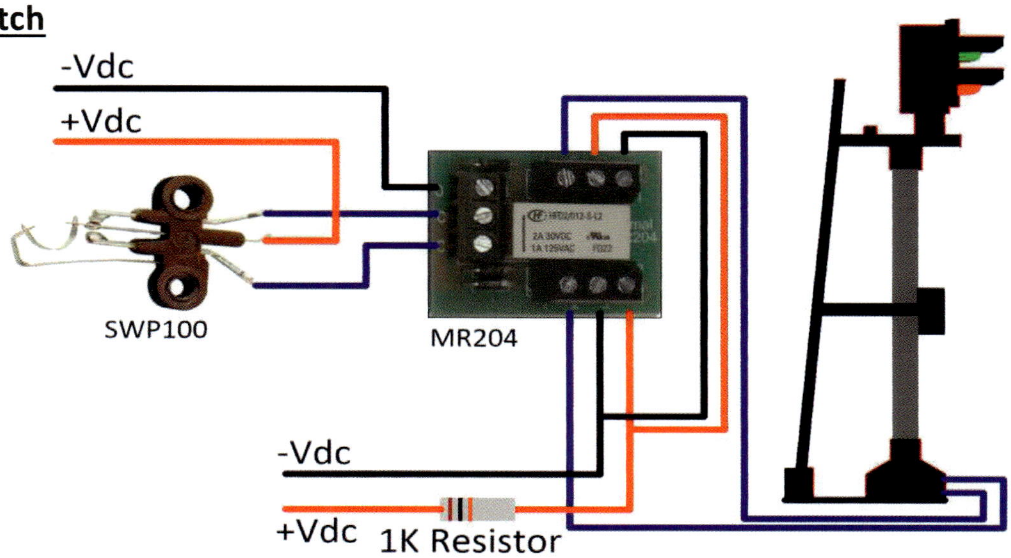

In this circuit we are using a Peco type Leaf Switch SWP100, this is a single pole changeover switch so cannot switch the Negative side. For this we use the MR204 Relay board. The leaf switch is activated by the Point Motor, this in turn activates the relay which can reverse the polarity for the LED Signal. Do not forget the Resistor installed as shown above. The Input to the Leaf Switch can be either 12vDC or 16vAC as the MR204 has built in diodes to rectify the AC. When connected as above the ON LED may not be correct for the position of the points, to correct it reverse the 2 wires going to C1 & C2 on the MR204.

Reed Switch SW928

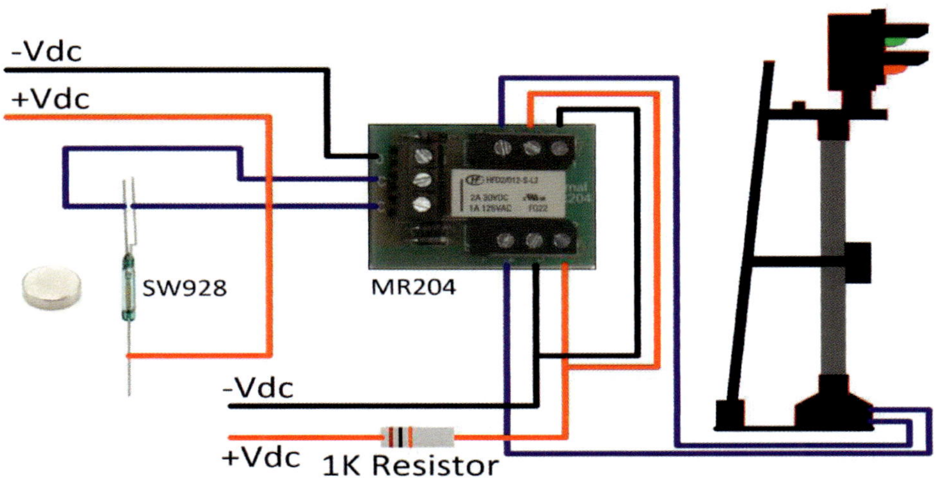

Here we are using a glass Reed Proximity Changeover switch SW928. In this case the Reed switch is activated b a magnet on the moving part of the Points. The Reed switch will be activated when the magnet is near the switch changing the state of the switch, therefore changing the Signal. When the magnet is moved away from the Reed switch the state of the switch will change again, this in turn switches the signal again. When connected as above the ON LED may not be correct for the position of the points, to correct it reverse the 2 wires going to C1 & C2 on the MR204.

In all the above cases a repeater indication can be sent to the Control Panel. This can either be 2 LED's as the signal, one bicolour LED, or on LED just to indicate when the Points are turned out. Each of the above will require a 2 core cable run back to the Control panel.

In the case of the Slide switch or Toggle switch the 2 core cable is wired into terminals 3 & 4. In the case of the MR204 the 2 core is wired into the same terminals as the signal.

Connection at the Control panel is as follows.

Repeater Panel 2 LED's

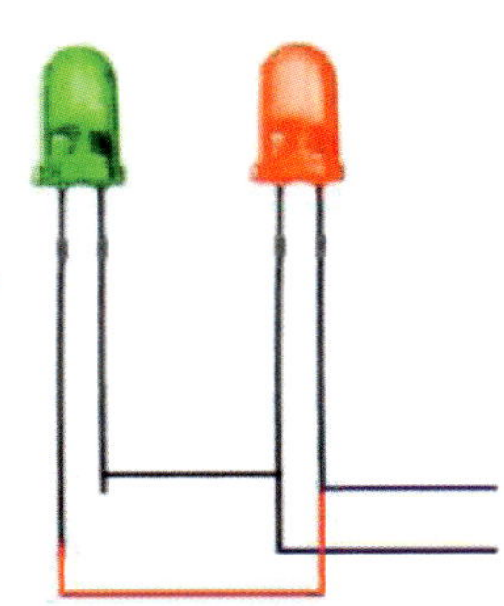

The Led's presumably Red & Green as the signal need to be wired as follows.

An LED has two pins, one short and one long. The short pin is normally the Negative or 0v the long pin is the Positive or +v. To connect them correctly first connect the short pin on the Green to the long pin on the Red. Next connect the long pin on the Green to the short pin on the Red. Now connect the 2 core cable from the signal to the short and long pins of the Red as shown

PROJECT 16

2 Aspect Filament Signals

A simple 2-aspect colour light signal (right) which would act as a Replacement for a semaphore stop signal. The Home signal would have Green & Red aspects The Distant signal would have Yellow & Red aspects. The white plate below the signal will display an identification plate using the reference letters of the controlling signal cabin and the signal number. There are several ways to control these signals on a Model Rail layout.

Fig: 1

Manual.

Individual Signal

A simple ON / OFF miniature toggle switch for each signal will do the job, see the below circuit

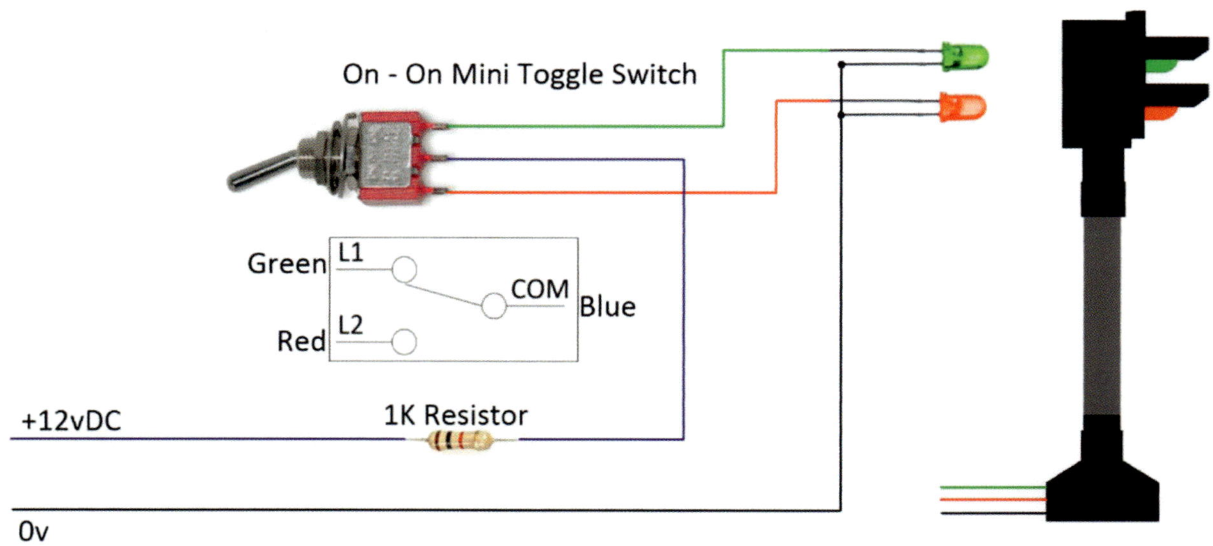

Fig: 2

Parts List

Mini Toggle Switch	Salecom T80-T Series T8013-SEBQ-H
1K Dropping Resistor	CR25 Series ¼ watt Carbon Film Resistor

In this circuit the bulbs are LED's so a 1K dropping resistor is required, the toggle switch is a simple SPDT ON/ON switch. If you are using Wheat Germ bulbs then the dropping resistor is not required, as long as the bulbs work off the same voltage as the supply voltage. The same circuit can be used for the 'Distant' signal by replacing the Green for Yellow.

Note1. The switch can be either a toggle switch, slide switch, leaf switch, or the switch on some point motors.

Note2. The colour of wires on the proprietary manufacturers' signals may not be the same as above, please check the manufacturers instructions.

Dual Signals from 1 Switch

In this circuit both the 'Home' and 'Distant' signals are controlled by one toggle switch. Here we are using a DPDT Toggle switch (Double Pole Double Throw) SW312. The left side (Pins 1,2,&3) control the 'Home' signal, and the right side (Pins 4,5,&6) control the 'Distant' signal. There is a little conjecture regarding the sequence of the signals so changing the sequence can be done by swapping around pins 4 & 5, or replacing the colour of the bulbs.
The principle of the resistor and bulbs applies as above.

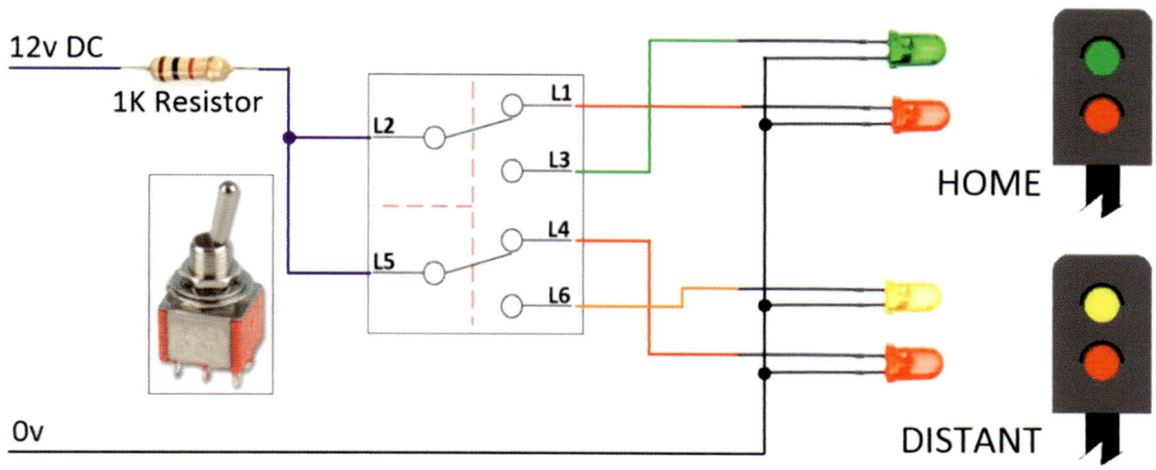

Fig: 3

Parts List

Mini Toggle Switch	Salecom T80-T Series T8011-SEBQ-H
1K Dropping Resistor	CR25 Series ¼ watt Carbon Film Resistor

Note3. LED's are polarity sensitive, therefore the short lead (Cathode) should always be Negative (0v), and only work on a small DC voltage of 2 or 3 volts hence the reason for the 'dropping resistor'. With the Wheat Germ Bulbs or LES bulbs the polarity is not important as they are miniature filament lamps, and rated at 12v DC.

Automating the 2 Aspect Signal.

There are a number of ways of switching signals automatically, these include switches on point motors, leaf switches, magnetic sensors or Infrared sensors.

Add on Switches.

The Peco PL-10 , the Gaugemaster PM-10 and the Hornby R8014 will all accept the Peco PL-13 Changeover switch. The following circuit shows how the PL-13 can be used to control a 2 aspect signal when connected to any of the above point motors.

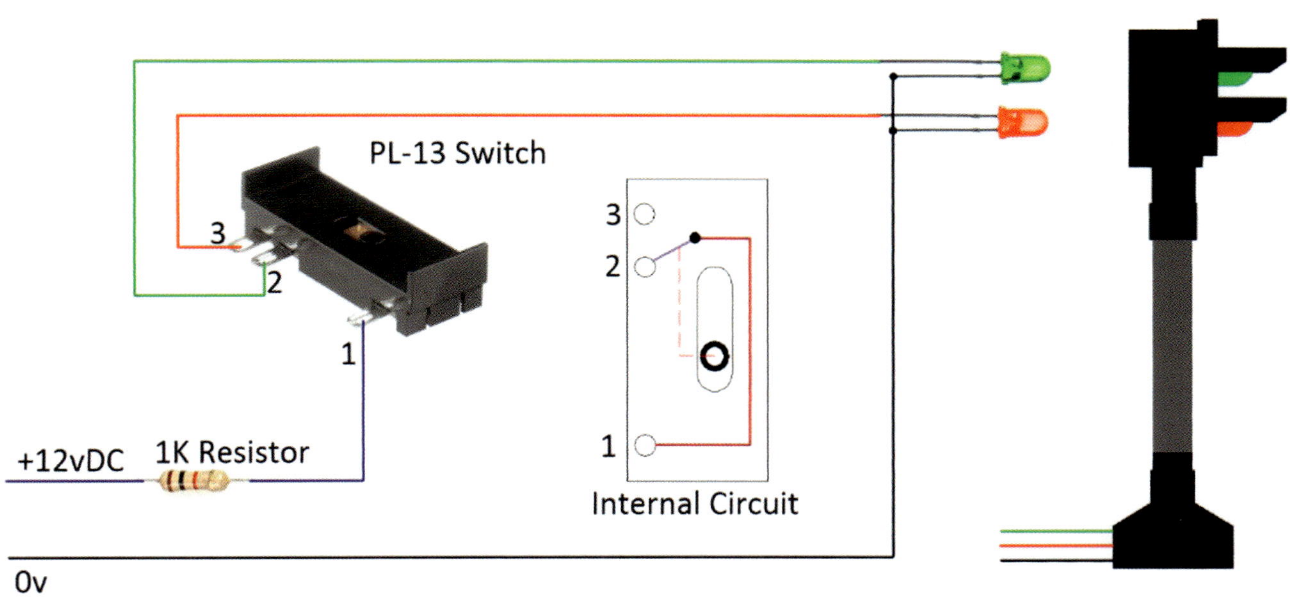

Fig: 4

In this circuit the PM-13 is controlling 2 signals, one on each line feeding into a Point set. When the points set at straight through signal 1 is Green signal 2 will be Red, with the points set at turn out signal 2 will be Green and signal 1 will be Red.

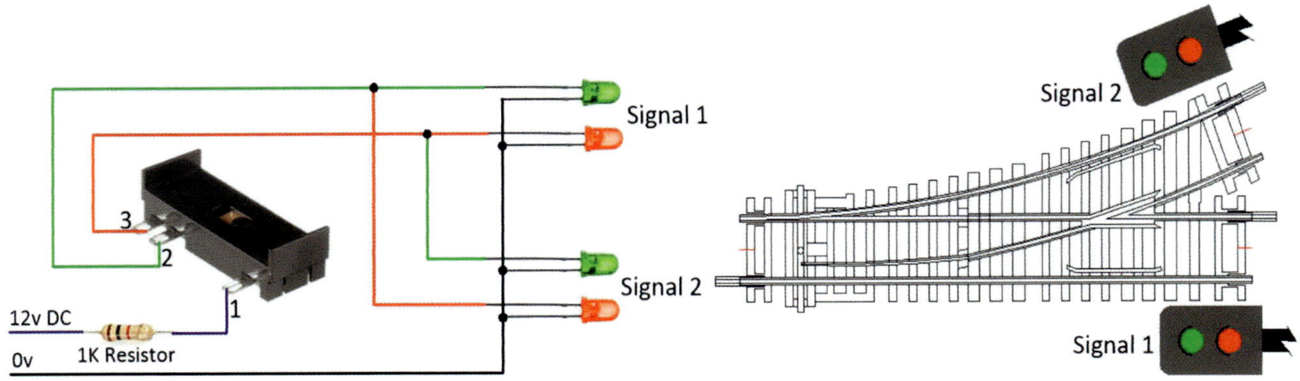

Fig: 5

Snap Action Switch (Spring Lever switch, Leaf switch).

The Snap Action Switch (SAS) is a single pole changeover switch. Fit the switch in the position shown below so that the point lever pushes the spring loaded lever down changing the state of the switch. Fix the switch in position with a screw nearest the points. You can now swivel the switch to get the best operating position, then fix the second screw to lock it in position.

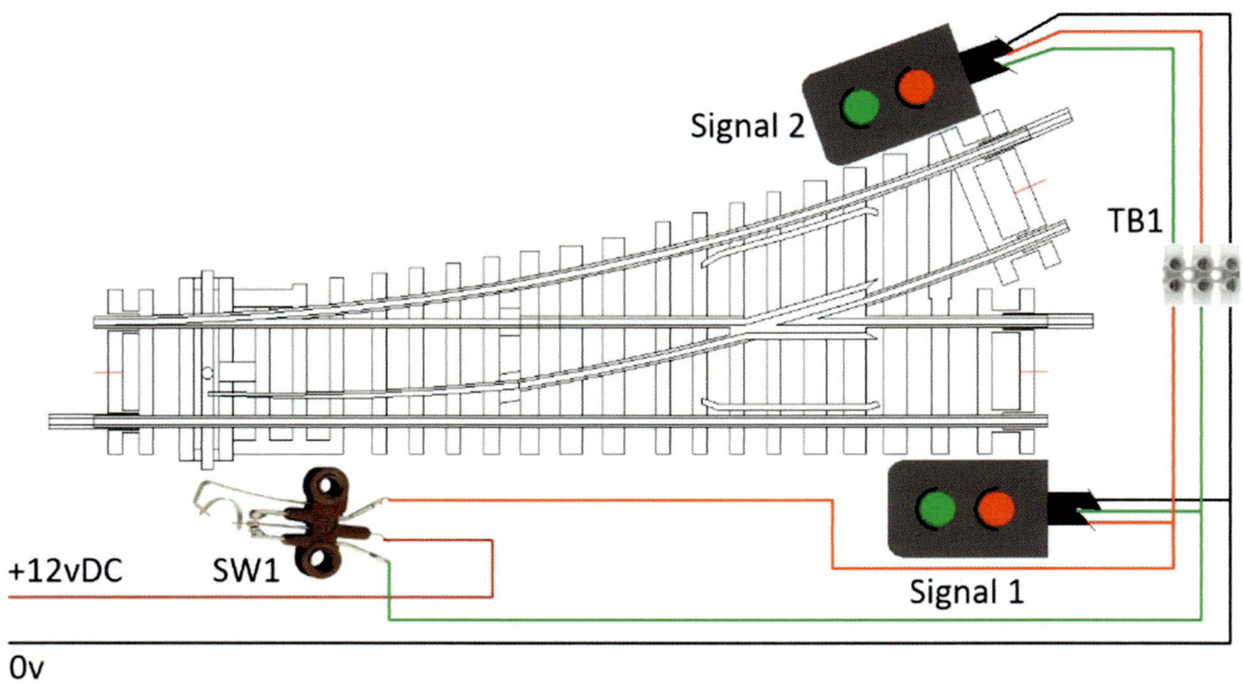

Fig: 6

MODEL RAILWAY PROJECTS

PROJECT 17

How to wire a Double Slip

As seen in the BRM magazine April 2020

A double slip is a narrow angled crossing of two lines combined with two sets of points, which allows the train to exit on one of two tracks. Here we show a range of Analogue circuits for DC operation, and a range of motors with DCC circuits.

You will see from the circuits that the DC wiring is a little more complicated than the DCC wiring, this is because all the switching and polarity changes happen in the DCC controller and are then sent to the Point Motor decoder.

The train travel sequences are:

Route A to B / B to A PM1 down PM2 down
Route A to D / D to A PM1 up PM2 down
Route C to B / B to C PM1 down PM2 up
Route C to D / D to C PM1 up PM2 up

Fig: 1

DC Coil Motors.

Coil Motors require a short pulse of power and will be damaged with a permanent voltage on the coils, this is why we use a Momentary switch such as the Salecom T8014A-SEBQ-H, or similar. This switch is called a Single Pole Single Throw (SPST) switch.

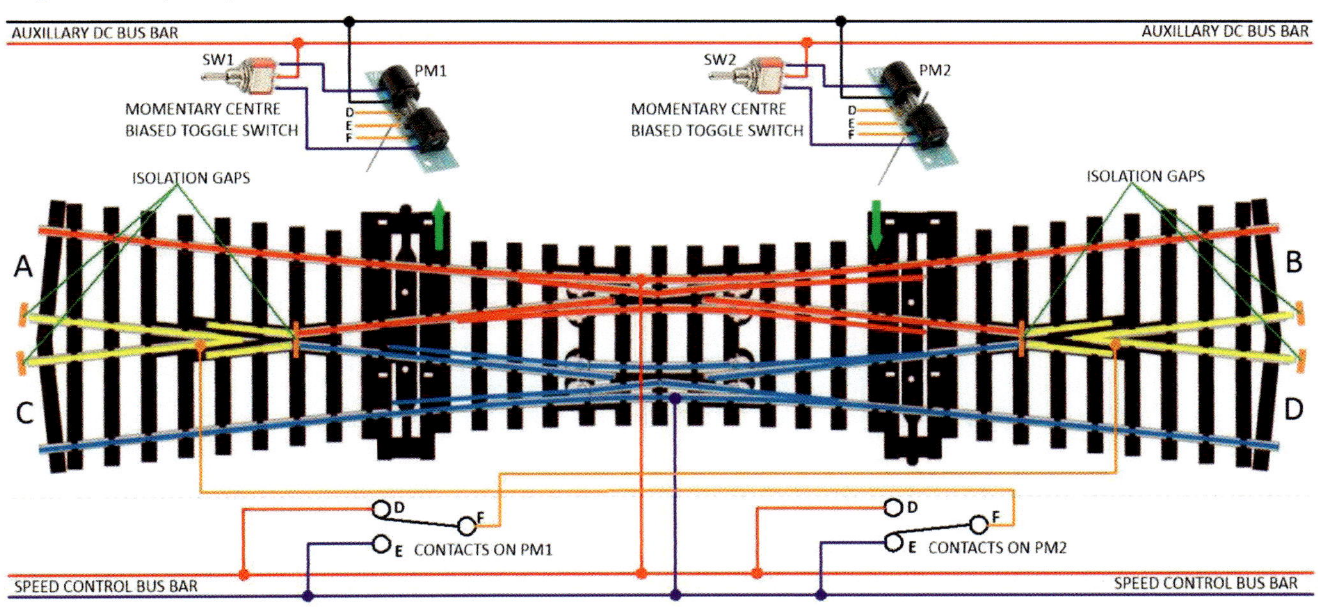

Fig: 2

Please note that PM1 switch goes to the right frog and PM2 switch goes the left frog.

In this diagram a train traveling from A to D must have PM1 in the Up position putting positive on the right frog through the PM1 switch via F & D, also PM2 is in the down position putting negative on the left hand frog through the PM2 switch via F & E. To make the Train go from A to B them PM1 must be in the Down Position putting negative on the right frog via PM1 switch E & F, PM2 remains in the down position putting negative on the left frog through PM2 E & F. The above circuit is using the Gaugemaster PM1 Point Motor. The same circuit can be used for the Hornby R8014 with a Peco PL-13 fitted, Peco PL-10 with a Peco PL-13 fitted, or the Gaugemaster PM-10 with a Peco PL-13 fitted, or a Hatton's HAT-PM-01.

Analogue Slow-Motion Motor.

These motors work one way with normal polarity, and the motor then reverses when the polarity is reversed. The motors also have a stall circuit built in which means that power can remain on the motor. The switch to use is a Salecom T8011-SEBQ-H double pole double throw (DPDT) Latching switch, or similar. In one position the polarity is normal, in the second position the polarity has been reversed.

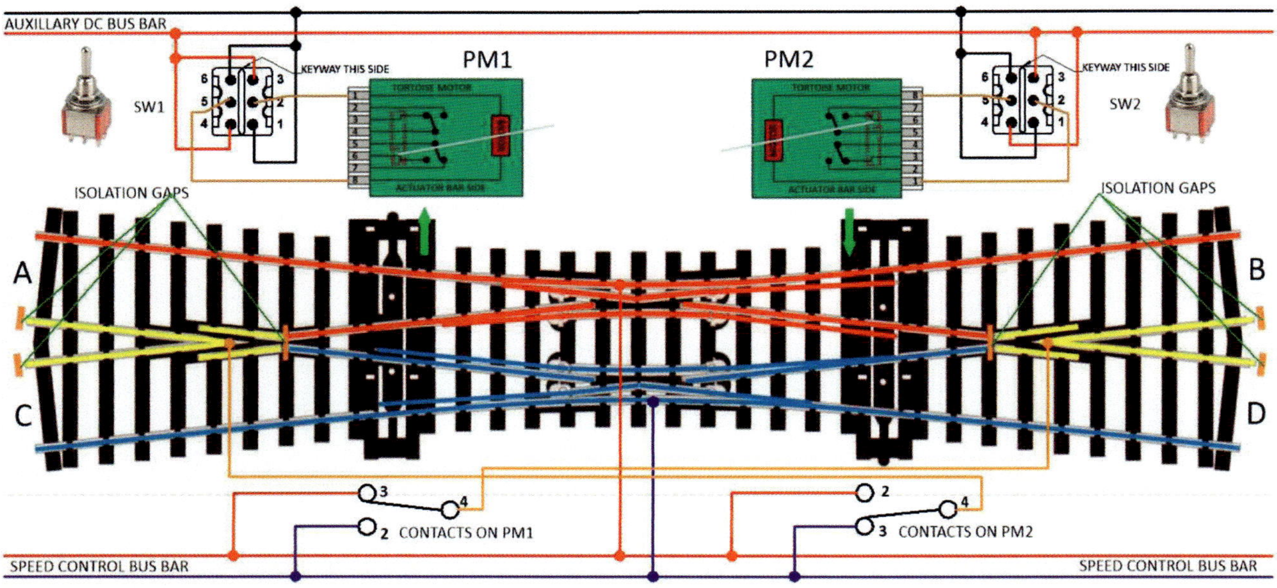

Fig: 3

In this drawing we are using Tortoise Slow Motion motors to change the points. The frog polarity switches are built into the motor housing, but the principle is the same. The same circuit can be used for the Cobalt IP Analog DCP-CbiP Point Motor with DC power via SW1 to pins DC In(1), DC In (2), PM1 contacts Red to S3-R, Blue to S3-L, and the Frog feed to S3-C. PM2 DC power via SW2 to pins DC In (1), DC In (2), Red to S3-L, Blue to S3-R, & the Frog feed to S3-C.

Analogue without Integral Switches

All the above motors have a change-over switches as part of the motor, the following do not have integral switches so a separate switch has to be introduced for the Frog Polarity. The Point motors that do not have integral switches are the one shown Hornby R8243, also the Gaugemaster GMC-PM20, Peco PLS-125, Peco PL-11.

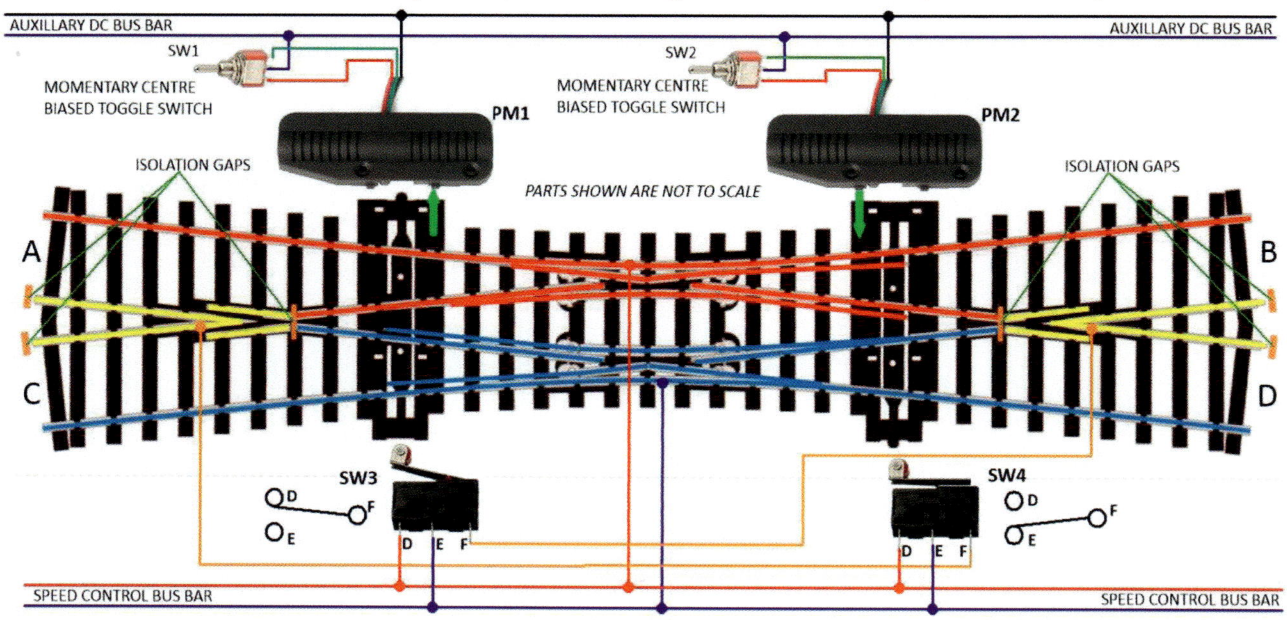

There are many types of switches available to switch the frogs, from Magnets Reed Switches, to Mini Micro switches with either roller actuators or button actuators. The switch shown is a Micro Switch with Roller by Camdenboss V4 PCB Type Roller Lever, it is activated by the Throw Bar on the points.

DCC Point Motors.

Digital Point Motors get their instructions from the same wires that power the tracks. This means the wiring is a lot simpler, however the signal from the Control Panel must first go through a Decoder which is mapped to that specific point motor. Some Point Motors have the DCC Decoder built into the casing as shown below. Other motors do not have the decoder built in, so you need to purchase one for each motor you want to convert to digital control.

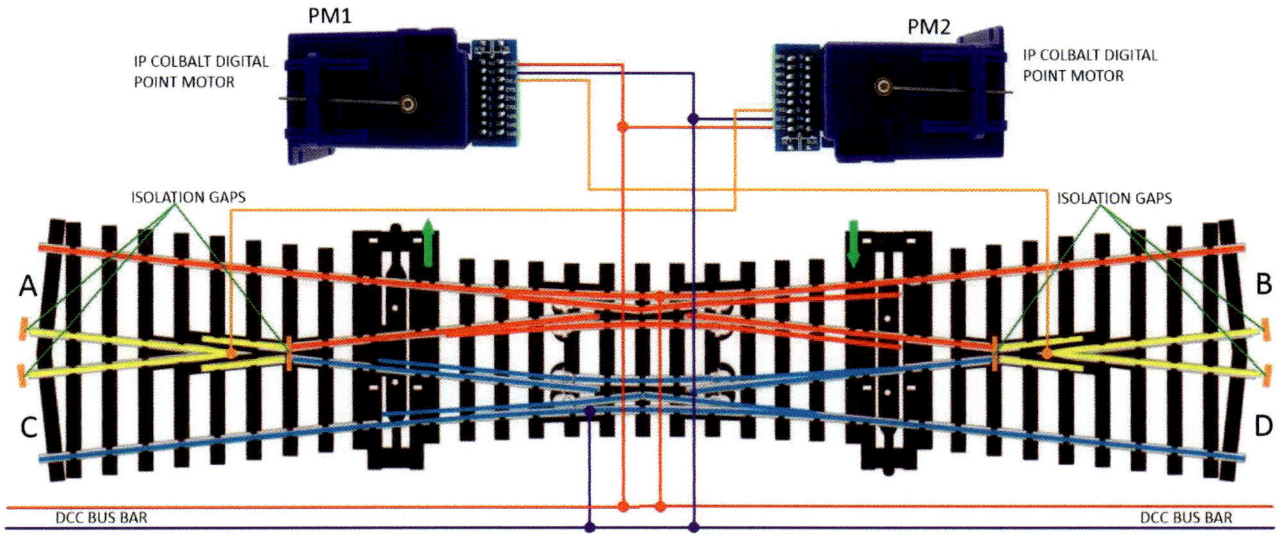

Fig: 5

The above circuit shows 2 Colbalt Digital Motors PM1 and PM2. Ensure these are the Digital version so that they have the decoders built in. As you can see the wiring is a lot simpler than DC as the frog switches are built into the Point Motor and the instructions for them come from the built in decoders.

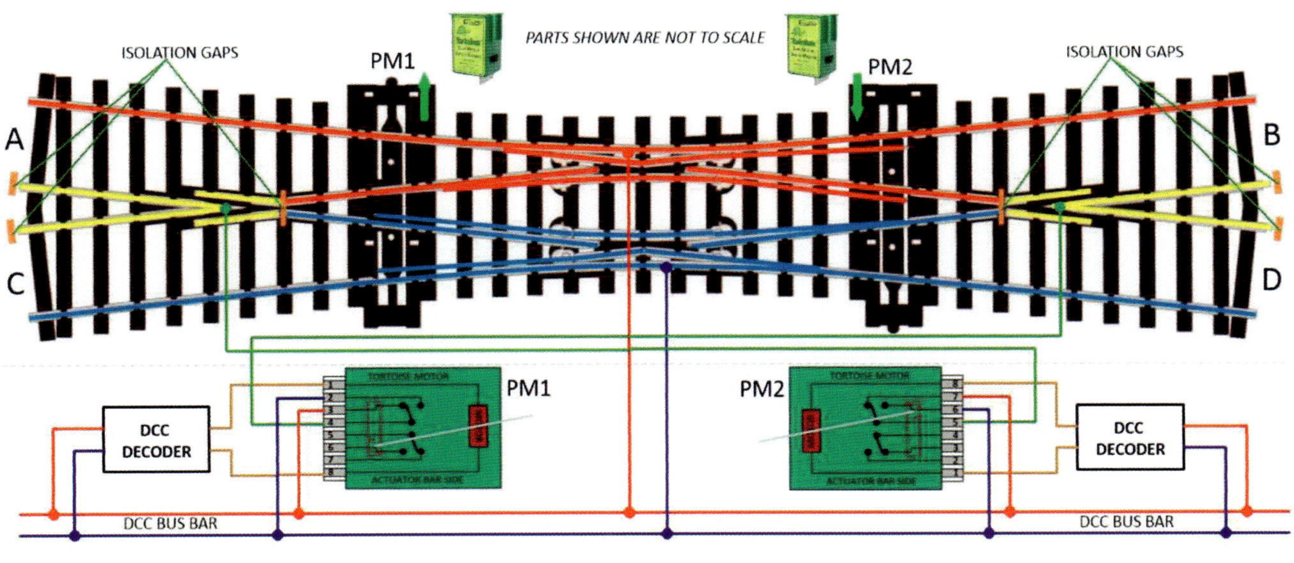

Fig: 6

In the above example the Point Motors are Slow Motion Motors that do not have DCC Decoders built in, so each motor needs a stand alone decoder. However they do have two sets of changeover contacts inside the casing. You will need to wire the decoders from the DCC Bus Bar to the Point Motor as shown. The Frog Power switch are the same as the DC connections as shown in the above drawing.

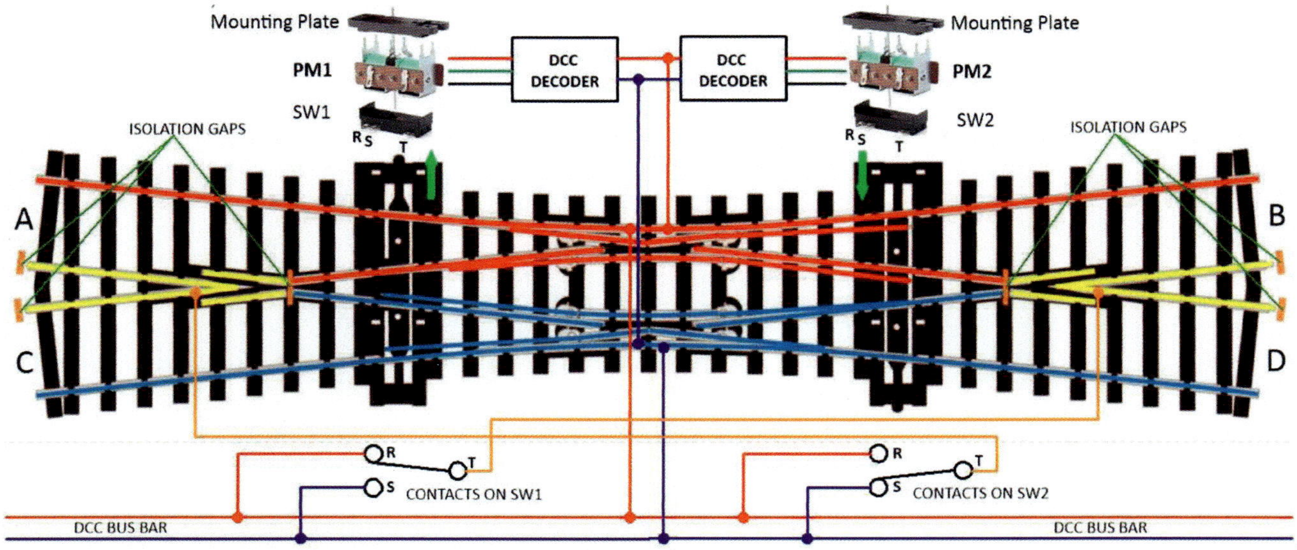

Fig: 7

In this example we are using coil type point motors (a list of which is under Fig 2). These motors do not have built in decoders so each motor requires it's own decoder, wiring for these is shown above. The switching of the frogs is dependant on a separate changeover switch.

Notes:

1) The colours of wires in all the circuits is for clarity only, you need to check the instructions from the manufacturer each time as they may use a different colour system.
2) The Bus Wires should all be run in 32/0.2mm wire and Spur Off units should be capable of handling in excess of 15 Amps at any one time.
3) The spur wires should be in either 24/0.2mm or 16/0.2mm to the equipment terminal blocks. Most proprietary manufactured products come with a short length of 7/0.2mm wire, so you will need to have a terminal block at this stage. Please note not all manufacturers use the same colour coding for their products, so check the instructions before switching ON.

Terminations.

Termination of one size of wire to a smaller or larger will require a connection system that is capable of taking both and creating a good connection. The termination system must also be able to cope with the current passing through the junction. Terminal blocks (Chocolate Blocks) are available in 3A, 5A, 10A, 15A, and 30Amp, you need to select the one that will cope with your worst case scenario of the number of points or CDU's activated simultaneously.

Controlling a 3 Aspect Signal

Controlling these on a Model Rail layout can be done with a Toggle Switch. Rotary switch, or automatically with magnetic switches. The 3 aspect signal is Green, Yellow, & Red. Green at the top means 'All Clear' Yellow in the middle means 'Warning – next signal could be Red', and the Red means 'Stop,

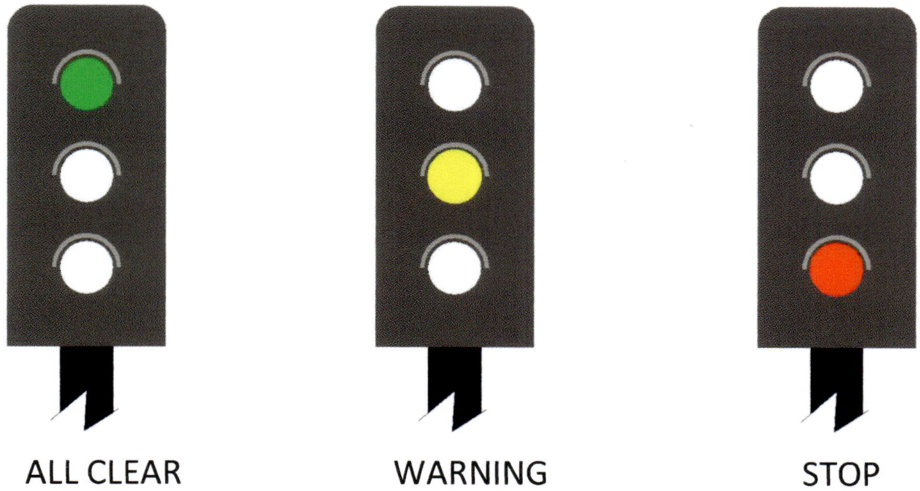

Fig: 1

Toggle Switch

Using a toggle switch requires the switch to have three 'ON' position and three lever positions. This is achieved with a TE Connectivity 3-1825139-4 switch. The terminals on the base of the switch are numbered 1 to 6. Please follow these numbers on the drawing carefully as the sequence of wiring is important.

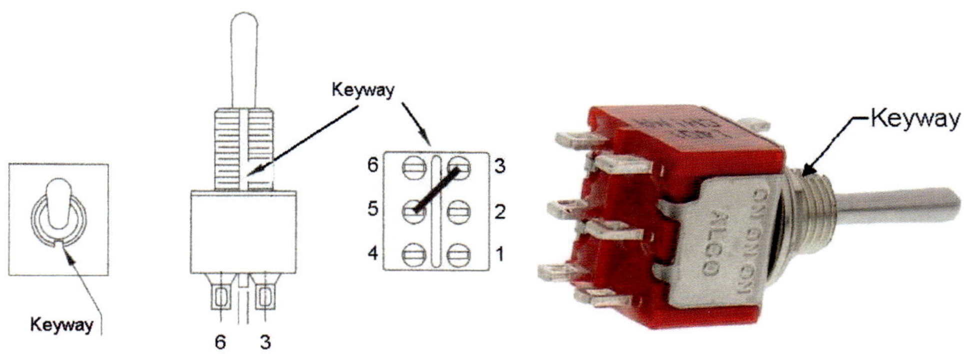

Fig: 2

The first thing to do is to ensure the Keyway is to the top of this diagram Then put a link between terminal 3 and terminal 5 as shown.

Start by connecting the Green LED to terminal 6 on the switch (Long lead on the LED), the Yellow LED to terminal 5, and Red to terminal 1. The short leads from the LED's are joined together and then connected to a 1K resistor before connecting to the negative supply. Now connect 12v DC supply to terminal 2. Your switch is now ready. (Note: If you are using filament bulbs such as Wheat Germ or LES or MES bulbs you do not require the Dropping resistor)

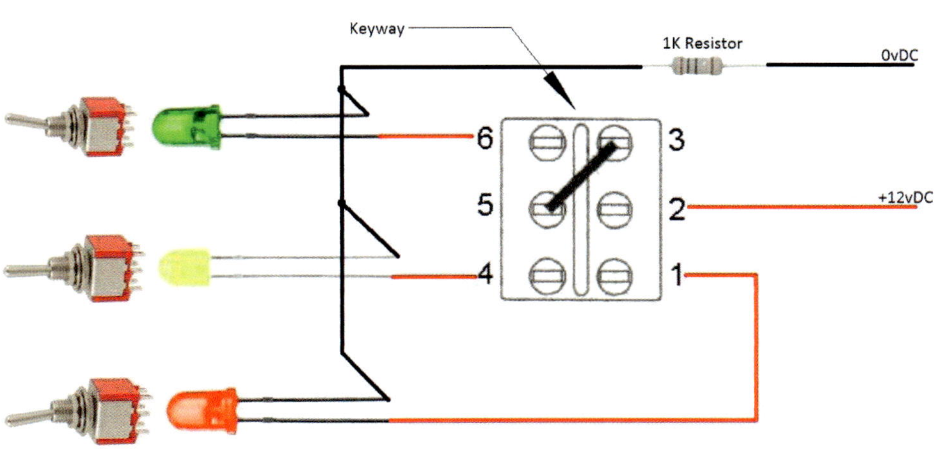

Fig: 3

Please note that this DP3T (Double Pole Triple Throw) has a special configuration on the inside of the switch (SW313), a normal DPDT will not work, even though they look the same. Due to the link between 3 & 5 it is advisable to use Heatshrink sleeving on the connecting wires, just to protect against short circuits.

The following is another combination of the 3 Aspect signal Light, where the Yellow & Green are ON at the same time.

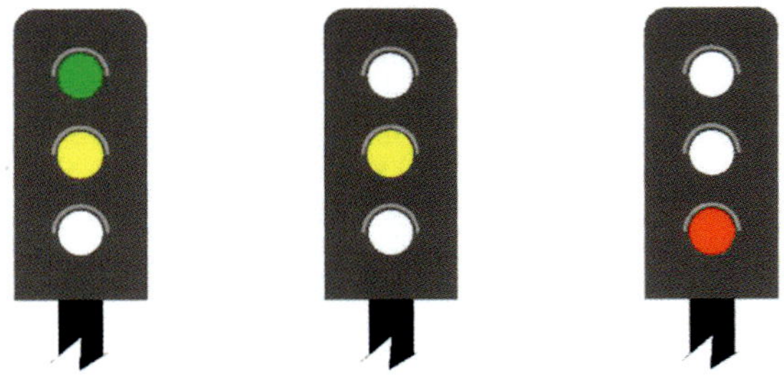

Fig: 4

In this sequence when the switch is in the Yellow position it also supplies power to the Green via a diode D1. This can be a signal diode such as a 1N4148, or a power diode 1N4002 (which you are more likely to have).

Please note the + of the diode must face the terminal 4. The 1N4148 has a black line to indicate the positive end, whereas the 1N4002 has a white line to indicate the positive end.

Again if you are using Wheat Germ of Filament lamps rated at 12 volts then the 1K Resistor is not required.

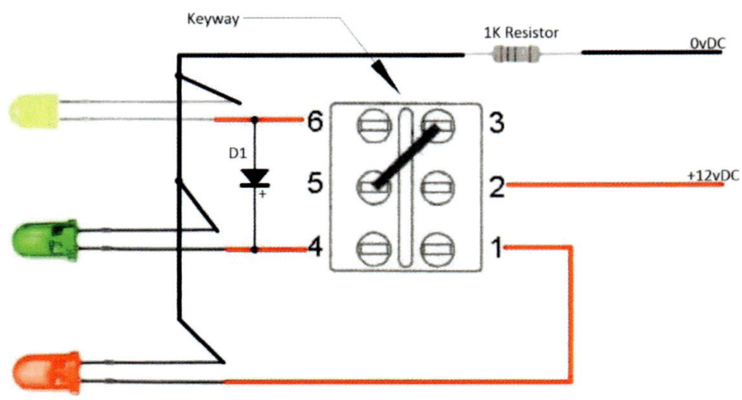

Fig: 5

Parts List

Mini Toggle Switch	TE Connectivity 3-1825139-4
Resistor	1K ¼ watt Carbon Film Resistor.
D1 Diode	1N4148 or 1N4002

Rotary Switch

You can also use a Rotary Switch to control this signal. Here we are using a 3 Pole 4 way switch. The 12v DC is fed to the common terminal on section A & B. So in position 1 the Red is ON, in position 2 the Amber is ON, and in position 3 the Green is ON. As we are using LED's don't forget the dropping resistor on the Negative line as shown. You can have the Amber on with the Green by adding the dotted orange wires. You can also use the 4th way to have just the Green ON by adding the dotted green wire joining terminals 3 & 4. You have enough space on this rotary switch to control at least one other 3 Aspect signal with a different sequence

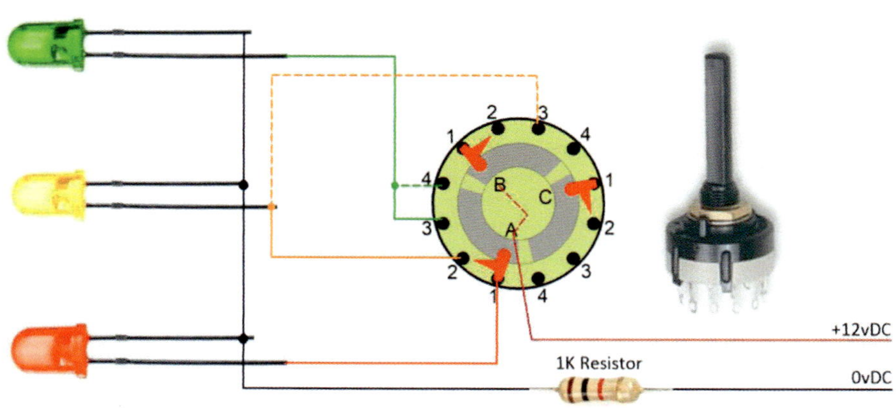

Fig: 6

So the sequence of the rotary switch is as follows.

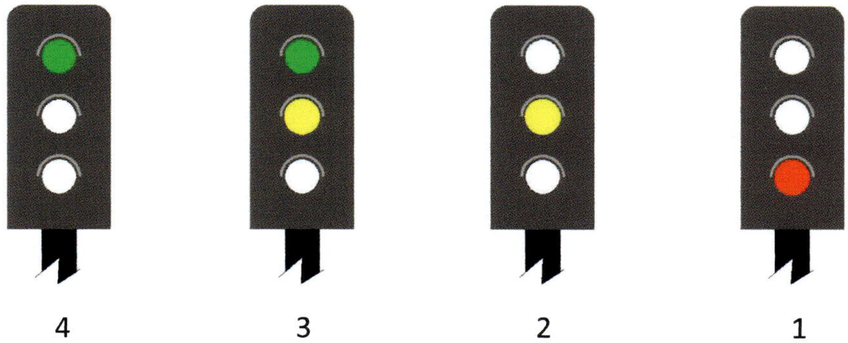

Fig: 7

Parts List

Rotary Switch	Alpha SR2611F 3P4W
Switch Knob	Your choice must accept 6.35mm spindle
Dropping Resistor	1K ¼ watt Carbon Film Resistor.

Automatic 3 Aspect Signal

It is possible to automate your 3 Aspect Signal or even a number of signals by using a series of Latching Relays and Magnetic Sensors. You will need 2 Relays and 3 sensors for each signal. This time the train activates the signal and changes each aspect as it travels along the track. There are three sensors along the track which are activated by the magnet on the underside of the locomotive. The distance between sensors should be at least the length of your train, to create safe blocks between the sensors for the trains to travel in. (see below Automatic Isolation) Because of the Latching properties of these relays, the signal should show a Green light, however it might show either no lights or a yellow light on initial switch ON. Easy to solve, you just need to reset both or one latching relay, do this by placing a magnet near SW3 sensor. Now you should have a green light showing.

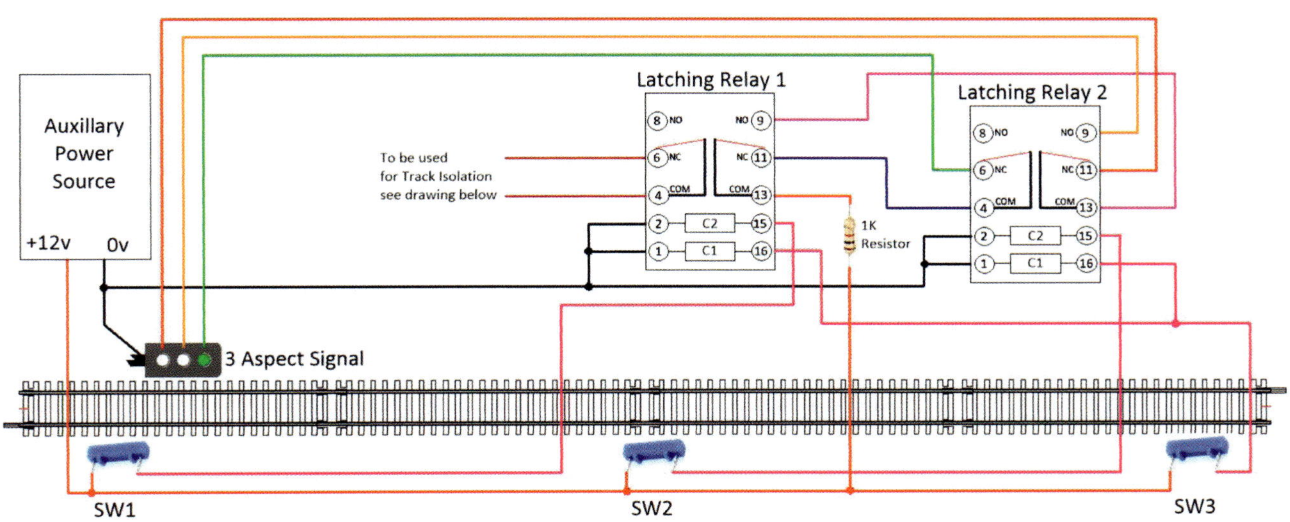

Fig: 8

Direction of Travel is from Left to Right. As the train passes over SW1 this will latch Relay 1 turning the Red light On and the Green Light Off. The train then passes over SW2 which switches Relay 2 On, this then turns the Red light Off and switches the Yellow light On. The train will then pass over SW3 which will reset both relays and switch on the Green light again.

Note 1: In automatic Isolation Mode the second set of contacts (6 & 4) on Relay 1 can be used to Isolate a section of track prior to SW1. This Isolation will remain in force until the train has passed SW3.

Note 2: The drawings have been prepared using LED's that require a dropping resistor. If your signal uses 12v filament lamps then the dropping resistor should not be used.

Note 3: The Latching relays can be purchased from Gaugemaster, Brimal, or a number of retails, as can the Magnetic Reed Switc

MODEL RAILWAY PROJECTS

3 Way Peco Point Set

This project tries to help with the wiring of the Peco PL-E99 3 way Electrofrog Turnout with 2 Point Motors. The turnout has 2 wires connected to the sections of rail that need to have the polarity changed depending on the direction of travel. The first wiring diagram shows the points wired using the PL-10 motors and the PL-13 switches which sit on top of the motors. These are used to change the polarity of the FROGS.
In the above image the 3 sections of track that are isolated are shown. ON the PL-E99 sections 2 & 3 are pre-connected, so in fact there are only 2 wires on the underside of the turnout. I have shown the position of the motors and designated them PM1 & PM2. I have also shown the 4 positions where you will need Isolating Fishplates, on the left of this image.

BASIC WIRING.
The following drawing shows how the Motors PL-10 and the switches PL-9 are connected to the Turnout set.
The Power to the track you may be feeding from a Bus Bar system. If this is the case you will have 5 wires going back to the toggle switches (SW301) at the control panel.
Please note how the control switches PL-13 are connected to the Motors and then to the mounting bracket PL-9, prior to fitting them to the underside of the baseboard.

The Second wiring diagram shows the same set of points wired using our MR204. The advantage to using the MR204 is that you can change the polarity of the FROGS and also send a status indicator back to the Control Panel.

This is the Peco SL-E99 3 way Electrofrog Turnout.

Fig: 1

This is the Peco SL-E99 3 way Electrofrog showing the sections that need to have their polarity changed.

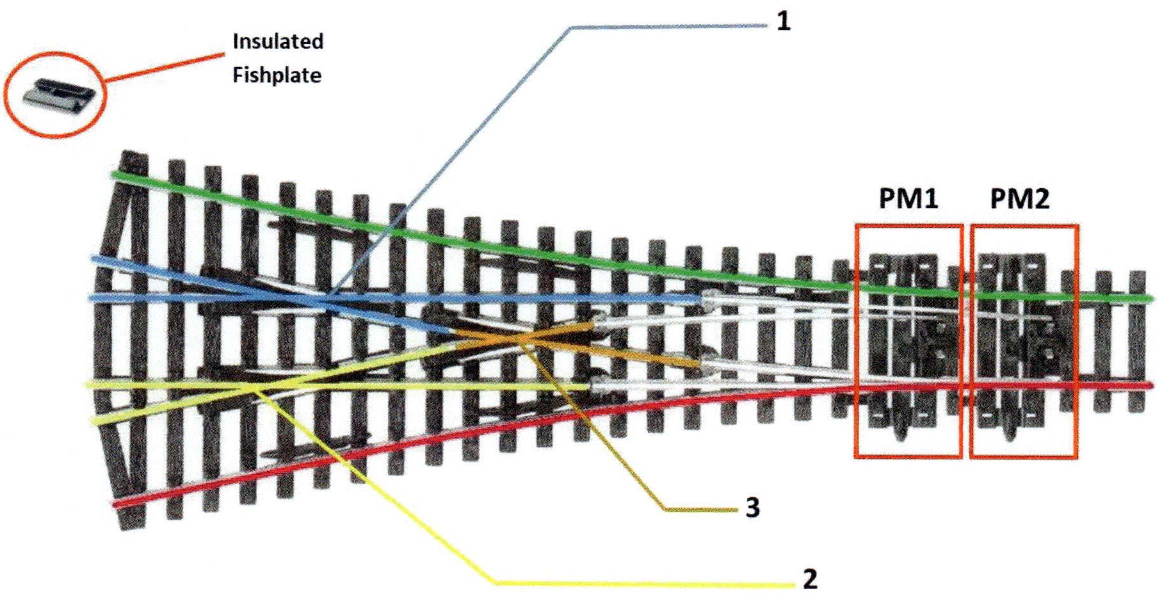

Fig: 2

In the above image the 3 sections of track that are isolated are shown. ON the PL-E99 sections 2 & 3 are pre-connected, so in fact there are only 2 wires on the underside of the turnout. I have shown the position of the motors and designated them PM1 & PM2. I have also shown the 4 positions where you will need Isolating Fishplates, on the left of this image.

BASIC WIRING.

The following drawing shows how the Motors PL-10 and the switches PL-9 are connected to the Turnout set. The Power to the track you may be feeding from a Bus Bar system. If this is the case you will have 5 wires going back to the toggle switches (SW301) at the control panel.

Please note how the control switches PL-13 are connected to the Motors and then to the mounting bracket PL-9, prior to fitting them to the underside of the baseboard.

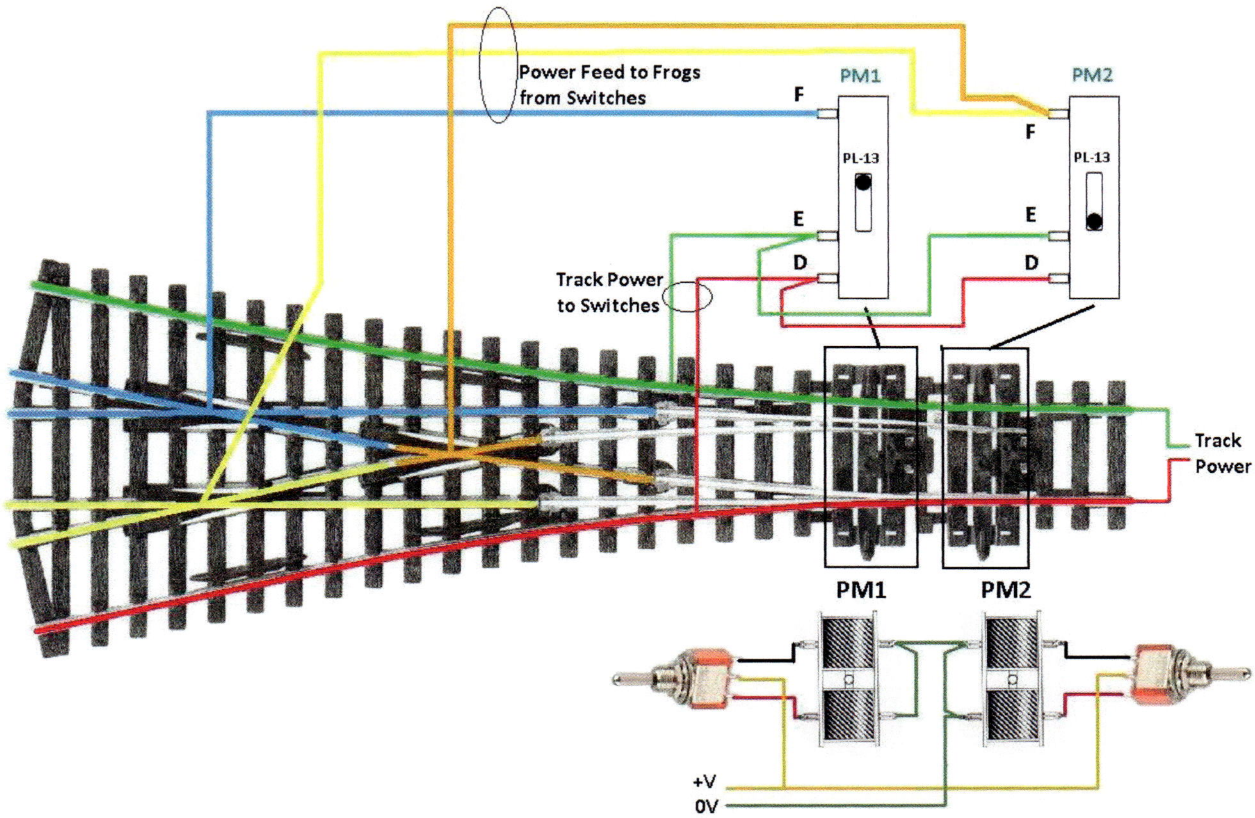

This drawing shows how the switch and Motor are made up prior to fixing to the baseboard. A substantial amount of wiring can be done prior to fitting.

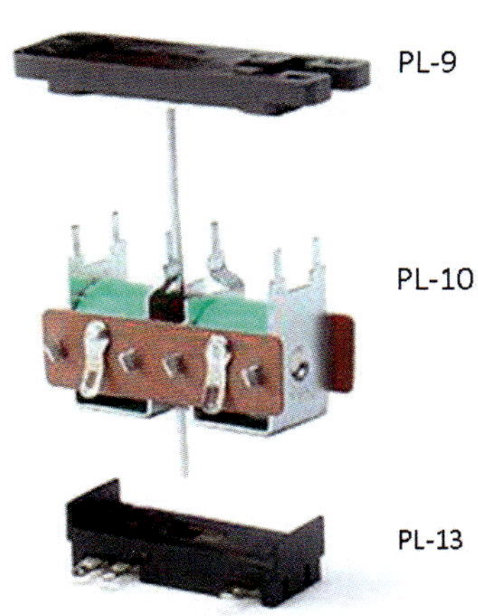

The second image shows the hole through The baseboard (1) 10mm for the actuating pin (2) to move the throw arm of the points.

An alternative method of fixing the motors is to cut a 80mm x 40mm hole in the baseboard and fit the motors directly to the point set. The Switch PL-13 will still fit onto the motor as above.

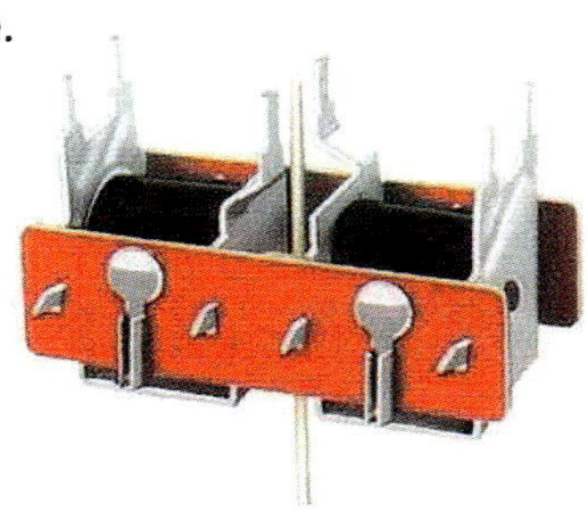

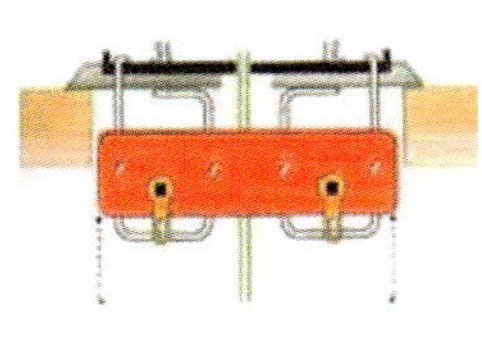

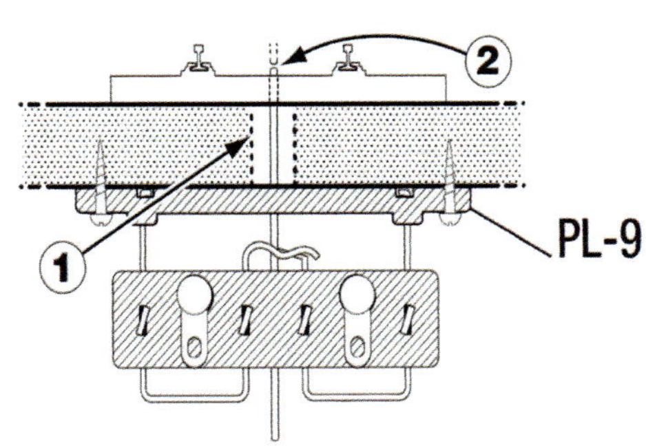

POINT POSITION INDICATOR.

Having wired the points as per the drawing above, we can now add a little extra to stop the 2 motors being out of sequence and giving an indication back at the Control Panel as to which turnout is live.

The table below shows the position of the point motor lever for each motor in the 3 possible turnout positions.

TURNOUT	PM1	PM2
STRAIGHT	DOWN	UP
LEFT	UP	UP
RIGHT	DOWN	DOWN

By using our MR204 Latching circuit you can provide a visual indication of the state of the points. This indication will remain even after all power is removed at the end of the day. The circuit below uses 2 No MR204 pcb's one for each motor. These circuits replace the 2 PL-13 motor mounted switches. One set of contacts of the relay controls the FROG polarity, while the other set of the relay contacts controls the LED indicator. The following table shows the LED colour for each position of the points.

TURNOUT	PM1	PM2	LED
STRAIGHT	DOWN	UP	ORANGE
LEFT	UP	UP	GREEN
RIGHT	DOWN	DOWN	RED

A few Pointers.

ITS NOT AS COMPLICATED AS IT LOOKS – YOU ARE ONLY ADDING AN LED, A RESISTOR, AND 6 SHORT PIECES OF WIRE ABOVE WHAT YOU WOULD HAVE TO DO TO POWER THIS TYPE OF POINTS. Oh & replacing the PL-13 with MR204's

2) Prior to wiring the Point Motors to the Toggle switches (sw301) and the MR204's, try to get the motors as follows PM1 in the DOWN position, and PM2 in the UP position.

The reason for this is so that when you wire the toggle switches and the MR204's you should get an Orange LED illumination.

If you don't then toggle PM1 switch down, and PM2 switch up, theoretically this should have no effect on the points but should have synchronised the MR204's to the points.

3) Double check the sequence from the table above to ensure you get the correct LED colour (sl110) with the points in the position shown.

4) If you are running a DCC system the MR204 will still work, or you can run a separate 12vDC supply for them and the LED.

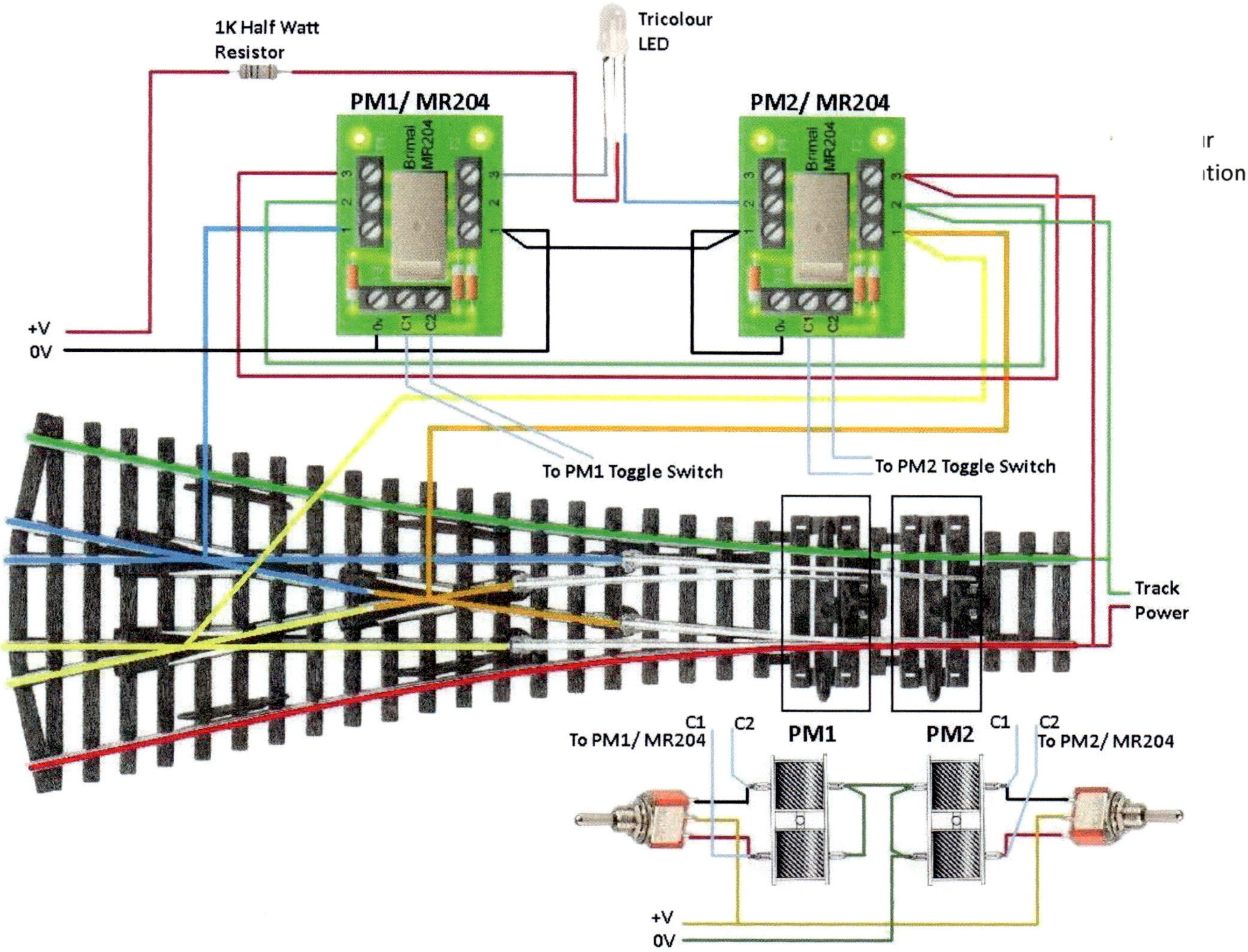

PROJECT 20

Alternating 2 Aspect Signal Display.

This circuit is used to display the changing state of a 2 Aspect Signal purely for a visual effect and is not connected to the layout in any way. In this circuit we are using the MR355 Pulse Timer to create an alternating Signal display. The 2 Aspect signals are connected to the relay outputs, So that the RED of A is OFF, and the GREEN of B is ON. When the Relay switches on the signals will change state so that A is now GREEN and B is RED. VR1 controls the Red ON time of Signal A, and VR2 controls the RED ON time of Signal B. There is approximately 180 seconds in each state. The Signals will change for as long as there is power to the timer.
You could also add an ON/OFF switch to control the Timer, as shown in the diagram.

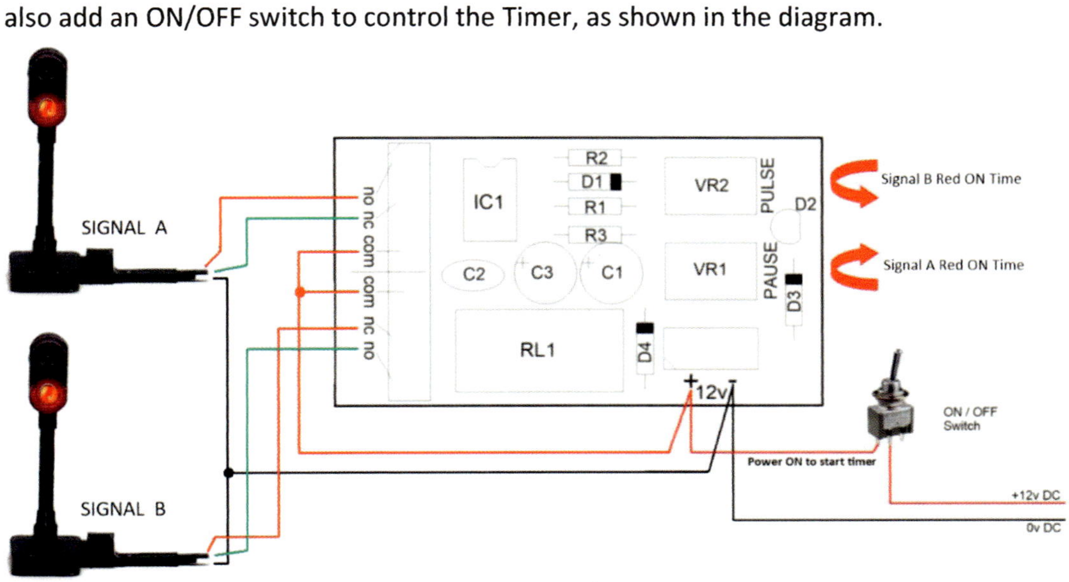

How to Isolate Sidings

The MR204 can be used to control the Track Power of a complete Siding System. In the diagram below the first MR204 on the right is controlled by the Points switch for PM1, this in turn is switching ON or OFF the power to the Track to all siding above PM1. So with PM1 in the straight through position the MR204 has removed power from the tracks above IS1. When the Points PM1 are changed to Turn Out power is restored to tracks above IS1. If you are removing a Locomotive from Siding 2, then PM3 Points should be in the Turn Out position switching power OFF to the tracks above IS3. This will allow the Loco to move from Siding 2 to the Main Line. Resetting PM1 to Straight Through will switch OFF Power to all the Sidings. *(Note 1)*

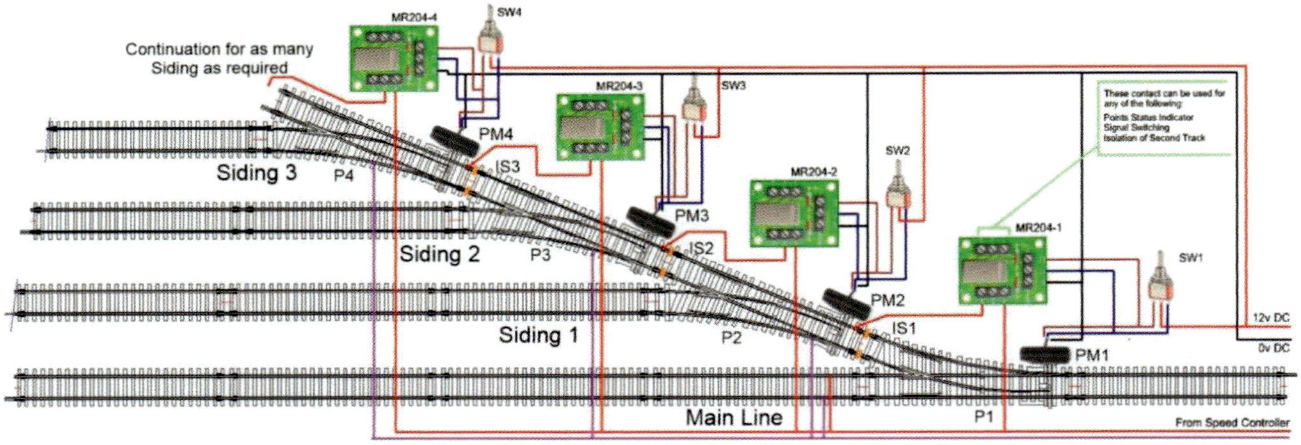

Start by fitting Isolating Fishplates to all the position shown by an orange line. Ensure you have Negative Feed to all the lower tracks of each siding (shown in violet). The positive feed from the Speed Controller goes to Terminal 1 on all the MR204's. As the drawing above shows there is no power on the tracks above the Main Line. PM1 In the position shown the contact on MR204-1 the wiring must come from the Normally open contact (3) to ensure there is no power on the Turn Out at IS1 and above.

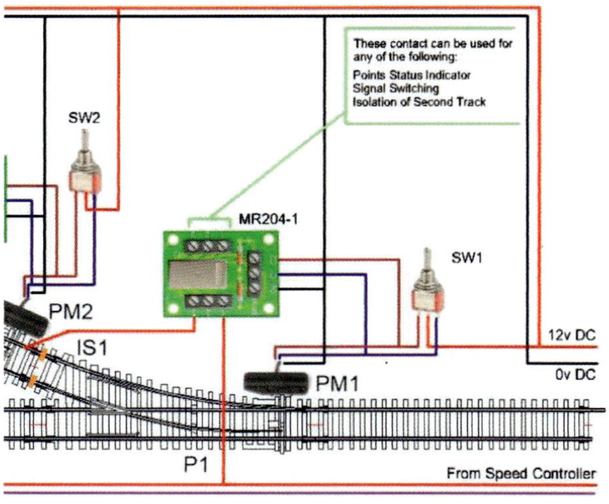

To remove a Loco from Siding 2, PM1 must be in the Turn Out position thereby putting power on the Siding Feed Track. PM2 remains the same as the drawing Isolating Siding 1. PM3 is now put in the Turn Out position giving power to Siding 2 and isolating everything above it. This gives a Speed Control path from Siding 2 to the Main Line with all other sidings are Isolated. The switch used to activate the points in this case is a Momentary (centre biased) mini toggle switch, this supplies a short pulse to the Point Motor and the MR204. The feed for the Point Motors comes from a separate Power source of a constant 12 – 16v DC.

The second set of Change over contacts on the MR204 (T2 Terminals 1 -3) can be used for a number of things.

1) A two aspect signal on each siding.
2) A 2 aspect indication back at the control Panel
3) Isolating the Negative track in each position.

Note 1: With PM1 in the Straight Through position, all the Sidings are Isolated, you could therefore have a separate Speed Controller connected to the siding layout so that shunting can be done independently of what is going on elsewhere. However before changing PM1 you need to ensure that the second Speed Controller is Isolated from the Tracks. This can be done by using a second MR204 paralleled to MR204-1, so that both the Positive and Negative Feed of Speed Controller 2 goes through the contacts first before feeding the siding tracks.

Controlling Electro-Frog Points

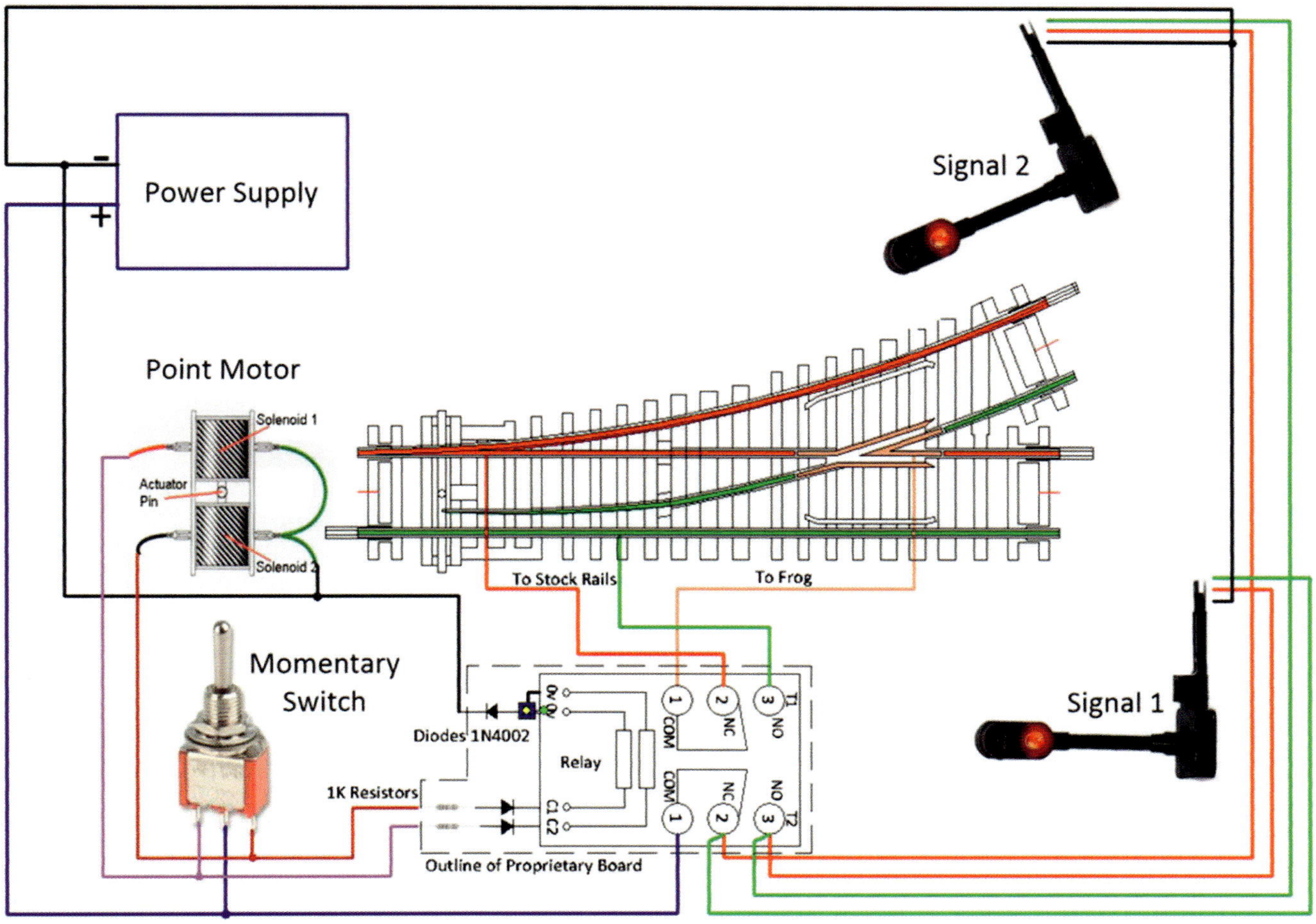

In this application the MR204 is used to control the polarity of the Frog in a set of Points, also a local Signal or Status indication back at the control panel. The type of motor used in this circuit is a twin coil type with a momentary toggle switch to change the state of the points. As the switch, and therefore power to the motor and the MR204 is only momentary, the MR204 is used to remember the status of the points.

The MR204 is powered from the Power Supply via the Momentary Switch, as shown in the circuit diagram. Positive power is placed on either C1 or C2 depending which way the switch is pushed, this in turn pulls the Point motor Lever Left or Right which changes the state of the Points. Power is then removed from the Points and the MR204, but the contacts on the MR204 remain in the last state they were energised to.

The circuit shows a wire from the RED track going to Terminals 3 of T2, and a wire from the GREEN track going to Terminal 2 of T2. The YELLOW frog has a wire going to Terminal 1 of T2. Because the Contacts in the relay are Changeover the Yellow wire will either be powered from the Red or the Green track. The other terminal set T1 can be used for anything – another set of Points, a Signal, Indication LED's back at control, or to lock out another set of Points.

IMPORTANT. The above drawing is powered for Straight Through therefore the power from the RED Track is running through the relay from Terminal 3 to 1 on T2. Because the Relay stays in the last state even when power is removed you must check the flow of power. (It could be that when you receive the MR204 the relay is in 2 to 1 state in which case you would be putting GREEN power onto the Frog, which is not what you want.) There are two ways to solve this.
1) Place a positive pulse on either C1 or C2 to change the relay, independent of the Point motor. You do not want the points to move.
2) Swap the wires around in Terminal T2 (3 to 2) and (2 to 3
The same as above will apply to anything connected to Terminal T1.

Controlling Electro-Frog Points in a Crossover

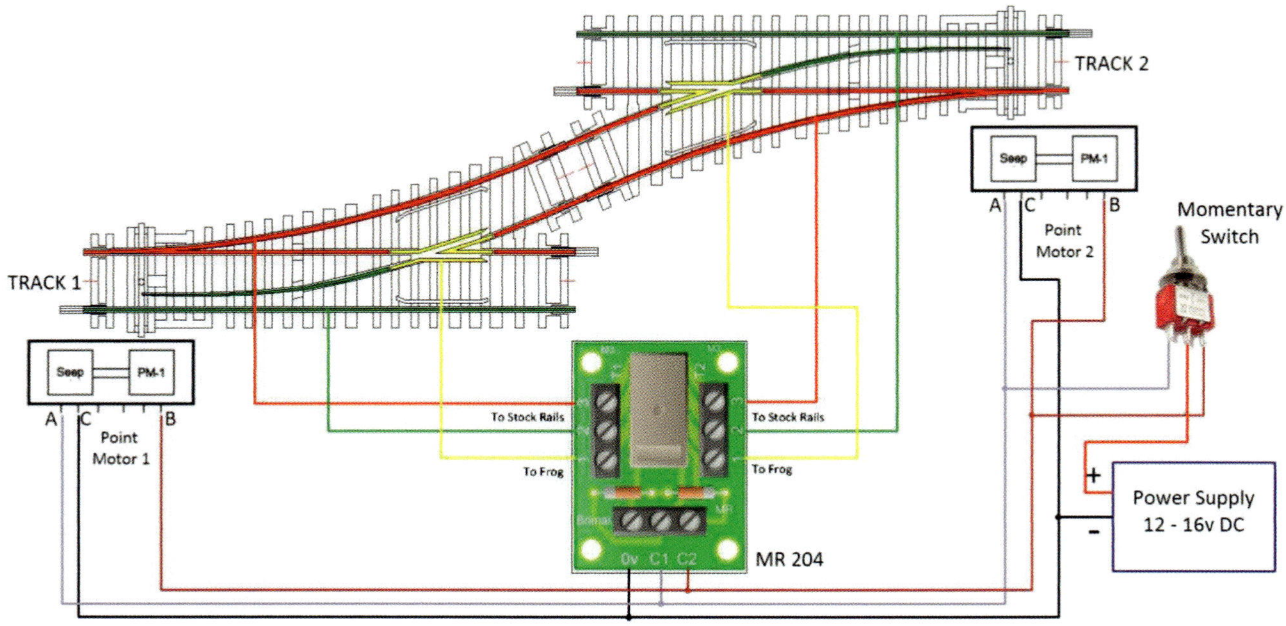

In this application the MR204 is used to control the polarity of the Frogs in two sets of Points. The type of motor used in this circuit is a twin coil type with a momentary toggle switch to change the state of the points. As the switch, and therefore power to the motor and the MR204 is only momentary, the MR204 is used to remember the status of the points.

The MR204 is powered from the Power Supply via the Momentary Switch, as shown in the circuit diagram. Positive power is placed on either C1 or C2 depending which way the switch is pushed, this in turn pulls the Point motor Lever Left or Right which changes the state of the Points. Power is then removed from the Points and the MR204, but the contacts on the MR204 remain in the last state they were energised to.

The circuit shows a wire from the RED track going to Terminals 3 of T2 & T1, and a wire from the GREEN track going to Terminal 2 of T2 & T1. The YELLOW frog has a wire going to Terminal 1 of T2 & T1. Because the Contacts in the relay are Changeover the Yellow wire will either be powered from the Red or the Green track. You will see that we are using Terminal set T1 for Track 1 Points and Terminal Set T2 for Track 2 Points. It is important that you use one Momentary switch for this operation, as forgetting to change the points of one set will cause a derailment.

IMPORTANT. The above drawing is powered for Straight Through therefore the power from the RED Track is running through the relay from Terminal 3 to 1 on T2. Because the Relay stays in the last state even when power is removed you must check the flow of power. (It could be that when you receive the MR204 the relay is in 2 to 1 state in which case you would be putting GREEN power onto the Frog, which is not what you want.) There are two ways to solve this.

1) Place a positive pulse on either C1 or C2 to change the relay, independent of the Point motor. You do not want the points to move.

2) Swap the wires around in Terminal T2 (3 to 2) and (2 to 3)

The same as above will apply to anything connected to Terminal T1.

Wiring of SEEP PMI Points Motor

Point Position Indicators using LED's

The first circuit shows how the points motor can be used to control signals around a set of points. You will see from the circuit that the LED's are wired opposite to each other so the signal on Green will have the other signal at Red, when the points change both signals will change to the new aspect. You could add a third set of indicators for the panel. Connection would be at points X & Y and the circuit would be the same as in the dotted box, but at the panel. The resister is essential if you are using LED' as they only require between 1 and 2 volts. Please note they are polarised, so the short lead is the negative' and the long lead is the positive'. If you are using filament lamps you will need to see the drawing below

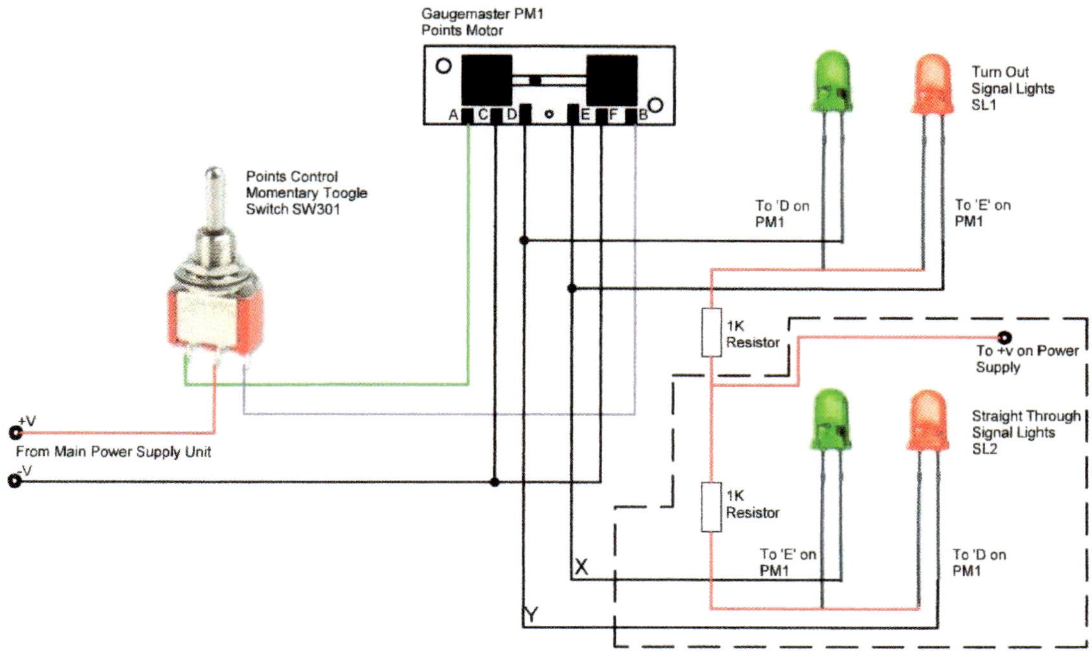

Filament Lamp Signal Control.

In the next case the signals are using filament lamps so the resistor is not required (bulbs should be 12v) The signals have three wires Red, Green, & Black. Logic does not hold in this case, check each wire, one will be the common negative the others will be the positive for the Red & Green lamps. With the points in the straight through position you want SL2 Green ON and SLI Red ON, in the Turn out Points Motor position you want the opposite should apply. The section in the dashed box is an example of Points Indication on the control panel Please note if you are using LED's on the panel then you require a resistor on the positive leg of each LED. The Negative of each LED is connected to the negative suppl

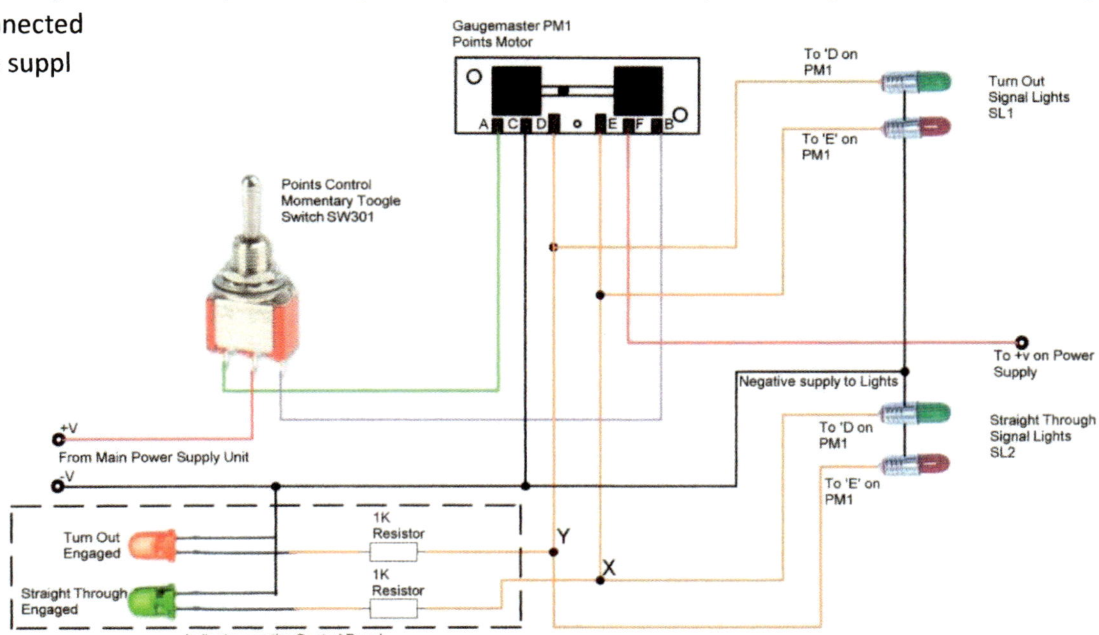

Automatic Points Switch

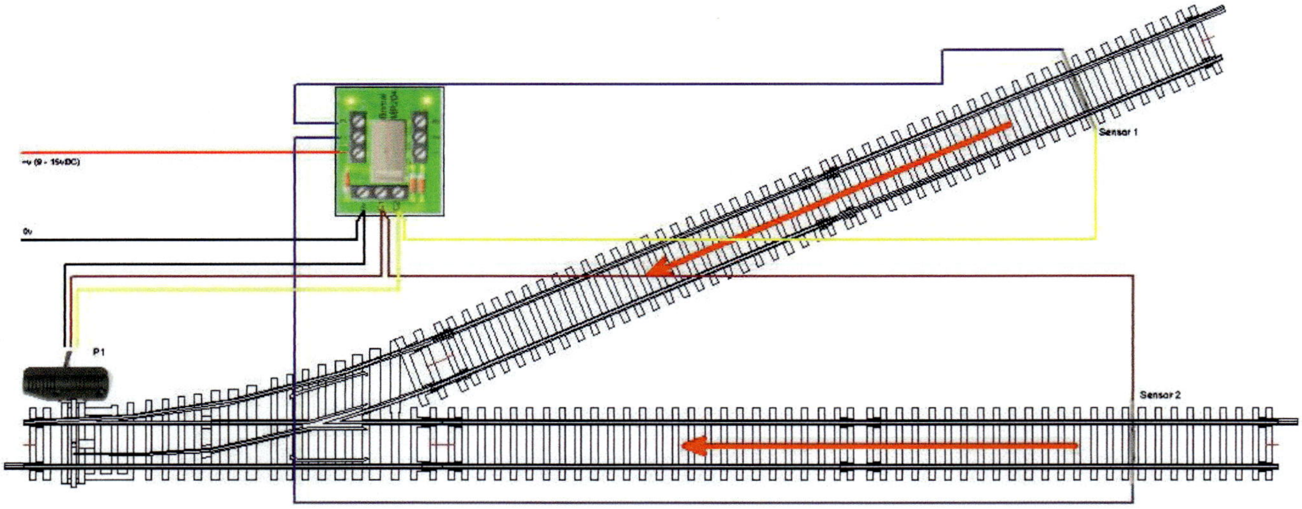

In this application the MR204 is used to control a Point Motor automatically. The MR204 is controlled by 2 Reed Switches (Sensor 1 & Sensor2) this means the Locomotive requires a Magnet fixed to the underside of the unit to activate the Sensors.

This can be used on systems where the fiddle yard is feeding into a Main Line. The Sensor 2 is activated by the Loco switching the points to straight through, the MR204 now removes power from the sensor so any subsequent passes over the sensor have no effect on the Point Motor. The points will remain in this position until Sensor 1 is activated.
As a Train passes over Sensor 1 the points will change and power will be removed from Sensor 1, and put back on Sensor 2. Further Trains coming from the sidings will have no effect on the points.

With this arrangement there is one spare set of contacts on MR204, this can be used to drive a signal set, isolate the track, give an indication back at the control panel, or block another set of points.
The relay has latching contacts, this means once energised and power is removed the contacts stay in that state until the second coil is energised.

Once you have the system wired as above, you may find the indicators are back to front, this is due to the state of the relay when you first switch ON. In this case you may have to swap 2 & 3 around (you will only have to do this once – after the initial wiring, after this it will always be correct)

Track Priority Switch with Indication.

There are going to be certain circumstances when you will want to use a switch to isolate / remove power from a section of track. An example of this could be power on your coding track (Test Track), and then removing it back to the main layout. Or switching power to a bank of sidings.

It is always better to switch ON & OFF both feeds to any piece of equipment or track, however in reality with a DC system we tend just to switch ON & OFF the positive feed. This is not advisable with DCC, it is best to switch both feeds.

Here are a few switch circuits that may help.

Most feeds only require a DPDT switch (Double Pole Double Throw) to achieve this.

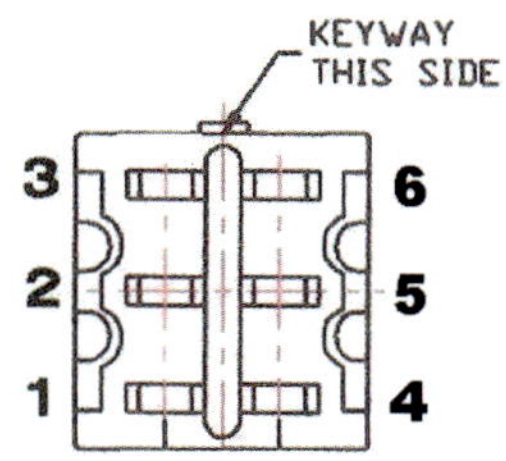

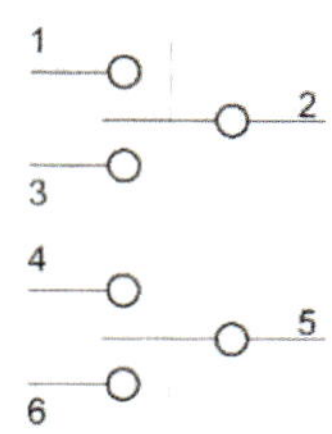

Double Pole
SW312 Mini Toggle Switch
ON – OFF - ON

SW315 Mini Toggle Switch
ON - ON

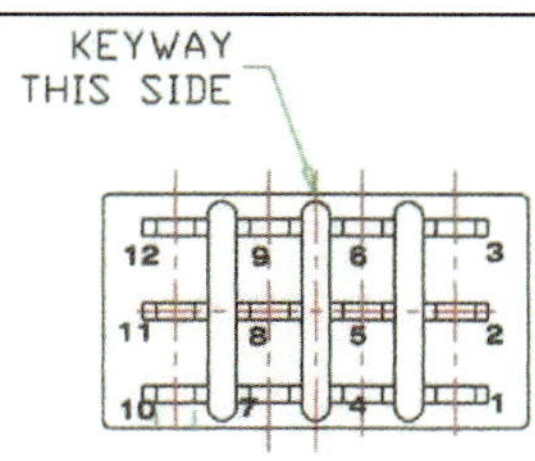

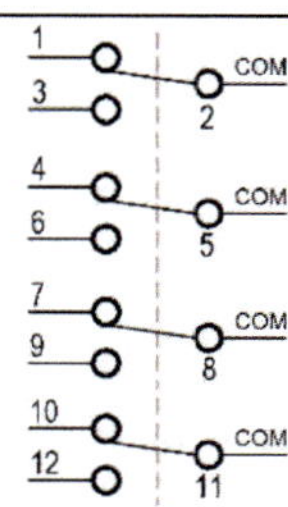

4 Pole
SW320 Mini Toggle Switch
ON – ON

SW321 Mini Toggle Switch
ON - OFF - ON

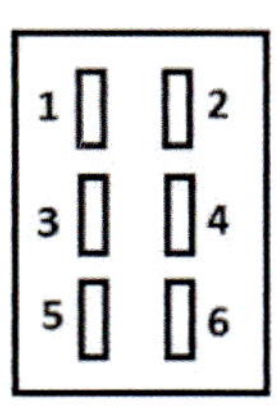

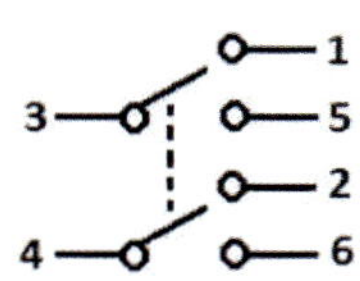

SW150 Standard Slide Switch
DPDT.

SW151 Standard Slide Switch
with centre OFF

Double Pole Double/Triple Throw ON-OFF-ON (SW312)

In this diagram we have DCC power coming from the controller to Terminals 2 and 5 on the double pole toggle switch. Track 1 or Coding track will be powered when the switch is positioned UP to 1 & 4. In the centre position both tracks are OFF. When the switch is positioned DOWN track 2 is powered through 3 and 6.

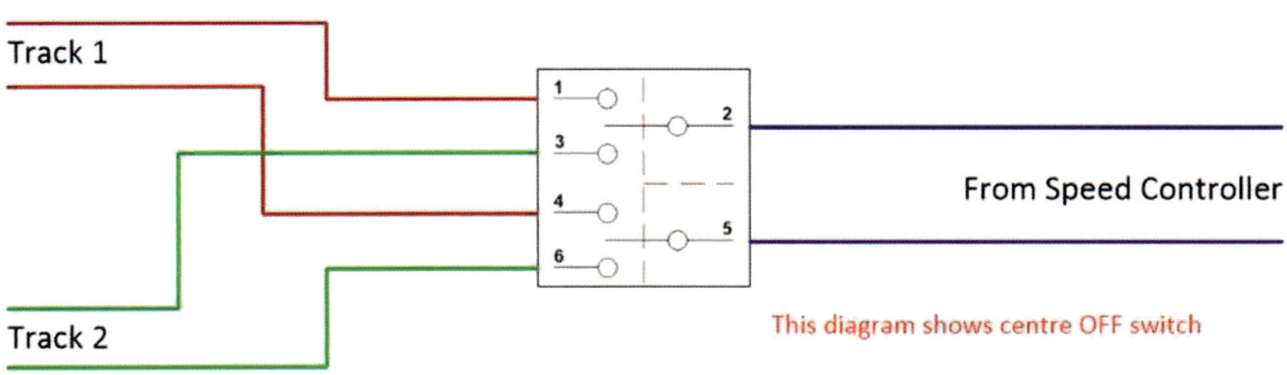

Double Pole Double Throw ON – ON (SW315)

In this diagram we have DC power coming from the controller to terminals 2 and 5 on the double pole toggle switch. In this circuit we have a positive wire and a negative wire, which must follow through the switch to the correct rail. If these wires are crossed over the train will go in reverse.

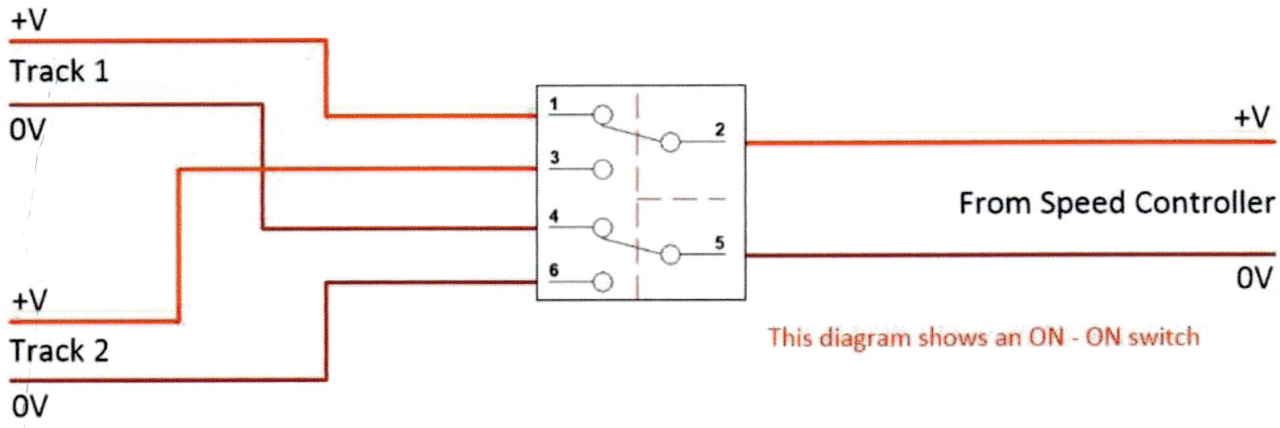

4 Pole Double Throw ON-ON (SW320)

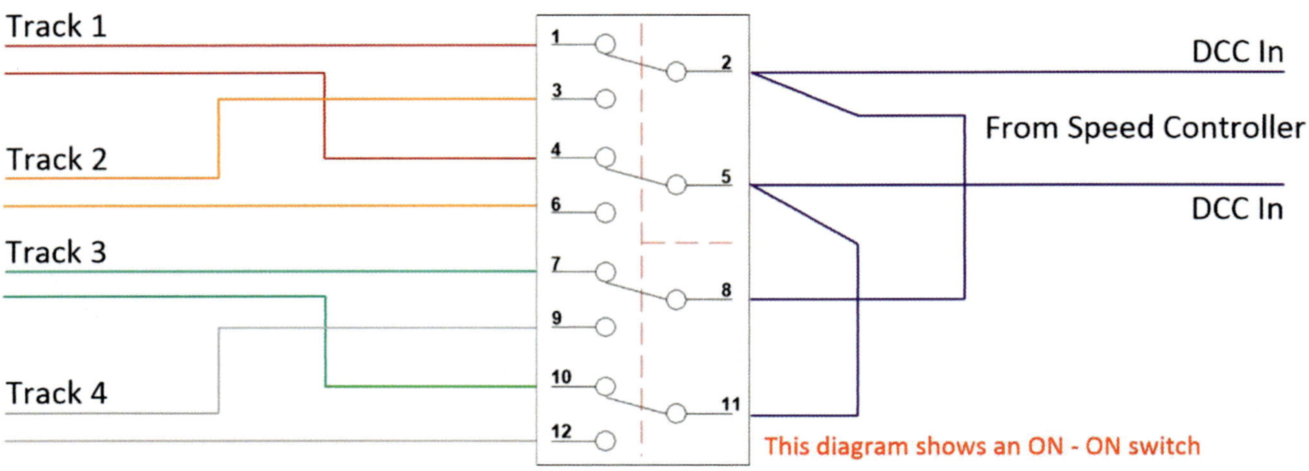

4 Pole Triple Throw ON-OFF-ON (SW321)

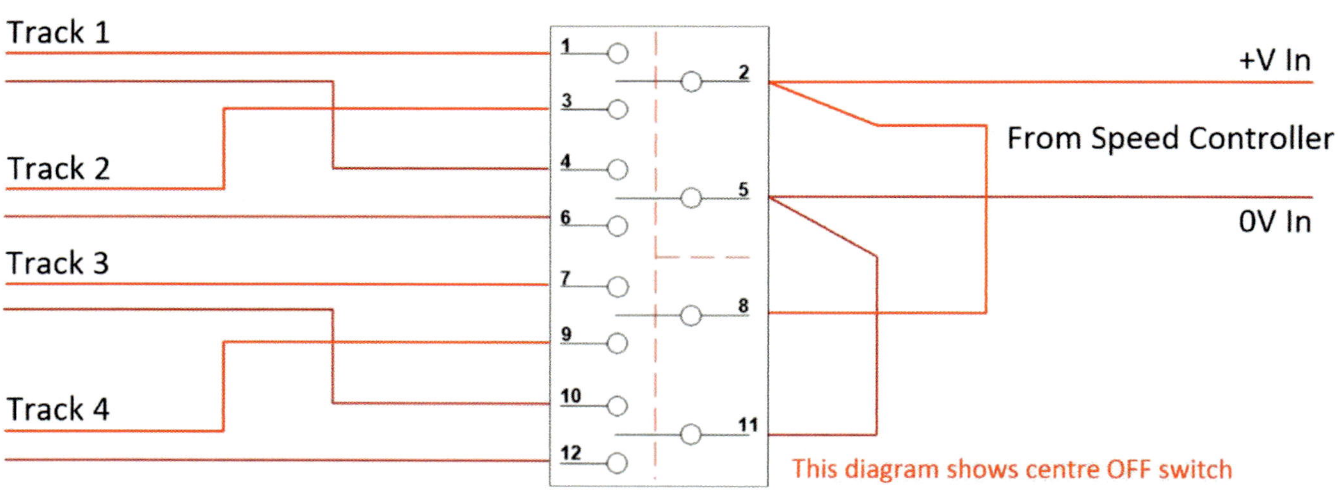

In this example we are using a 3PDT (3 Pole Double Throw) switch to control 2 separate Layouts or Tracks from one Speed Controller, with an LED indication back at the Control Panel, indicating which Track / Layout is Active. This switch will work just as well on DCC as it does on an Analogue layout. Each track is switched through the toggle switch as shown using terminals 1 to 6. The Indicator LED's us the terminals 7 to 9, and are powered by a separate Power Supply at 12v to 5v. A Dropping Resistor of 1K is required for the LED's which can be fitted on the Negative 0v wire. The Negative 0v pin on the LED is the short Pin. The switch has a centre OFF position which can be used if you want. You can get just a straightforward ON – ON if you prefer.

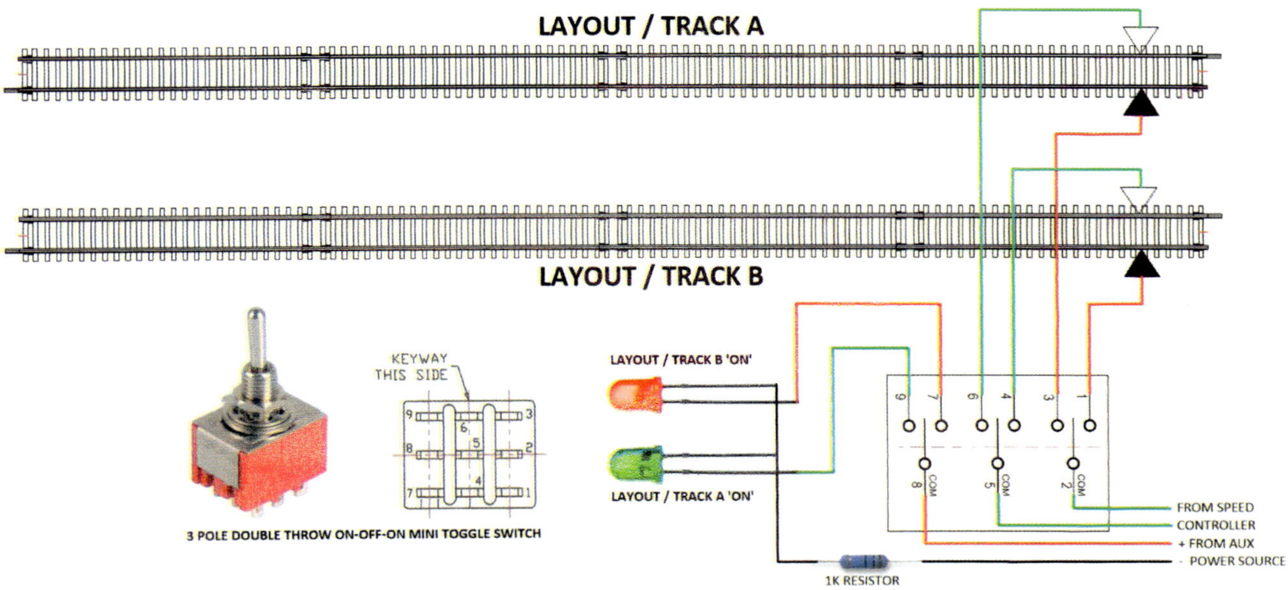

In this circuit the Indication has been replaced with a Bicolour LED, which means we have to change the 3 pole switch to a 4 pole switch, so that we can use the switch to reverse the polarity for the LED. The wiring of the Track A & B is the same on this switch. The difference with this switch is, it does not have a centre OFF position. This means that either Track A is live or Track B is Live. You could, if you wanted, have a centre OFF switch.

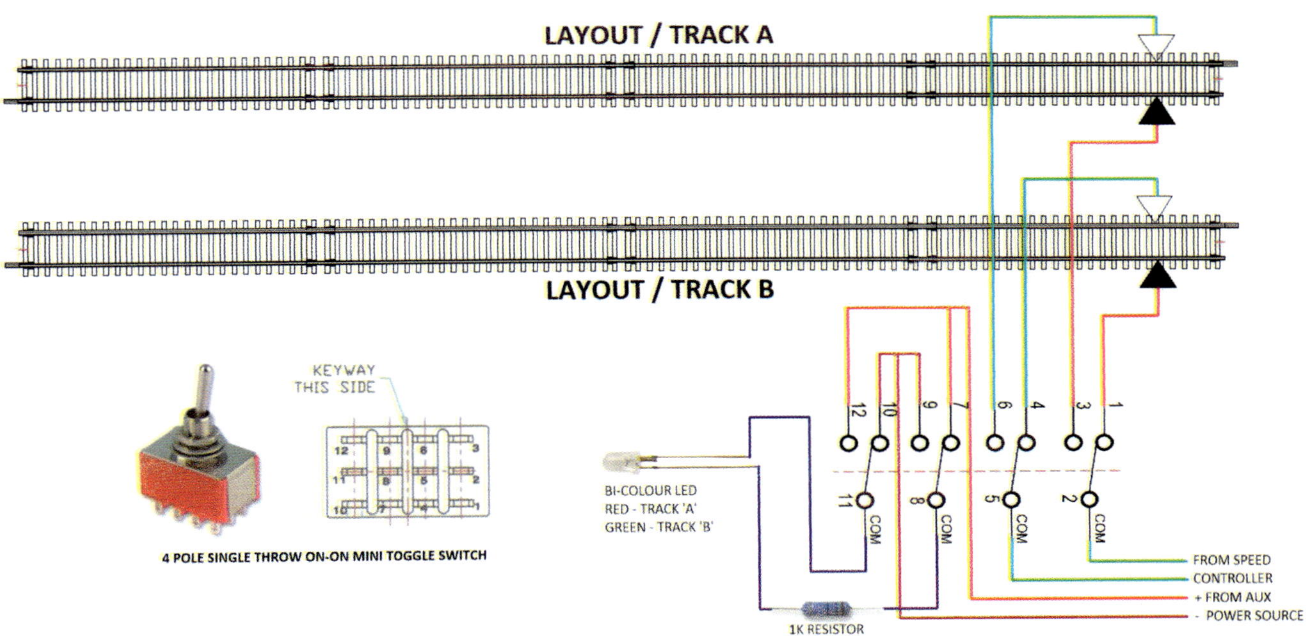

PROJECT 27

Signals Driven by DC Track & Reversing Polarity

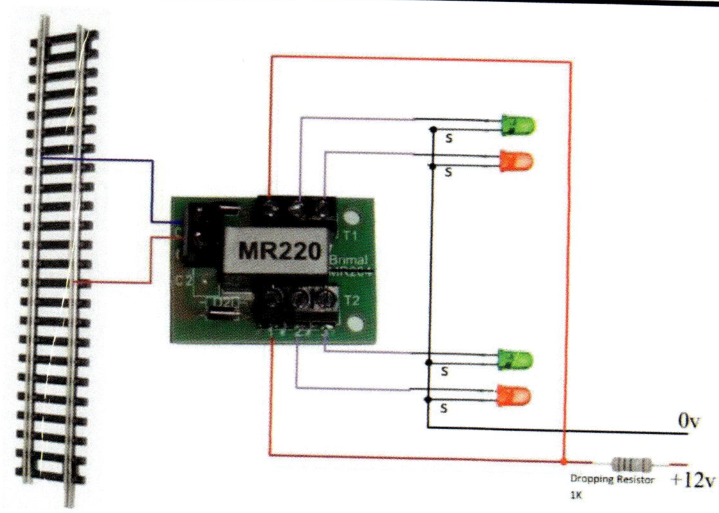

Positive Switching of 2.2v LED's

In this circuit the Positive and Negative comes from the DC track. With the polarity in one direction the relay is energised, in the opposite direction the relay is unenergized. If using 12v LED's don't use the Dropping Resistor

Please note the wiring of the LED's on T2 are the opposite to T1 **The 'S' stands for SHORT lead on the LED.**

Negative Switching of 2.2v

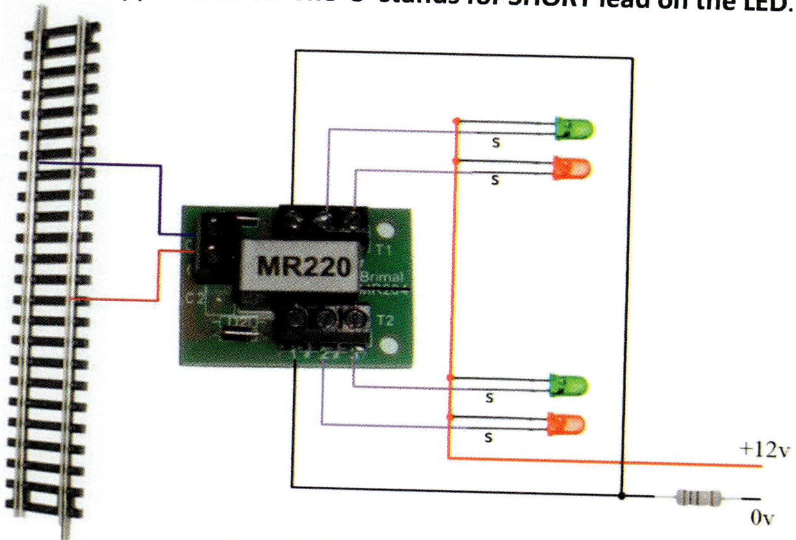

Negative Switching with 2.2v LED's

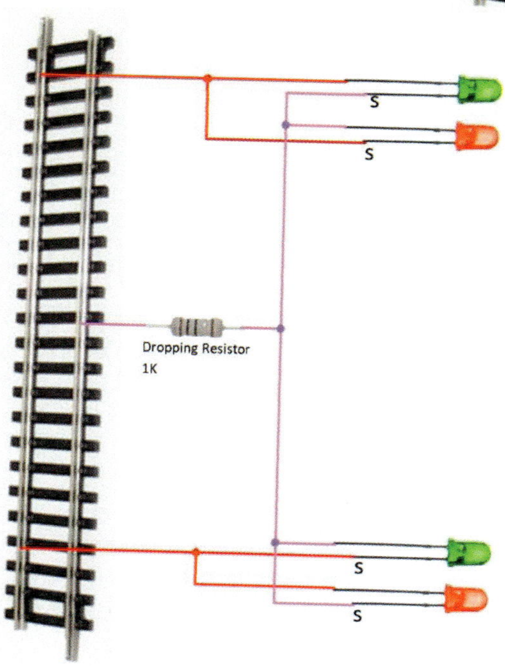

In this circuit the LED's are wired directly to the track.

Again check the polarity of each LED

Capacitor Discharge Unit CDU

Most types of point motors are not in fact motors but are solenoids. When two solenoid coils are placed end to end a forward and reverse motion can be created. A solenoid requires a short sharp punch of current to switch them. These high currents can damage switches and indeed cause points motors to overheat and burn out. A Capacitor discharge unit gets over this problem by supplying this high current as a high energy pulse to the points motor solenoid which in turn operates the points. The purpose of capacitor discharge units is to store up electricity in a capacitor. The electrical charge is released, on throwing a switch, as a pulse of a much larger current. A Capacitor Discharge Unit is normally powered with AC, generally a voltage of around 16 Volts. Note that whether you power the CDU from AC or DC the output of the CDU will be DC. The CDU may be operated from any AC voltage up to 24 volts. Using a high voltage increases the power from a CDU. Operating from 24 volts instead of 12 volts gives 4 times the power.

Why do you need one:

All Model Rail layout have a power source, and this power source has a limited capacity. Not all layouts will require a CDU unit. The best way to judge it is, if your points have problems switching over, then you probably need a CDU. The larger the system the more drain on the power source, also the further away the points are from the power source then the voltage drop is greater. The point motor requires a precise voltage and current to energise it. The CDU achieves both these. As this pulse is short it avoids the problem of motor burn-out, the current burst is over by the time the switch contacts open, thus eliminating the back EMF which can weld the switch contacts together. After the pulse has fired the CDU will not allow recharging of the capacitors until the switch reopens or is released. Then the cycle can start again with the capacitors recharging.

The Circuit:

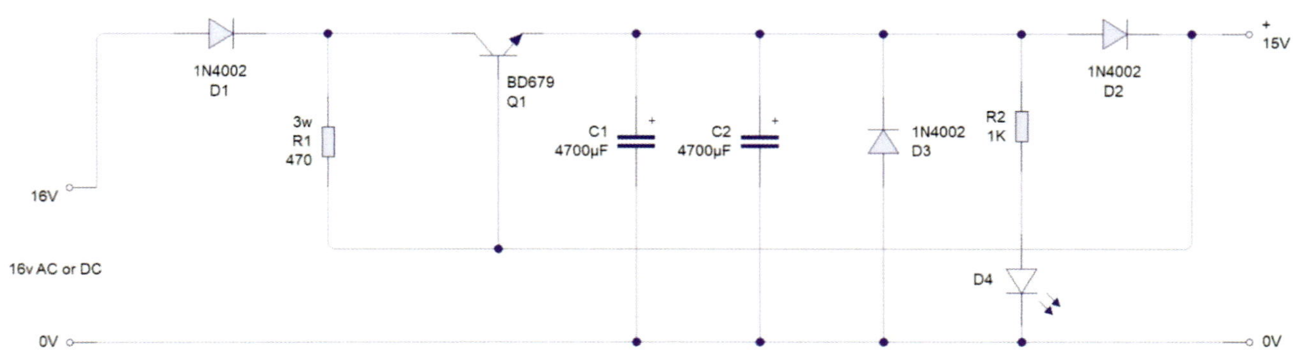

How it works:

The AC voltage (16v) at the input of the CDU is rectified by D_1. This diode passes every positive half-cycle of the AC and blocks the negative half-cycle. Assuming no solenoid is connected to the CDU, R_1 pulls the base of the Darlington transistor high, switching it ON and allowing current to flow through it (from C to E), to charge the 1000u capacitors. These are the reservoir capacitors that will supply the surge of current to the solenoid. D_2 and D_3 are protection diodes that prevent any back EMF from damaging the transistor or capacitors.
This is what happens when a solenoid is connected across the output of the CDU: The reservoir capacitors will discharge through D_3 into the solenoid. The low impedance of the solenoid (typically 3 ohms) is now holding the base of the transistor LOW, switching it OFF. The only current now flowing is going through R_1 and the solenoid. This current is less than 50mA. The transistor remains OFF preventing the charge-current reaching the solenoid. Removing the solenoid from the output of the CDU will allow the base of the transistor to be pulled HIGH by R_1. The transistor will turn on and charge the reservoir capacitors again, ready for the next operation. Recharge time is less than half a second.

Wire Size:

The CDU delivers a short sharp jolt of power to the Motor, and therefore requires the appropriate wire size. The smaller diameter wire suffers from 2 problems, voltage drop due to its diameter and or distance from the CDU to the points, and this could affect the performance of the Point Motor. You should wire from the CDU to the points in either 16/0.2 or 24/0.2 size wire. If you are changing two points at the same time you will be drawing approximately 3 Amps at that point in time, the standard 7/0.2 or 1/0.6 wire will not cope with that so you need a larger wire size. The short piece of wire the motor may come with should have no effect on the overall performance, but keep it as short as possible when using capacitor discharge units.

Basic Wiring:

The CDU inputs can be connected to any AC power supply up to 16volts. The most common connection point would probably be the 16V AC auxiliary output usually found on model railway speed controllers. With DC supplies, be sure to connect them with the correct polarity to the CDU. The minimum supply voltage is 12V AC or 15V DC, as below this level the CDU will no longer improve the action of the points. The output terminals are connected to the points switches, with the CDU negative output generally connected to the common, centre point, of the points motors.

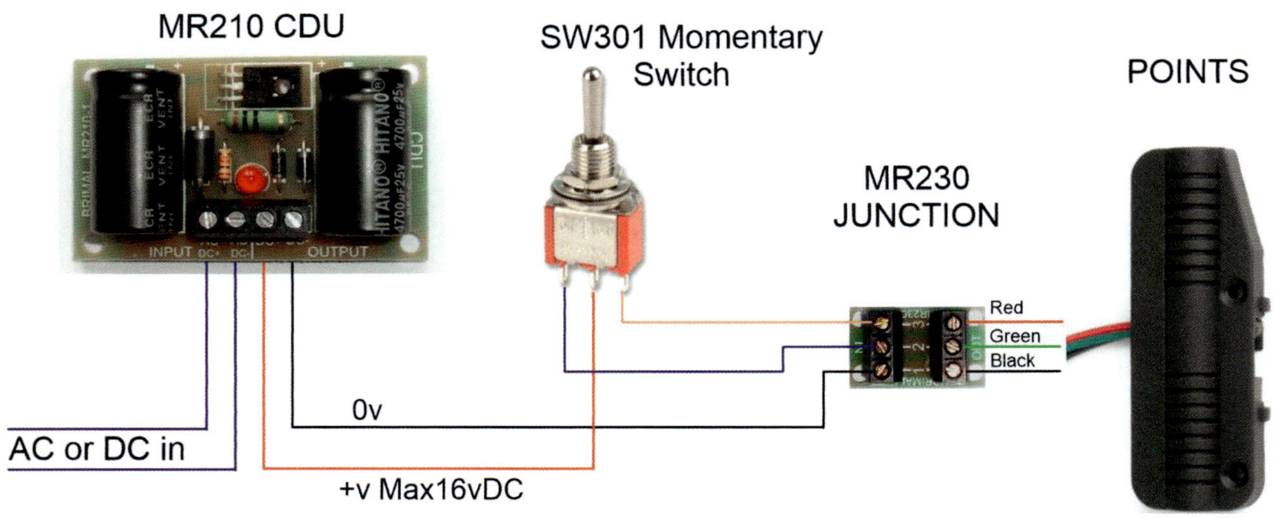

The current from the CDU will make the point motor move up or down depending on which coil is energised. Some point motors have four terminals (wires), because each coil has 2 wires. Some point motors such as Seep & Hornby have three because the manufacturer has connected one end of each coil to give a common return connection.

Multiple Motors:

The following picture shows the connection of multiple Point sets. The wiring is basically the same for one as it is for many, just follow the Red and Black wires on the drawing. As you will see the black wire is the common 0v and it runs between all the points and then back to the CDU. This is a good case for a 0v (Negative) Bus Bar, which will be either 24/0.2 or 32/0.2 wire, saves running a separate Negative wire to each set of points. See our Bus Bar section. You cannot run the positive (Red) on a Bus Bar as each set of points requires 2 separate wires.
The image also shows a few alternative Point Motor types.

Multiple & Crossover Points:

The following image shows a single switch used to activate 2 sets of points, this would be in a crossover situation, of in the Fiddle Yard. In this situation you are changing two points at the same time you will be drawing approximately 3 Amps at that switch, the standard 7/0.2 or 1/0.6 wire will not cope with that, so you need a larger wire size. The short piece of wire the motor may come with should have no effect on the overall performance, but keep it as short as possible when using capacitor discharge units. As you will see the black wire is the common 0v and it runs between all the points and then back to the CDU. This is a good case for a 0v (Negative) Bus Bar, which will be either 24/0.2 or 32/0.2 wire, saves running a separate negative wire to each set of points. See our Bus Bar section. You cannot run the positive (Red) on a Bus Bar as each set of points requires 2 separate wires.

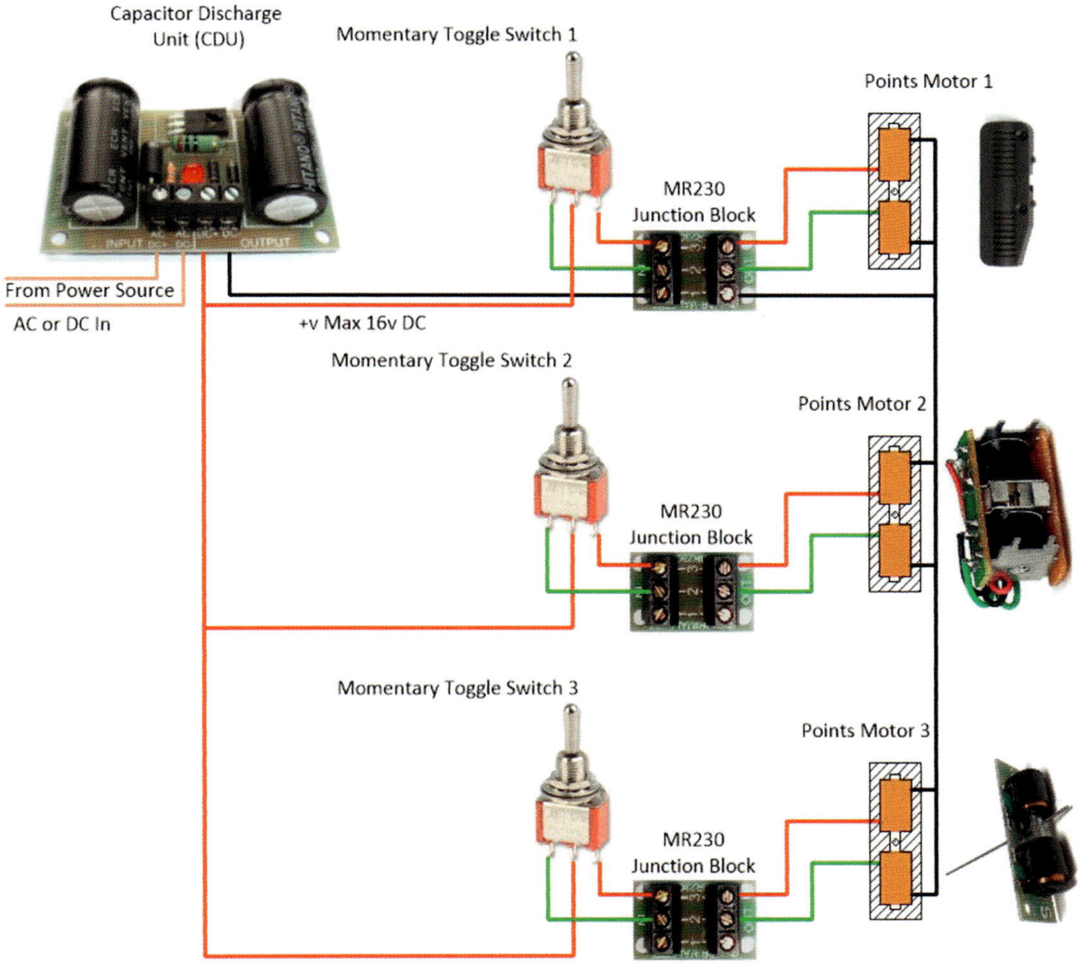

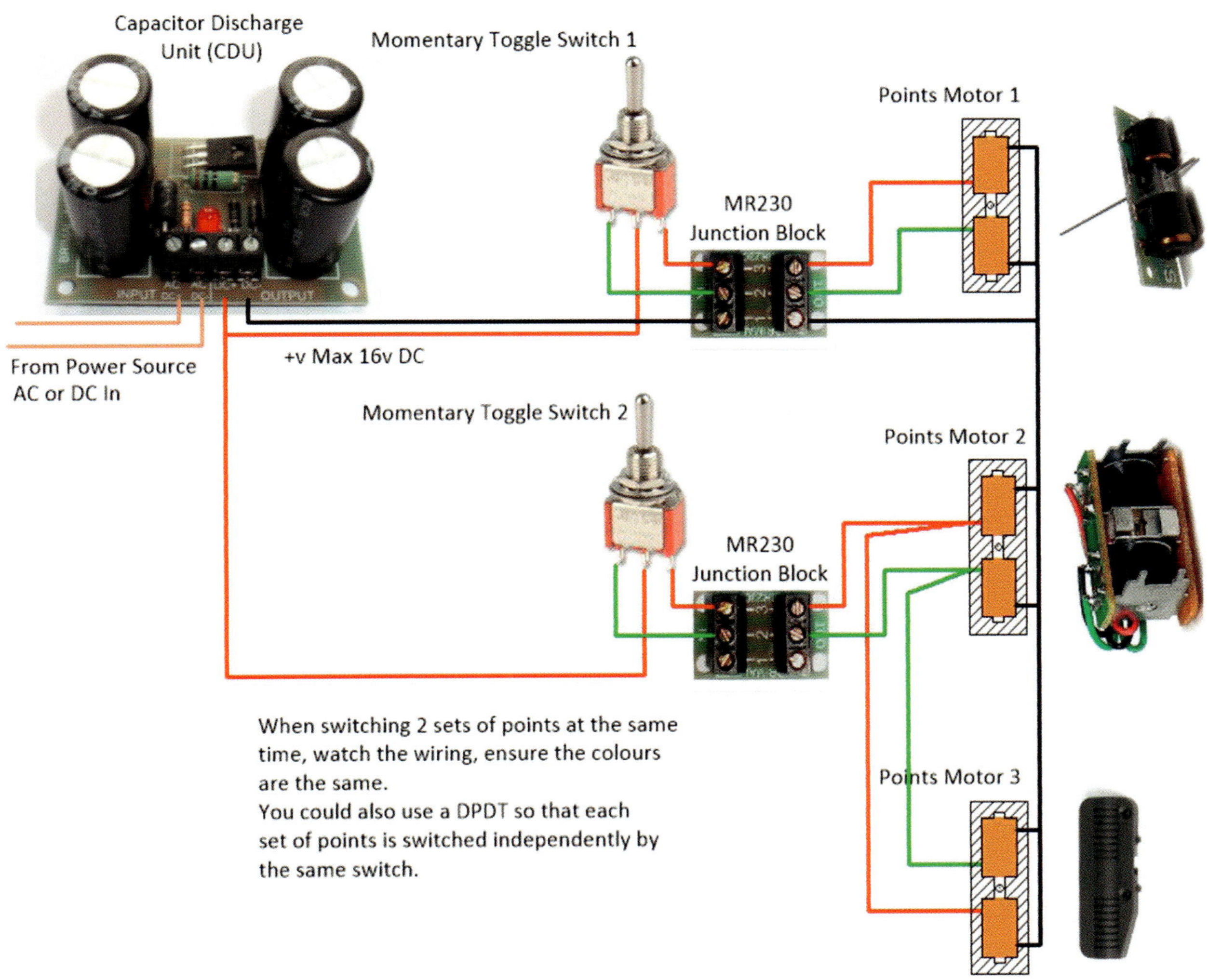

When switching 2 sets of points at the same time, watch the wiring, ensure the colours are the same.
You could also use a DPDT so that each set of points is switched independently by the same switch.

PROJECT 29

Track Isolation.

WHY

In a DC system track isolation is important otherwise all trains will move when the speed controller is used.
The most common way of isolation is via the points, when the points are closed the points also break the power connection to one of the tracks, this isolates all power to that section, and therefore all locomotives in that section.

In Figure 1 tracks A, B, & D are live, track C is isolated because the points are set for straight through. This means that any train on the track CD has no power.
In Figure 2 tracks A, C, & D are live, track B is isolated because the points are set from the straight through. This means that any train on the track AB has no power.

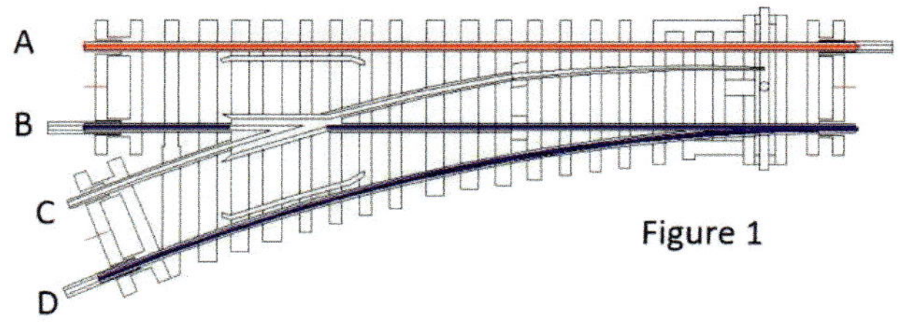

Figure 1

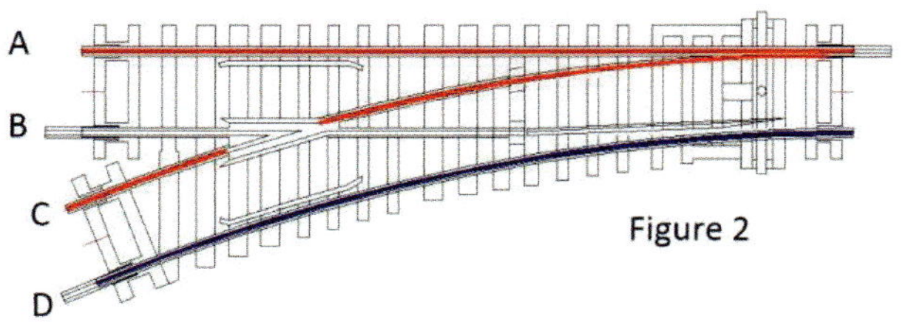

Figure 2

HOW

A more permanent way to isolate a section of track is to use plastic fishplates. These are used to join two tracks sections together with a 1mm gap. Most proprietary manufactures produce plastic fishplates.

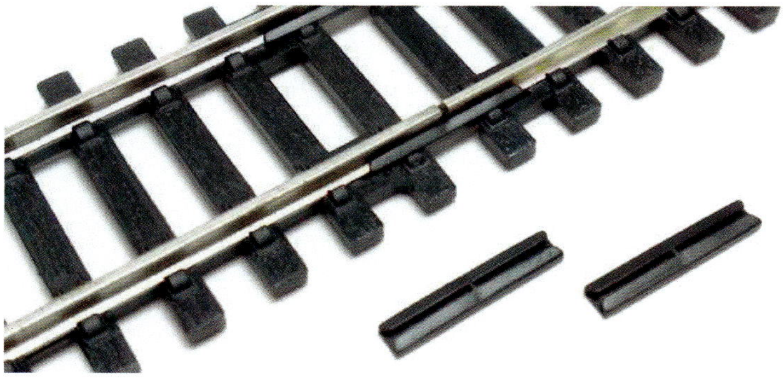

Fig: 3

Another way is to use a Track Isolator section as shown below. Here the left and right tracks have been separated & on the top track a loop of wire is used to continue the circuit. On the lower track a switch can be used to energise or isolate the right section of track.

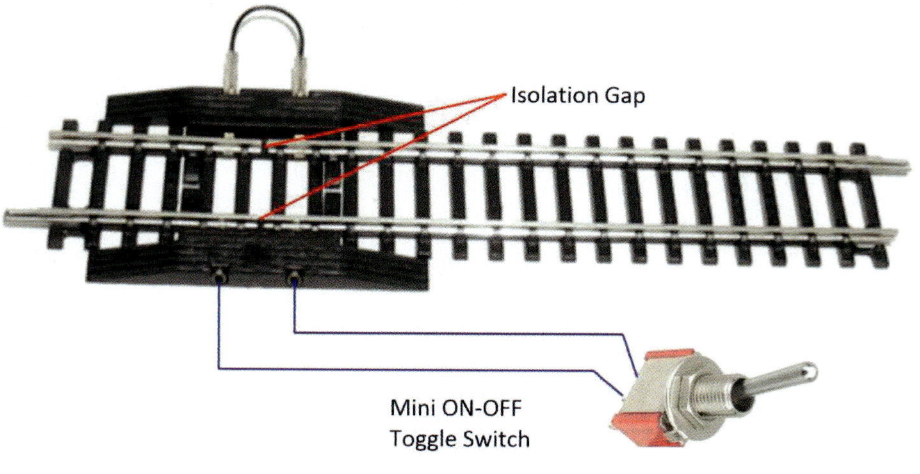

Fig: 4

In this example only one track is being switched to create the isolation. The top track has a link to maintain the circuit. If you want to switch both tracks then use a double pole double throw switch as shown below.

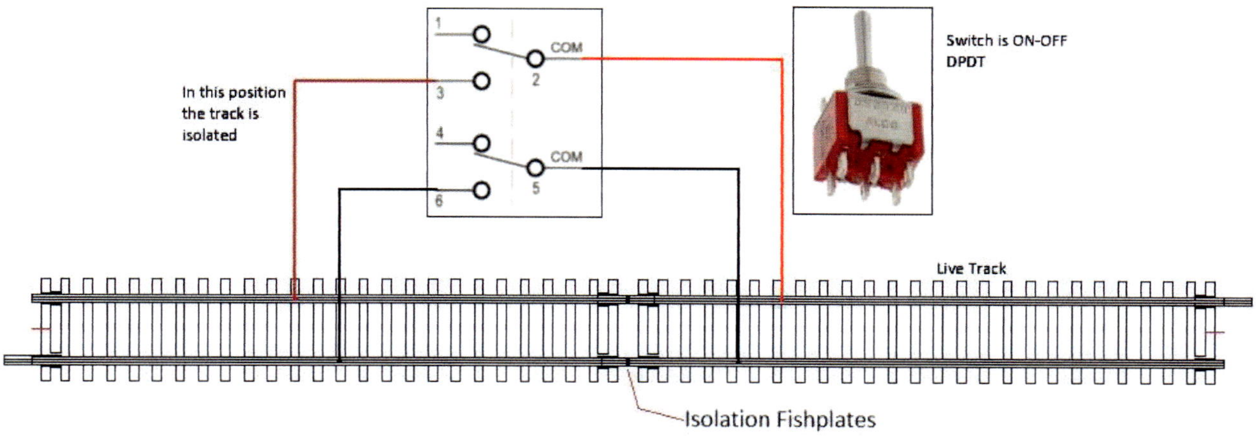

Fig: 5

In this drawing the isolation is created by using plastic fishplates and the connecting wires are either soldered directly to the track or a power connector clip can be used both left and right of the isolation point.

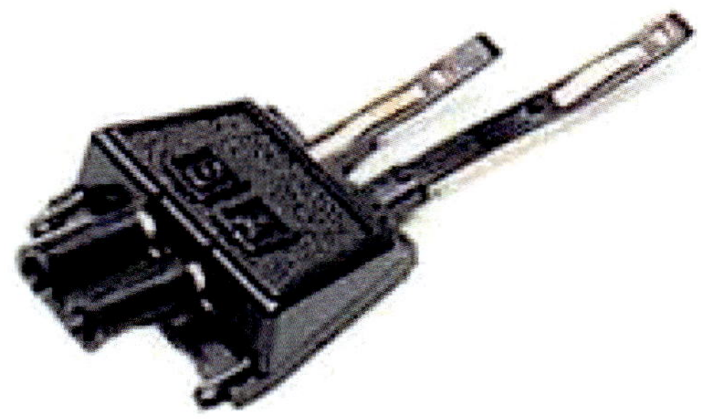

Fig: 6

Power Connection Clips come in all shapes depending on the manufacturer, but the function is the same.

For switches SW312, SW151, MR326, & MR601

If you require to Isolate a section of track for any reason, then the above switches will do this. In Fig 4 the diagram shows how to isolate track using the above switches, as they all have a centre OFF. This allows you to Isolate the left section of Fig 4, and then either Forward or Reverse.

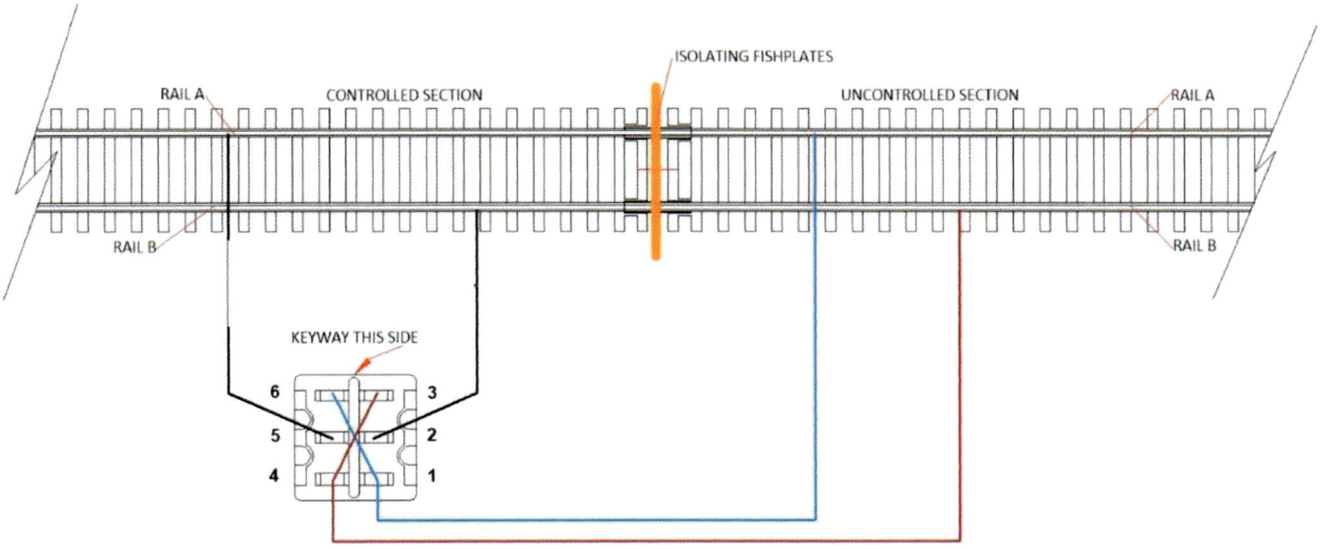

Fig: 7

How to wire a Point Motor

There are many different types of Point Motors available for your Model Railway Layout. They range from Twin Coil Motor, Stall Motors, Reverse Polarity Motor, Reverse Polarity Coil Motor, and finally the Servo Motor. (Please note I have used Miniature Toggle Switches in all these examples, but there is nothing stopping you using proprietry switches by each manufacturer.)

Twin Coil Motor   Stall Motor   Reverse Polarity   Reverse Polarity Coil   Servo Motor

Twin Coil

Let's look at the Twin Coil Motor, probably the most commonly used motor, which is in fact not a motor but 2 coils. These come in many different shapes and sizes, for above and below baseboard mounting. Some have auxiliary switches built in other have the facility to have auxiliary switches fitted to them. The basic principle is you switch ON one coil (for a second) to move the actuator bar one way, and then switch ON the other coil (for a second) to move the actuator bar the other way.

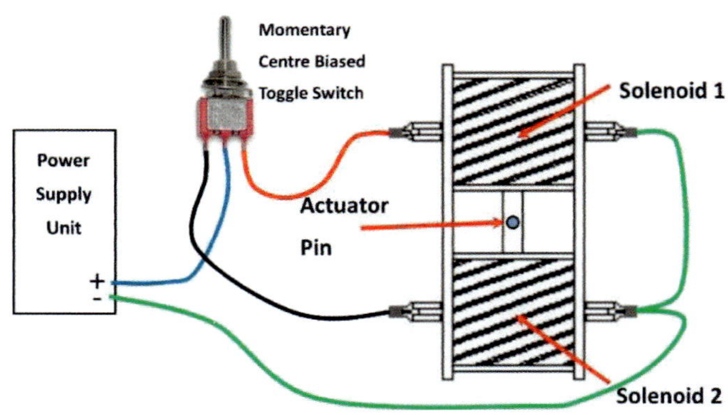

The wiring of this type of motor is as follows. The Negative is common to both coils and is shown in Green from the Power supply. The positive from the power supply goes to the centre terminal on a Momentary (centre biased) Toggle switch. (Salecom T8014A-SEBQ-H). One side of the switch (Black) goes to one coil, and the other side of the switch (Red) goes to the other coil. When the switch is pushed left the red coil is energised, pulling the actuator bar towards Solenoid 1. When the switch is pushed to the right the black coil is energised, pulling the actuator bar towards Solenoid 2.

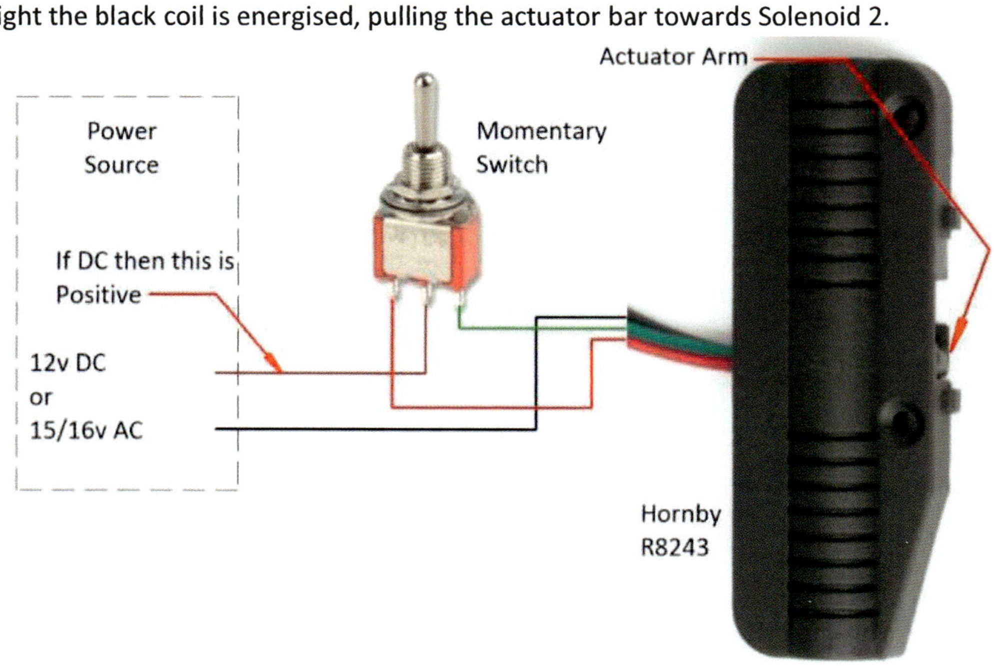

Hornby R8243

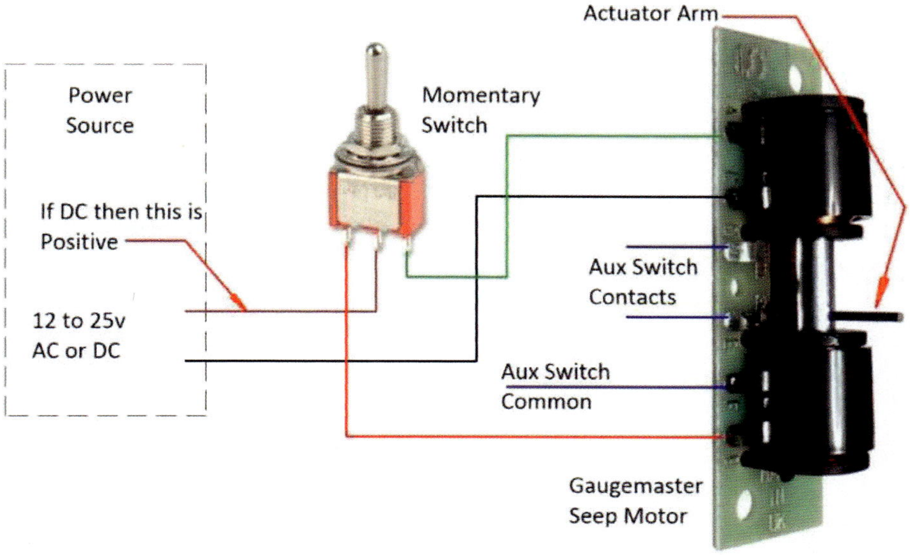

Gaugemaster Seep Motor

It must be noted that each manufacturer has a different colour code system so please read the instructions that come with the motor, an example of this in the Hornby R8243 where the Negative is Black. The Gaugemaster does not have any wires pre-installed so you can decide which colour goes where.

Note: This type of Point Motors are in fact solenoids so you can use a CDU if required.

Using a CDU with Coil Point Motors.

Under normal circumstances the coils will energise using a 12vDC or 16vAC power supply (depending on the type of coil motor) through a momentary switch, however sometimes you may want to switch more than 1 motor at a time. In this case to ensure all the coils energise it is advisable to use a Capacitor Discharge Unit (CDU). The purpose of a CDU is to store an electrical charge and release it in one bust, enough to power all points connected to it.

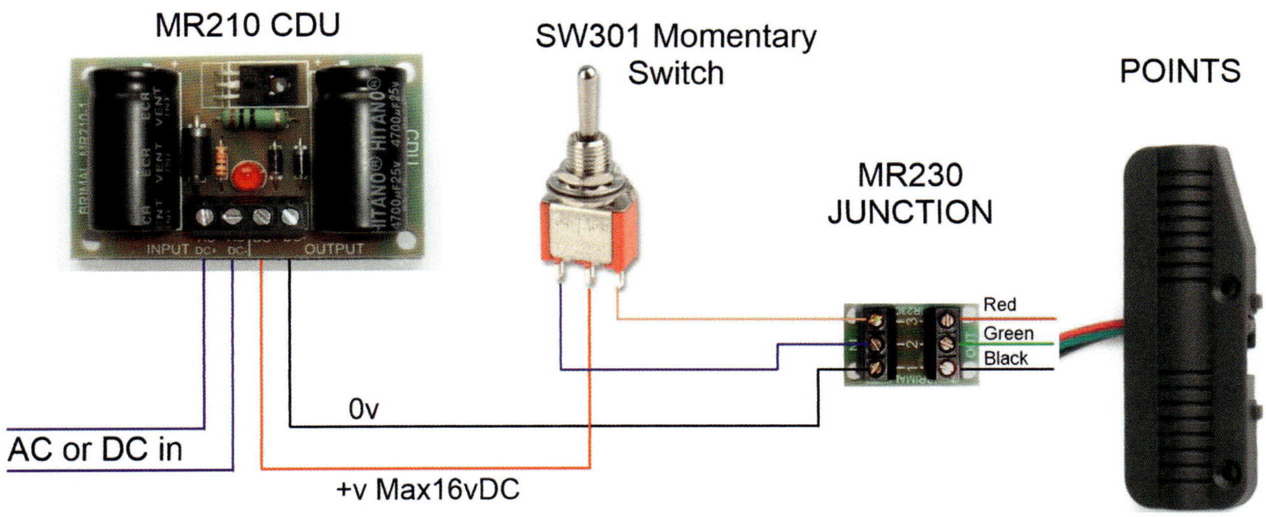

Stall Motors Tortoise

Tortoise Motors sometimes called Stall Motors or Slow Motion Motors work with a permanent current to the motor coils, so when it reaches its limit it simple stalls and remains there until the polarity is reversed, changing the direction of the motor.

The Power supply can be very basic 9v to 12v unfiltered. The polarity is changed by the Double Pole Double Throw (DPDT)Switch, (Salecom T8011-SEBQ-H), the switch could also be a DPDT Slide Switch. The toggle switch has a Keyway on one side of the shaft, position this as the drawing before you start soldering wires to it. (A keyway is a groove in the shaft). Connection to the Tortoise Motor is via Terminals 8 and 1. The wires can be soldered to the printed circuit board, there are also push on terminal blocks available for this.

Wiring is as follows. Positive from the power source goes to pins 3 & 4 on the Switch. Negative goes to 6 & 1. Pin 2 Goes to Terminal 8 on the motor, & Pin 5 goes to Terminal 1. Terminal 2 to 7 on the motor are two separate

Change-over contacts activated by the motor. These can be used for panel indications, signals etc. They can be used to drive LED's directly without the use of dropping resistors.

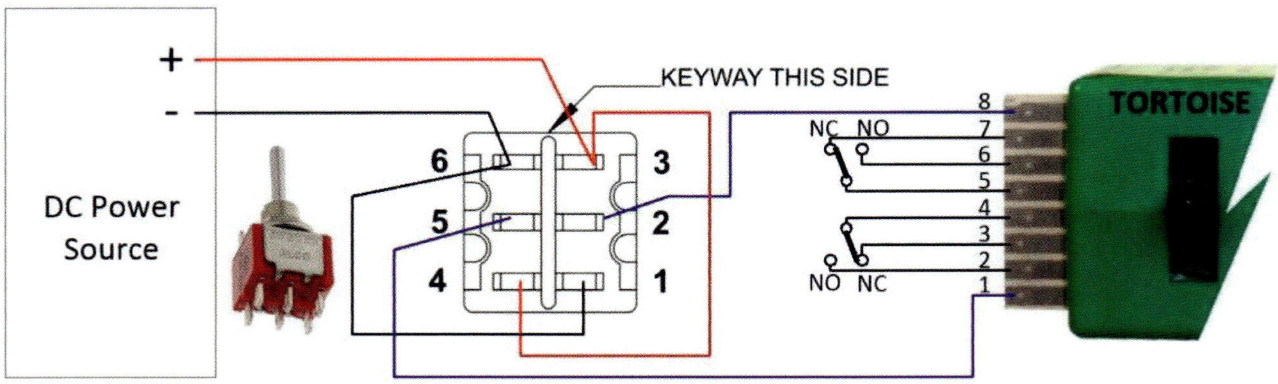

The DCC Connections

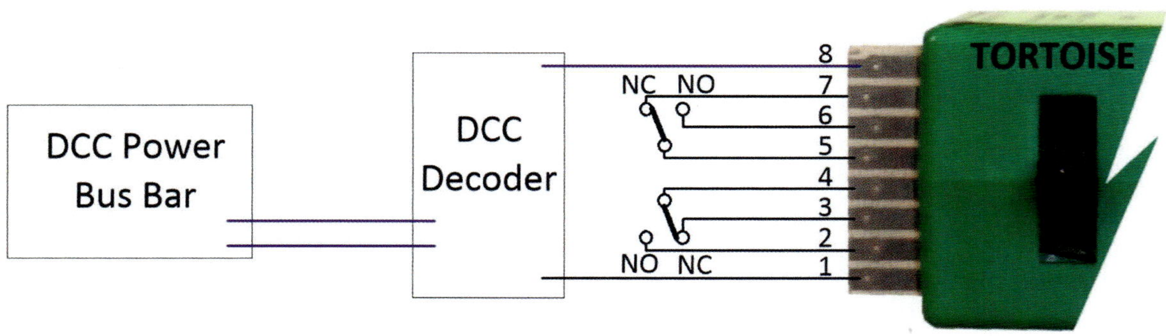

This is the wiring when using a DCC system. Each manufacturer has its own way of wiring so please read the manufacturer's instructions

<u>Note: This type of Point Motors are in fact motors so do not require a CDU</u>

<u>Stall Motor Cobalt Omega</u>

Cobalt Omega Motors sometimes called Stall Motors work with a permanent current to the motor coils, so when it reaches its limit it simple stalls and remains there until the polarity is reversed, changing the direction of the motor. The Power supply can be 9v to 12v or 12v to 18v by using the miniature switch to the right of the terminal block. The polarity is changed by the Double Pole Double Throw (DPDT)Switch, (Salecom T8011-SEBQ-H), the switch could also be a DPDT Slide Switch. The toggle switch has a Keyway on one side of the shaft, position this as the drawing before you start soldering wires to it. (A keyway is a groove in the shaft). Connection to the Cobalt Omega Motor is via Terminals 1 and 2. The wires should be 16/0.2mm and are push fit into the spring terminals.

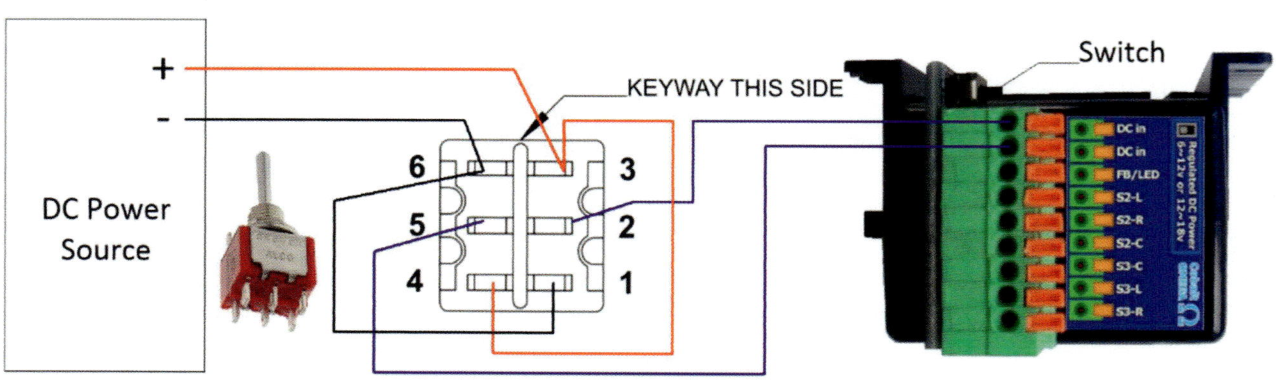

Wiring is as follows. Positive from the power source goes to pins 3 & 4 on the Toggle Switch. Negative goes to 6 & 1. Pin 2 Goes to Terminal 1 on the motor, & Pin 5 goes to Terminal 2. Terminal 3 can be used to wire LED's or Signals. Terminal 4 – Left rail, Terminal 5 – Right Rail, Terminal 6 – Common Terminal 7 – Common, Terminal 8 – Left, Terminal 9 – Right

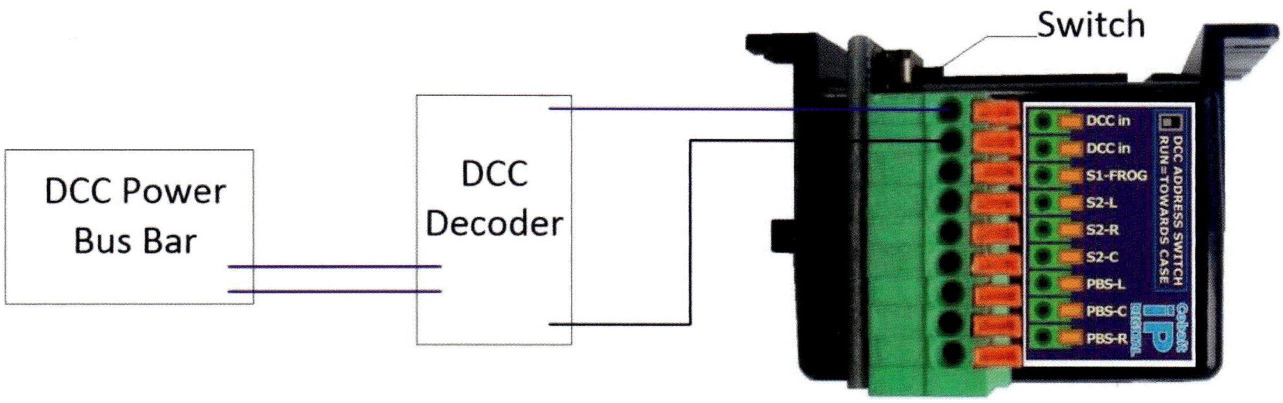

DCC Wiring.

This is the wiring when using a DCC system. Each manufacturer has its own way of wiring so please read the manufacturer's instructions

Note: This type of Point Motors are in fact motors so do not require a CDU

Single Coil Kato Motor

The Kato Point motor is a single Solenoid Coil which works the same way as the twin coil motors. The difference is that by Reversing the Polarity feeding the coil changes the coil from push to pull. The switch must be a Momentary action with centre biased, as the coil only requires a short pulse. So activating the switch in one direction makes the single coil push the actuating lever, and activating the switch in the other direction makes the coil pull back the actuating lever. The polarity is changed by the Double Pole Double Throw (DPDT)Switch, (Salecom T8012A-SEBQ-H), the toggle switch has a Keyway on one side of the shaft, position this as the drawing before you start soldering wires to it. (A keyway is a groove in the shaft).

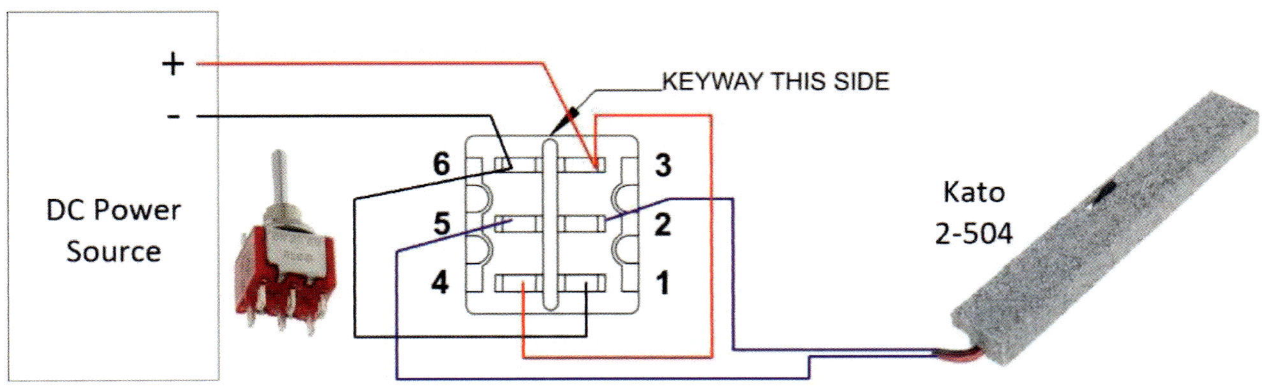

Kato also do a Point motor installed on the underside of a set of points. The circuit is the same as above.

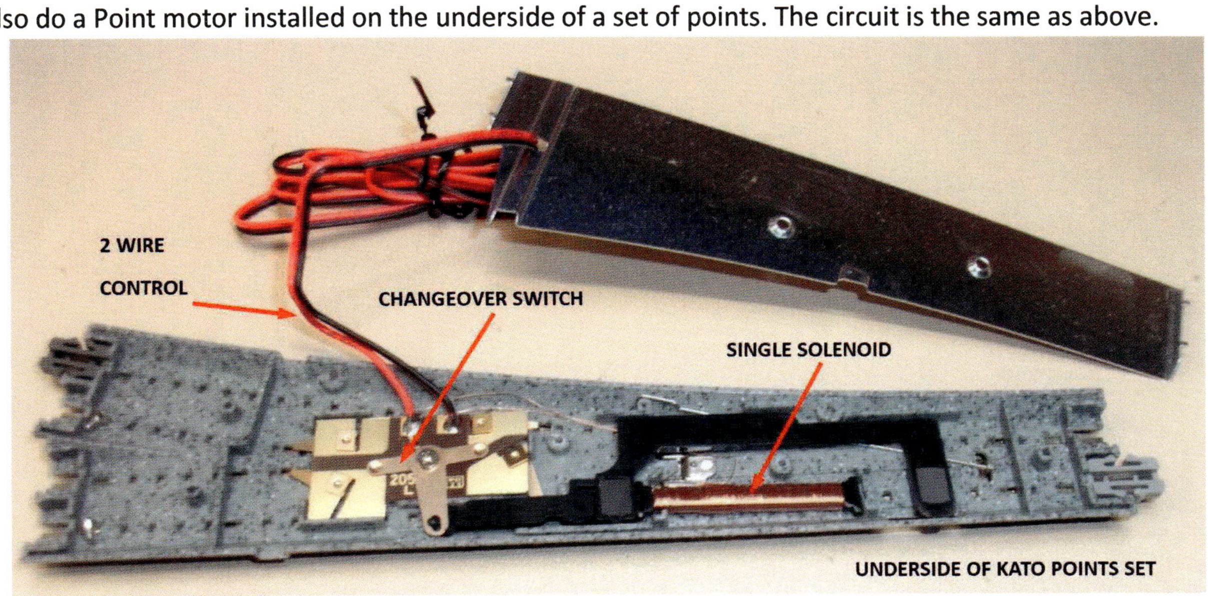

Note: This type of Point Motors are in fact single solenoids but do not require a CDU

Servo Motors

A servo motor is a rotary actuator or a motor that allows for a precise control in terms of the angular position, acceleration, and velocity. Basically, it has certain capabilities that a regular motor does not have. Consequently it makes use of a regular motor and pairs it with a sensor for position feedback . A typical servo motor comprises of three wires namely- power, control, and ground. They are becoming more popular in Model Railway layouts due to their lower cost.

The Servo motor can be used above the baseboard as shown or below the baseboard. The control circuit will come with 3 variable resistors, (pre-sets), one to adjust the limit of the Forward motion of the actuator The second one to control the limit of the Reverse motion of the Actuator, and the third to control the transition speed. Once these are all set to your requirements the mini momentary toggle switch is used to send the signal to the Servo Motor. As always please read the manufacturers instruction to get the best out of your controller.

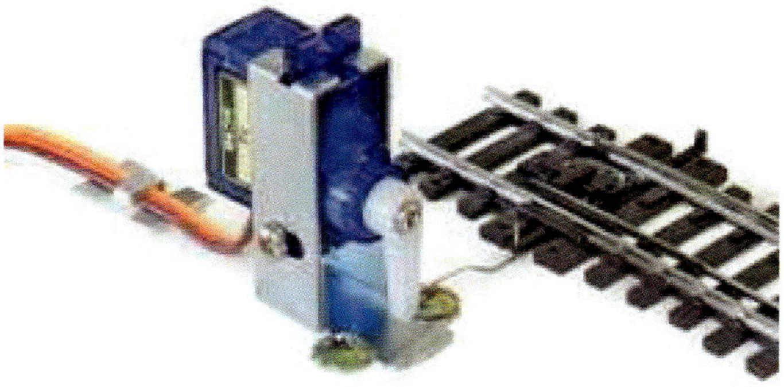

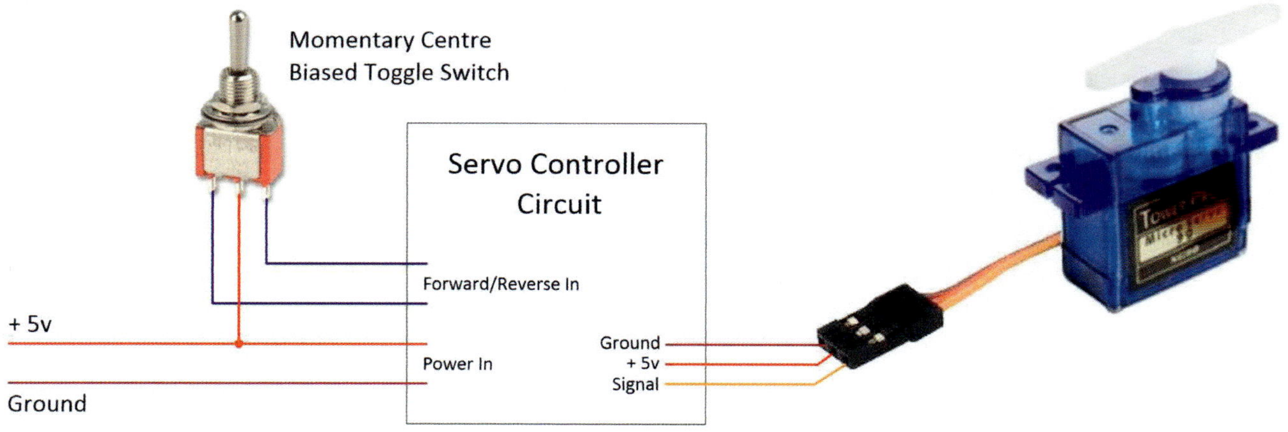

For Circuit Details see Project 46

This diagram shows what the control circuit is sending to the Servo Motor. You will have set the motor so that the 0' is with the points open (Straight Through), so when the switch is placed in the Forward position the signal sent to the motor is as the 'Neutral Position'. When the switch is placed in the Reverse position the signal sent to the motor is as the 'Minimum Pulse', this turns the actuator arm and the points go to the turn out position.

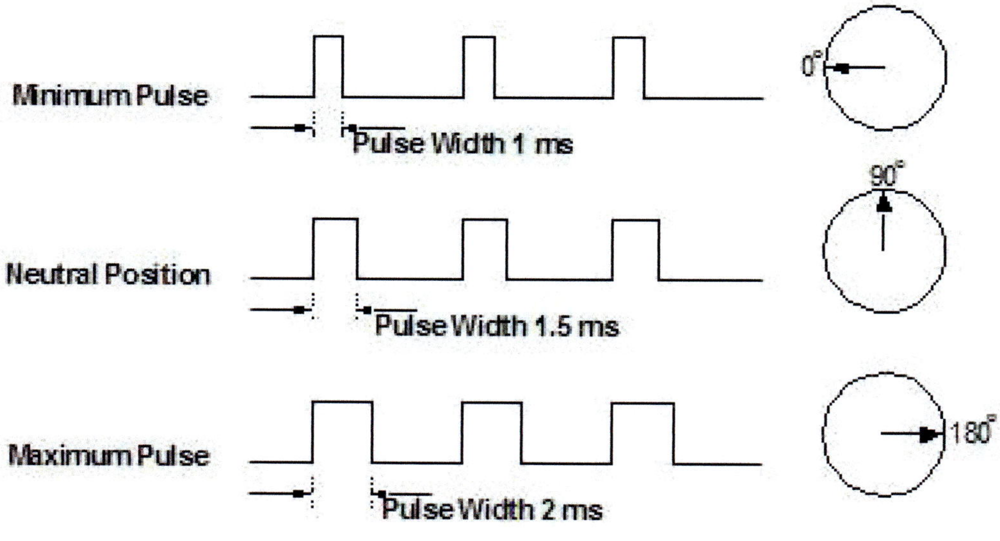

PROJECT 31

Peco SL-99 & Peco PM1 Motors

Turnout Indication Circuit

The Peco SL-99 has 3 turnouts, so it would be handy to know which one is active at any one time. This circuit shows how you can wire 3 LED's or 3 Lilliput lamps to the point motors. The Indicator could be either next to the points or back at the control panel.

The switch part of the point motor PM1 is D,E,&F, with F being the common. It is not important where the point actuator pin is while wiring up as long as you follow the drawing. If you are using LED's you will need to incorporate the 1K Resistor as shown. If however you are going to use 12v Lilliput bulbs then leave the resistor out.

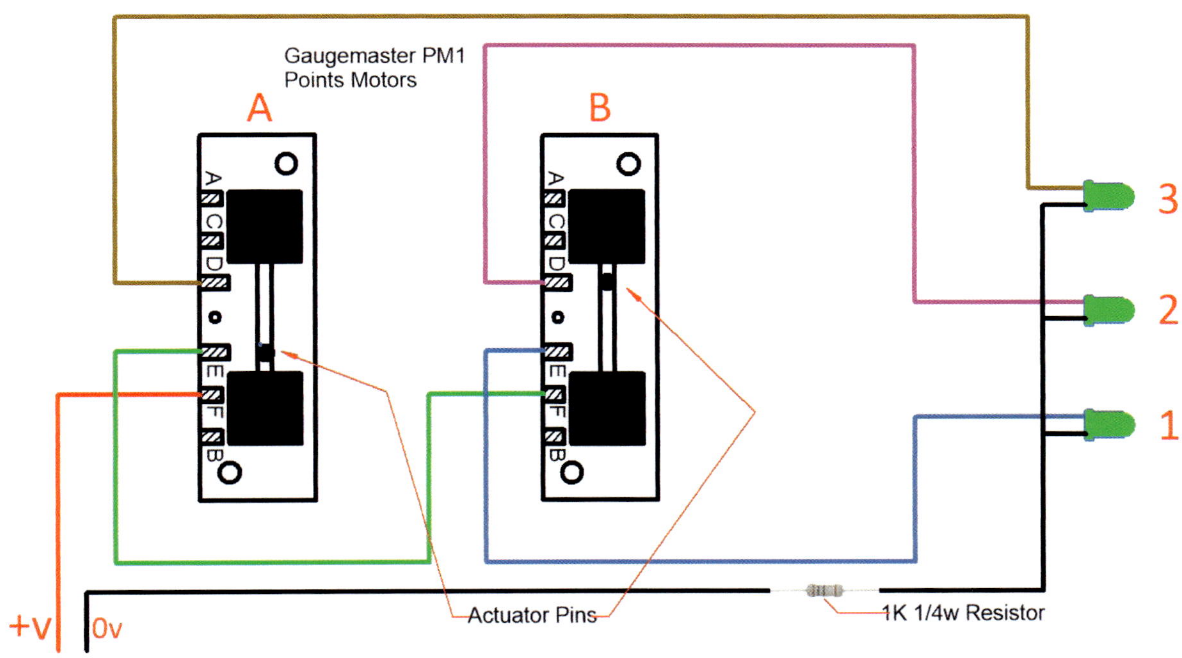

NOTE: The Negative (0v) on an LED is the shorter lead and the one next to the flat on the casing.

Ground Signal Control

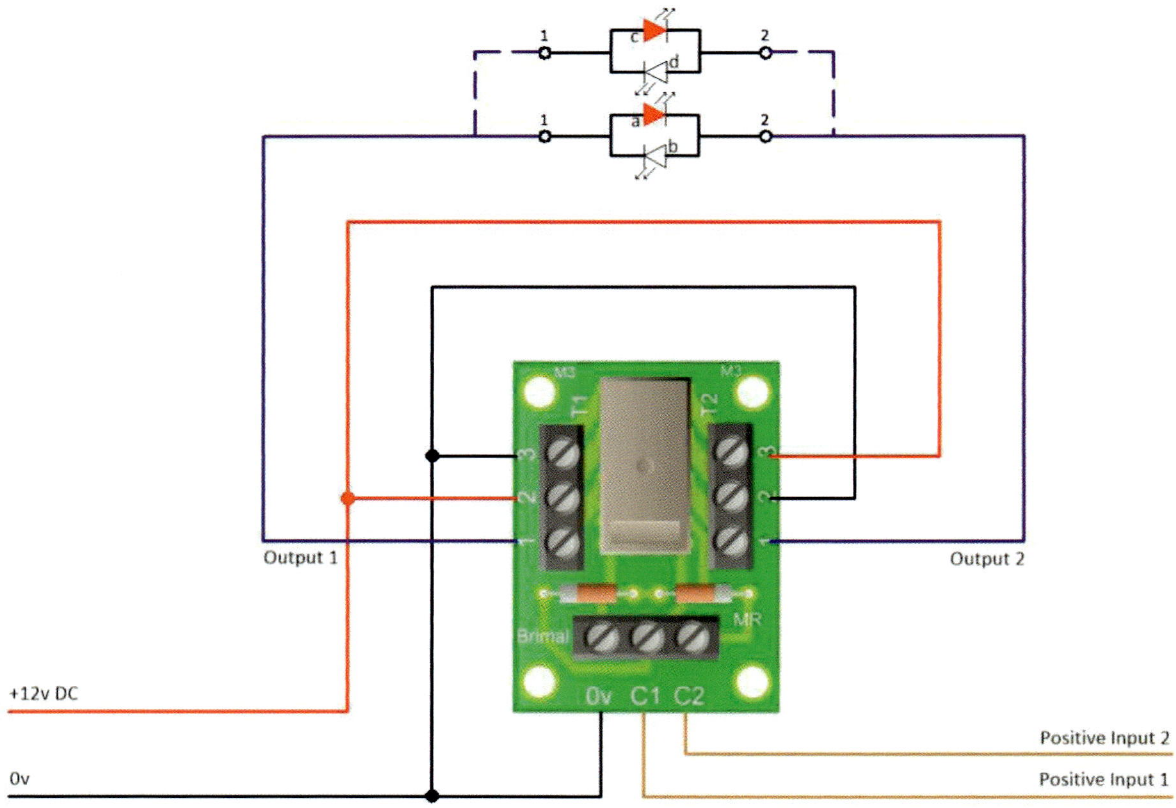

This is basically a REVERSE Polarity switch.
The Inputs at 1 and 2 could be any form of contact that goes from nothing to Positive Voltage, such as a Momentary Switch, Magnetic Switch, Leaf Switch, Microswitch, Relay Contact, InfraRed Output, and so on.

When Input 1 goes positive momentarily the relay latches in one position. This makes Output 1 Positive and Output 2 Negative, therefore the Red LED's are ON and the white LED's are OFF.

When Input 2 goes positive momentarily the relay latches in the opposite state to above. This makes Output 1 Negative and Output 2 Positive, therefore the White LED's are ON and the Red LED's are OFF.

Diode Matrix for Coil Type Point Motors.

A Diode Matrix is simply a set of Diodes placed in an order between a switch and a set of Points. You will remember that a diode only allows current to pass in one direction. So we can use this ability to set a number of points to change to create a path for the train to travel, all from one switch. As you will have in certain cases more than one switch connected to a point motor, the diode stops the current flowing to a point set that you do not need at that point in time. As you can see from the drawing below you have sidings A to G all feeding from the Main Line. In each case there are a number of points that need to be set for each siding.

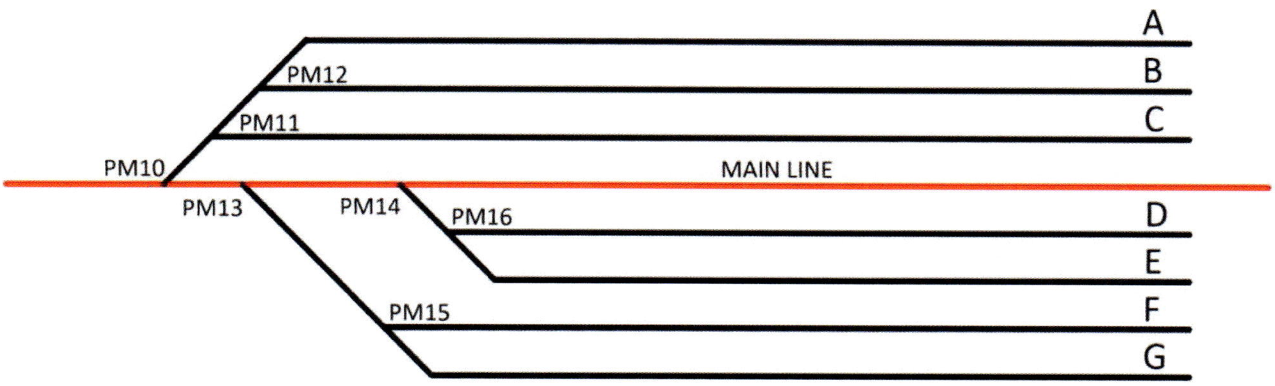

For the purpose of this example we will call a **straight through points ST**, and a **Turn out points TU**. The first thing to do is create a Truth Table.

example: To get from the Main Line to siding A the following must be true. PM10 must be Turn out TU, PM11 must be straight through ST, PM12 must be straight through ST.

So for this to happen 3 sets of points need to be activated from one switch.

If you now look at switch A row you will see there are three 'Y', this means that three sets of points need to be set for this to work as described above. If you now look at Fig 2 and follow row 'E' you will see there are 3 connections starting from this row, one of which is a link (you could use a diode here if you wish)

ROUTE	PM10		PM11		PM12		PM13		PM14		PM15		PM16	
SWITCH	ST	TU	ST	TU	ST	TU	ST	TU	ST	TU	ST	TU	ST	TU
A		Y	Y		Y									
B		Y	Y			Y								
C		Y		Y										
D	Y						Y			Y				Y
E	Y						Y			Y			Y	
F	Y							Y				Y		
G	Y							Y			Y			
ML	Y						Y		Y					

On the table above you will notice the top line shows the Points designation number, the next line has 2 columns for each set of points ST & TU. On the left hand side is a column with the siding letter which is also the control switch letter.

We want to place the Loco and Wagons in siding A.

So the first set of points to be changed to TU is PM10 as shown in the table above.

The next set of points to change will PM11 to straight through as shown in the table.

The final set of points to change is PM12 to straight through as shown above.

PM12 Straight through does not have any other 'Y' in the column so you do not need to use a diode, a link wire is placed here. However using a diode will not affect the circuit in any way, so if you prefer use a diode.

Repeat this for each siding until you have a Truth Table similar to above for your fiddle yard.

Now we need to transfer this information onto a Strip board Blank and add the diodes in the correct places. First mark the top of the strip board blank with the switch positions and the Point Motor ST & TU. This will help you get the diodes and links in the right place.

Below is the stripboard template you will receive with the Matrix Kit

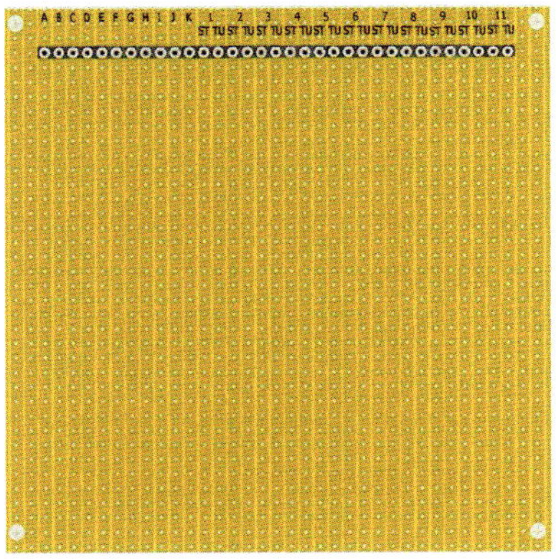

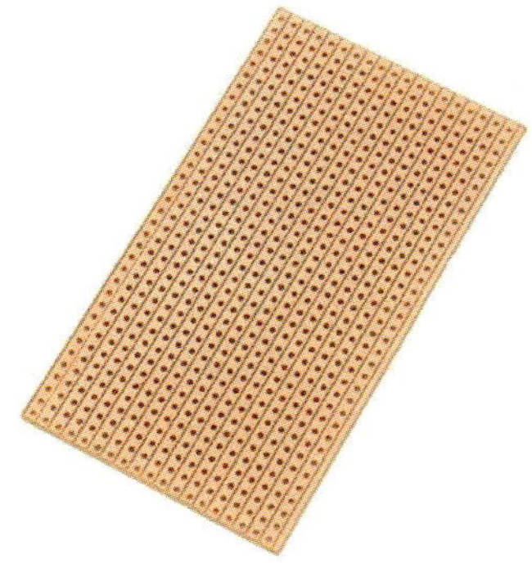

Below is the strip board with the diodes and links in place for the example layout above. As you can see Line A on the far left has three connections.
First: A diode from A to PM10 TU
Second: A diode from A to PM11 ST
Third: A Link from A to PM11 ST (If you follow this line down to the bottom you will see no other onnections - this is why a link is OK.

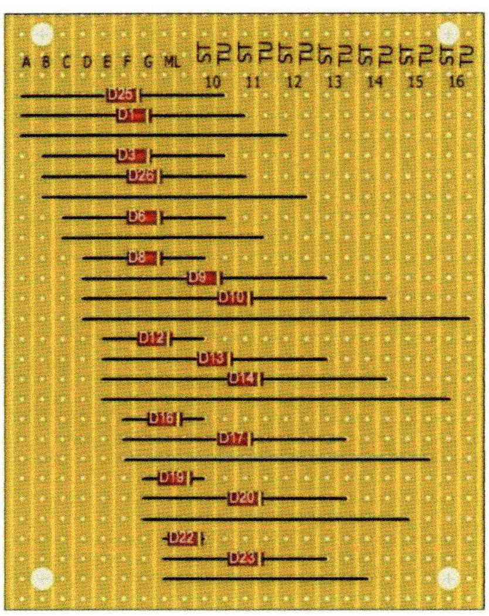

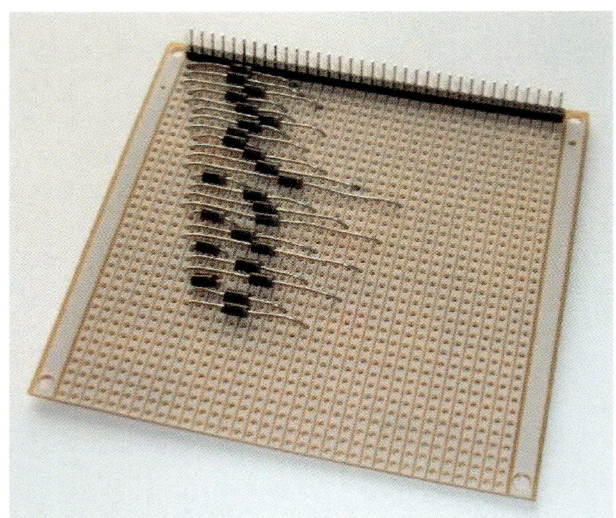

Now continue down the strip board fitting the diodes in the correct places as per the Truth table.
You will notice there is one switch called ML. After you have completed your work in the siding you will have to set the MAIN LINE (ML)back to straight through. The example has 3 sets of points on the main line, so all 3 sets must be now straight through, hence the ML switch.
The next stage is to connect the switches and the points to the diode matrix board as shown below.

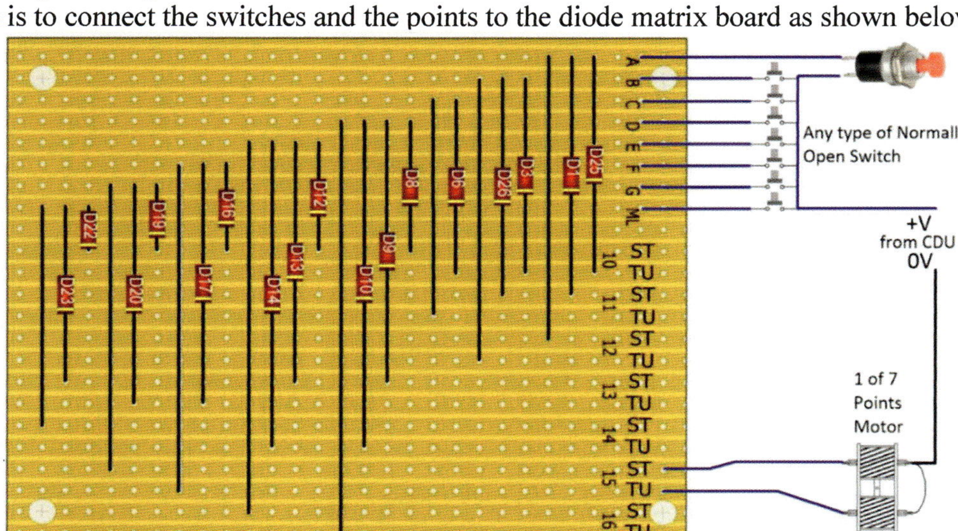

Position the board so the runs of cable are as short as possible.

The switch can be any Normally Open (NO) contact switch - this could be a push button as shown, a stud connection, or a momentary toggle switch OFF-(ON). One side of the switch is connected to the positive supply voltage and the other side to the corresponding siding pin.

The points are connected as shown. One coil to the ST and the other coil to the TU pins. The negative (Ov) side of the points is connected to the Ov of your power supply.
CDU as you are energising a number of points simultaneously your power supply is not likely to be able to cope with the power required, it is therefore advisable to connect a CDU as shown.

The diodes supplied in the kit are 1N4002 which are rated at 1 Amp at 100volts.

Diode Matrix Truth Table.

	P1		P2		P3		P4		P5		P6		P7		P8		P9		P10		P11	
switch	ST	TU	ST	TU	ST	TU	ST	TU	ST	TU	ST	TU	ST	TU	ST	TU	ST	SU	ST	TU	ST	TU
A																						
B																						
C																						
D																						
E																						
F																						
G																						
H																						
I																						
J																						
K																						

Diode Matrix Strip Board Layout.

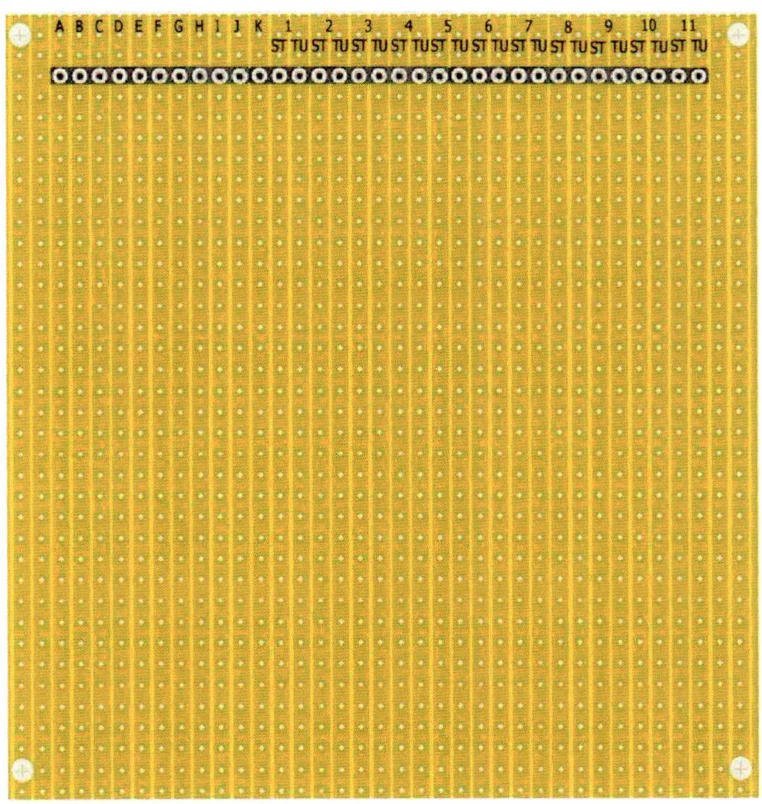

Station Stop Timer from 5 sec to 240 seconds.

This project adds a Station Stop Timer to your layout. This will allow you to run your train on a continuous loop with it stopping each time it gets to a station.
The basic principle is to have two sections of track inside the station isolated from the power, and switched ON and OFF by a electronic timer.

How to Install the system.

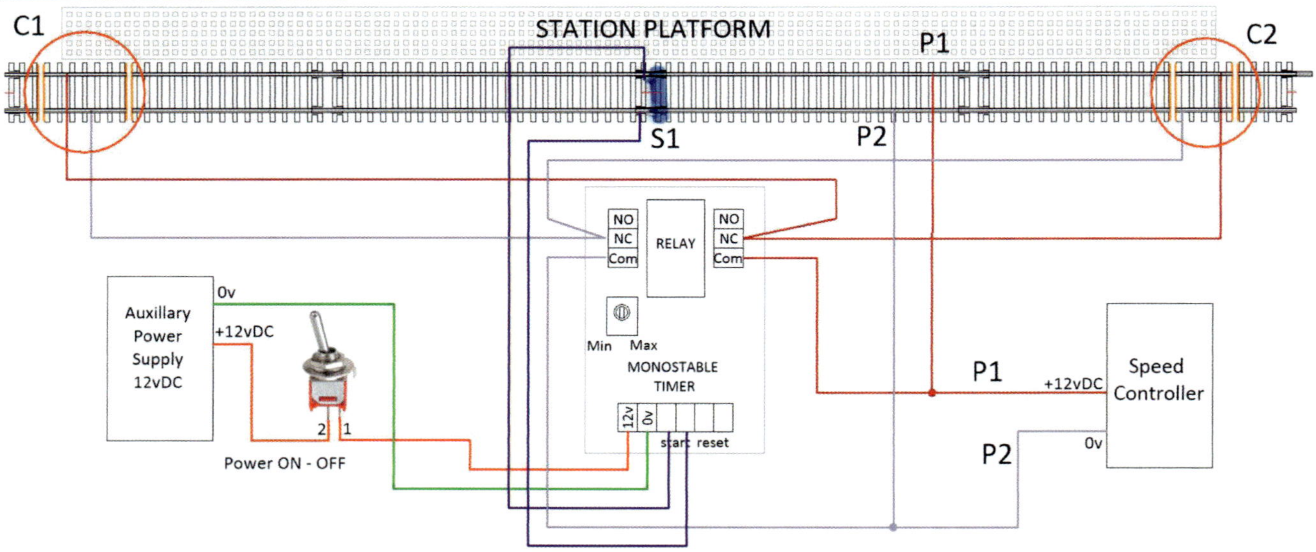

The first thing you need to do is replace either the track fishplates with 'Insulated Fishplates' in positions C1&C2 to the nearest joint.
Next connect a wire to each rail within the area between C1 and C2 shown as P1 and P2, back to the Speed Controller. Now connect the brown wires to the top track in C1 and C2 and run them back to the NC contact on the Timer Relay. Repeat this for the Grey wire from the bottom rail in C1 and C2 back to the NC contact on the Timer Relay. Then take a Grey wire from the Relay COM to the Speed Controller, and a Brown wire from the Relay COM to the Speed Controller.
At this stage the train should run normally as though there is no added circuit.
You need to solder a wire to each of the pins on the Reed Switch S1, long enough to get back to where you are positioning the timer. Now drill 2 holes (2mm) between the sleepers at the distance the pins are apart (12mm). You now need to fit the reed switch to the space between the sleepers, and check the clearance by running the loco over the reed switch.

Now connect the Auxiliary Power Supply positive via the switch to +12v on the timer. The 0v from the Power Supply goes tothe 0v on the timer.

The kit comes with 1 miniature magnet which should be fitted on the under side of the locomotive.

PARTS LIST	
MR350	Timer Kit
SW927	Reed Switch
SW932	Magnet
SW305	Mini Toggle Switch
	Track Insulators (by others)
	Power Connectors (by others)

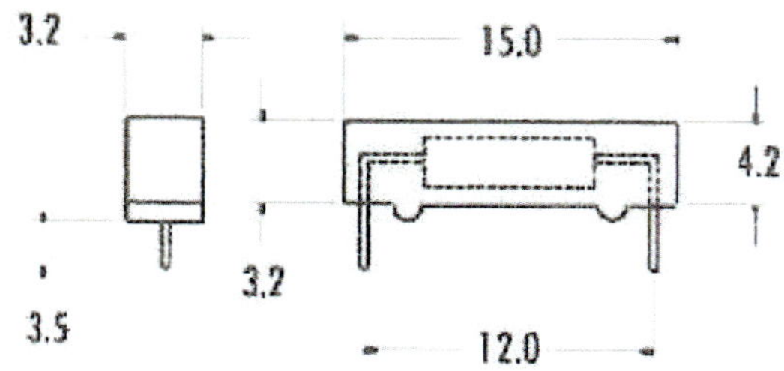

Simulated Long Tunnel

In this project we are using a MR350 Monostable timer to extend the time a train is in a tunnel, to give the effect of a longer tunnel.

In this layout the train enters the tunnel from either the right or left and energises the timer by passing over 'Timer Start Sensor'. The timer has now started so the relay on the timer has gone from 'Normally Closed' to 'Normally Open', thereby removing power from the tracks in the 'Isolation Area A & B'. When the train arrives at Isolation Area it will stop as there is no power on the tracks. To be effective the stopping area should be positioned so that the Train can not be seen from either end of the Tunnel entrances. When the timer has completed it's cycle the relay will be de-energised, putting power back on the track and the train will move out of the tunnel.

The timer is powered by 12v DC from your auxiliary Power Source. The positive feed should go through a Mini Toggle Switch at the Control Panel so you have an ON / OFF switch. Using the spare set of contacts on the relay you can wire a remote LED back at the control panel to show when the timer is active. (see drawing below). The Speed Control output is fed to the track as normal. A section of track will need to be isolated using plastic fishplates, and the feed from the speed controller will go to this section of track via the relay on the timer board, as shown.

The sensor can be one of many different types from Reed Switches to Infra-red switches. In this example we are using a Reed switch imbedded between the sleepers, and a small magnet on the underside of the Locomotive. Which ever method you use to initiate the timer it is important to remember the Start sequence only requires a short NEGATIVE PULSE.

Note: When you see Normally Closed (NC), or Normally Open (NO) for a relay or switch, this is the state the relay or switch is in with no external effects, or straight from your supplier.

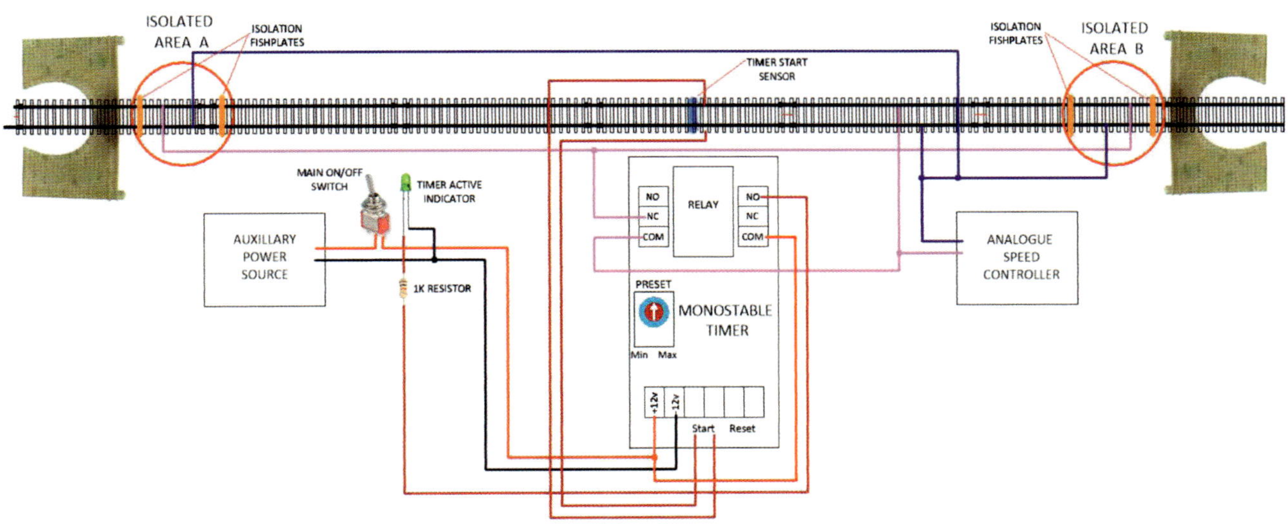

KIT PARTS LIST

MR350	Timer	1
SW932	Neodynium Magnet 6mm x 2mm	1
SW927	SPNO Encapsulated Reed Switch	1
SW305	ON – OFF Switch	1
SL101	Standard Green LED	1
E137	Resistor 1/4w 1K	1

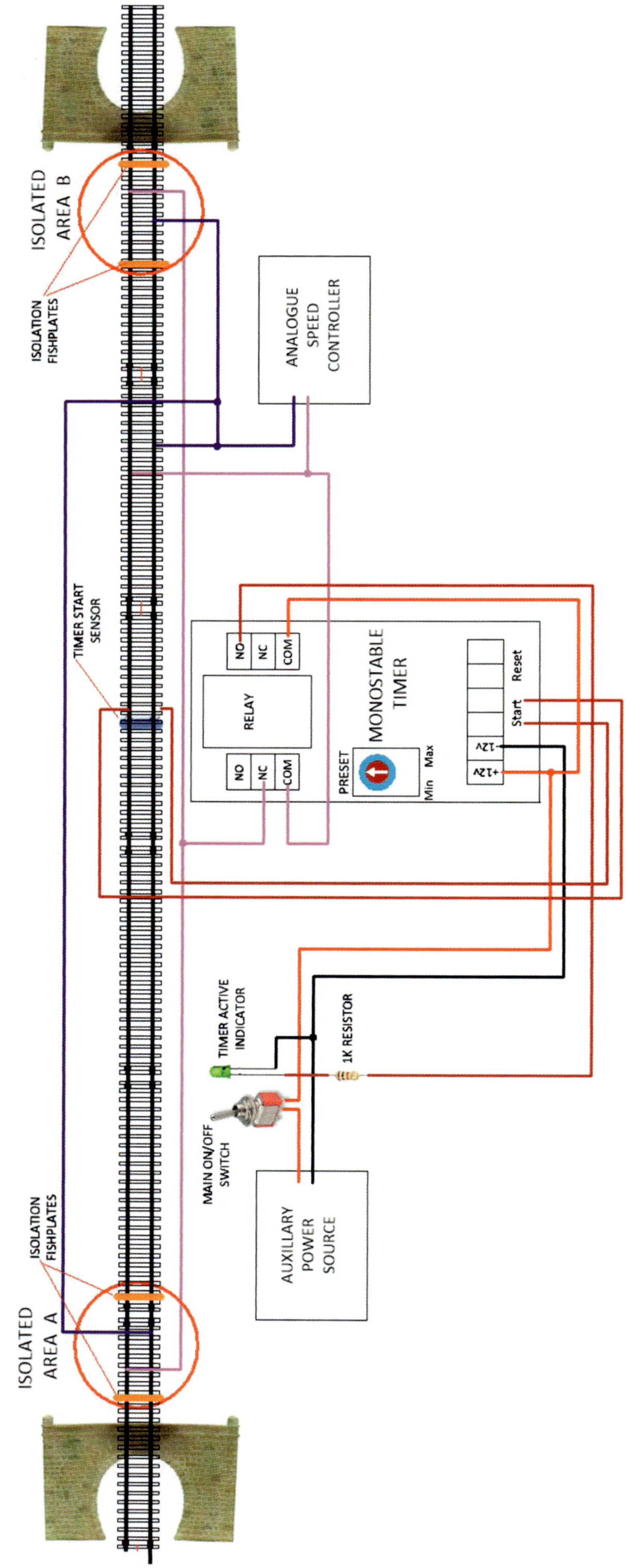
ISOLATED AREA B
ISOLATION FISHPLATES
ANALOGUE SPEED CONTROLLER
TIMER START SENSOR
NO
NC
COM
RELAY
MONOSTABLE TIMER
PRESET
Min
Max
-12V
+12V
Start
Reset
TIMER ACTIVE INDICATOR
1K RESISTOR
MAIN ON/OFF SWITCH
AUXILLARY POWER SOURCE
ISOLATION FISHPLATES
ISOLATED AREA A

PROJECT 36

Control of Running Lights

In this application the MR204 is used to control the signals after a train has passed, each MR204 informs the next MR204 of the status of the last signal. This allows a cascade effect so each signal shows the correct aspect at all times. It is however limited to 2 aspect signals.

As the train passes over Sensor 1 the MR204 will change state which in turn changes the Signal 1 from Green to Red. Also an indicator back at the control panel if required. At this time Signal 2 should be at Green as should all signals left of this.

When the train passes over Sensor 2, Signal 2 will change from Green to Red, and Signal 1 will change from Red to Green. This effect will continue as the train passes over the next sensor and so on, until it gets back to Sensor 1 where the cycle will start again.

The distance between Sensor 1 and Sensor 2 will be dependent on the size of your Layout, it could be every 300mm or 500mm and so on

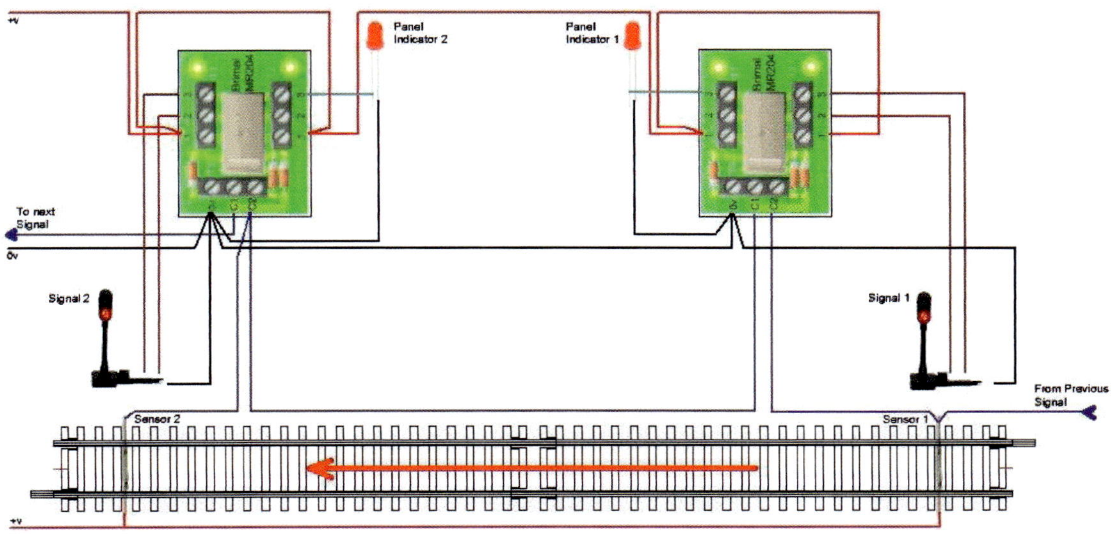

PROJECT 37

Station Stop with Manual Start

In this application the MR204 is used as a Station Stop with Manual Override. As the Train passed over the sensor the MR204 cuts power to the rail and the train will stop. You must insert 2 Isolating points as shown. The critical point is how far from the left Isolator do you place the Sensor. Too close and the train may over run the Isolator and just continue. Too far and the train will not stop at the station. So there is a little trial and error until you find the correct position.The Push Button changes the state of MR204 and allows power back on the track so the train can move forward. Replacing the Push Button switch with a timer will give an adjustable stop period, see other circuit for the wiring of a timer.

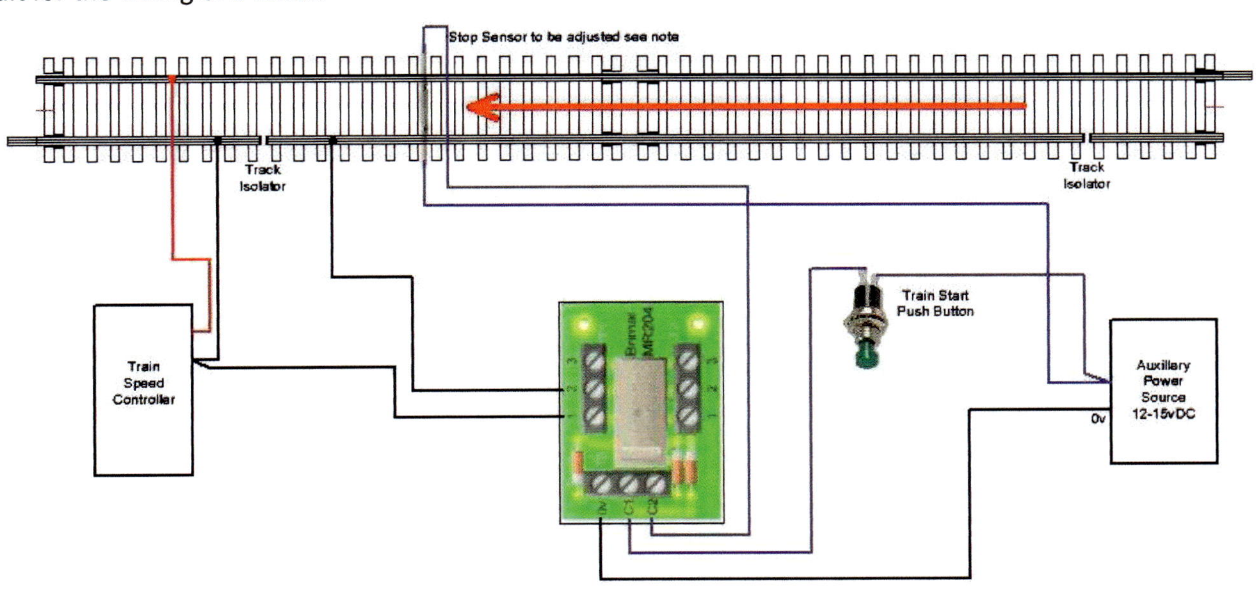

PROJECT 38

Automatic 3 Aspect Signal Control with Isolation.

Previous projects have shown how to wire a 3 Aspect Signal using a toggle switch or a rotary switch, this project takes this one stage further and automates the signal. This time the train activates the signal and changes each aspect as it travels along the track. There are three sensors along the track which are activated by the magnet on the underside of the locomotive. The distance between sensors should be at least the length of your train, to create safe blocks between the sensors for the trains to travel in Because of the Latching properties of these relays, the signal should show a Green light, however it might show either no lights or a yellow light on initial switch ON. Easy to solve, you just need to reset both or one latching relay, do this by placing a magnet near SW3 sensor. Now you should have a green light showing.

<u>Direction of Travel is from Left to Right.</u> As the train passes over SW1 this will latch Relay 1 turning the Red light On and the Green Light Off. The train then passes over SW2 which switches Relay 2 On, this then turns the Red light Off and switches the Yellow light On. The train will then pass over SW3 which will reset both relays and switch on the Green light again.

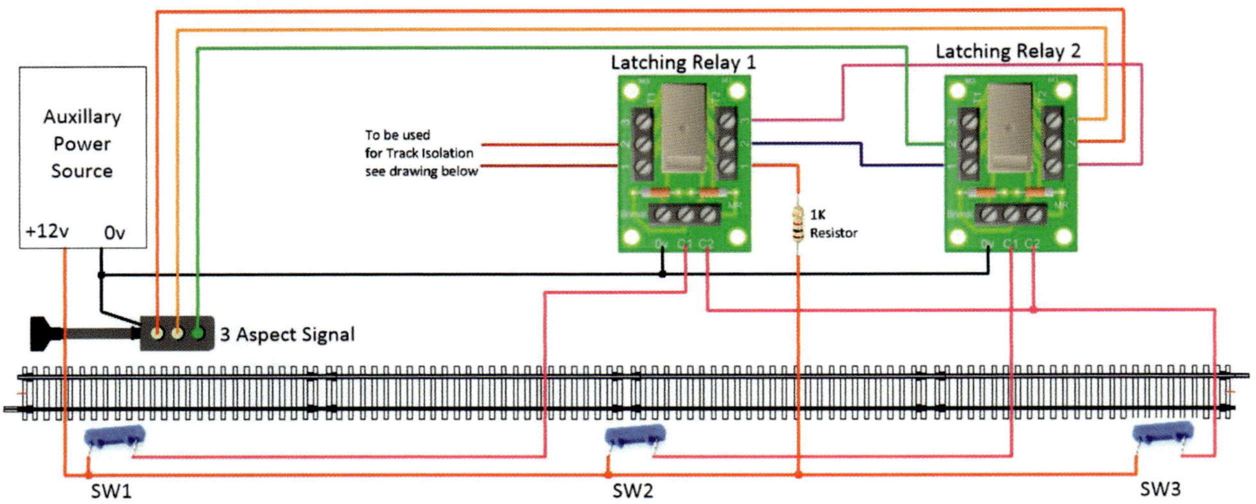

PROJECT 39

Home & Distant Signal Control

In this application the MR204 is used to control a Point Motor, a Home Signal, and a Distant Signal. The switch is a Momentary action Mini Toggle Switch, (this can be replaced by 2 mini Push Button switches).
Ideally the MR204 should be fixed near the set of points it is controlling, as the Signal will also be in the same area.
You will require a 2 core cable back to the control panel
The colour code for the wiring is 0v Black, +v Red, please see the individual product instruction sheets to see the colour code they are using.
The relay has latching contacts, this means once energised and power is removed the contacts stay in that state until the second coil is energised.
Once you have the system wired as above, you may find the indicators are back to front, this is due to the state of the relay
when you first switch ON. In this case you may have to swap 2 & 3 around.

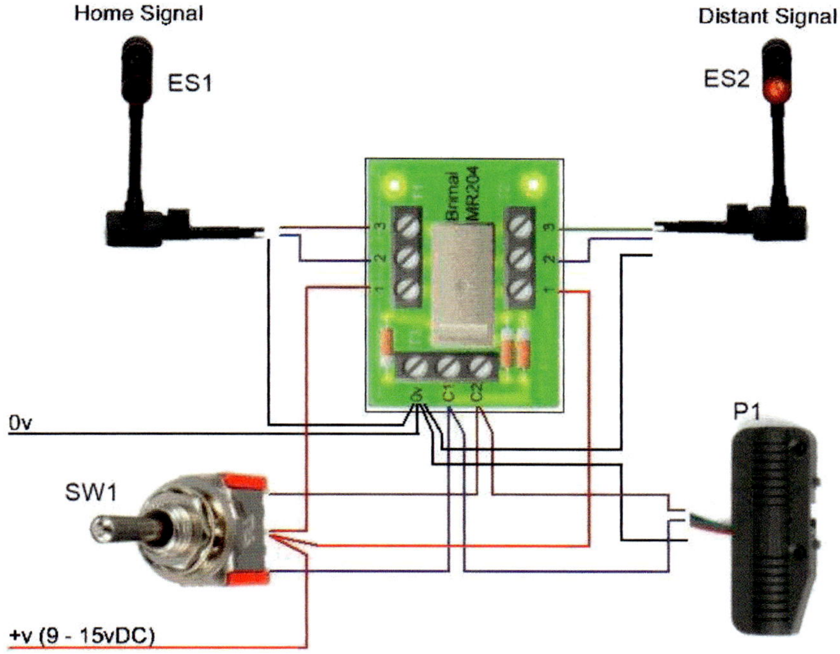

Know the Points

PROJECT 40

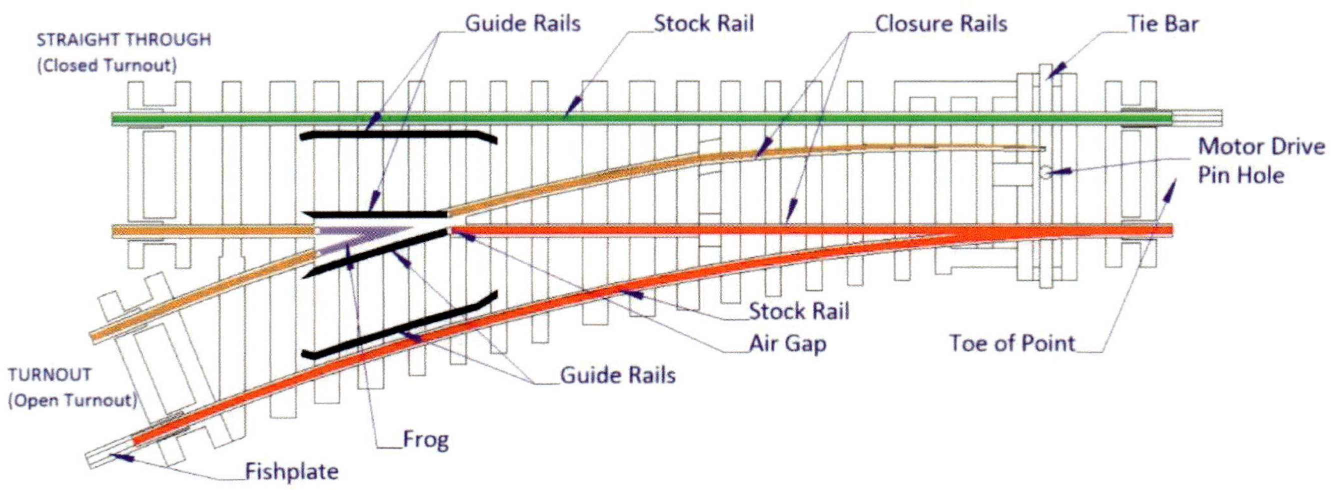

Most points have two states Straight Through (Closed Turnout) or Turnout (Open Turnout). There are other points that do have 3 states which we will cover later. All points have a 'Frog', this is an area of the points which is either a dead area or requires the electrical supply to be changed depending on the position of the points. The following image shows all the parts of a simple set of points. As you can see the Frog needs to be either Red or Green depending on the position of the 'Closure Rails', otherwise the Locomotive will not have power at this point.

Using Toggle Switches with Solenoid Points

The SW301 switch is momentary action UP & DOWN from the centre. In operation try to limit the 'ON' period to 1 second or less (prolonged power will overheat and therefore damage the Point Motor Coils). For ease of operation rotate the switch when in the control panel, so that up gives the straight through line. This will help you to know which way to move the switch by looking at the points. You can also add a relay to power an indicator on the control Panel.

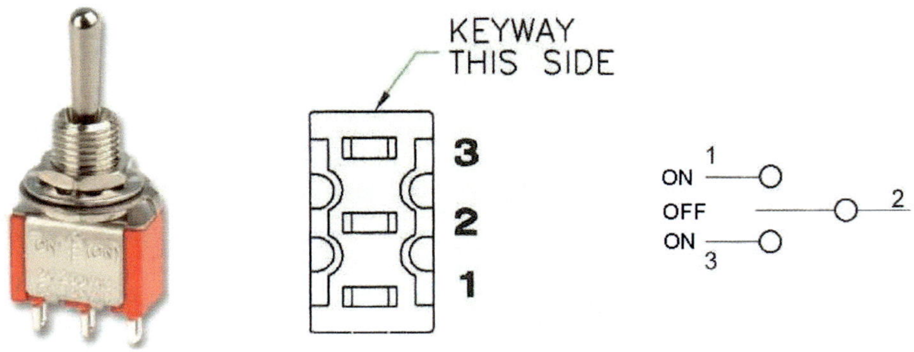

Fig: 1

Point Motors.

Point Motors are available in three types from a number of manufacturers, Circuitron, DCC Concepts, Gaugemaster, Hornby, Kato, Peco, Traintronics, Solenoid Coils, DC Motor, Servos

Solenoid Points

Most Manufacturers have one or two Solenoid points in their range, from the realistic Hornby R8243 to the Gaugemaster skeleton under baseboard type GMC-PM4. Solenoid points have two miniature coils that move a bar from left to right, and back again. Each coil requires a common Negative feed and a Momentary Positive feed. It would therefore follow that the point motor will have 4 wires or 4 solder or Terminal connections to it. In some cases, the manufacturer has joined up the Negative side of the coils in the housing, so there will only be 3 wires from the motor. Not all manufacturers use a standard colour code coding for these wires, so please check the literature that comes with the motor. In our circuits we use Black for Negative, Blue for Positive, and then other colours to show different connections, these may not be the same as the colour coming from the motor.

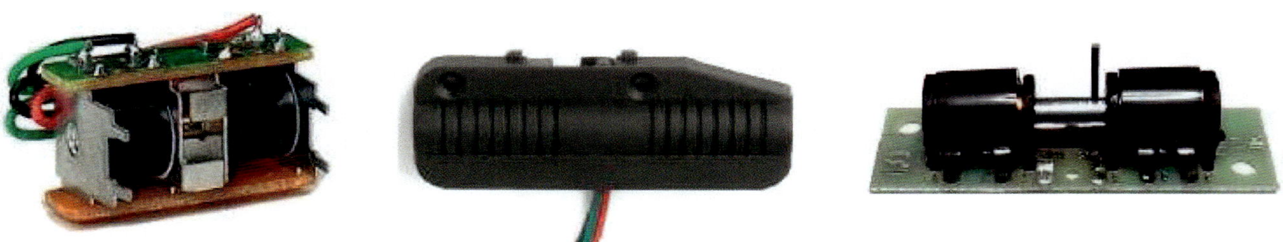

1 2 3

Fig: 2

Here are a few examples of Solenoid type Point Motors. Item 1 is the Hornby R8014, the Gaugemaster GMC-PM10 is very similar. Item 2 is the Hornby R8243, and item 3 is the GaugemasterGMC-PM4

Single Point Motor with One Switch

This circuit shows a single Momentary toggle switch controlling a single point set. The Negative comes from the Power supply to the coils. The Positive (Blue) goes to the centre (2) terminal, via a CDU if required. As shown the Red then goes to one coil, and the Green goes to the other coil. When the switch is pushed up the Green becomes live and coil 1 is activated, and visa versa.

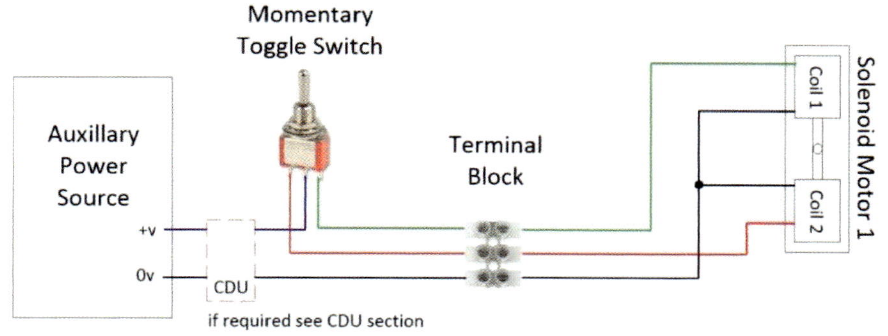

Fig: 4

Single Point Motor with One Switch Continuation

This shows the wiring if you have more than one switch for points. You would use the +V and 0V as a bus bar to feed all the switches and solenoid coils.

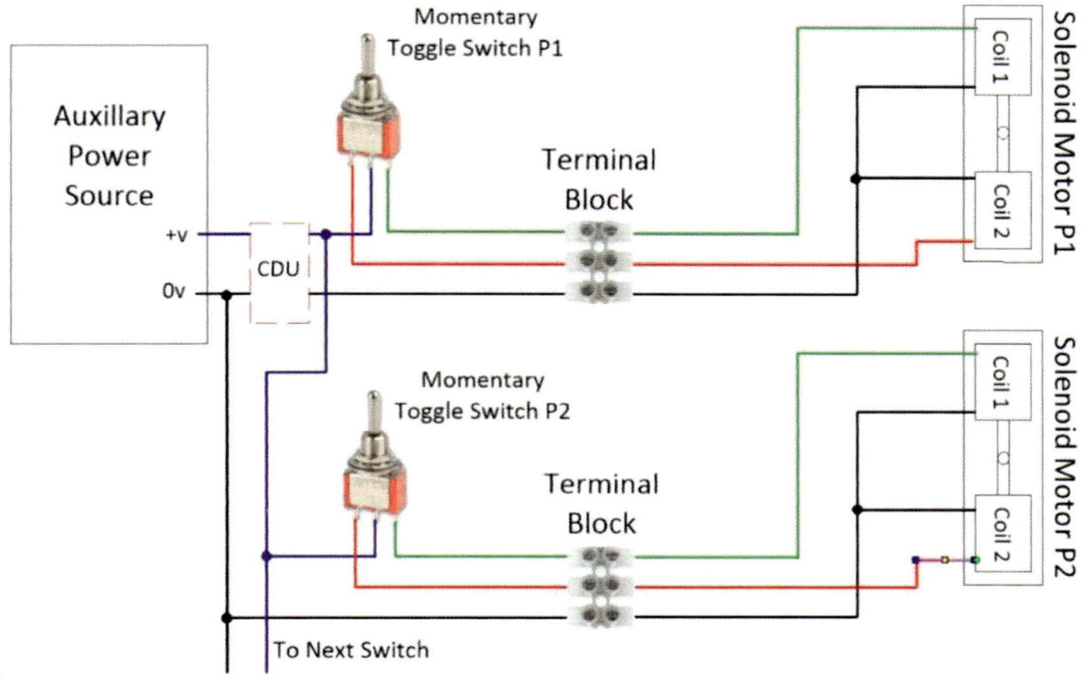

Fig: 5

Twin Points with One Switch

In this configuration both points must operate together, so check the operation after you have wired the points, you may find that one motor needs to be wired the opposite to the other.

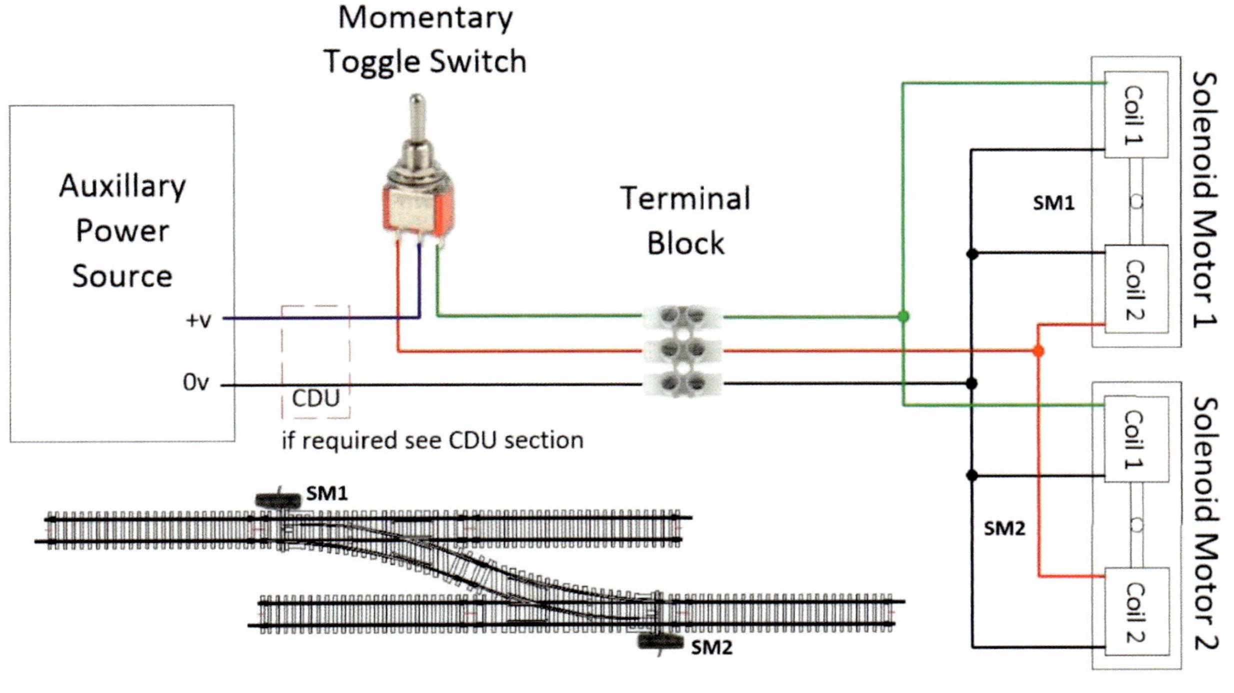

MODEL RAILWAY PROJECTS

Latching Relays

The problem with using a toggle switch is that the switch always returns to the centre OFF position, so you have no indication as to where the points are after you have switched them. We need to introduce a memory circuit to indicate the position of the points. This can be done by simply adding a Latching twin coil relay.

1 2 3 4

Fig: 7

Product List

Item 1	Hongfa Latching Relay 12vDC HFD2012SL2
Item 2	Gaugemaster GM500 Latching relay with solder tags for connection
Item 3	Brimal MR204 Latching relay with Screw Terminals for connection
Item 4	Brimal MR319 Latching relay, Bi-colour LED and Momentary switch with Screw Terminal connection

With both items 2 & 3 (Fig6) some of the circuit is on the printed circuit board (PCB) so you will need to follow the manufacturers instruction. Item 4 (Fig 6) has everything on the one PCB so you only have 4 wires to connect the Positive and Negative from the Power Supply, and the 2 wires going to the Coils. The Negative for the coils goes directly from the Power Supply.

Single Point Motor with Latching Relay & Indication

In this circuit we are using the basic Latching relay. The relay is shown with the pins facing up and the wiring to each pin. The diodes are across the coils of the relay and are used to reduce the Back EMF of the coils. They are used to avoid damaging some nearby components sensitive to high voltages. This voltage is generated in the coil when the current flow is interrupted. The dropping resistor is 1K ¼ watt Carbon Film, and is wired to the Negative side of the 2 LED's. You will notice on the right of the relay there are 3 pins unused. This is the second changeover contact in the relay. This could be used for a number of things such as, Track Isolation, Secondary Indication.

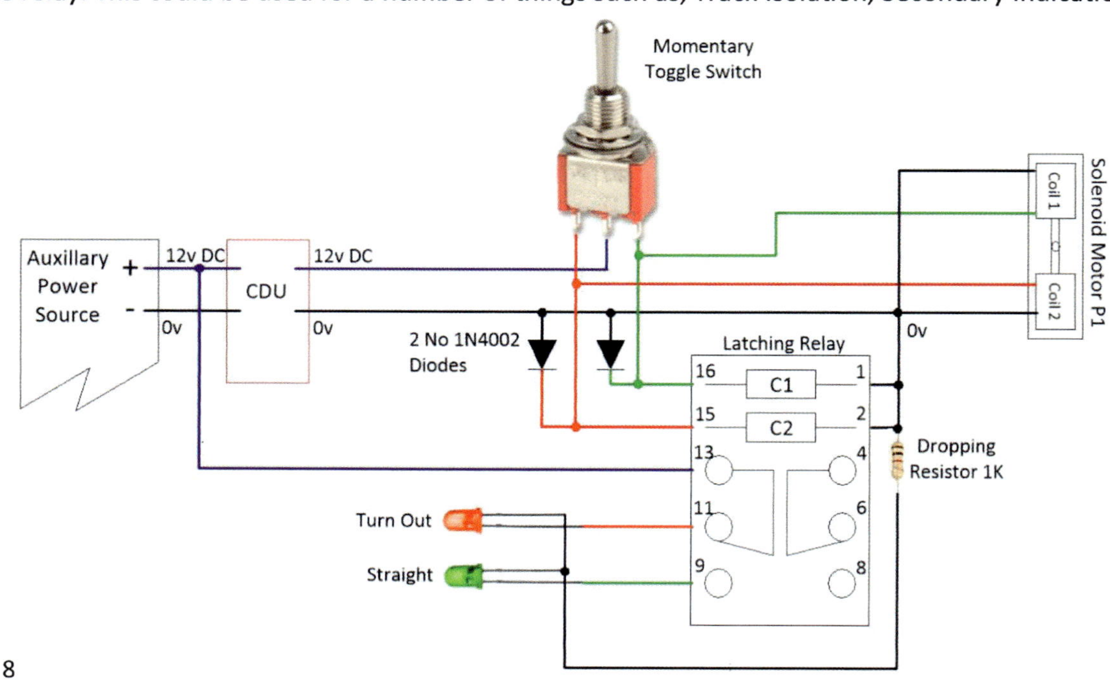

Fig: 8

Single Point Motor with Latching Relay & Bi-colour Indication

In the next circuit Fig 9 we are using a Bi-colour LED to show the Indication. A Bi-colour LED in this case has 2 pins and by reversing the polarity we can change the colour. However, we have to use both sets of contacts to reverse the polarity. You will see that the Negative supply is connected to the Normally Open on one side and Normally Closed on the other side of the relay, and visa versa for the Positive supply. The LED is fed from the common from both sides of the relay. This is so when the relay is activated the polarity on the LED is reversed changing the colour from Green to Red. It is not important which side of the LED you put the 'Dropping Resistor' as the polarity will change anyway.

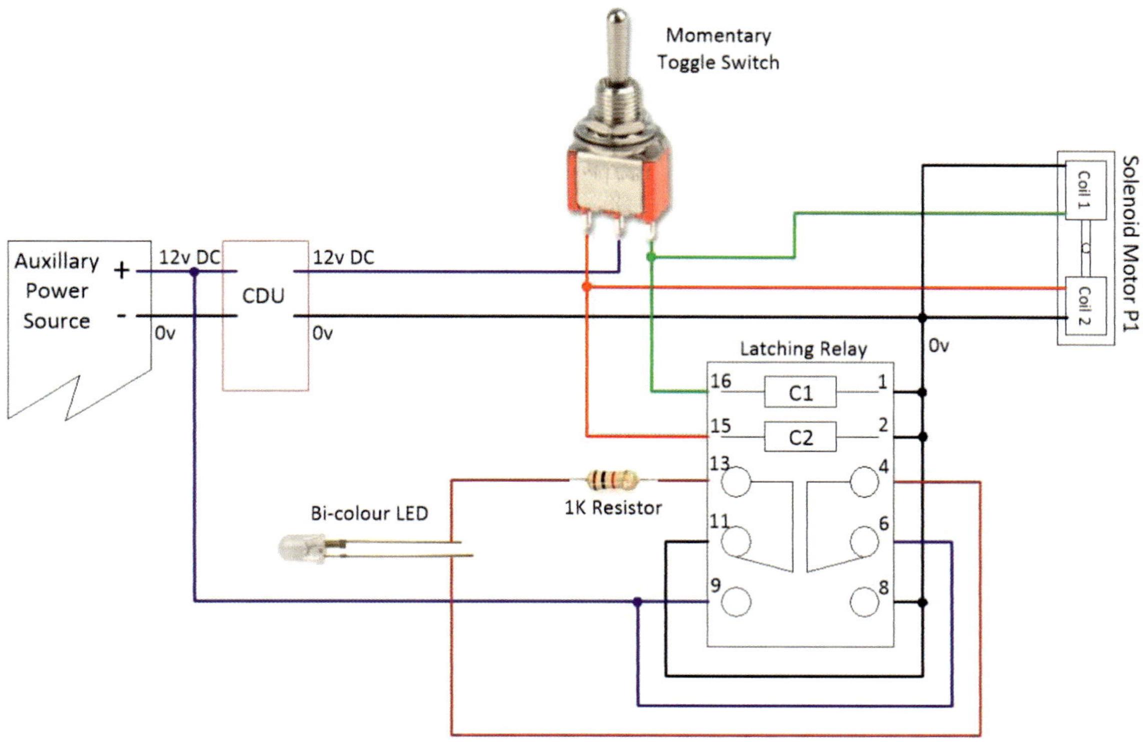

Fig: 9

Single Point Motor using Gaugemaster GM500

Fig: 10 This is the basic circuit using the Gaugemaster GM500 Latching Relay Board. This circuit uses a Momentary switch to change the Point Motor and the Relay is used to give an Indication back at the Control Panel. The other contacts 4,5,6 can be used to either control a signal or control the polarity of the Frog on a set of Points.

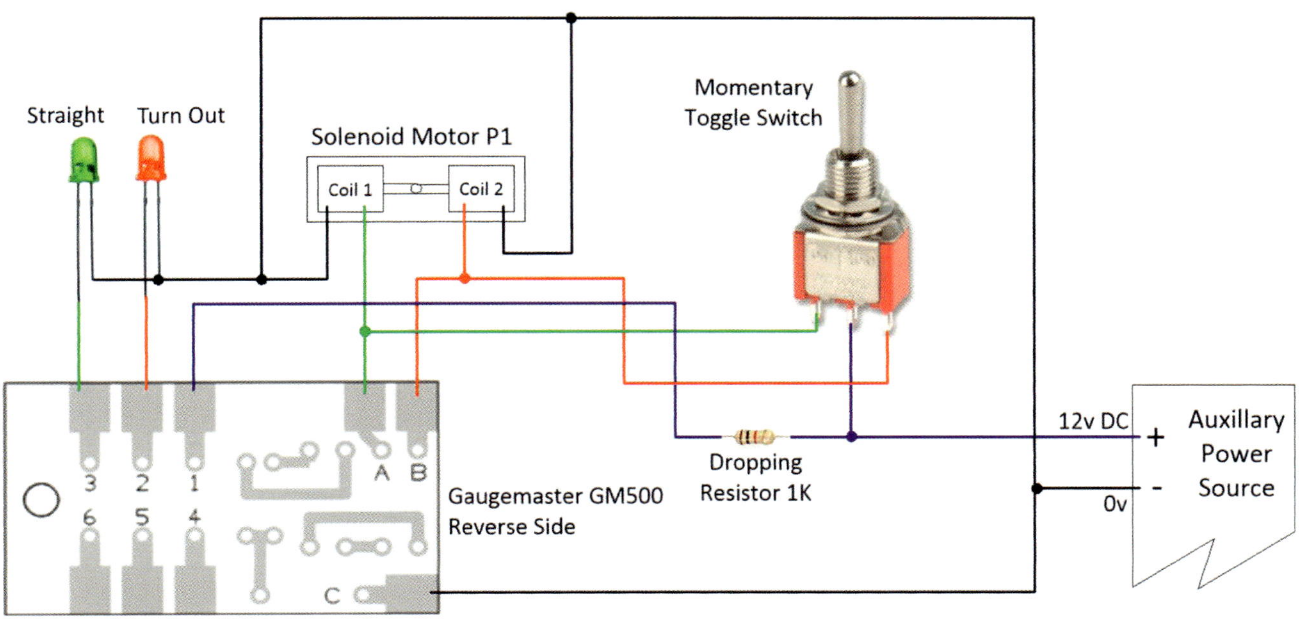

Fig: 10

In the following circuit Fig 11 we have added a 2 Aspect Signal to the second set of Changeover contacts on the GM500. We have left the LED's so you still have an indication back at the Control Panel. This signal is wired to be positioned on the Turnout, so when the signal is Red the Control Panel indicator is Green to show the points are Straight Through. You could add a second signal on the Straight Through line with the second signal Red wired into Terminal 5 and the Green into Terminal 6. This gives full signalling into the points.

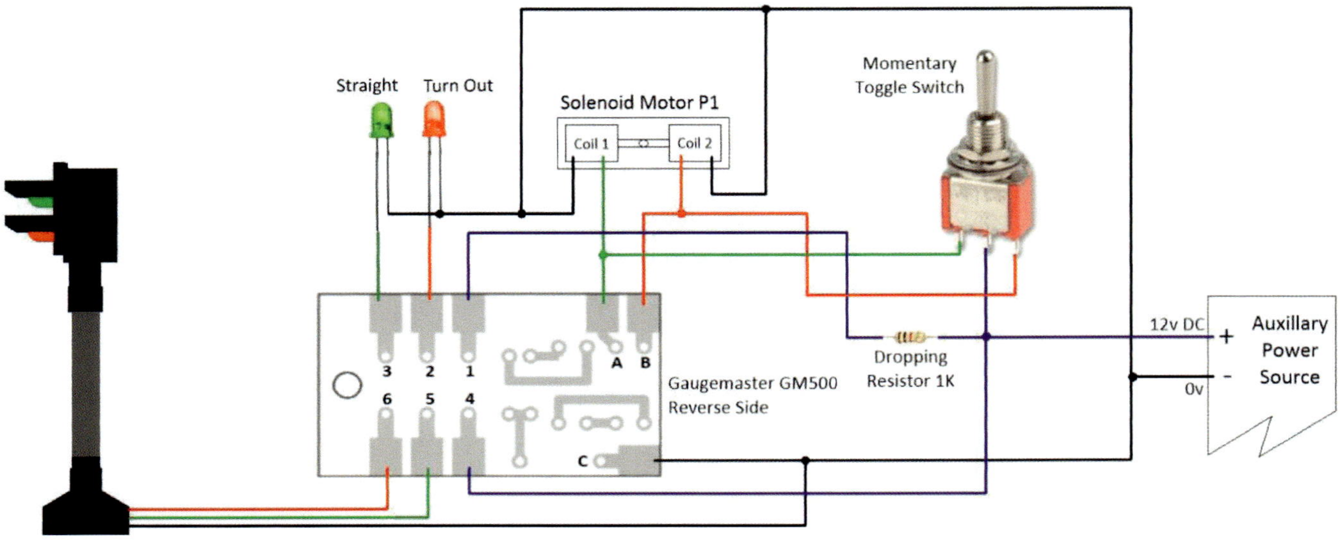

Fig: 11

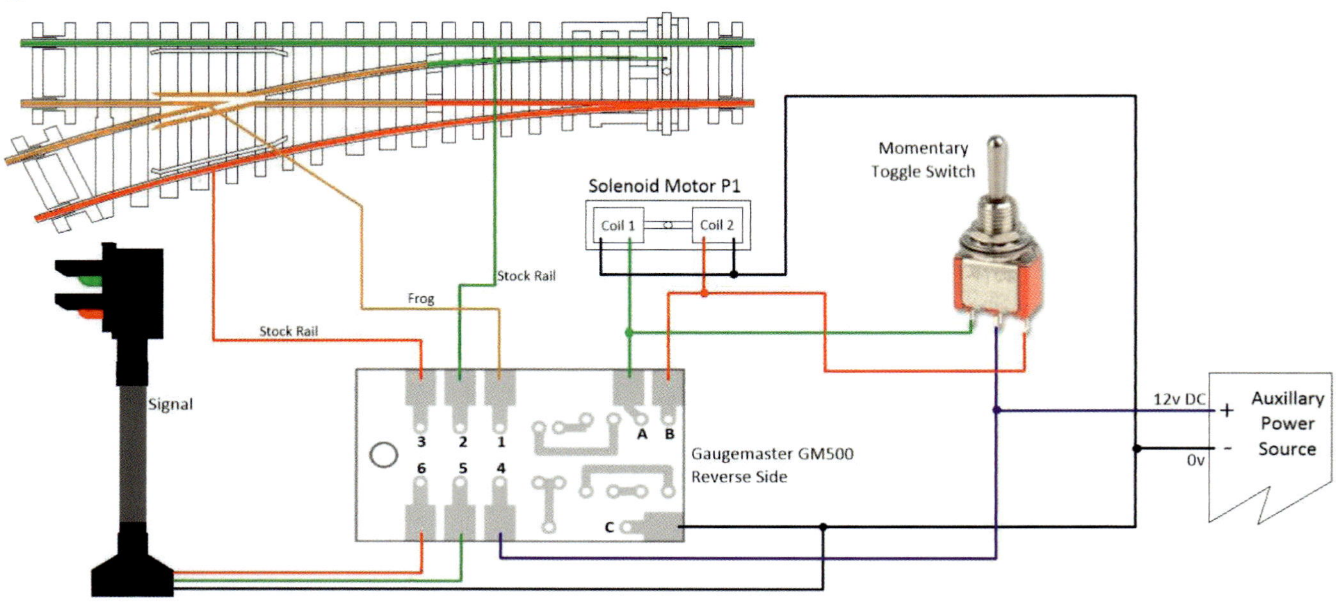

Fig:12

Single Point Motor using Brimal MR204

This is the basic circuit using the Brimal MR204 Latching Relay Board. This circuit uses a Momentary switch to change the Point Motor and the Relay is used to give an Indication back at the Control Panel. The other contacts on T1 can be used to either control a signal or control the polarity of the Frog on a set of Points Fig: 13

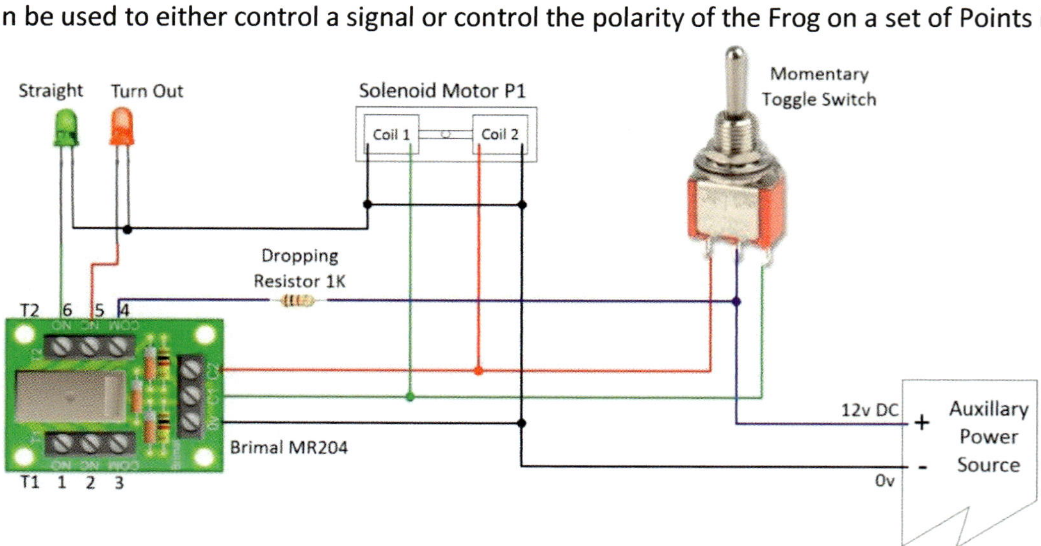

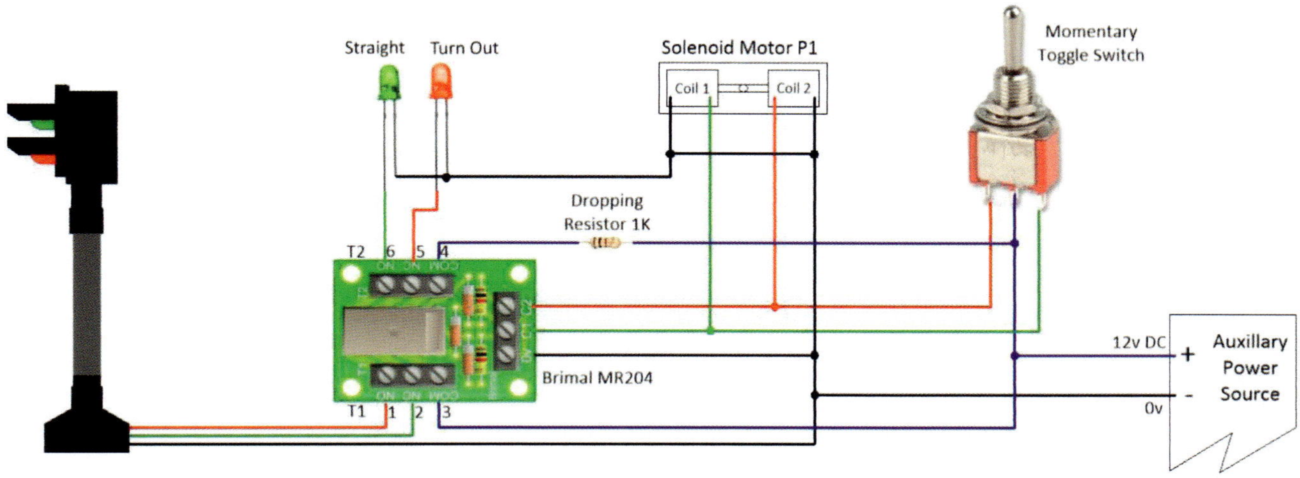

Fig: 14

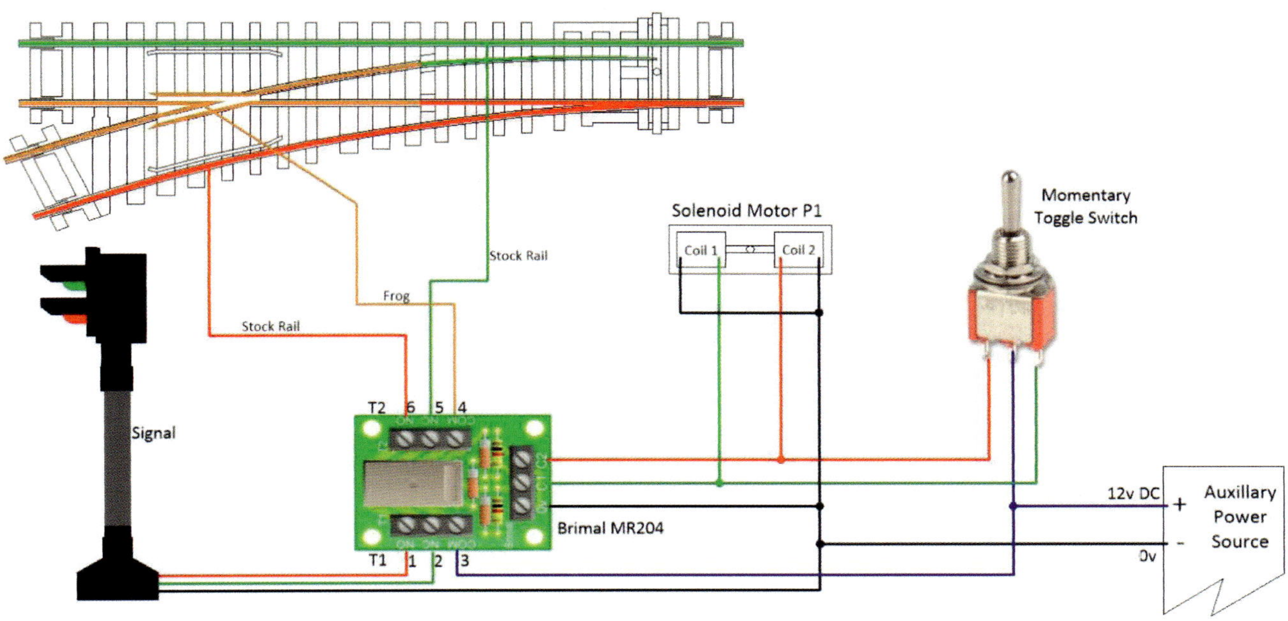

Fig: 15

You could also use a SW310 (Double Pole Double Throw) Momentary Switch in the above circuit

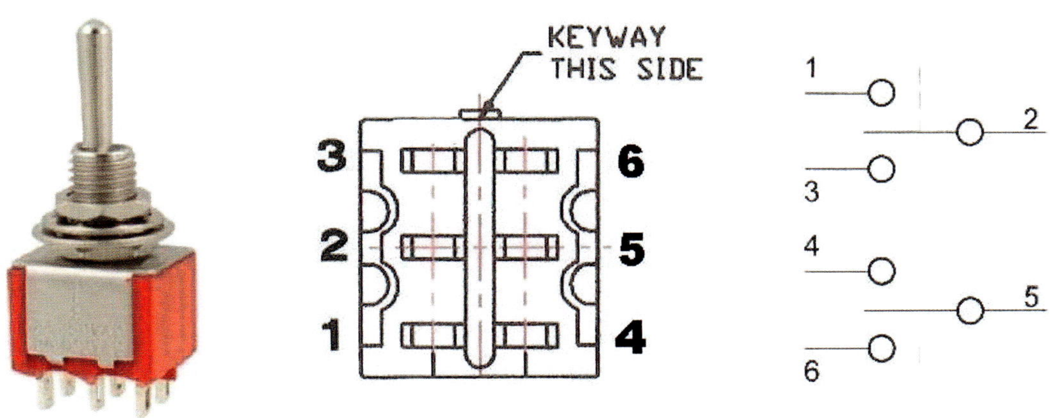

Fig: 16

The above circuits will work for all Solenoid type Point Motors, but should not be used on Stall Motors, Servo Motors or Reverse Polarity Motors

MODEL RAILWAY PROJECTS

Using a Bistable Timer

Basic Pulsing LED or Bulb

Lets start with a very basic flashing LED (or bulb – just wire the same but remove the 1K resistor). If connected as shown to the NO (normally open) contact the LED will switch on for the time set by the PULSE VR2 pre-set, and the OFF time will be set by the PAUSE VR1 pre-set. The timer will start pulsing as soon as you switch power ON, it does not need a trigger, and will continue until power is removed.

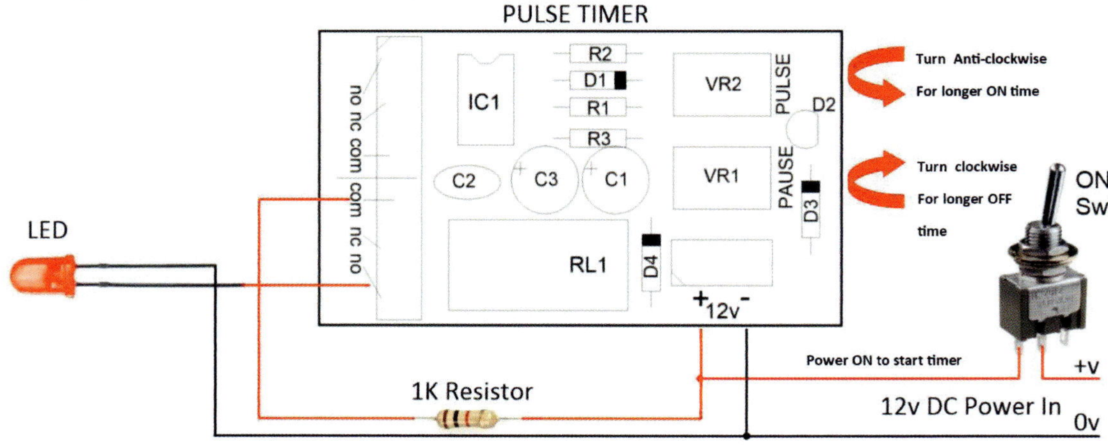

Alternating Flashing LED's

In this circuit we have added a second LED or bulb, so now the Green and Red will alternate, so when one is OFF the other is ON. By adjusting VR1 and VR2 you can have them flashing at the same rate as each other, or one ON longer than the other.

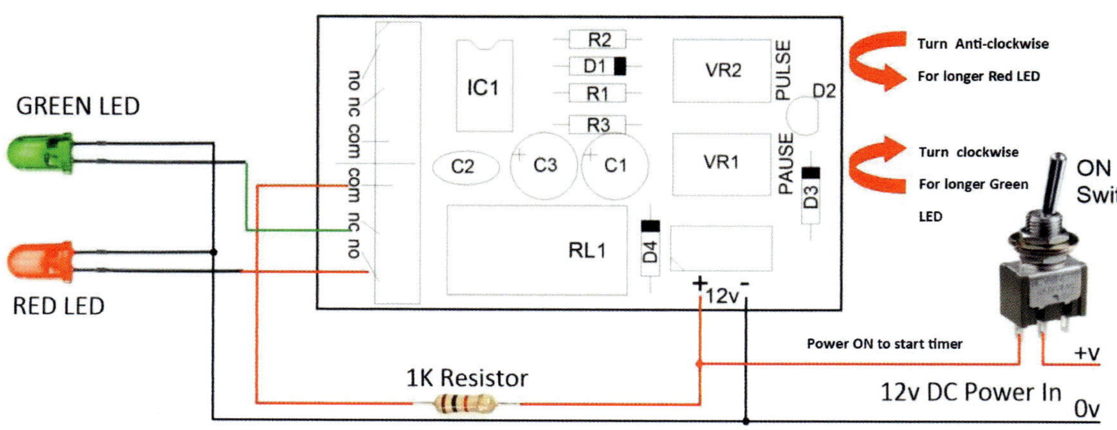

Pulsing Buzzer.

In this circuit we have connected a miniature buzzer to the NO (Pulse) contact so you can have a short Beep. By adjusting VR1 you can vary the OFF time of the buzzer.

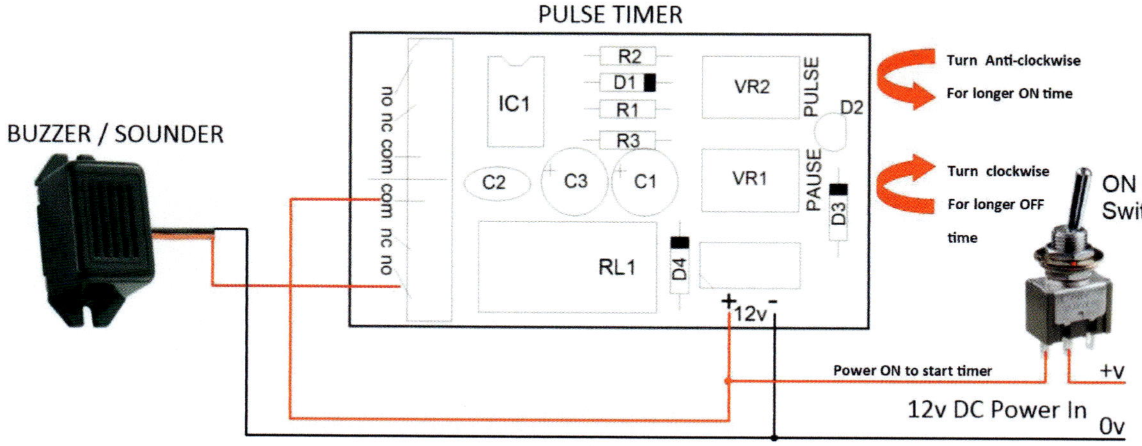

Welding Simulator

A very simple Welding Simulator consists of an Ultra bright White LED and a Standard blue LED, they can be either 5mm or 3mm. The circuit shows the white LED connected to the NC contact which is the Pause variable, and the Blue connected to the NO contact which is the Pulse variable. By adjusting these you can create a very passable simulator which can be placed inside a factory building. The drawback is that the simulation is repetitive and has no light variation.

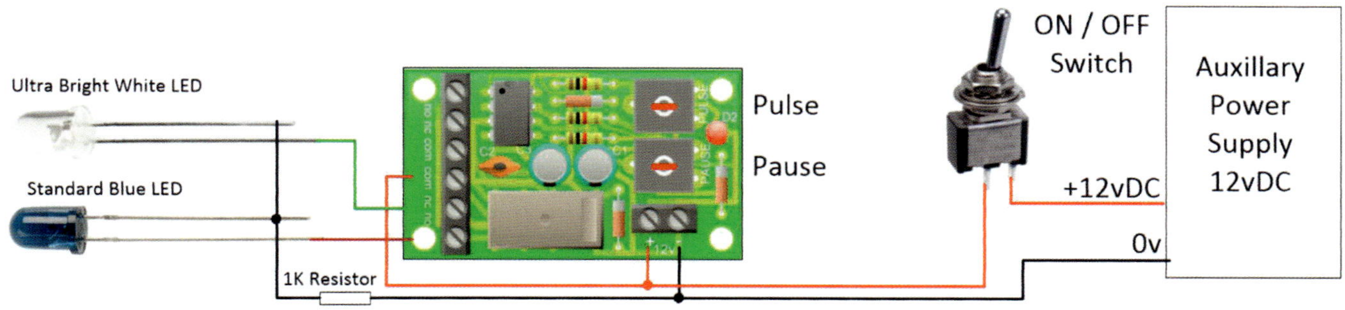

Fig 4

Light House beacon

In this circuit you can use either a 5mm LED or a 3mm LED, depending on space restrictions. Both LEDs are available in high brightness, the 5mm you can get up to 40,000 mcd and the 3mm you can get up to 20,000 mcd. Set the Pulse (ON) to about 1 second and the Pause (OFF) to about 5 seconds. (*The light output of LEDs is rated in either* candelas *(also candle) or* lux, *with the candela being the more common. Both are a measure of luminous intensity. The higher the candelas/lux, the brighter the light. Standard LEDs emit only a modest amount of light, not even 1 candela. They're rated in millicandelas, or thousandths of a candela. Millicandela is typically abbreviated as* mcd. *Typical intensity of a Standard 5mm red LED is about 50 to 75 mcd.*)

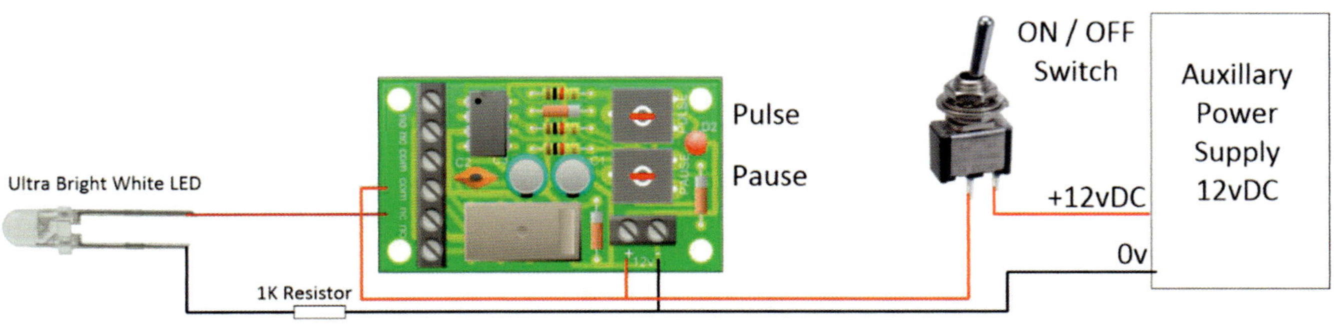

Fig 5

Simple Pelican Crossing

In this first circuit the Lamps in A & B come on at the same time. You will notice there are no resistors as these Lamps normally use a 12v filament bulb rather than an LED.

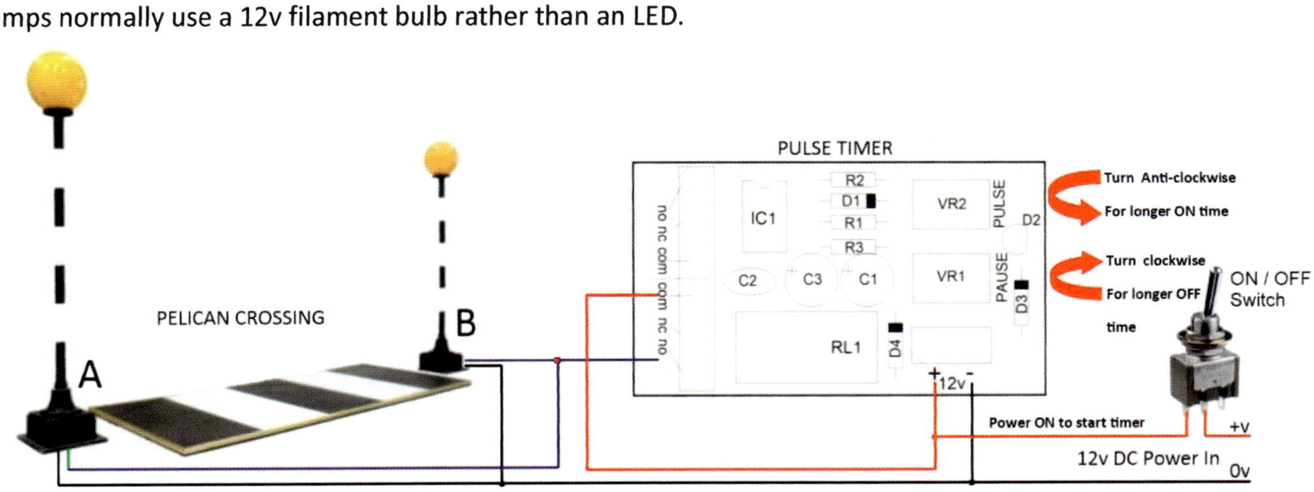

Fig 6

Simple Alternating Pelican Crossing.

In this circuit we have wired each lamp to a separate contact on the relay so that the lamps A & B alternate ON and OFF. Note no dropping resisters are used as these are normally 12v filament Bulbs.

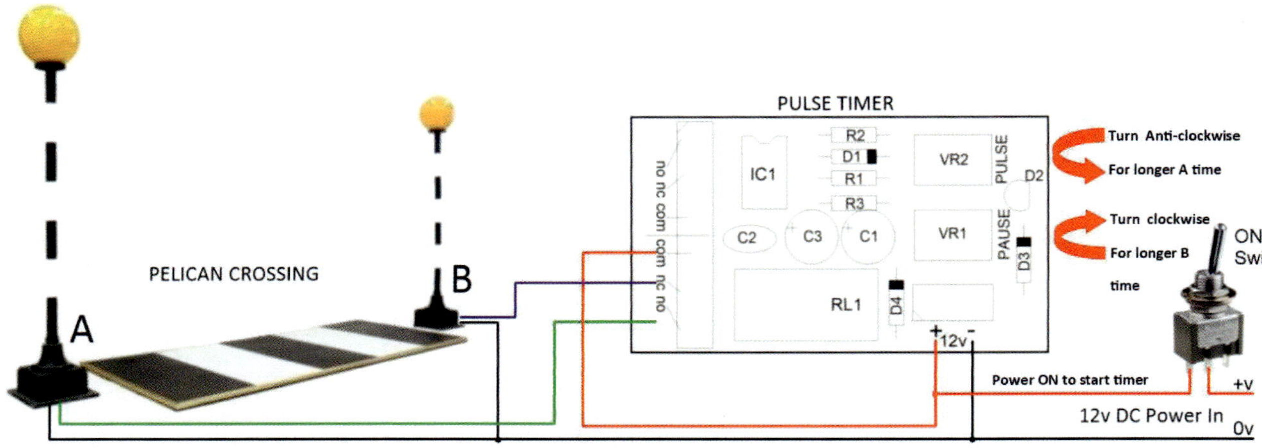

Fig: 7

In all the above circuits we have a second set of contacts that are unused. This could be used to give a repeat indication back at the control panel if required.

Level Crossing Basic

A level Crossing controller using a Pulse Timer (Astable). Power is fed from the 12v DC Supply through an ON – OFF switch to the timer. Each Left LED is connected to the timer via the Blue wire, and each Right hand LED is connected to the timer via the Blue wire, this will give a Left / Right Pulse similar to the real thing. The Pulse and Pause variables should be set for equal ON and OFF, so that when the timer is in Pause the Red wire is connected switching ON the Left Lamps, and when the Timer is in Pulse the Blue wire is connected switching ON the Right Lamps.

The 1K resistor is for all LEDs that are low voltage, if you are using LEDs or Filament Bulbs at 12v then do not use the Resistor.

The Lights will flash only when the Power switch is in the ON position.

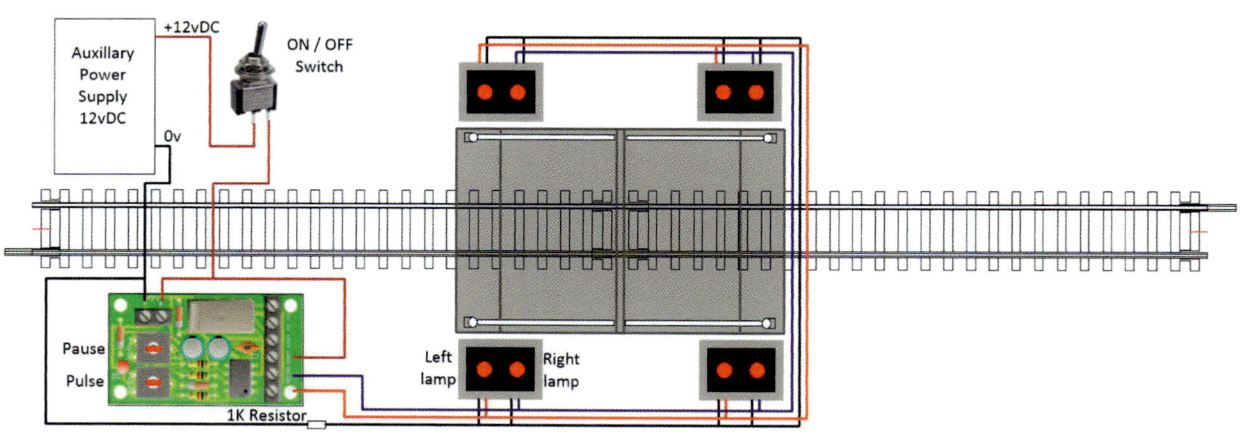

Fig 8

Fully Automatic Level Crossing.

Here we have added 2 sensors and a latching relay. The sensor S1 will be triggered by the train and switch the Latching Relay which in turn will start the Pulse Timer. The wiring for the pulse timer is exactly the same as the above circuit except the Positive Power (Purple wire) is coming from the Latching Relay. When the train reaches the second sensor S2 it will switch the Latching relay OFF which will switch the Pulse timer OFF. The system is now ready for the next train to energise it. In the bottom left corner of the image is a green dotted box. If you add the switch circuit here you can change the direction of travel, so the sensor S2 starts the operation and S1 switches it OFF.

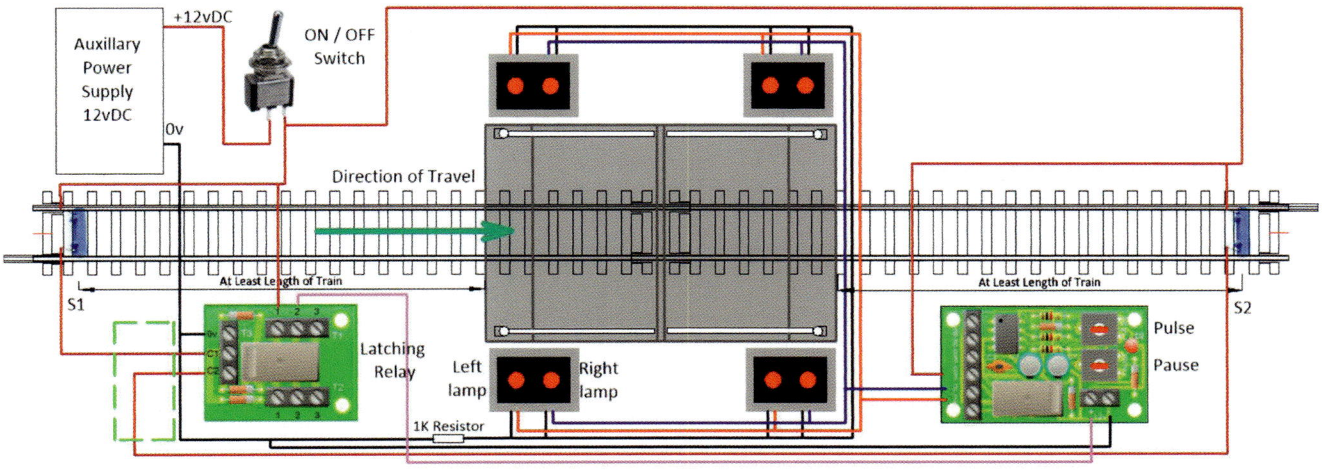

Fig 9

See the Green dotted box above.
This switch will change the direction that S1 And S2 sense the Train. So S2 will become S1 and S1 will become S2, this allows the level crossing to work when the Train is traveling Right to left.

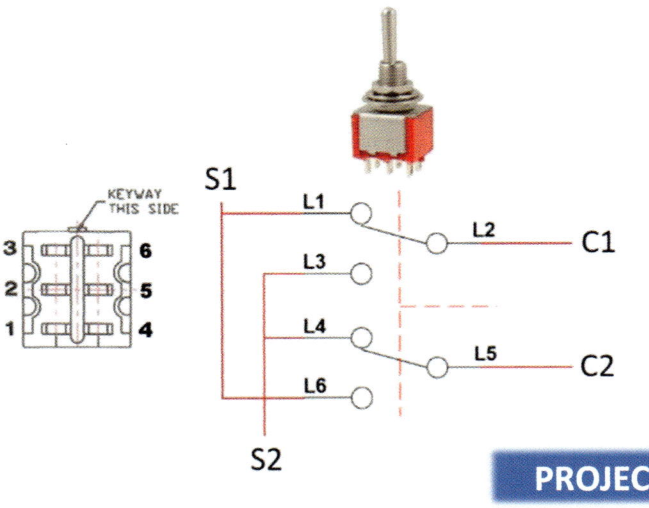

PROJECT 44

Zebra Crossing

Here we are using the Timer to run 2 Belesher beacons at a Zebra crossing. The Beacons normally are supplied with an LED or small filament Lamp. Check the voltage they require before you switch ON. If they are 12v then remove the 1K resistor. In the circuit below each Beacon is wired to the relay separately so when one is ON the other is OFF and visa versa, so set the Pause and Pulse times to the same length. If you want them both to flash ON and OFF at the same time then wire them both into either NC or NO of the Relay Output, this will allow you to adjust the ON and OFF times independently.

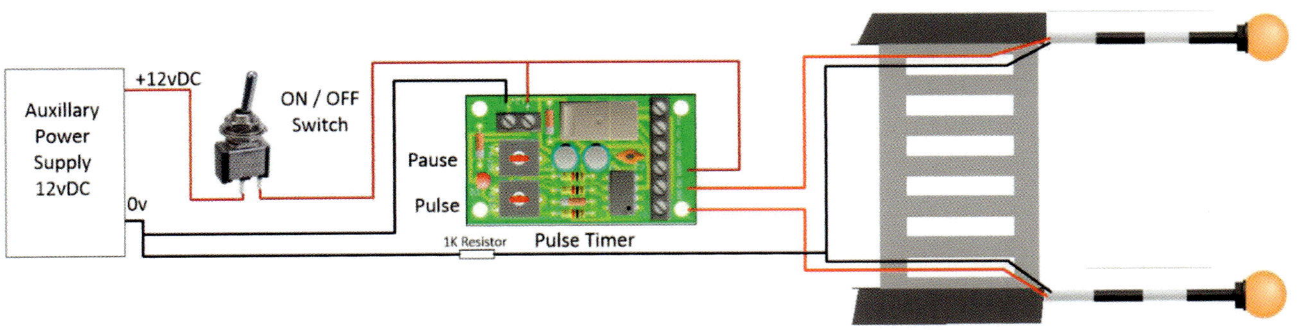

Fig 10

MODEL RAILWAY PROJECTS

Anti-Collision Crossover

In this project we show how to Isolate sections of track to avoid collisions at a simple crossover. The basic idea is that the train switches on a timer after passing over a sensor, which isolates the other track for a period of time while the train goes through the crossing.

Let's assume the train is on Track A coming from the left.

At this point in time all signals are Green and all Isolated Areas are active.

As the train passes over Sensor 1 this starts Timer A. Timer A will now isolate Track Areas 2 and 3, and switch all Signals to Red.

Any Train travelling on Track B will be stopped at Area 2 or 3 depending on which direction it is travelling.

The Timers are set to work for a period of time decide by how long it takes the full train to go through and clear the crossing.

The Timer A will now reset, putting power back on the Tracks and changing all the Signals to Green again.

The Train on Track B can now proceed forward. This will activate Timer B isolating the Track areas 1 & 4 on Track A and changing the Signals Red.

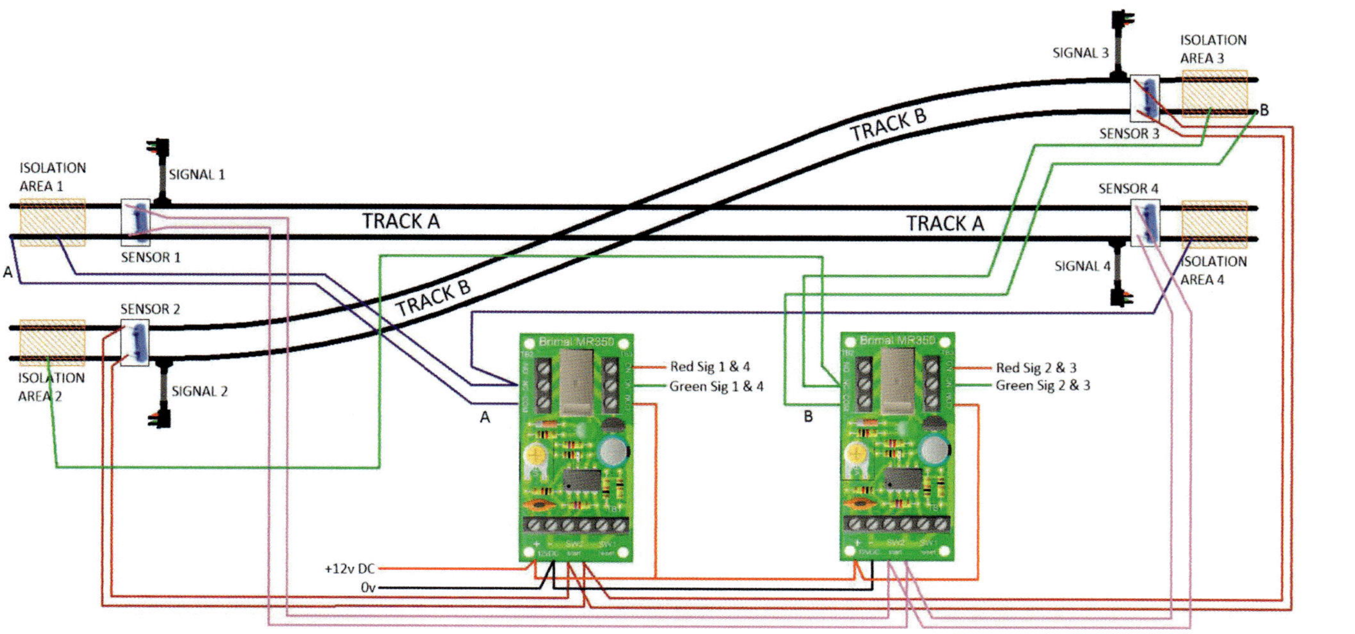

Sensors.

There are four sensors so that the system will work no matter which direction the Train is travelling. For example Sensor 1 and Sensor 4 are connected to the Timer in Parallel so that either sensor will activate the Timer, also Sensor 2 and 3 are connected in Parallel to activate Timer B. Depending on the physical shape of the sensor will determine the position. Remember the operating distance between sensor and the magnet on the underside of the Train is 4 to 5mm. Here are two examples of fixing the sensors.

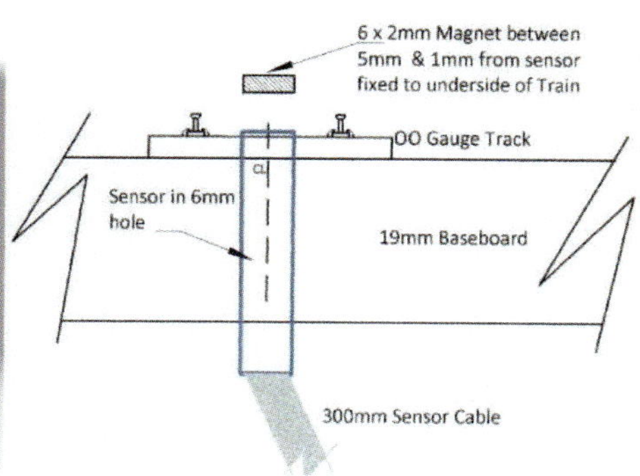

Isolation Areas

The isolation areas should be far enough back to not allow the train to stop on a Sensor or affect the other trains. As shown the power from the track comes from point A before Isolation Area 1 into the Common on the Timer, the feed to the Isolated areas 1 & 4 is connected to the NC (Normally Closed) contact. When the timer is activated the power is disconnected to these areas.

How you achieve the isolation areas is your choice, we have shown below a few examples. On a DC system we are only disconnecting one rail, preferably the positive rail.

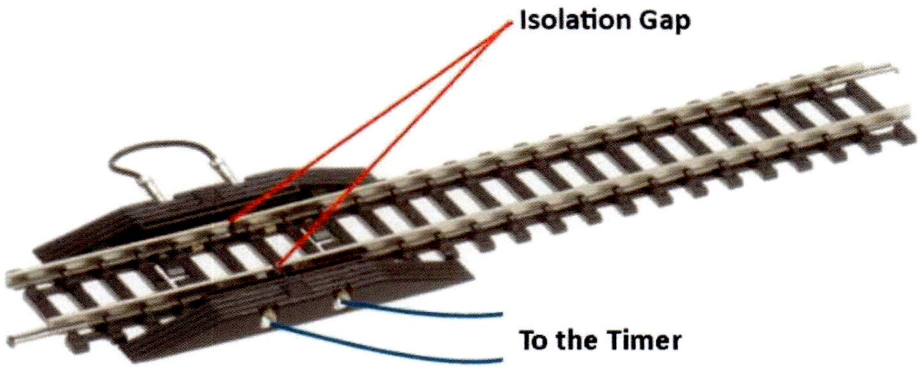

Signals

The signals are an added extra if you require, and will be dependant on the type used. They will all start Green and change to Red irrespective of where the train is coming from and which track initiates the Timers.

Wiring

The best way is to wire Track A Sensors in parallel and then two wires back to the Time A, and the same for Timer B.

If using signals, again if they are wired in Parallel and then back to the Timers this will reduce the amount of wiring to and from the Timers.

The Timers require a permanent 12v DC supply from your auxiliary supply. A ON/OFF switch in the supply could be added if you want to disable the system for any reason.

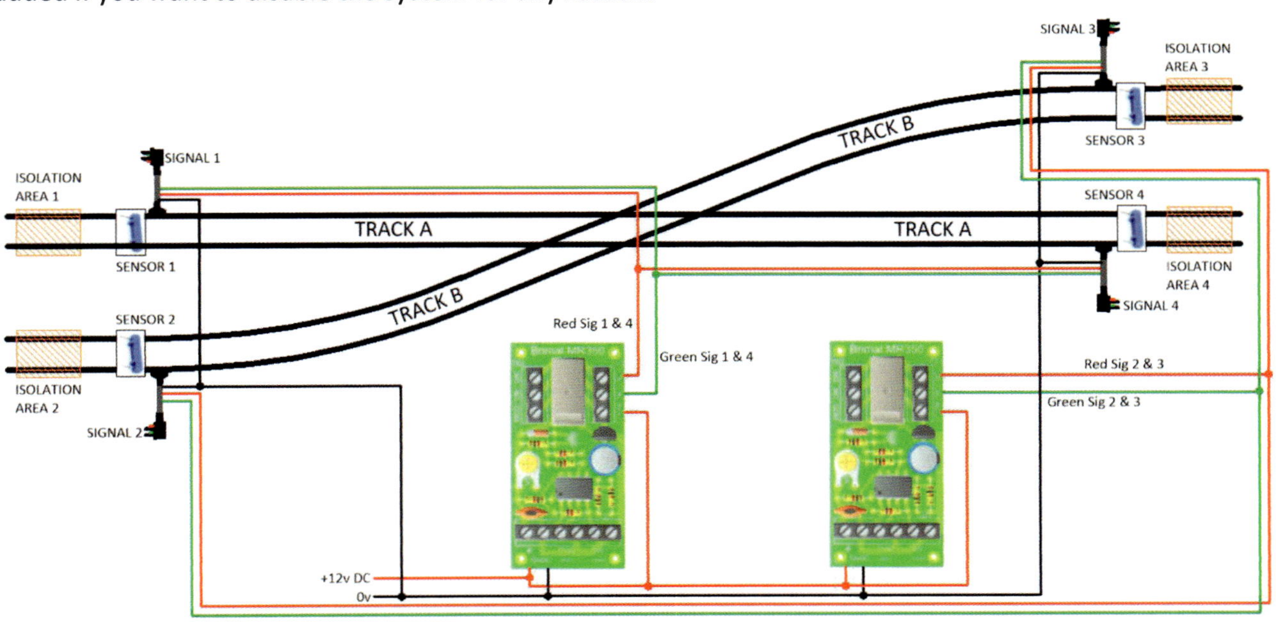

In this drawing we have removed the wiring for the sensors and Isolation Areas, for clarity. Although the drawing shows wires crossing each other they are not joined unless there is a dot on the join.

PROJECT 46

Servo Motor Controller

A servo motor is a rotary actuator or a motor that allows for a precise control in terms of the angular position, acceleration, and velocity. Basically, it has certain capabilities that a regular motor does not have. Consequently it makes use of a regular motor and pairs it with a sensor for position feedback . A typical servo motor comprises of three wires namely- power, control, and ground. They are becoming more popular in Model Railway layouts due to their lower cost.

The Servo motor can be used above the baseboard as shown or below the baseboard. The control circuit will come with 3 variable resistors, (pre-sets) , one to adjust the limit of the Forward motion of the actuator
The second one to control the limit of the Reverse motion of the Actuator, and the third to control the transition speed. Once these are all set to your requirements the mini momentary toggle switch is used to
send the signal to the Servo Motor. As always please read the manufacturers instruction to get the best out of your controller.

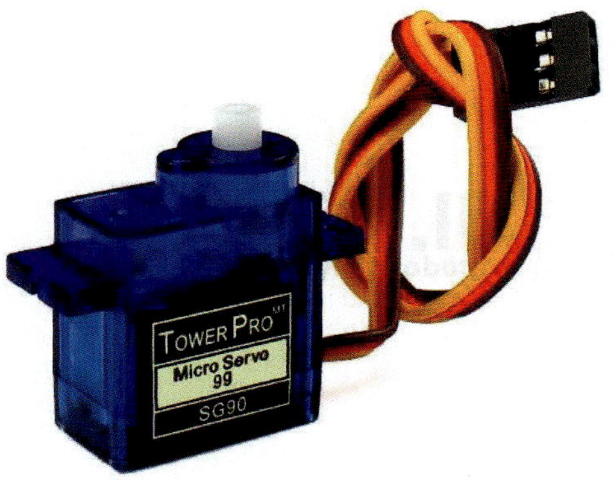

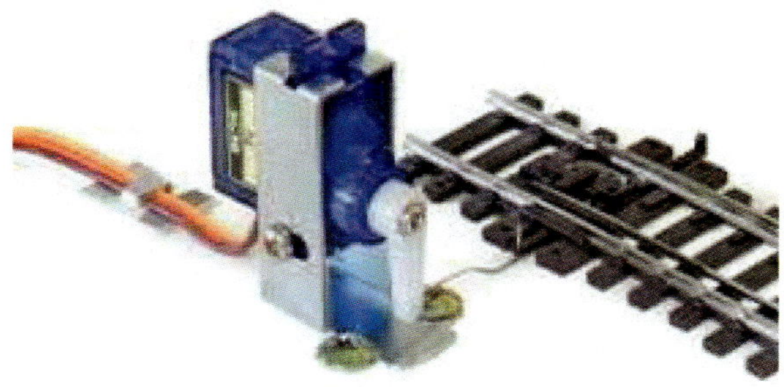

The first circuit below is the very basic driver, or could be used as a Servo bench tester. As you can see there is no way to adjust the travel, just straight forward Push Button SW1 for Forward and SW2 for Reverse

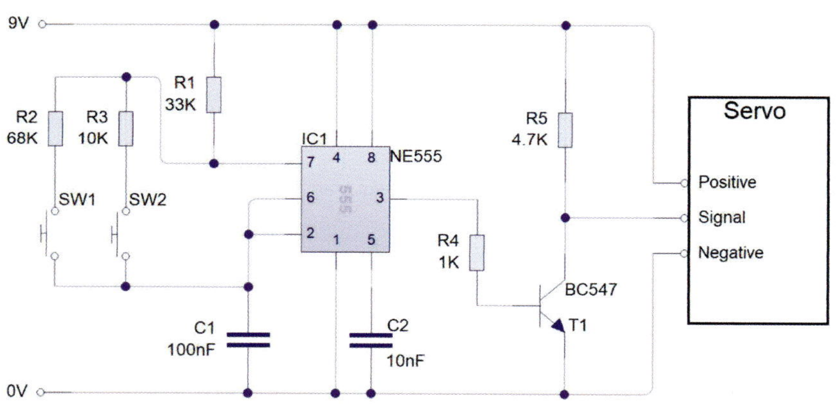

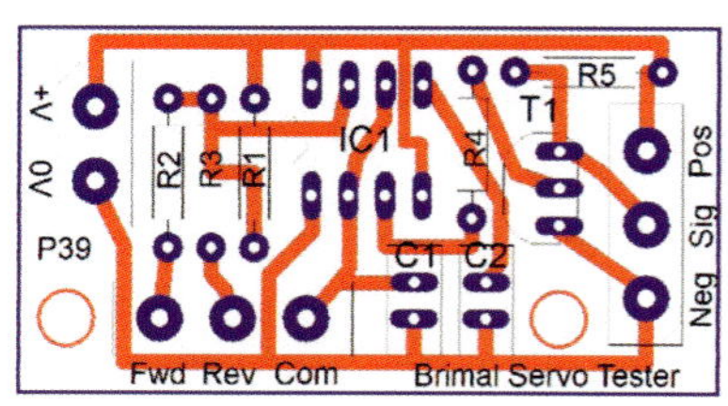

This next circuit is almost the same as above but we have added some variable resistors so that the travel of the arm can be adjusted.

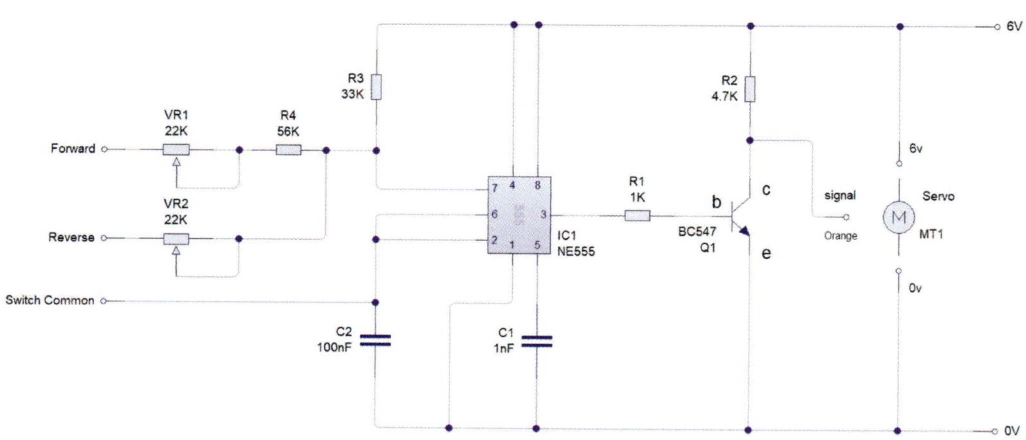

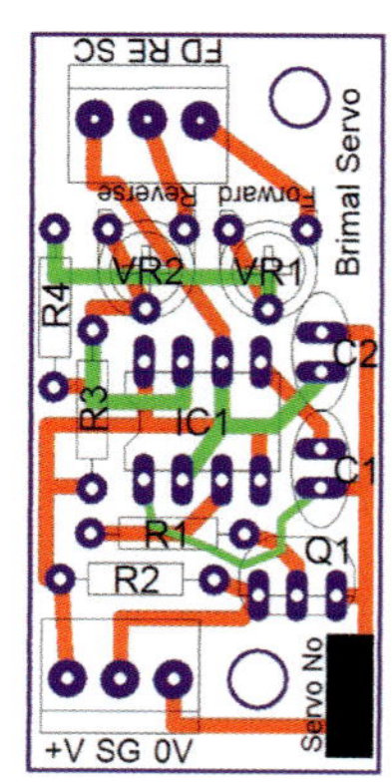

The next alternative is to purchase ready made unit. The Sparkfun WIG 13118 is a very good little controller

MODEL RAILWAY PROJECTS

The SparkFun Servo Trigger is a small robotics board that simplifies the control of hobby RC servo motors. When an external switch or logic signal changes state, the Servo Trigger is able to tell an attached servo motor to move from position A to position B. To use the Servo Trigger, you simply connect a hobby servo and a switch, then use the on-board potentiometers to adjust the start/stop positions and the transition time. You can use a hobby servo in your projects without having to do any programming!

Trigger-
Low input causes the motor to move to its set end position.
High Input causes the motor to return to it's set start position.

More than one motor can be controlled by one trigger unit.
The Diode at the entrance to the Trigger is optional

The Variable Resistor (Presets)

A) Sets Motor Stop Position
B) Sets Motor Stop Position
T) Sets Motor Transition Speed

Approx 3 seconds at slowest Speed and maximum sweep angle.

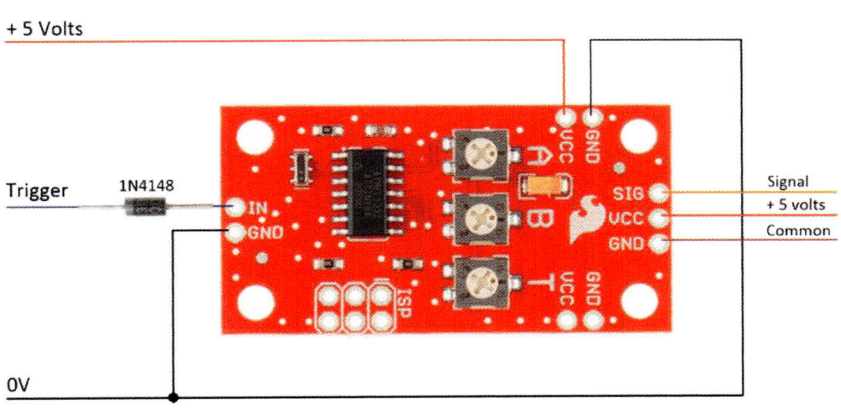

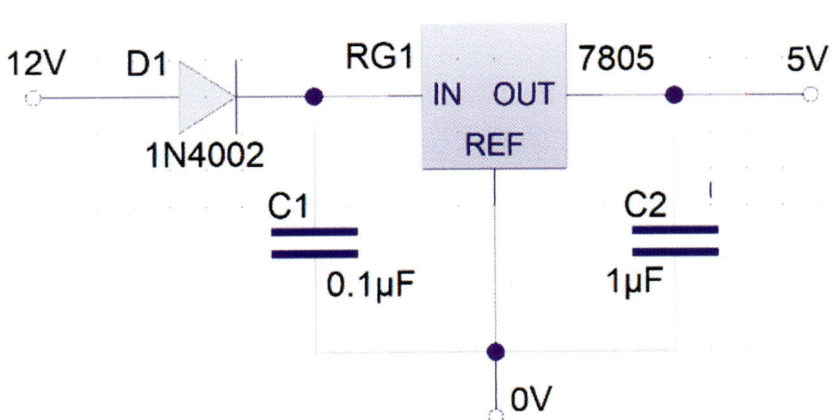

This circuit will give you the 5 volt supply required by the sparkfun card, from a nominal 12 volt DC supply.

Transistor to Transistor Logic

There will be times when you purchase a circuit that does not appear to work no matter what you do. This is more than likely a circuit with a TTL output. (Transistor to Transistor Logic)

A case being the Infrared Sensors shown below where the output is TTL

Here is a very simple circuit which will convert the output into a signal that you can use to power either some LED's or a relay. This circuit will work fine on any voltage from 5v to 24v, in this case the Infrared sensor requires 5v so best power this from the same power source. The only item you will need to check is the relay. This should have a 5-6v Coil.

PARTS LIST	
R1	1K 1/4w Resistor
D1	Diode 1N4148
D2	Diode 1N4148
TR1	Transistor BC547 npn
RL1	In this case a Miniature 5v Relay with 2 C/O sets

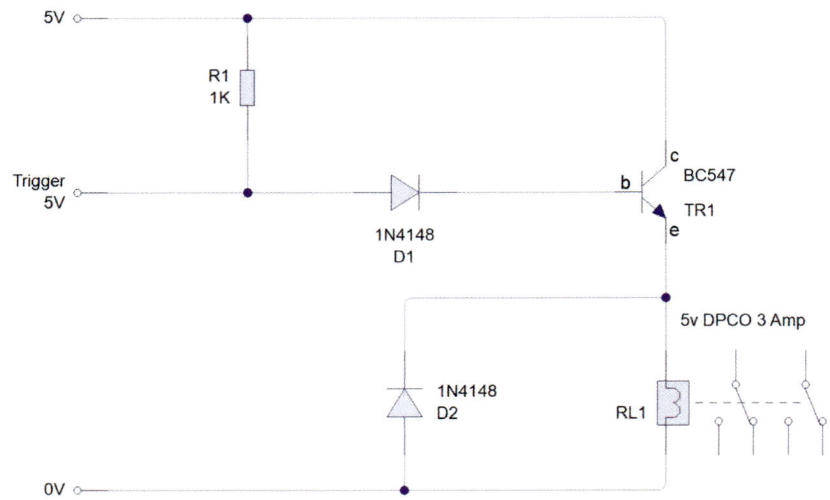

If you want to put this onto a PCB then here is the Copper Layout and the Component Layout.

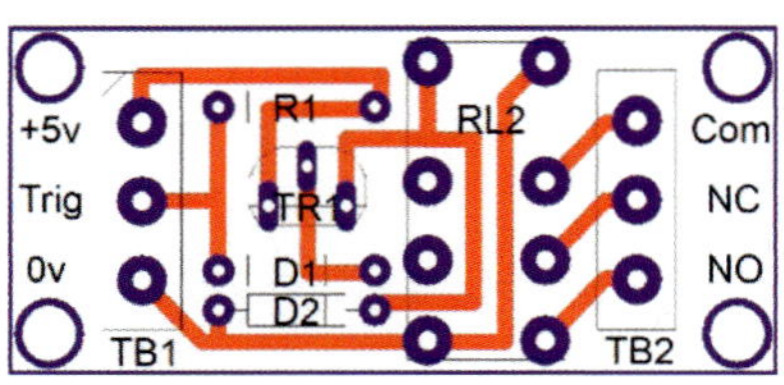

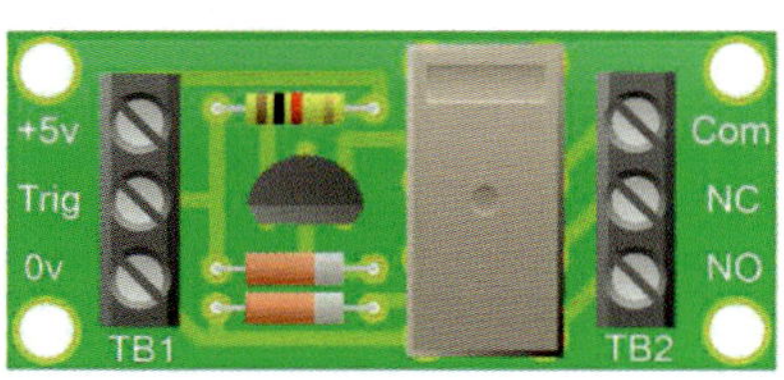

Additions to the Parts List

PARTS LIST	
PCB	Printed Circuit Board Single Sided 50mm x 22.0mm
TB1	3 way Terminal Block
TB2	3 way Terminal Block

Most sensors available at the moment are similar to the one opposite They appear to be good value for money, however they will not Trigger anything other than a logic circuit. The circuit above will convert the trigger signal into something that can switch on a relay. From the relay you can now switch virtually anything you want, from a warning LED, to Buzzer, Point Motors, and so on. The above circuit is so simple it could all be fitted on the pin side of the Relay, so not needing to produce a Printed Circuit Board. The following diagram shows how the Infrared circuit is wired to the above Interface circuit.

Infrared Sensor

Interface Circuit

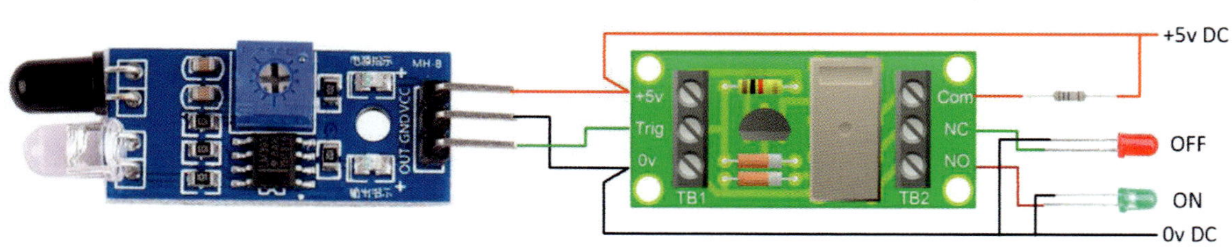

The Infrared Sensor could be any type of Logic output circuit. Here it is wired to a 5v DC supply and the trigger is wired to the centre terminal on the interface circuit. The output from the Interface is wired to a Green (ON) and Red (OFF) LED's. As the supply is above the working voltage of the LED's, a dropping resistor must be used to reduce the voltage to the LED's.

Power Supply Equipment

Most layouts require three forms of Power Source. The first is a variable 12v supply to control the speed of the train, the second is a fixed 12v supply to power all ancillary equipment such as points, signals, etc, and the third is 16vAC for some types of Points and signals.

How much power do you need.

Electrical power is a function of voltage and current (literally: Power in Watts is equal to the current in Amps multiplied by the voltage in Volts, or P=IV). Power for model trains and accessories is typically measured in thousandths of an Amp, or milliAmps (mA) Note: one milliAmp of current at 12 volts provides 12 milliWatts of electrical power.

What really matters in a model train is the torque produced by the motor (which varies with current) and the power to move a train ("power in rotational motion", which is at it's maximum at about half the full unloaded speed). Torque is used to overcome friction, and is particularly important when starting a stationary train, this we will cover in the chapter Control panels, but you need the power available to run the Speed Controller.

The Power Source.

There are many types of Power Supplies on the Market today. What you are looking for is a 12vDC supply with a current rating of between 2 to 5 Amps. The current rating required will depend on the size of your layout and how many Locomotives you are running at the same time, for very large layouts you could go up to 10 Amps or higher You will also need a 16v AC supply if you are using certain types of Point Motors and Signals.

The first example is a Power Supply delivering 12 volts DC and rated at 3 Amps.

Fig 1

The second example is a PSU delivering 12 volts and rated at 5 Amps

Fig 2

The third example is a PSU delivering 9v to 15v and rated at 10 Amps.
This unit has a potentiometer for you to set the voltage you require

Fig 3

The fourth example is a 16v AC power unit with a separate circuit to convert the 16vAC to 12v DC at 1.1 Amp, if required

Fig 4

Which ever one you decide to use you will now have to distribute the power to certain equipment on your layout, the below diagram gives an idea of how this could be done. You must however bare in mind the current capabilities of the PSU. The fourth example would appear to be the logical one as you have the 16v AC and the 12v DC all in the one unit. However the 12v DC is only rated at 1.1 Amp so will be limited to what it can power.
The circuit diagram for the fourth example is as follows.

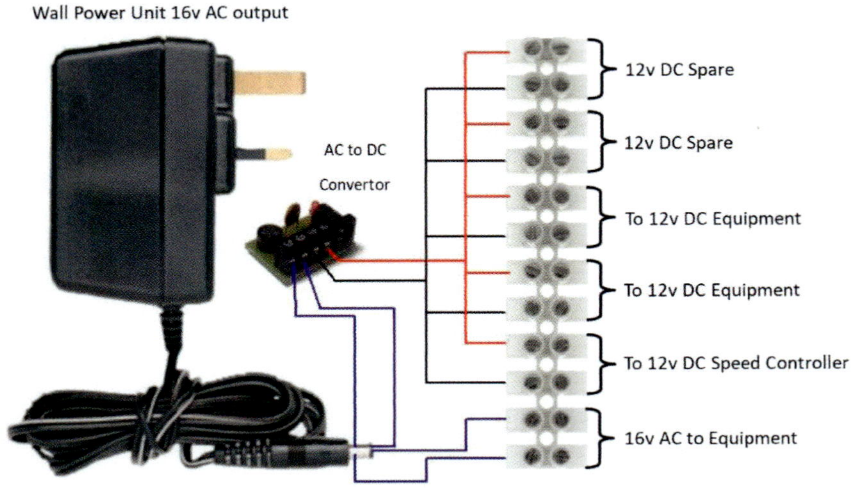

Fig 5

A better Power Supply system is as follows.

Here we use the 16v AC Power Pack just for the AC supply, and introduce a high current Power Unit for everything else. Now you have enough power to run a number of Speed Controllers and all the other 12v DC equipment.

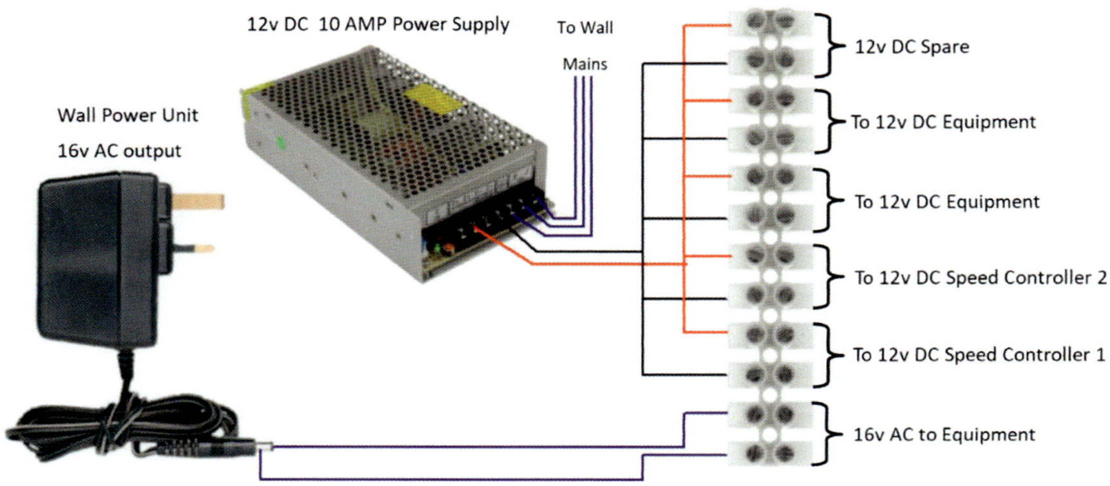

Fig 6

In all drawings Blue is shown as AC, Red is Positive (+) DC, and Black is Negative (0) DC.

Now that the Power is sorted out, we need to look at the Speed Controller.

<u>Speed Controllers.</u>

Most Propriety manufactures make their own Speed Controller, here are a few examples. They all supply a variable voltage to the tracks and most have a Forward/Reverse switch to change the polarity on the tracks. Some speed controllers will be supplied with the Power Unit built in so you may not require a Power Supply Unit. However these will be limited to the amount of current they can deliver, so at some stage you may have to invest in a separate PSU.

Examples of Speed Controllers, (Please note this is just a small sample of Speed Controllers)

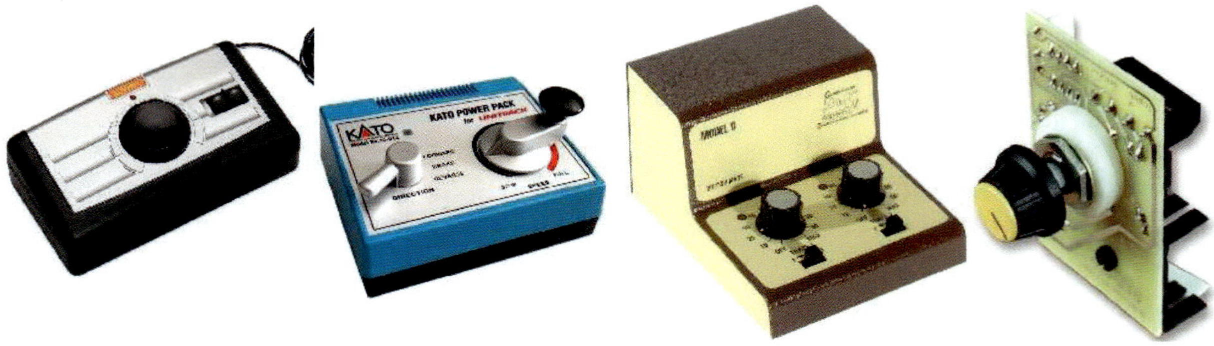

We now have the basis for the Power System for the Layout.
The wiring of these is straight forward and all will follow the circuit below.

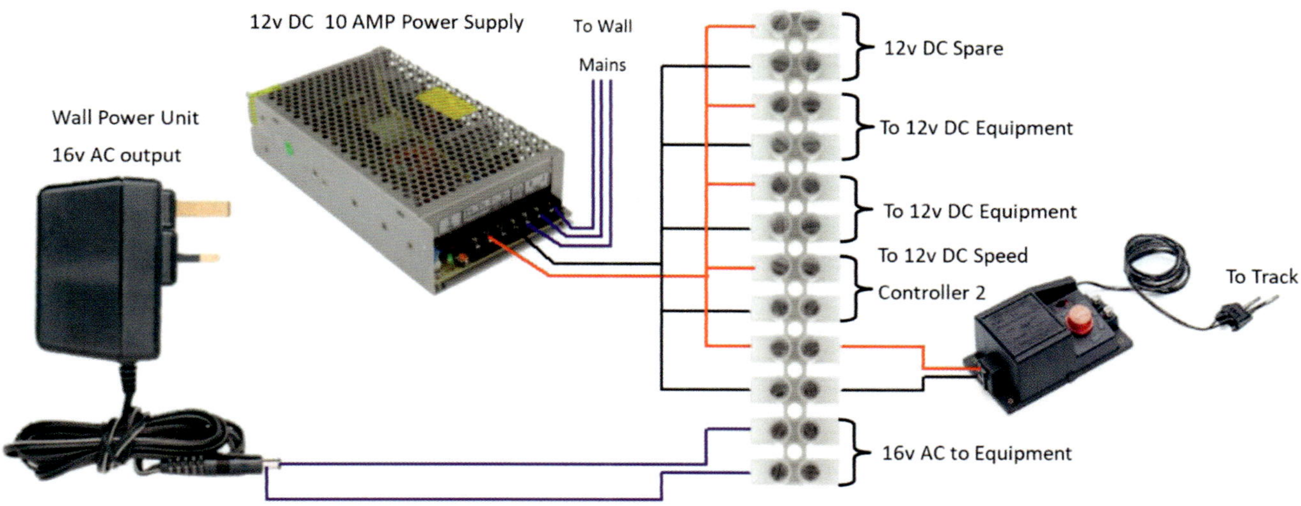

In all drawings Blue is shown as AC, Red is Positive (+) DC, and Black is Negative (0) DC.
Fig 11

As your system becomes larger and you put more equipment on the layout you may find that some of these items only require 5v DC. This is ideal for powering LED's and as you fit more it would be a good idea to have a separate Power Supply Unit for them, this will be a 5v DC and is available as a plug in unit.

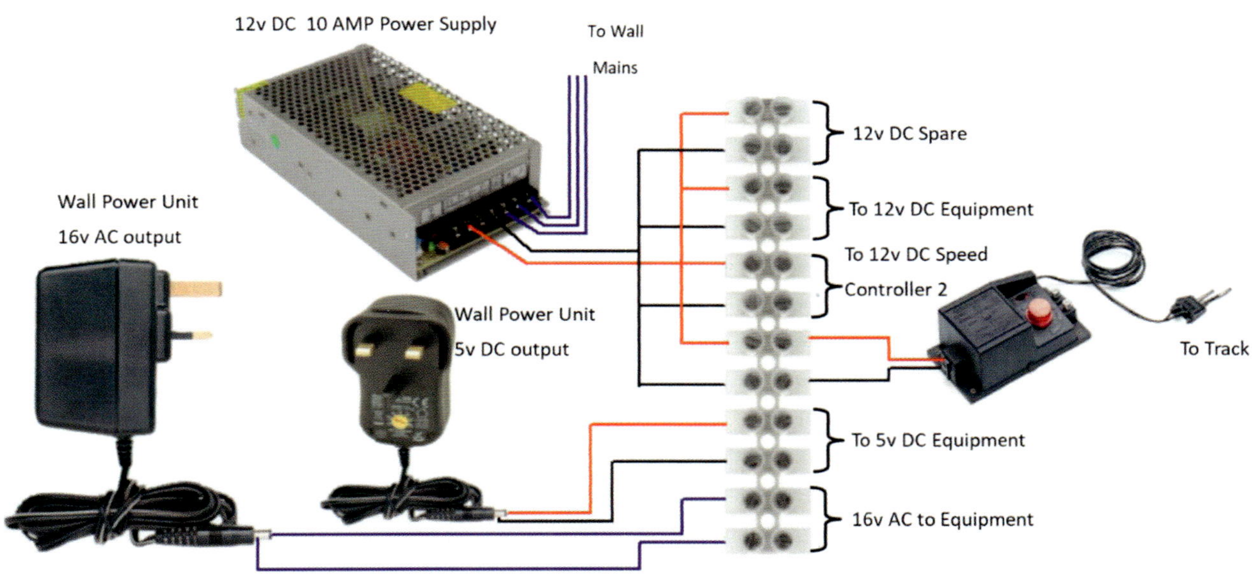

Fig 12
While looking for a Speed Controller you will come across the phrase 'Pulse Width Modulation'

<u>Pulse Wide Modulation</u>.
PWM is a modulation technique used to convert a voltage into a pulsing signal. This modulation allows the control of the power supplied to electrical devices, especially to loads such as motors. The pulse width modulation speed control works by driving the motor with a series of "ON-OFF" pulses and varying the duty cycle, the fraction of time that the output voltage is "ON" compared to when it is "OFF", of the pulses while keeping the frequency constant. The power applied to the motor can be controlled by varying the width of these applied pulses and thereby varying the average DC voltage applied to the motors terminals. By changing or modulating the timing of these pulses the speed of the motor can be controlled, ie, the longer the pulse is "ON", the faster the motor will rotate and likewise, the shorter the pulse is "ON" the slower the motor will rotate.
Also the amplitude of the motor voltage remains constant so the motor is always at full strength. The result is that the motor can be rotated much more slowly without it stalling.

Add an Ammeter

As mentioned before the voltage is not the problem with a Layout it is the Current drawn. As your layout grows so does the demand for power whether it be your 12vDC, 5vDC, or 16vAC supply. The current you draw may need to be monitored if you are expanding. A panel mounted 10 Amp meter is readily available and is connected into the Positive wire as near to the Power Supply Unit as possible. Where the positive wire goes into the Terminal Block, remove it and connect to one of the terminals on the back of the Ammeter. Fit another wire from the second Terminal to the Terminal block. The circuit below shows the position from each PSU where you can break into the supply and fit an Ammeter.

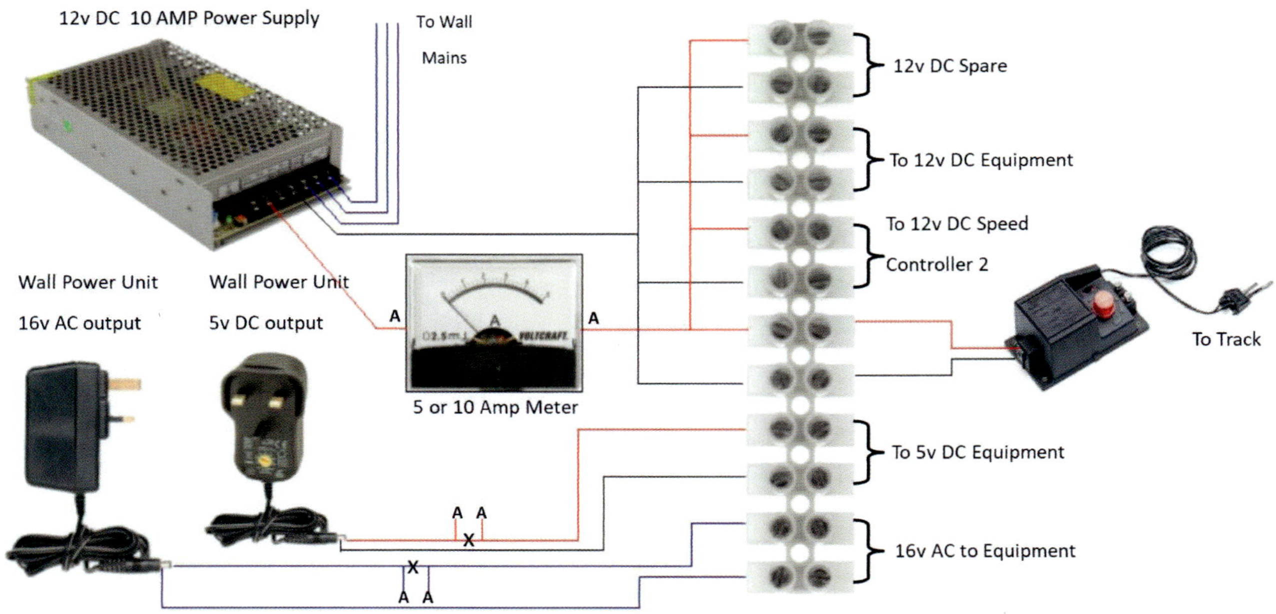

Fig 13

You could also use your Multimeter or purchase a Clamp Ammeter all will do the job. The Clamp Ammeter is the only one that does not require any rewiring.

Build your Own PSU.

You may wish to build your own Power unit and speed controller from scratch.

The circuit below shows a typical Power Supply circuit where the Track Speed Controller does not have a Transformer included.

The transformer would be a 12 volt AC output at 4 Amp, The Circuit Breaker should be rated initially at 3.0 Amp to protect your circuits and equipment from short circuits. The Rectifier converts AC to DC and must be capable of carrying at least what the transformer is delivering 4 amp or above.

The speed controller can be any transformer-less unit from any proprietary manufacturer.

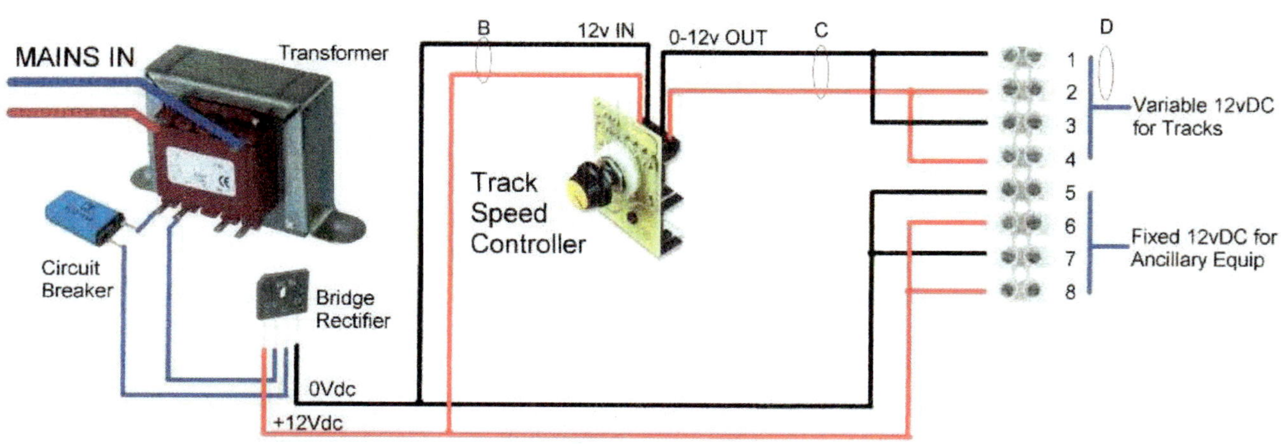

Fig 14

Note: A) All wiring should be no less than 16/0.2 Equipment Wire.

Note: B) The DC power supply above is unregulated and not stabilised and will work fine for most Railway systems, and will run ancillary equipment fine. It however is not recommended for use on sophisticated electronic circuits. The following circuit will do this job.

Connection to the Household Mains

All this needs to be connected to a domestic socket where ever your layout is.
A few points to remember.

1) Start with an RCD in the domestic socket.
   What is an RCD.
   A residual-current device (**RCD**), is a device that instantly breaks an electric circuit to prevent serious harm from an ongoing electric shock. RCD's are designed to quickly and automatically disconnect a circuit when it detects that the electric current is not balanced between the energized (line) conductor(s) and the return (neutral) conductor. Under normal circumstances, these two wires are expected to carry matching currents, and any difference can indicate a short circuit or other electrical anomaly is present, such as leakage. Leakage can indicate a shock hazard (or shock in progress) which is a potential danger to a person.
2) A Multiway Connector. There are many types and styles on the market, some even come with built in RCD's. Keep the cable from the Household socket – RCD – Multiway Connector as short as possible. Do not use a coiled extension lead, or if you do, uncoil the lead before you use it.
   Plug all your Power Units into the multiway and keep the wires to the control Station as short as possible.
   Why uncoil extension cables.
   A powered up extension cable is the making of an electromagnet, albeit very crude, however the coil can heat up, this could then cause a fire. I must stress this is very unlikely with the currents you will be using, but it is always better to be safe than sorry.

Train Blocking

The MR204 can be used to detect the position of a Train in a BLOCK, change the signal behind the train from Green to Red, & stop a following train in the Isolation Section. With 3 or 4 MR204's you could run 3 or 4 Trains on the same track without any collisions. As the train travels along the track the signal will be at Green. When the Locomotive passes over sensor A the Relay will change over. This puts the signal at Red now, and the other side of the relay removes power from the track in the 'Isolation Section'. When the locomotive reaches Sensor B, the relay will change again. This puts the signal back to Green and restores power in the 'Isolation Section'.

The drawing below has condensed everything onto one page. In real life the distance between Sensor A and Sensor B should be the length of your train plus a little more. The 'Isolation Section needs to be no more than 300mm, as the Locomotive is not likely to travel that distance without power. The 'Buffer Section' should be a little longer than your train length. The power for the 'Isolation section' is through the MR204 relay. Pin 1 (T2) picks up power from the track and passes through the relay to Pin 2 (T2), so when sensor A is activated Pin 2 (T2) is deactivated until Sensor B is activated

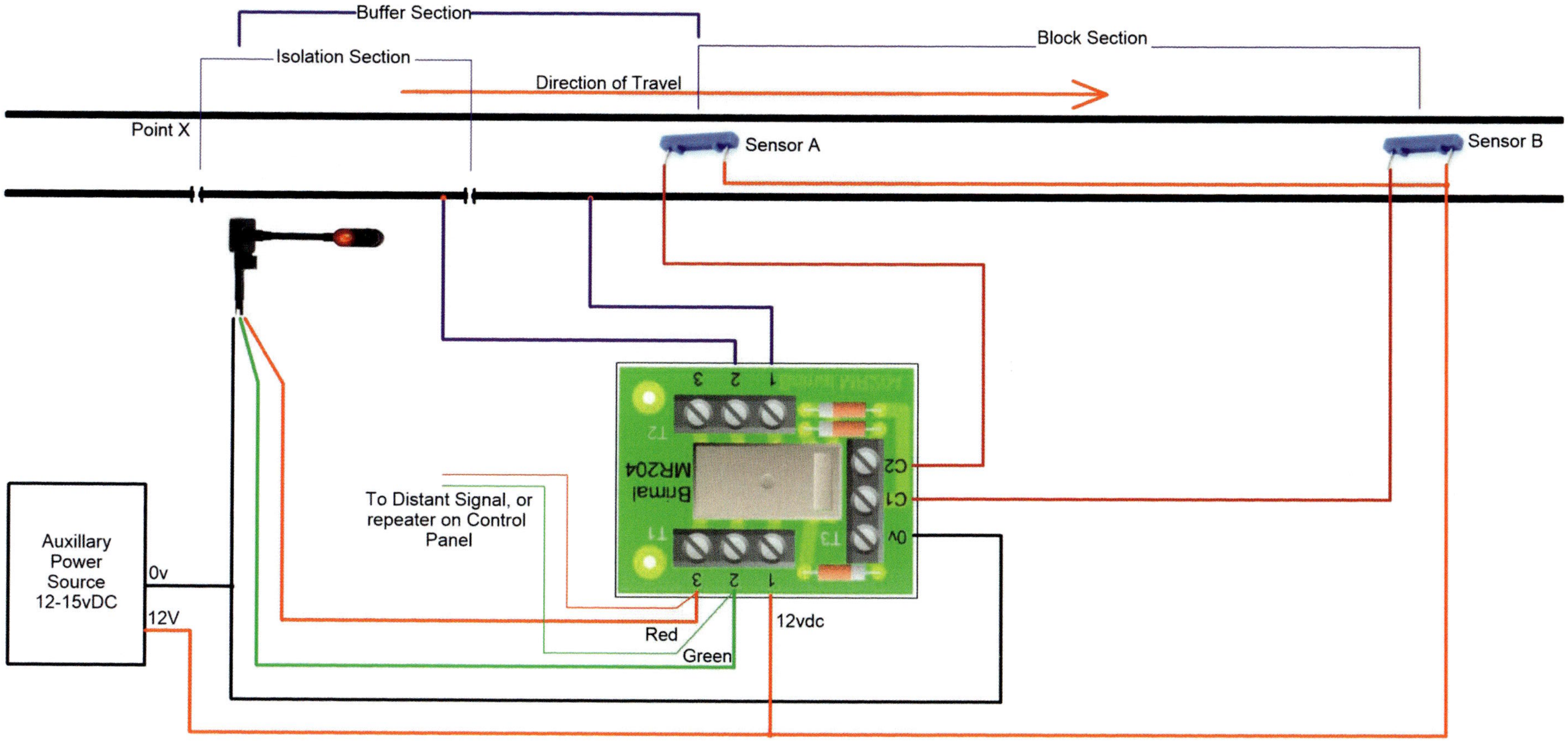

Using Toggle Switches

Push Pull Solenoid

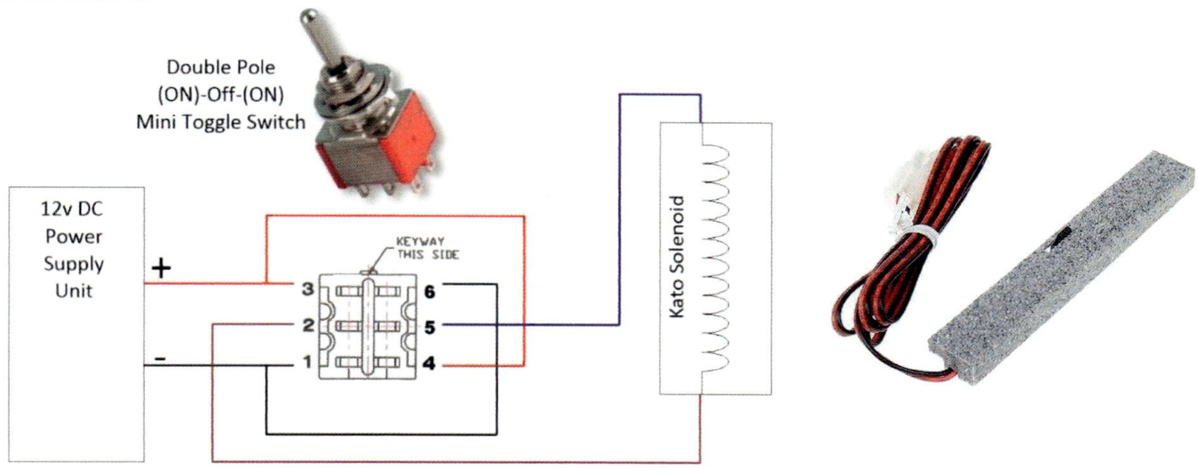

Stall Point Motors

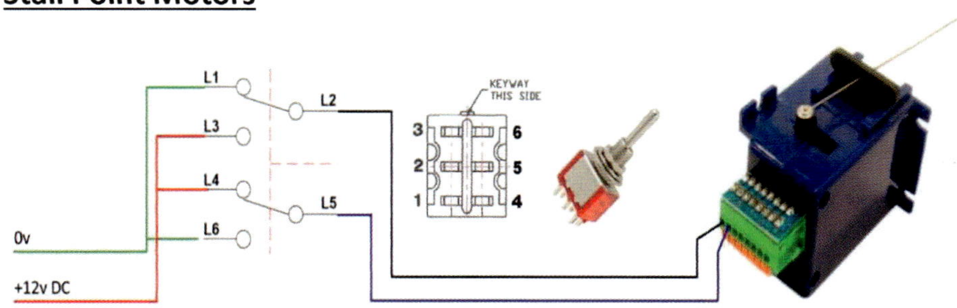

Dual Stall Motors

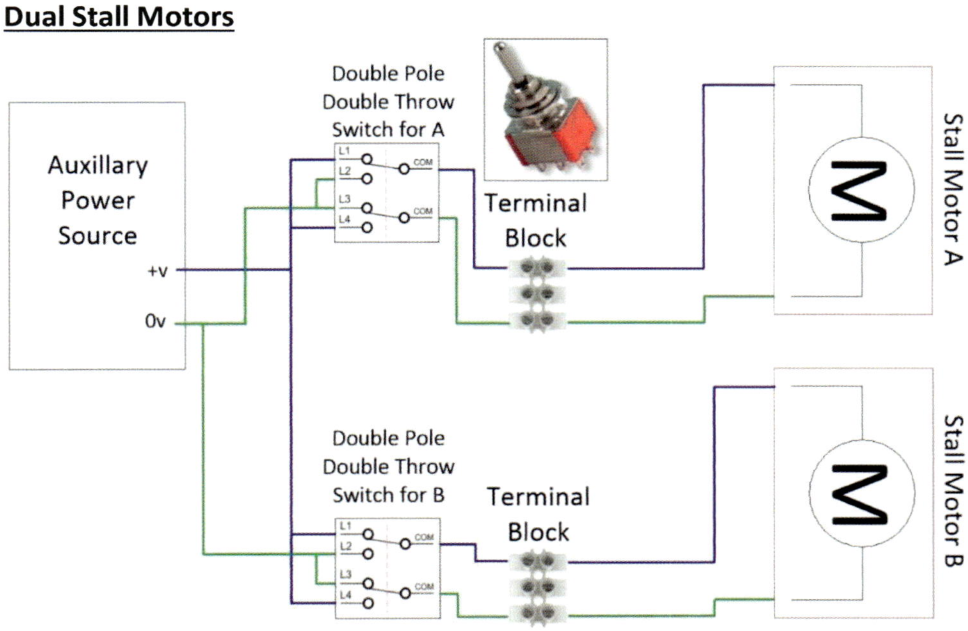

2 Aspect Signal

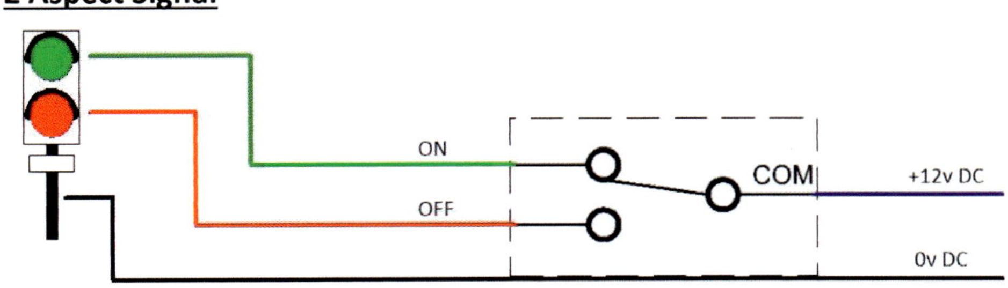

2 Aspect Signal using LED's

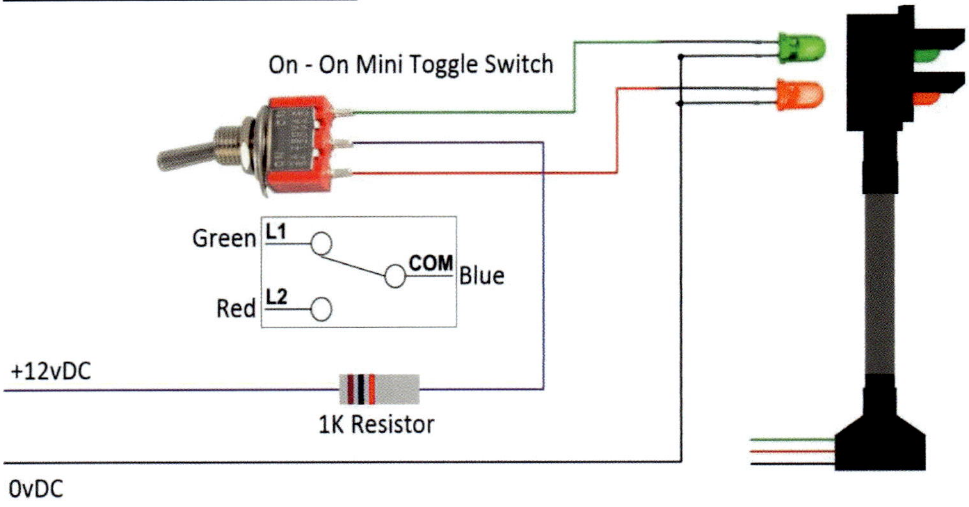

Home & Distant LED Signals

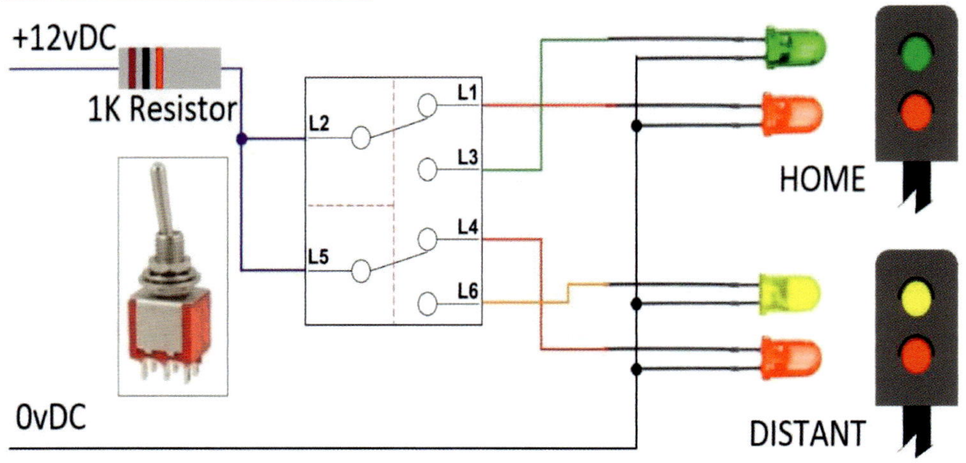

3 Aspect Signal

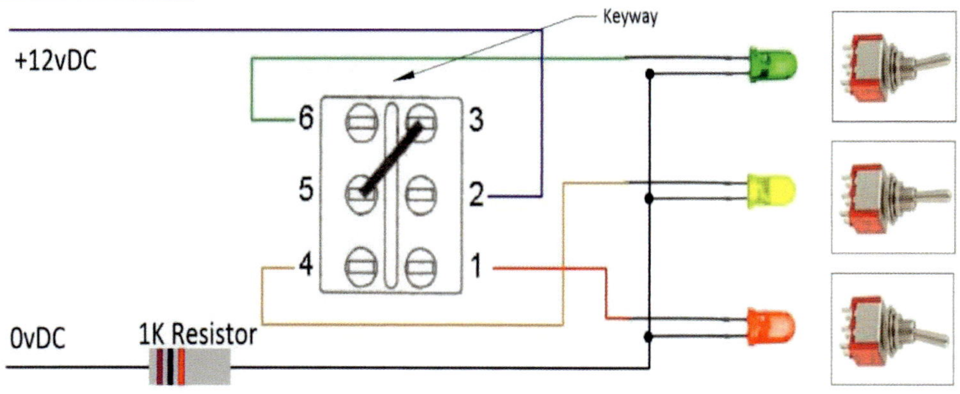

Track Isolation Single Rail

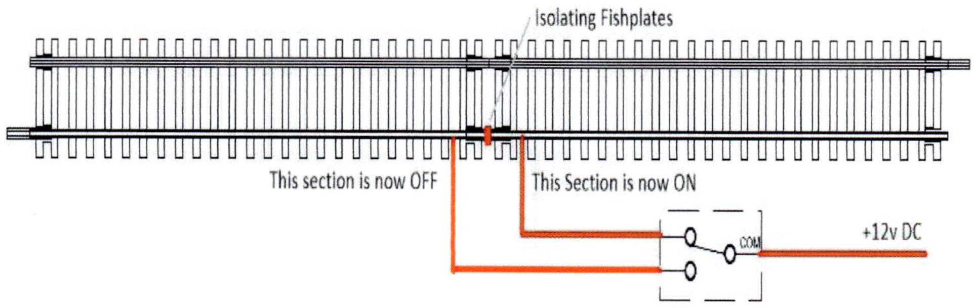

Track Isolation Dual Rails

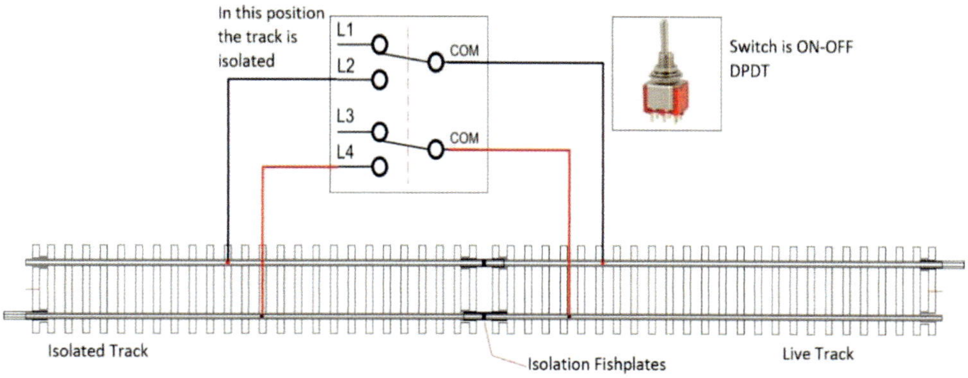

Forward Reverse Switch

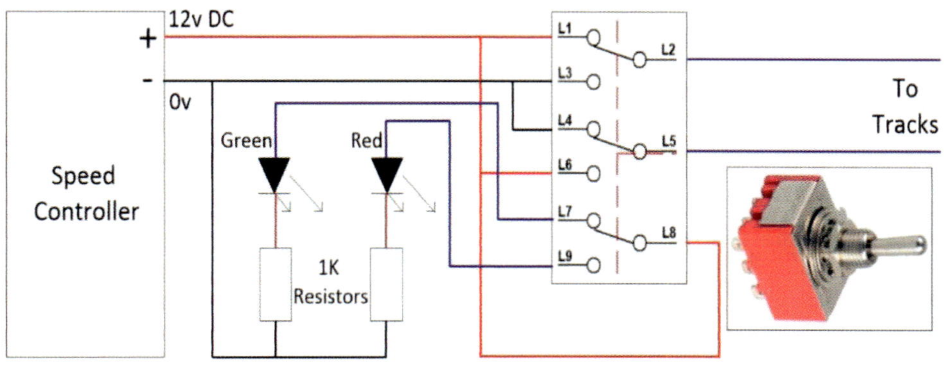

Street Lights

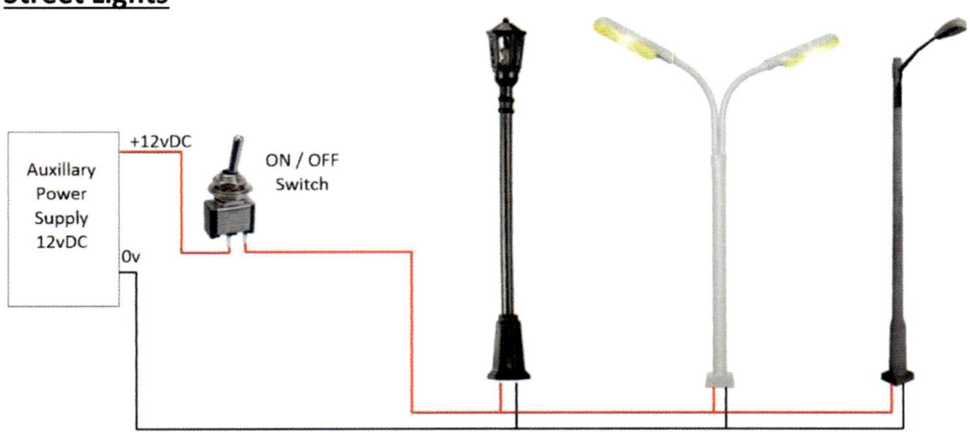

Building Lights

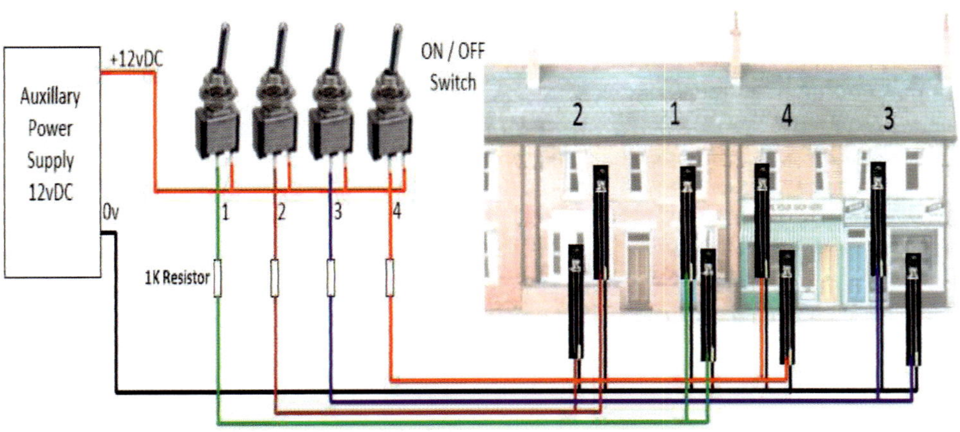

Point Arc Flash

This circuit is designed to simulate the Arc Flash made by electric Trains as they cross points and crossings. The flash can be triggered by the train using a magnet on the underside of the train and a sensor between the tracks. The Ultra bright Blue or White LEDs (or a combination of both) are set into the baseboard so they just protrude to the height of the sleepers. The sensor is set in place as near to the LEDs as possible between non moving parts of the points. The ideal situation is that the LEDs flash from under the Locomotive.

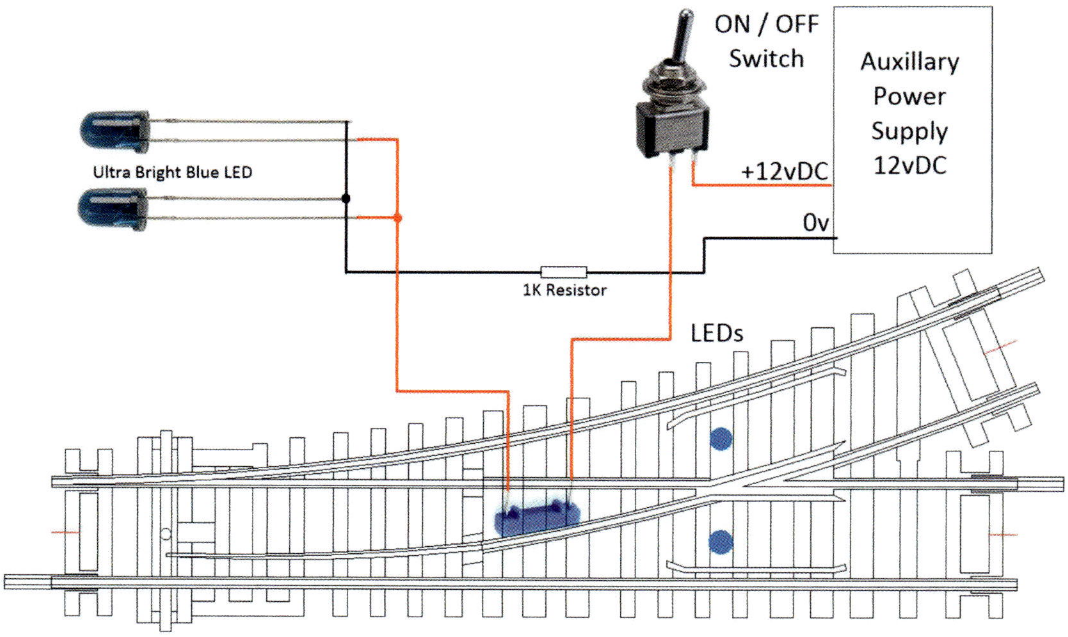

Fig 8

PROJECT 52

Heavy Duty Equipment Switch using a Latching relay

In this application the MR204 is used to switch ON/OFF a High Power Motor or some other piece of equipment. The ON and OFF push buttons are both momentary Push for ON switches, (these could be magnetic Sensors, Limit switches, timer contacts, pressure switches, etc, as they only need to give a momentary action). The ON/OFF indicators again could be LED's at 2.2v up to filament lamps at 240vAC – the limitation will be the current drawn by the Indicators can not be more than 2 Amps. On the other side of the relay the other changeover contacts can be used to switch ON or OFF a DC or AC appliance, such as a water pump, fan, siren, solenoid, and so on.
By introducing a Timer into T2 contacts the equipment can be switched ON for a specific period irrespective of the switch status, for example an alarm that is only required to be on for a short time.

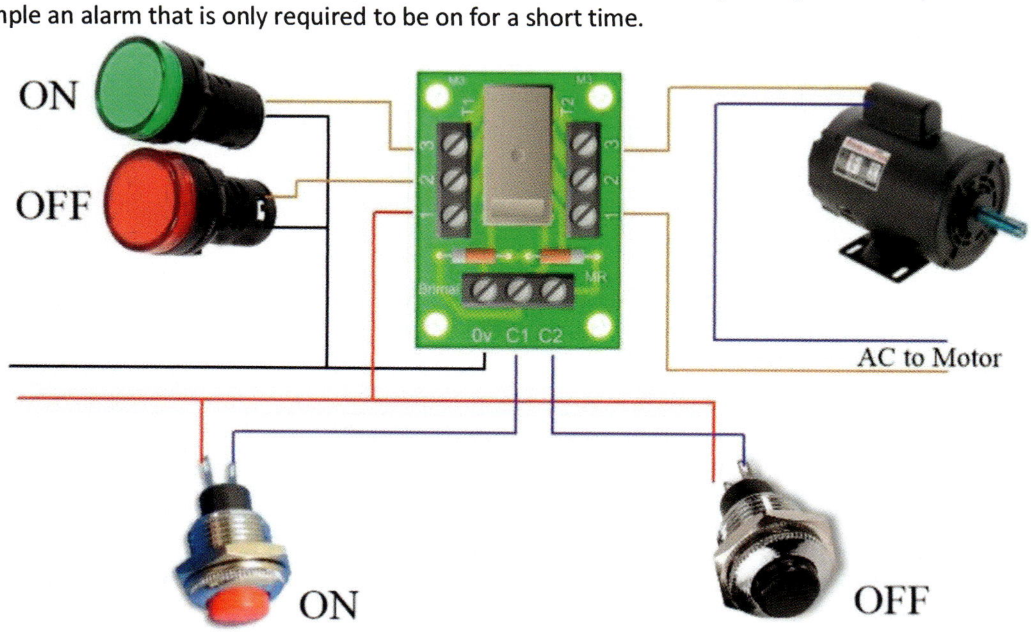

MODEL RAILWAY PROJECTS

MR365 Automatic Shuttle Timer.

PROJECT 53

The MR365 does not require any sensors on the track or magnets on the Locos. The analogue speed controller is simply connected to the track via the relay on the timer board. The system will work just as well on a complete loop or a straight section. On a straight section you would need to set the Forward time and the reverse time the same. On a loop layout you could set the forward time longer that the Reverse, this will then make the 'stop to reverse' position different each time. If you had two stations on a loop layout you could have the train shunting between stations. In a siding situation you could have the train moving between 2 points via a series of points, and back again, for as long as the timer is on. When the timer is switched OFF the power is still going to the tracks via the relay on the timer board.
Please note there is no slow down or slow start up in this circuit. The train will immediately change direction at the speed set on the controller.

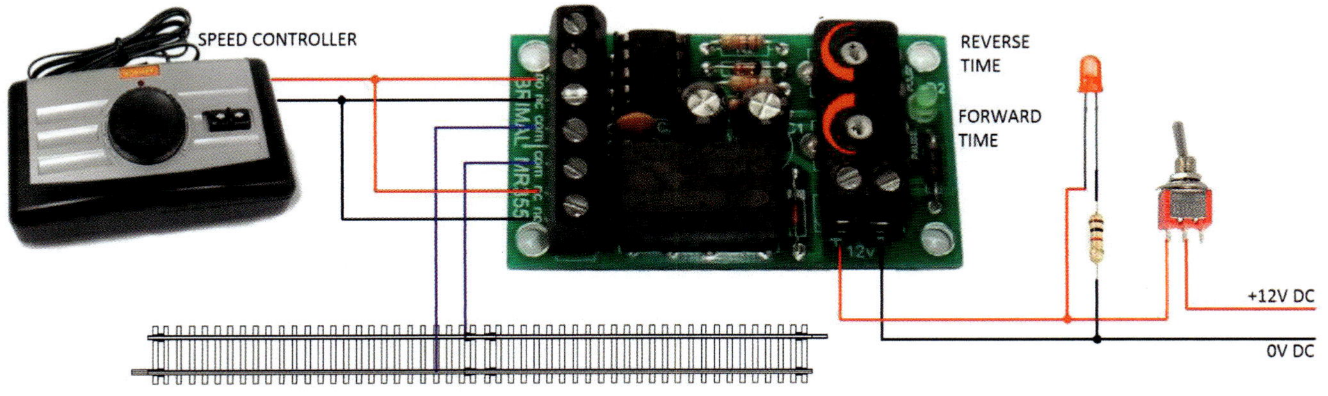

The MR365 comes complete with an ON/OFF switch, an indicator LED and dropping Resistor.

In the Loop layout below connection is very simple, instead of taking the speed control feed to the tracks, they are taken to the terminals on the MR365 as shown above. The two 'COM' wires are then taken to the tracks. When the MR365 is switched ON nothing will happen (the train will move forward) for the period set by 'Forward Time'. When this time has elapsed, the relay will switch over and the train will be put into reverse for the time set on the 'Reverse Time' preset. This will continue for as long as the MR365 is switched ON. When switched Off the train will revert to normal forward travel.

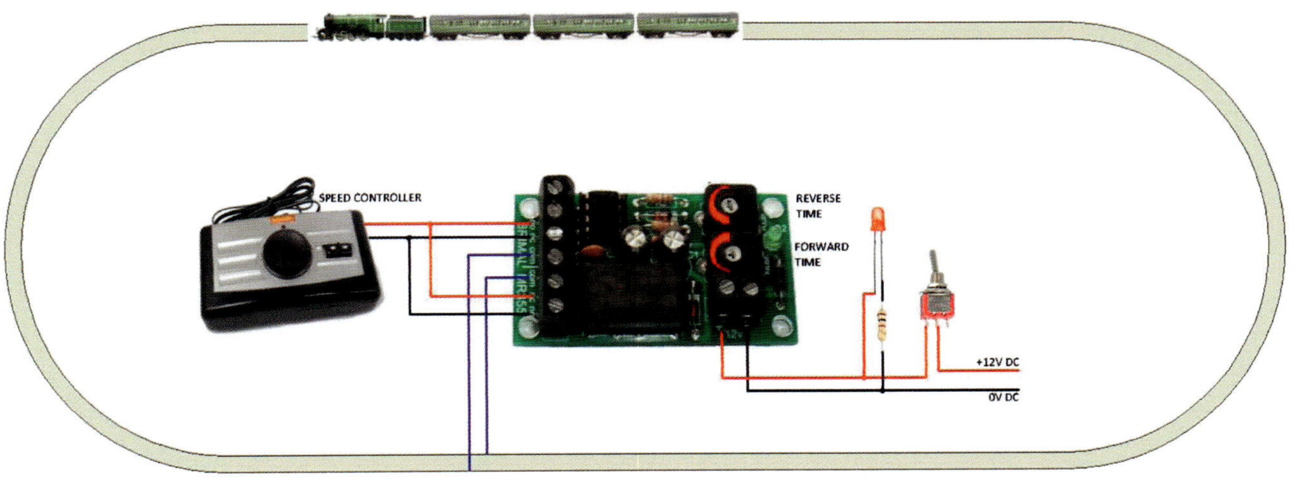

In the next drawing a single line track can be used to allow the train to move left to right and back. The important thing to remember here is that the 'Forward time' and the 'Reverse time' must be the same otherwise the train will start to creep. The common of the relay is connected to the rails as shown in the figure below.

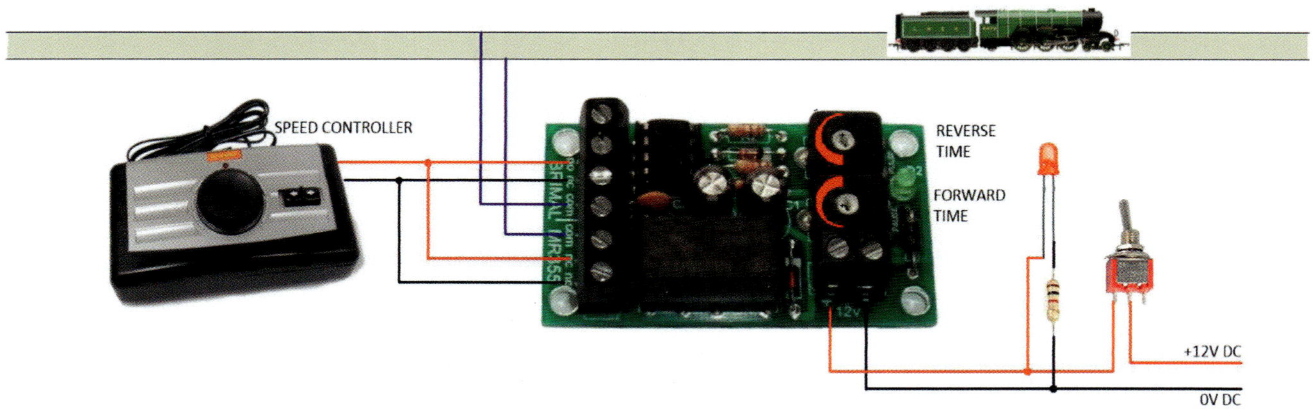

In the next application the Shuttle Timer is used to allow a Loco to travel trough a fiddle yard and then back. The fiddle yard would have to be isolated from the rest of the layout so it can run independently. How simple or complicated the Loco movement is, is up to you.

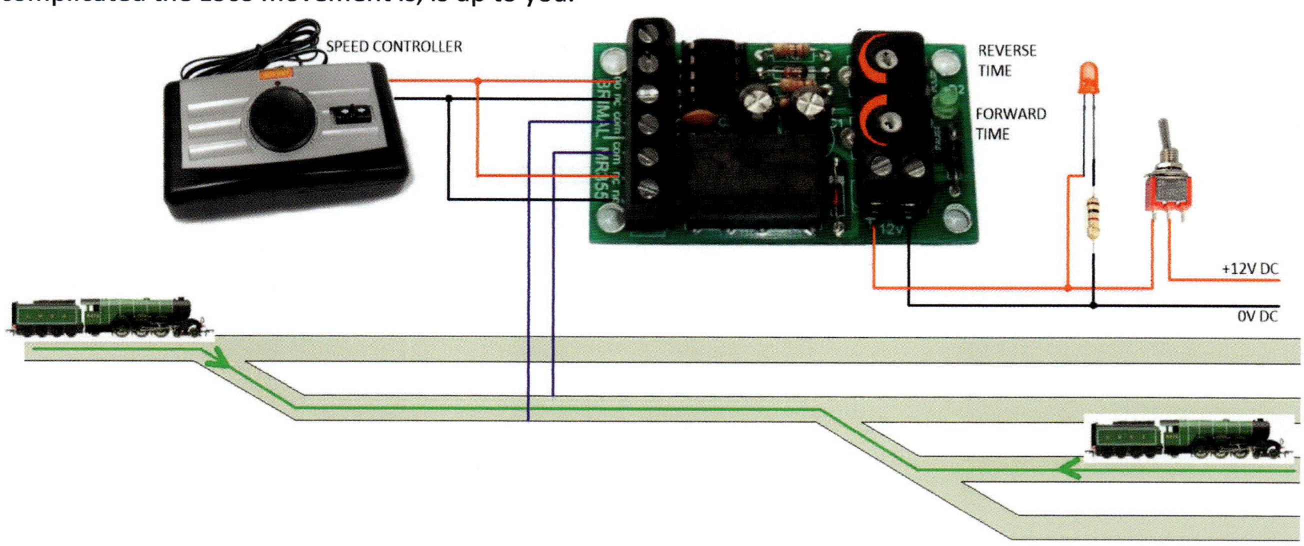

MODEL RAILWAY PROJECTS

BUS Bar Connections

PROJECT 54

DC Connection

The Bus bar wiring is designed to provide the maximum amount of current to a specific point in the track, so the more spurs you have the less likely you are to get voltage drop. The ideal solution is to have a 'ring main' so the far end comes back and is joined to itself as close to the power source as possible. The drawing below shows a Base Board with the bus bars running around the entire board. The spurs are as often as needed and details of connection are shown below.

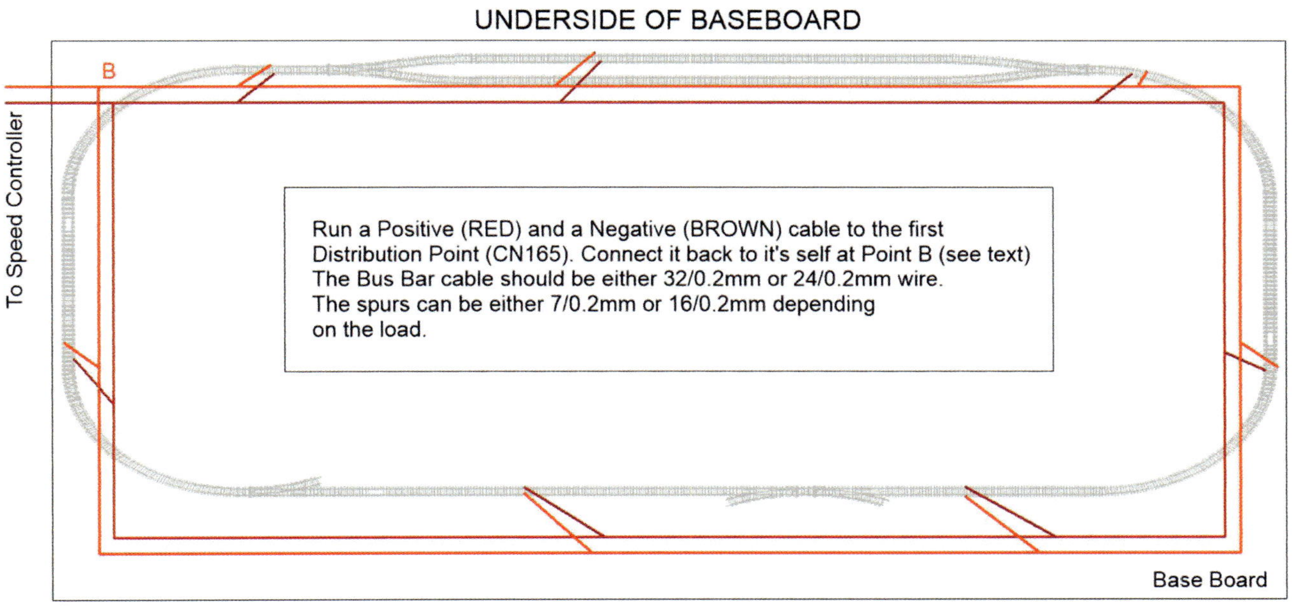

Connection using a Quickclip.

Connection will still need a terminal block at the end of the spur to feed the equipment. (see detail C)

The main Bus bar wire is inserted into the clip so that it is in the rear through slot. The spur wire (yellow) is then inserted into the front through slot. Press down the metal cutter with a pair of pliers so the top of the metal is level with the plastic holder. Now fold over the plastic retainer until it clips to the body. Job Done. Repeat, this for the Brown wire, and all the spurs you require.

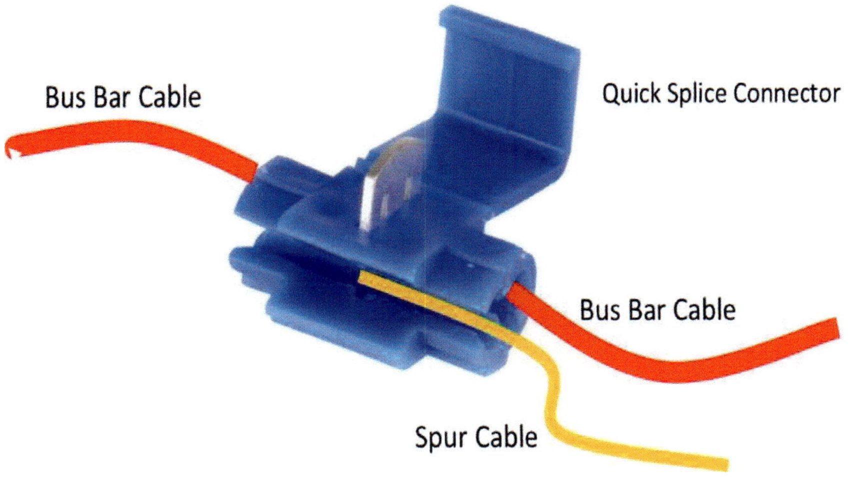

Connection using a Multiway Terminal Block (CN165)

With this type of Distribution unit you will have to break into the two Bus Bar cables and connect them on the left and right. The advantage of this unit is that you can wire the equipment directly into the terminals. Coming from the distribution unit you will use cable that is appropriate for the equipment, in most cases this will be 7/0.2mm or 16/0.2mm

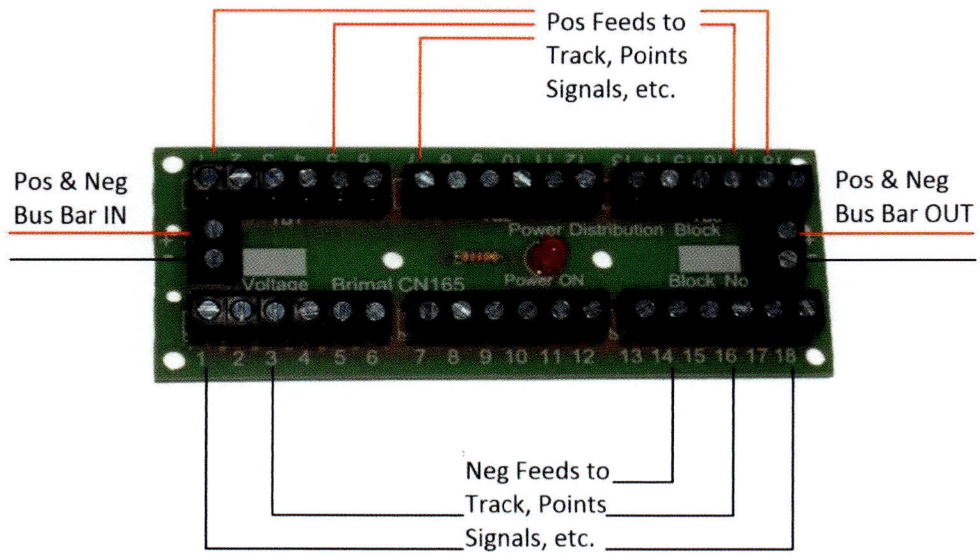

DCC Connection

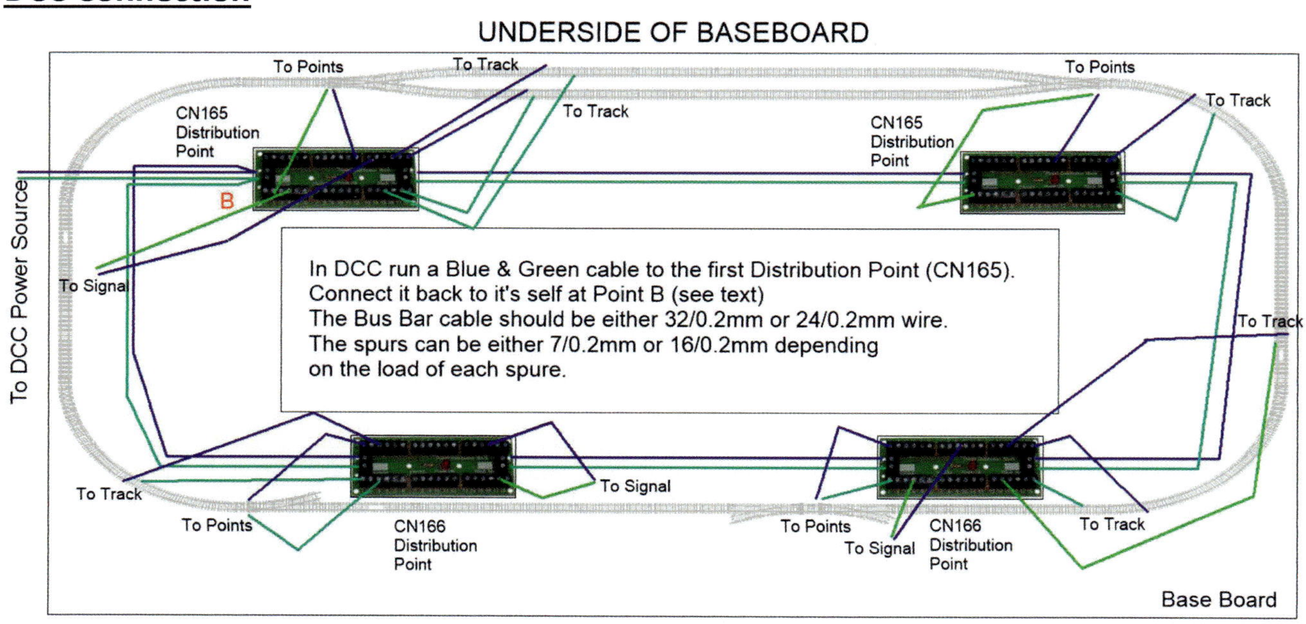

With a DCC system the two wires from the controller go to each section of track and each piece of equipment such as points and signals if all are DCC controlled.

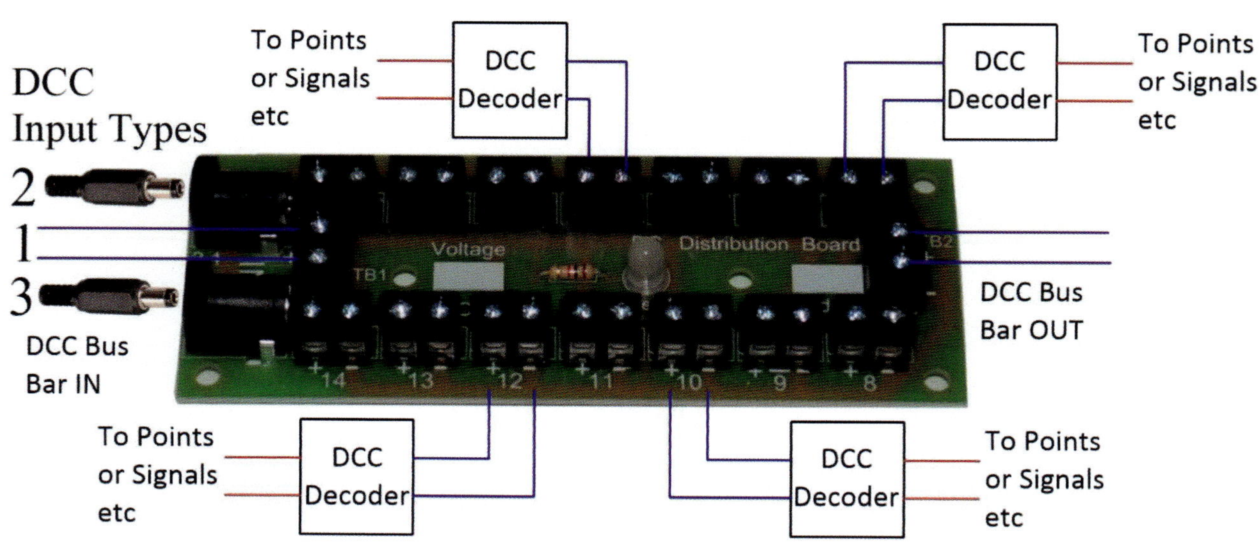

Remote Indication

In most cases this Distribution board is going to be on the underside of the baseboard. This means that you are not going to see the ON LED. If you want you can install a remote indicator on your panel. The Positive (RED) feed to the short pin on the LED, the negative feed through a dropping resistor to the long pin. The circuit below uses a Bi-coloured LED to give the three indications as mentioned above. You can if you want cut the Resistor in the centre of the board out to switch off the LED on the board, either way this circuit will work.

Fixing the Cable to the underside of the Baseboard.

There are a number of ways to fix your cables to the underside of your baseboard. The first one is a cable zip tie with a self-adhesive base, start with the zip tie at its maximum diameter so it's easy to thread the cables. The second one is an aluminium clamp which you just bend over the wings when you have your cables in place. The third one, is my preferred solution. The P clamps are screwed to the baseboard where required and the cable is threaded through. If the P clamp is a large diameter you can add cables at a latter date, and remove cables easily when you have a change of layout.

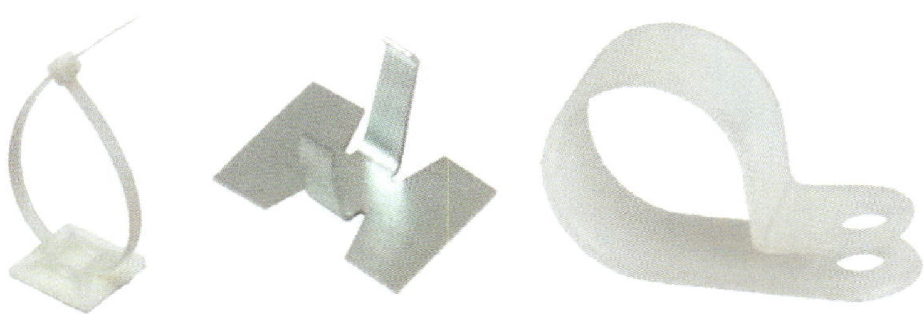

Detail C Terminal Connection

Short Equipment Wires.

The equipment you purchase will normally have short wires (100 to 200mm long) which inevitably will not reach your spur end point. In some cases you will have to have a secondary terminal block to extend the wires, care should be taken here as getting the polarity wrong just became a lot easier. The proprietary manufactures do not all use the same colour coding for Live, Neutral, and Da

MODEL RAILWAY PROJECTS

Automatic 2 Aspect Signal Control

The most common form of signal in Model Layouts is the 2 Aspect, this is because it is the easiest to wire up. In this project we will show you a few ways to automate this signal.
The basic way is to use the switch provided by the points manufacturer which sits on or is clipped to the point motor, some have a change over switch built into the motor.

1 2 3 4

This is a small sample of available Point Motors, No 1 has no switch capabilities so the switch needs to be placed elsewhere. No 2 can accept clip on switches. No3 has the switch on the printed circuit board. No 4 also has the switch built in.

1 2 3 4 5

Here are a few examples of switches No 1 Peco PL-15, No 2 Micro Roller Switch Brimal SW054, No 3 Leaf switch Brimal SWP100, No 4 Peco PL-14, No 5 Reed Switch Brimal SW926.
We will now show how to wire these switches to create automatic signals.

Peco PL-15 (1)

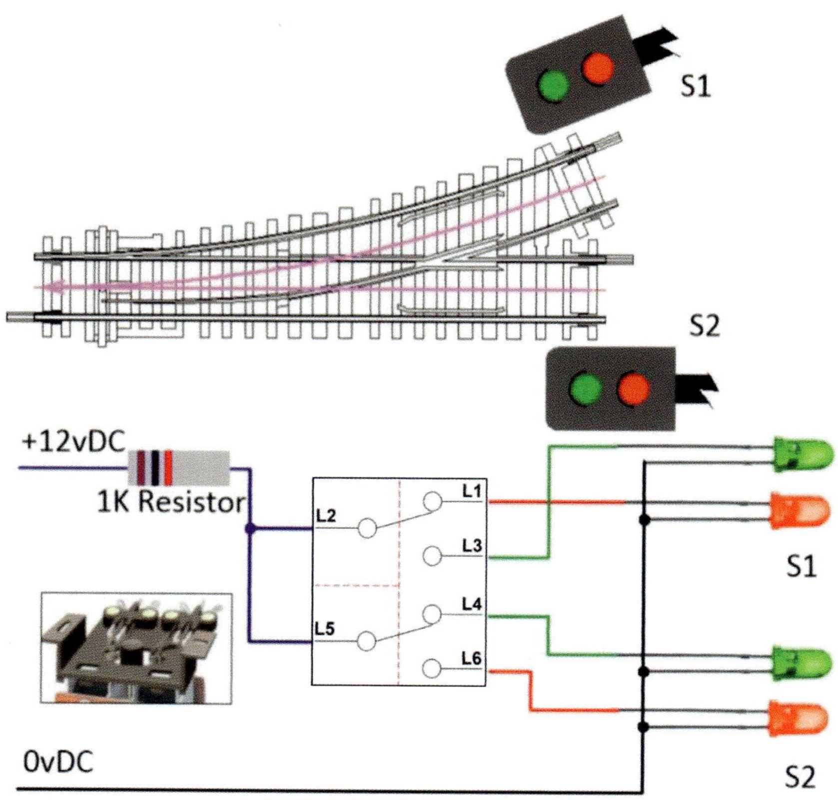

Fig 1

In the above circuit the PL-15 has two leaf switches which are controlled by the throw bar of the Point Motor.

These 2 leaf switches are changeover contacts so can control 2 signals giving the correct status.

Brimal SW054 (2)

This switch can be fixed next to the TIE BAR on the points, so as this moves it pushes against the Roller lever to change the status of the signal(s). The best way to fit this switch is to screw down through the top hole. You can then swivel the switch to get the best operation before fixing through the second hole.
Please note this example is using filament lamps so there is no dropping resistor on the 12v supply

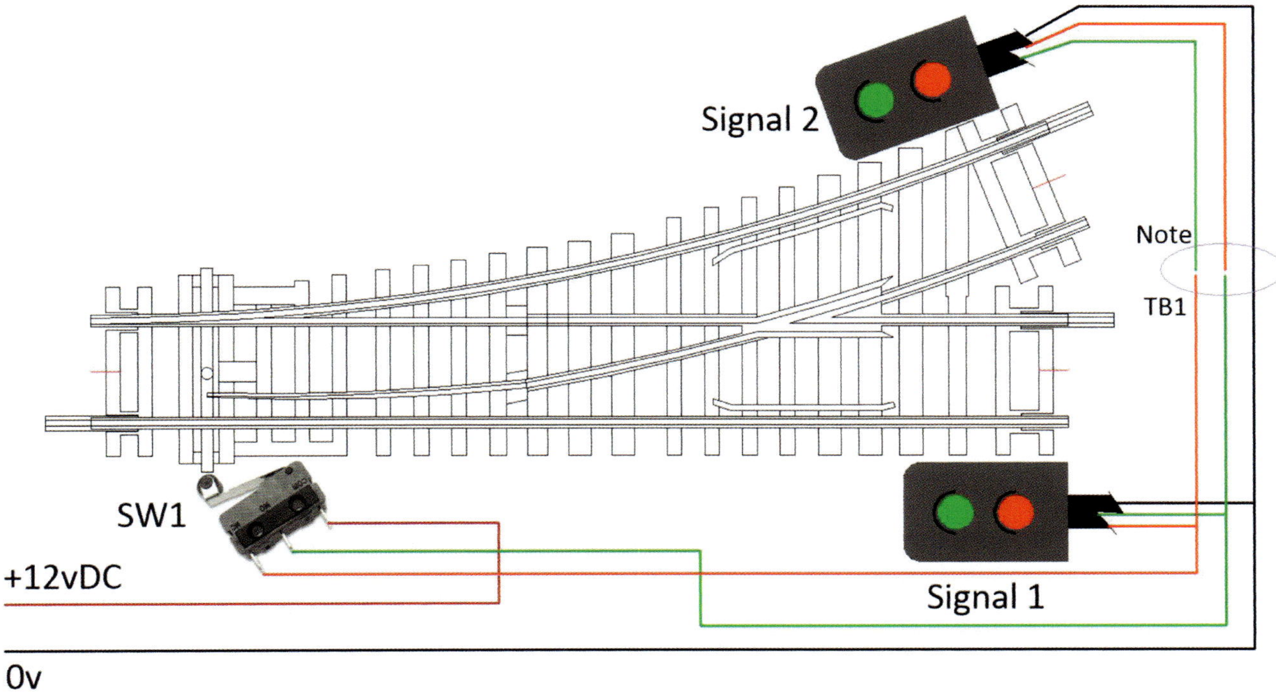

Fig: 2

Brimal SWP100 (3)

This switch is called a leaf switch or xxxxx, it is the same switch that Peco use in their PL-15, but sold separately. This switch can be fixed next to the TIE BAR on the points, so as this moves it pushes against the leaf switch to change the status of the signal(s). The best way to fit this switch is to screw down through the top hole. You can then swivel the switch to get the best operation before fixing through the second hole.
Please note this example is using filament lamps so there is no dropping resistor on the 12v supply

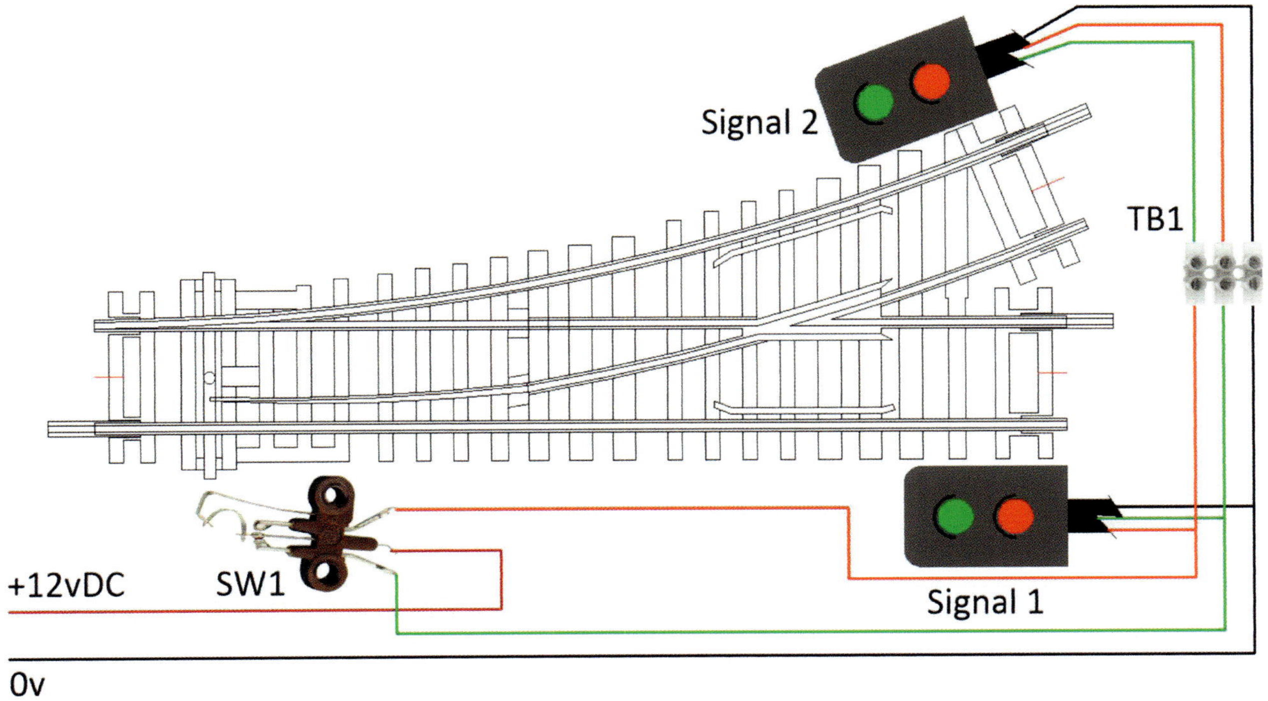

Fig: 3

Peco PL-13 (4)

The Peco PL-13 clips onto the Peco PL-10, Hornby R8014, Gaugemaster GMC-PM10, & Hatton PM-01 point motors. The circuit is as shown below, using a dropping resistor if you are using LED signals. The manufacturer will provide full wiring details with the product.

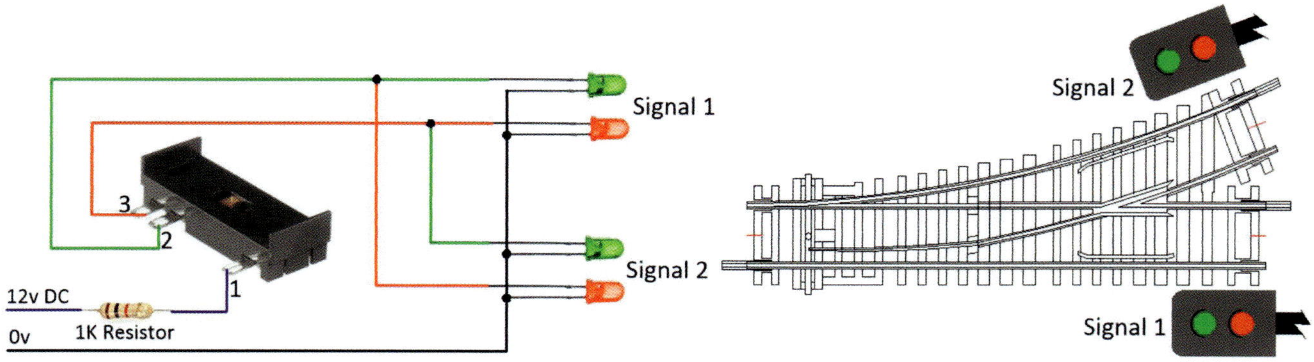

Fig: 4

Brimal SW928 (5)

Here we are using the SW928 Changeover Reed Switch to achieve the same as all the above.

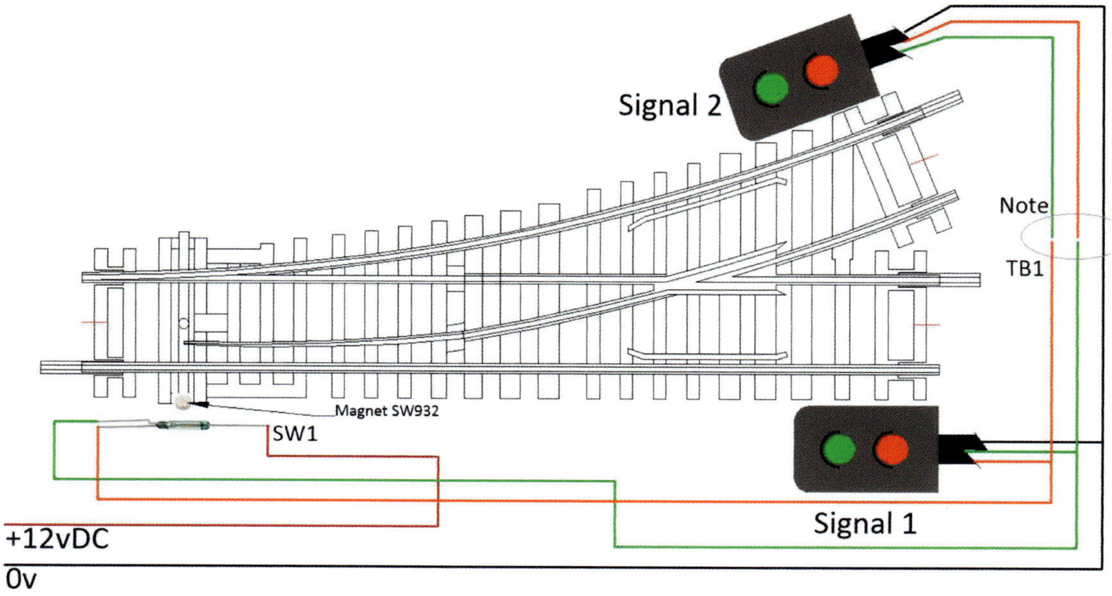

Fig: 5

Brimal SW929

The same circuit using the SW929 Encapsulated Changeover Reed switch.

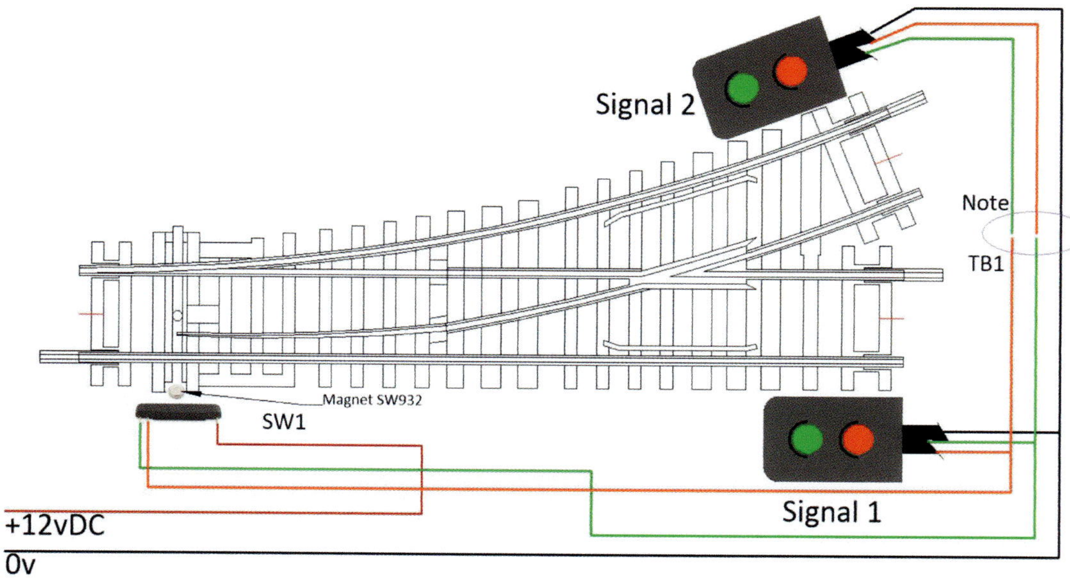

Fig: 6

High Current Relay

All the above have automated the signals by using a switch either on the point motor or beside the Tie Bar.
There will be cases where the switching capabilities of these switches is not enough to switch the signal lamps and you may have to introduce a relay to carry the higher current of the signal lamps. The MR221 is ideal for this. You now only need a NO (Normally Open Contact on the Reed switch, Leaf switch or Microswitch. This then powers the relay which in turn changes the status of the signals.

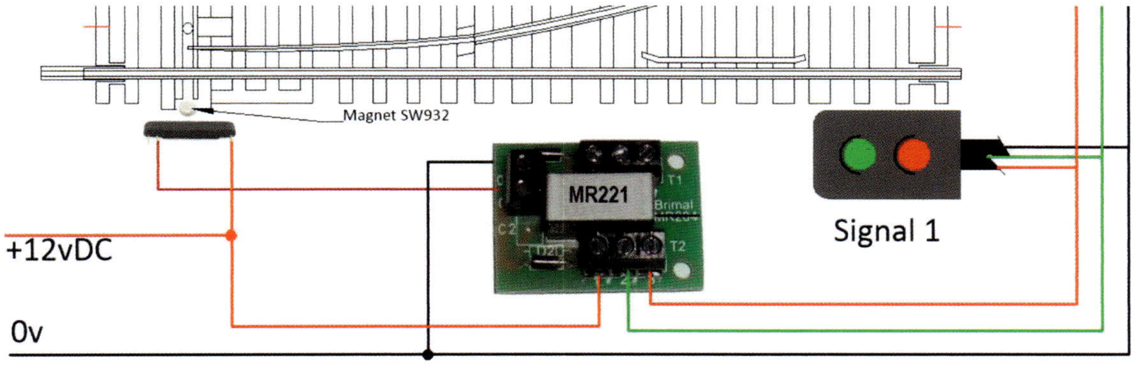

Fig: 7

Note: You will notice a 'Note on the above circuits this is to show that Signal 1 RED becomes Signal 2 Green, and Signal 1 Green becomes Signal 2 RED as the path through the points can only have one Green at a time.

Main Line Signals.

To automate main line signals the Loco must do this as it passes the signal. As the Loco is only going to be over the switch for a fraction of a second you will need something to keep the signal ON.
Firstly you need to fit a magnet to the underside of each Loco that is using this line. This could be the SW932 or the SW933, both need to glued to the underside of the Loco so that the gap between it and the switch is no more than 5mm.

Fig: 8

Fig: 9

The next is to fix the sensor between the rails. This will depend on the type of sensor being used, here are a few examples. The Blue sensor above will fit between the rails on HO,OO (SW927), the Blue cylindrical sensor can be fitted as shown from the underside with a 6mm hole. (SW901)

Fig: 10

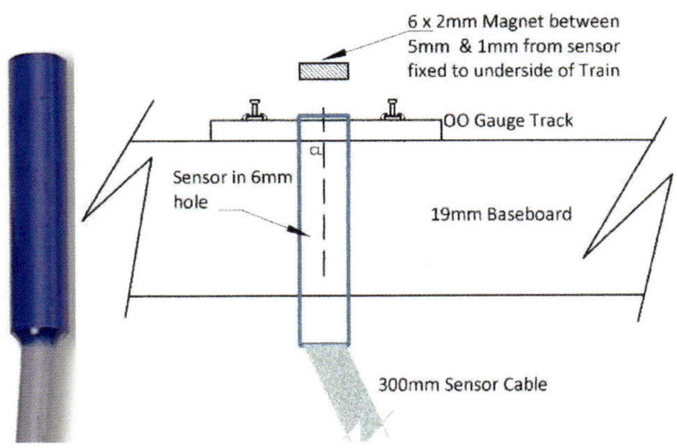

Fig: 11

The black sensor above is the same as the blue rectangular sensor. The cylindrical Blue sensor should be fitted as shown above right (SW925)

In the Next drawing the timer MR350 is powered by 12vDC supply which you could have switched ON/OFF locally. The sensor is placed between or on the sleepers, or if using the cylindrical sensor a 6mm hole through the baseboard, as shown above, The two wires from the sensor are wired into the timer unit START terminals 3 & 4, from the left. The 2 aspect signal is wired into one set of contacts on the relay. Note the Negative to the signal is directly off the common 0v Bus Bar. The positive to the relay can also come from a Bus Bar or connected as shown into the +v of the timer. The NC (Normally Closed) terminal is wired to the Green Lamp on the signal. The NO (Normally Open) terminal is wired to the Red Lamp. You will see that you have a spare set of contacts on the Relay, which could be used for another signal, isolating a section of track, or something else.
As the Loco passes over the Sensor this activates the timer, and changes the signal from Green to Red. It will remain Red now for a set time using the variable resistor (Preset) on the timer board. Set the length of the ON time or RED time to allow the full length of the train to pass the signal plus a little more.

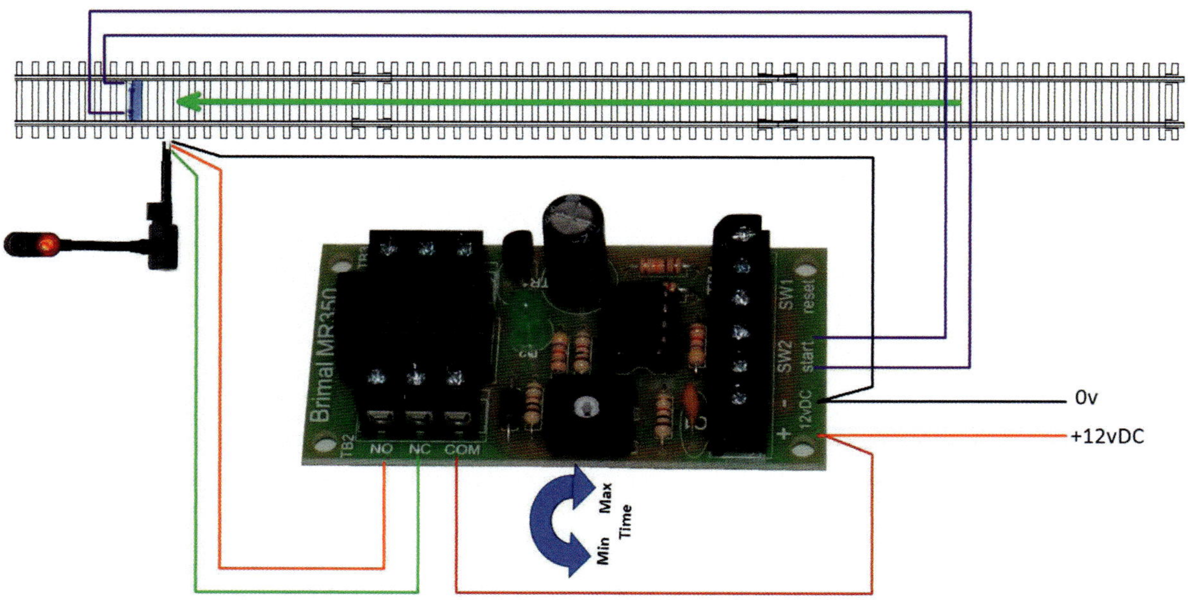

Fig: 12

If you have a large layout, you may have a number of Signals on the same line. In this case you can cascade the timers so that one Timer controls the next in line and so on.

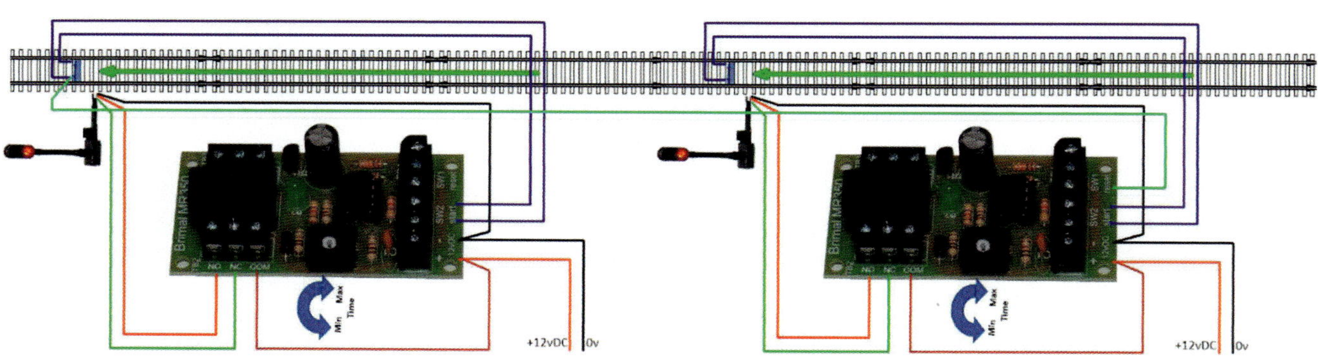

Fig: 13

The Light Green wire joins the two timers. In the above circuit when the left signal goes Red this will RESET the right hand timer to Green irrespective of the time left on the that timer. This can be repeated all around the layout if required.

Track Isolation

In all the above circuits there is a spare set of changeover contacts which can be used to Isolate the track behind the Train. If you have already used the above circuits on your layout then adding Isolation only requires inserting 'Isolation Fishplates' and a few wires. Let's see how this is done.

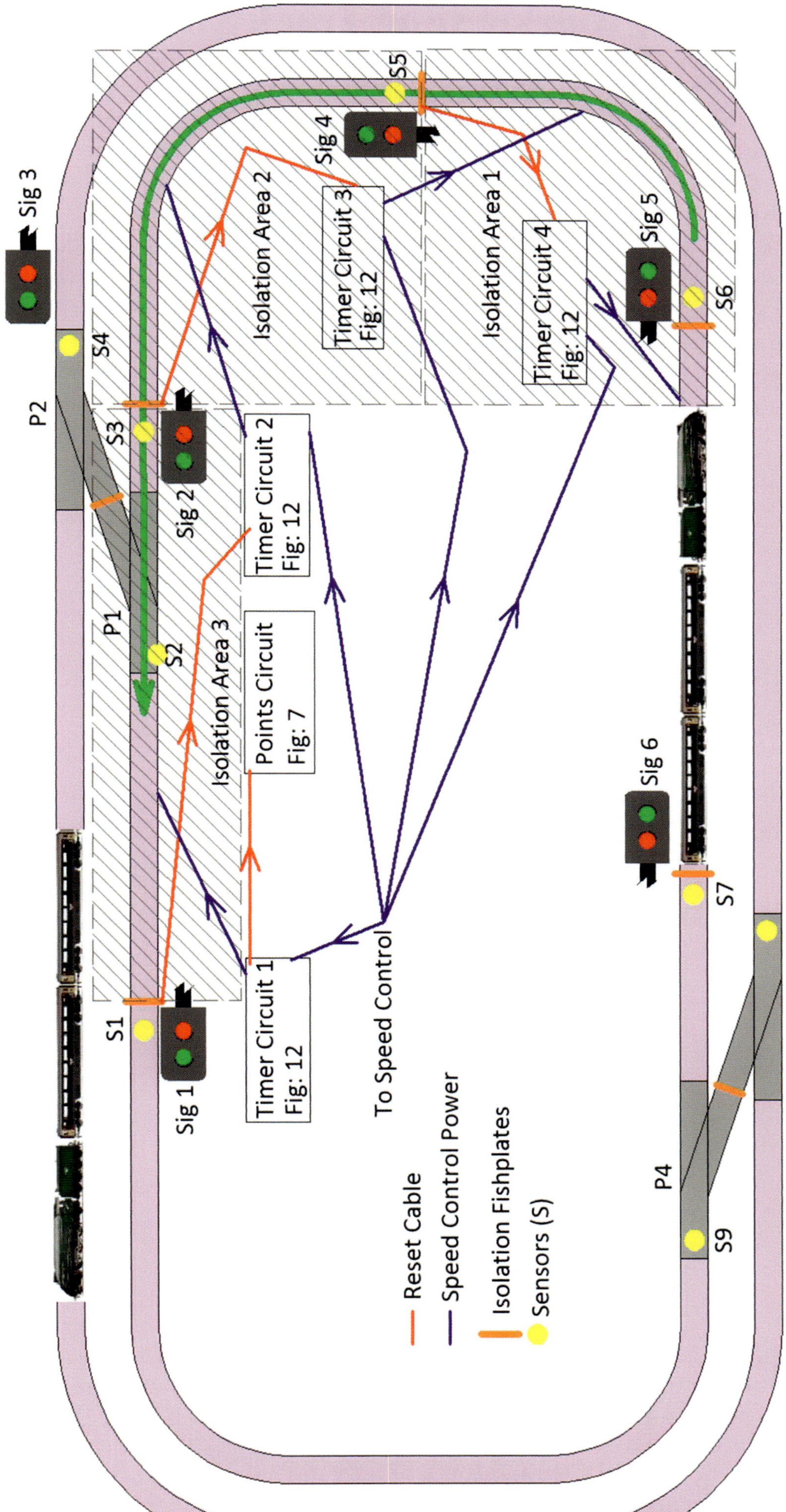
Sig 3
P2
S4
S3
Sig 2
P1
S2
S1
Sig 1
S5
Sig 4
Isolation Area 2
Timer Circuit 3
Fig: 12
Isolation Area 1
Timer Circuit 4
Fig: 12
Sig 5
S6
Timer Circuit 2
Fig: 12
Isolation Area 3
Points Circuit
Fig: 7
Timer Circuit 1
Fig: 12
To Speed Control
Sig 6
S7
S8
P3
P4
S9
Reset Cable
Speed Control Power
Isolation Fishplates
Sensors (S)

Programming Track Switch

Non Dedicated Programming Output

A Programming Track aids in programming multifunction decoders. They can be an independent segment, or a spur on your layout. They are used to safely program Multifunction Decoders using Service Mode. It is easier to have a portion of your layout track to double as a programming track, this allows you to simply drive your loco to the programming section, and read/change values of the decoder. It is best to have your programming track near the programming device (Command Station). Every layout should have a program track. It does not have to be on the layout, it could be a test track at the workbench. A dedicated programming output is usually only found on more sophisticated (very expensive) controllers. To prevent a locomotive from accidentally shorting the program track you need a section of track as shown below. The programming segment needs to be at least 50% longer than your longest locomotive and the isolating segment must be longer than your longest locomotive. The longer the programming track segment, the more useful it will be.

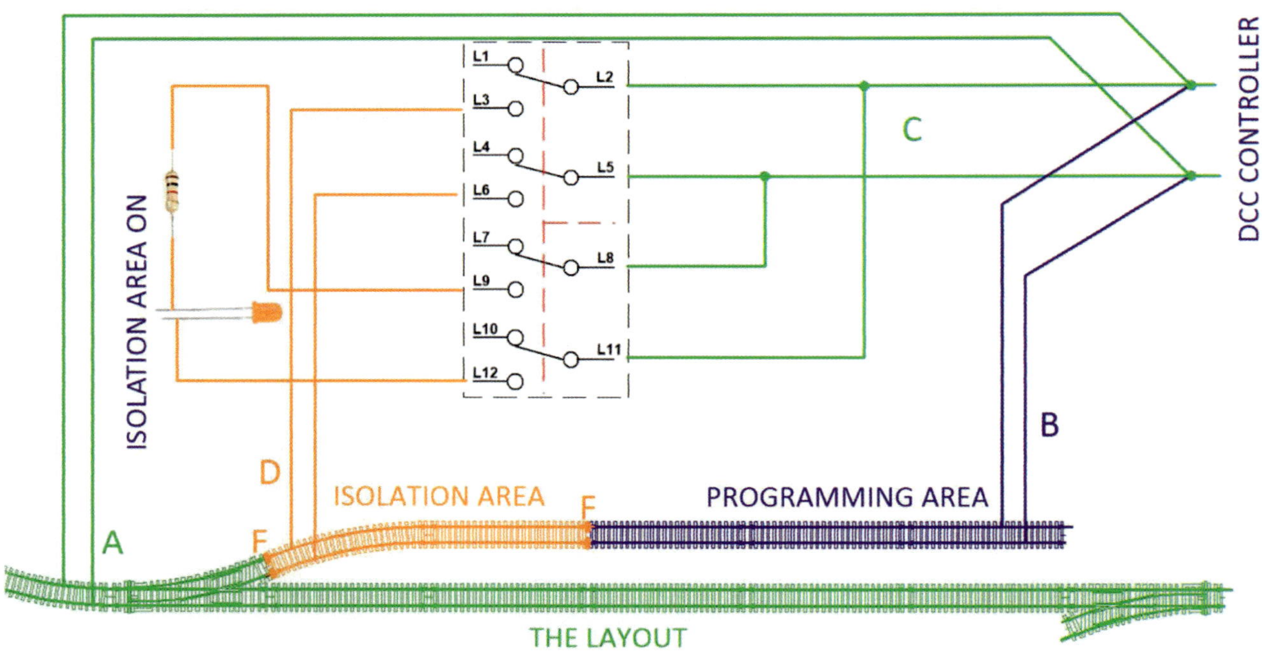

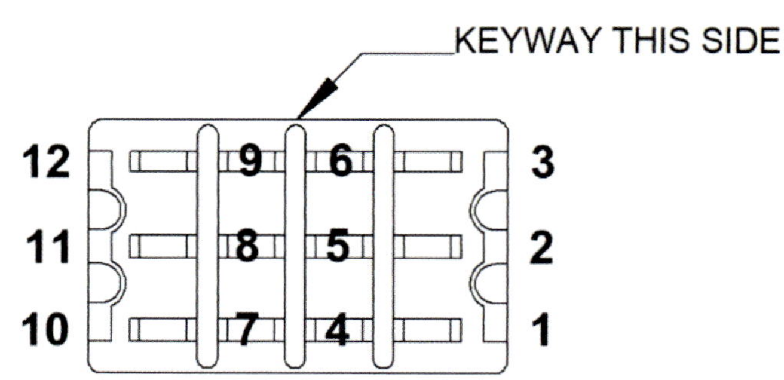

The switch being used here is a 4PDT (4 Pole Double Throw ON-OFF) switch, if you don't require the LED indicator a DPDT (Double Pole Double Throw) switch can be used. In the up position the Isolation Area is Live and the Amber LED is ON, in the down position the Isolation Area is OFF (isolated) and the LED is OFF.

The LED used is a Bi-colour red which will show Amber when connected to DCC, see parts list later

A) Wires from the Controller to the Layout.

B) Wires from the Controller to the Programming Area.

C) Wires from the Controller to the Control Switch.

D) Wires from the Control switch to the Isolation Area.

F) Isolation Points – either cut the track so there is no electrical connection or use the plastic Fishplates.

Dedicated Programming Output

If your DCC Controller has a dedicated 'Programming Output' then this circuit will switch it ON or switch it to Normal programmed Output. Any new, untried multifunction decoder install should *never* be placed on the layout, but first on the programming track. Should there be an error, the multifunction decoder will not be destroyed on the program track, due to the current limiting feature. The PROGRAM output on a Controller must never be connected to the **TRACK** Layout output!

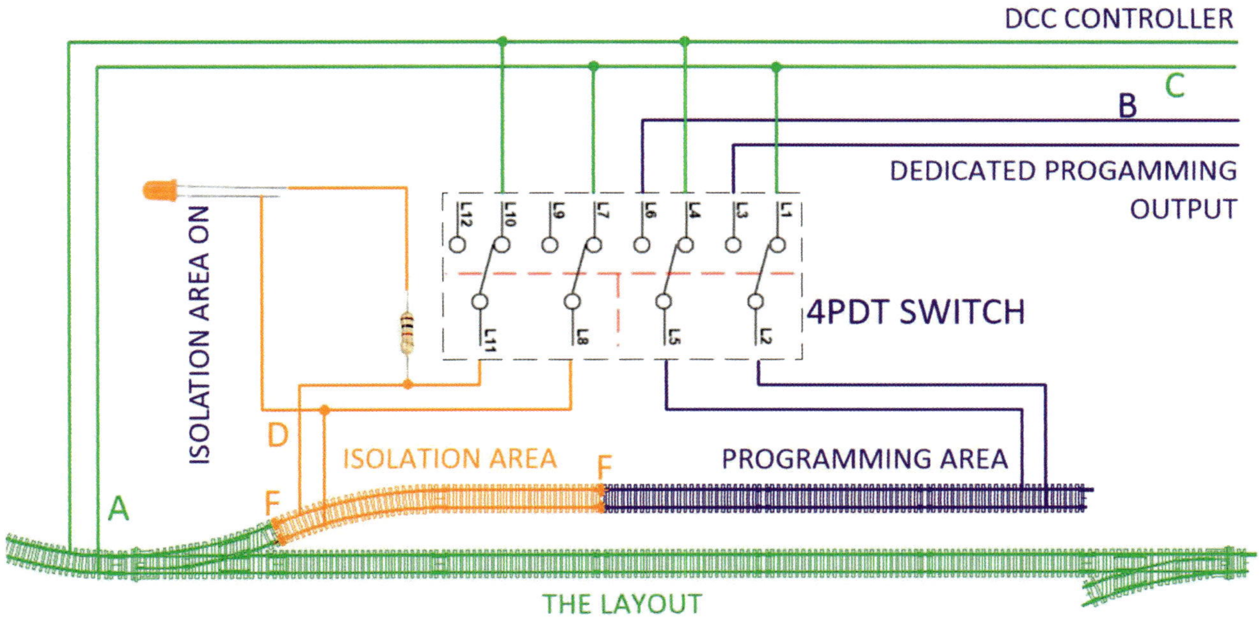

You will notice the wiring is somewhat different in this circuit. With the switch in the UP position all tracks have the DCC Controller connected as Green. When the switch is in the DOWN position the Green area is as shown the Isolation Area is not disconnected from the DCC controller and the Programming Area is connected to the Dedicated Programming Output of the Controller. The Amber LED is only ON when there is power on the Isolated Area.

Part List.

4DPDT Switch	Salecom T8401-SEBQ-H 4PDT	Brimal SW320
DPDT	Salecom T8011-SEBQ-H DPDT	Brimal SW315
Resistor	CR25 Resistor 1K	RE137
LED	Kingbright L-59EGW	LS111
Plastic Fishplates	By others	

3 Signal Junction

In this project we are using the point motor switches to simultaneously switch On & Off a relay which controls the Signal and Isolation. In the layout the trains travel from right to left, the Main Line being the centre line with signal S2 on it. With both P1 & P2 'Straight Through' signal S2 must show Green & S1 & S3 must show Red. If the train is conning from S1 then Both S1 & S3 should be Red, and if the train is coming from S3 then both S1 and S2 should be Red. Because this is controlled by the Point Motor switches then the points will be in the correct alignment with the signals.

	Sig 1	Sig 2	Sig 3
Straight	R	G	R
Turn P1	G	R	R
Turn P2	R	R	G

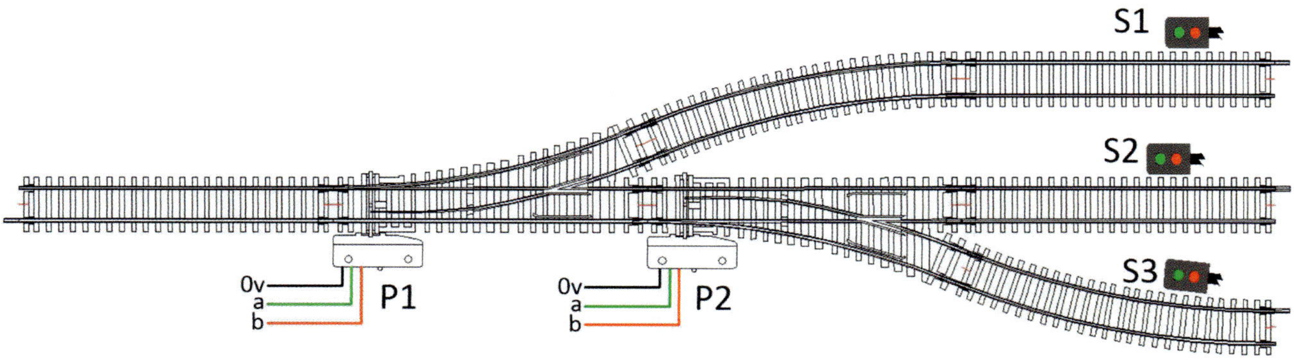

The circuit below shows the Point switches also controlling the 3 Relays, one for each signal. There is a spare set of changeover contacts on each of the relays, this could be used to isolate the track behind the signals. On the right of the circuit is the printed circuit board layout at actual size.

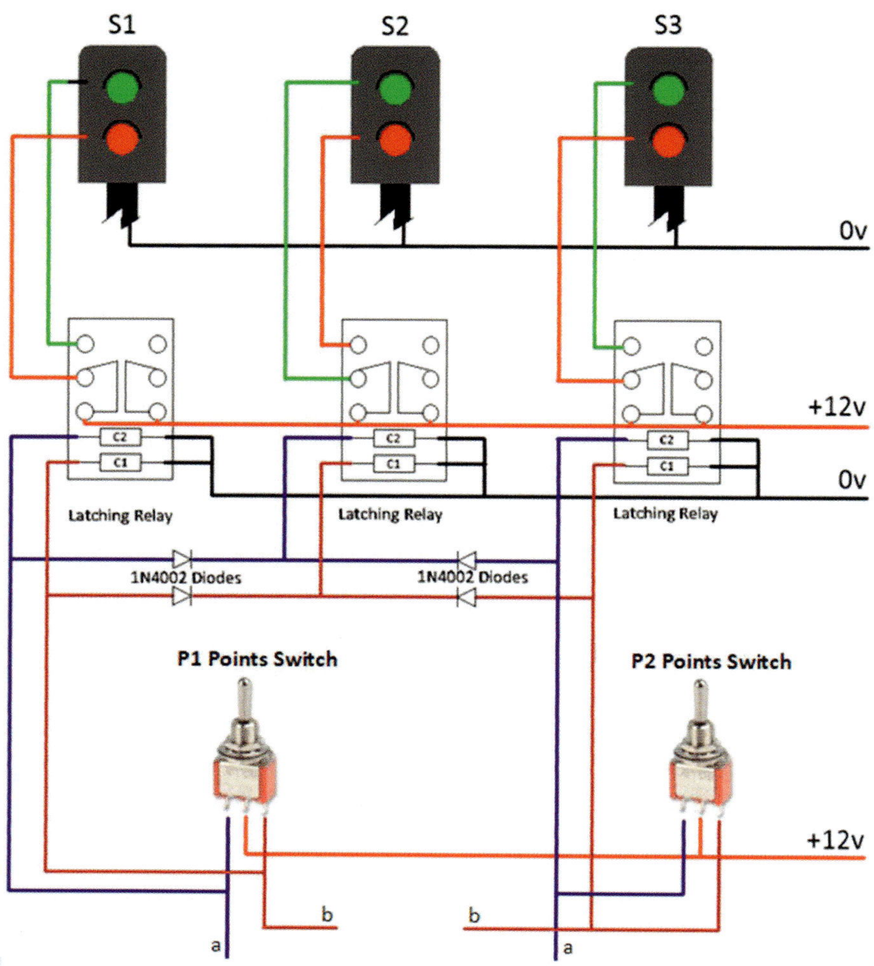

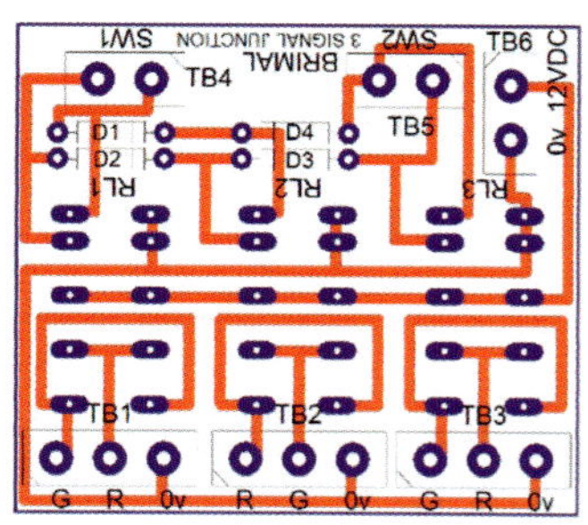

Using Infrared Sensors

PROJECT 58

Infrared sensing is fast becoming one of the more popular ways to sense movement on your model Rail layout. It is however a little more expensive than the traditional reed switch and magnet. There are many different types of sensors to suit all applications, but all need an interface circuit between them and the equipment you are controlling.

Here are a few sensors.

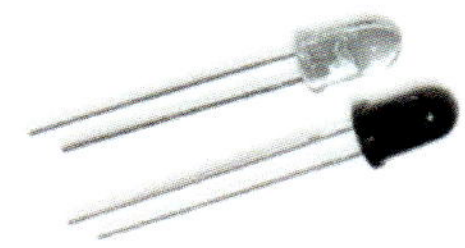

QRD1114 TCRT5000 QTR-1A IR LED's

These all need an interface circuit to operate them as shown below.

BOD2-RLY Brimal MR208/9 IOASM

The basic principle is the Infrared transmitter is continuously emitting a signal that is picked up by the Infrared Receiver. When this signal is received it activates the interface circuit.

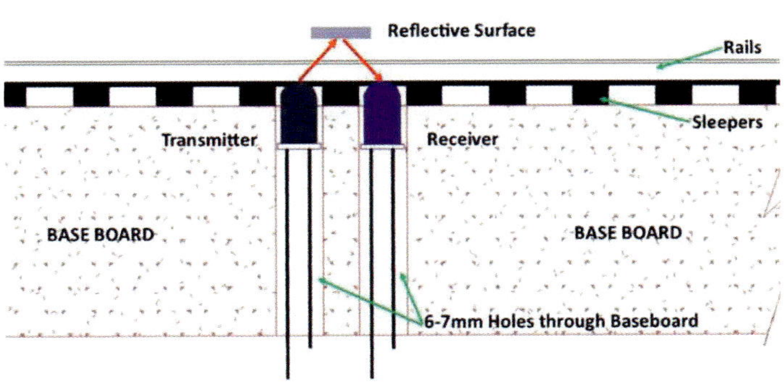

Individual IR LED's

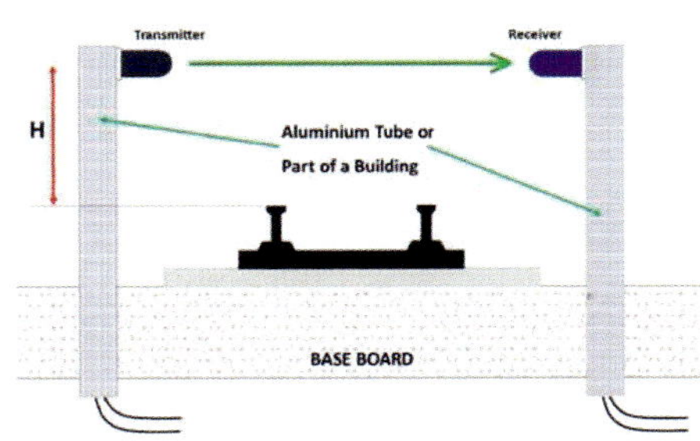

LED's fitted to Posts

In the following examples the sensor has been placed between the sleepers. The Loco is using magnets as the reflective surface as there are also reed switches in other parts of the layout .

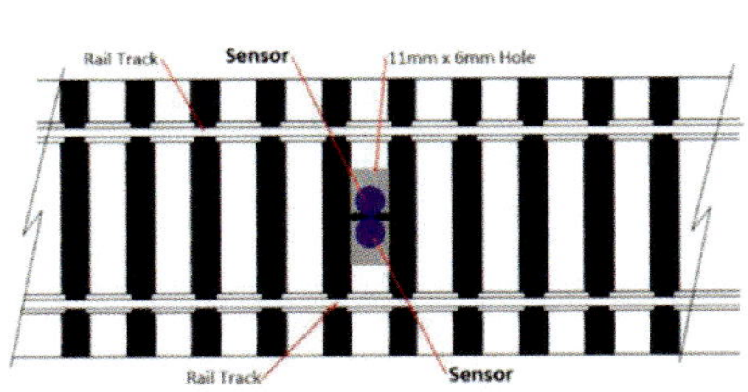

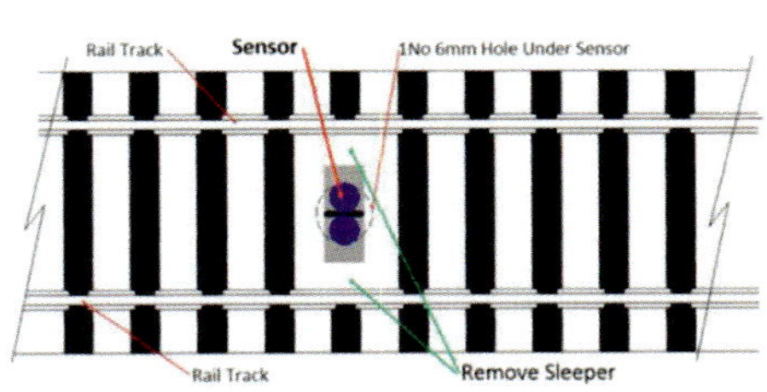

Images showing the TCRT5000

Now let's look at some applications.

The BOD2-RLY has a built-in infra-red detector which can "see" in the dark and can detect trains in these situations. The module has a small relay built-in. When a train crosses the sensor, the relay coil is energised and the relay common contact (labelled COM) moves from the normally-closed (NC) position to the normally open position NO. After the train clears the sensor, the module de-energises the relay and the relay contact moves to the normally-closed position.

MODEL RAILWAY PROJECTS

A delay can be set before this occurs to allow a train indication to remain present for a period, or the indication can immediately reset. The module can also be set to ignore the gaps between carriages. With a delay, the module can operate a two aspect signal, switching to red when a train crosses the sensor, and back to green a preset time after the sensor is cleared.

There are several programming options available (see later).

You can power the module from 8V-25V DC.. The module reduces the supply voltage down to 5V to feed attached led's, etc.

<u>Here it is used to drive a 2 Aspect Signal</u>

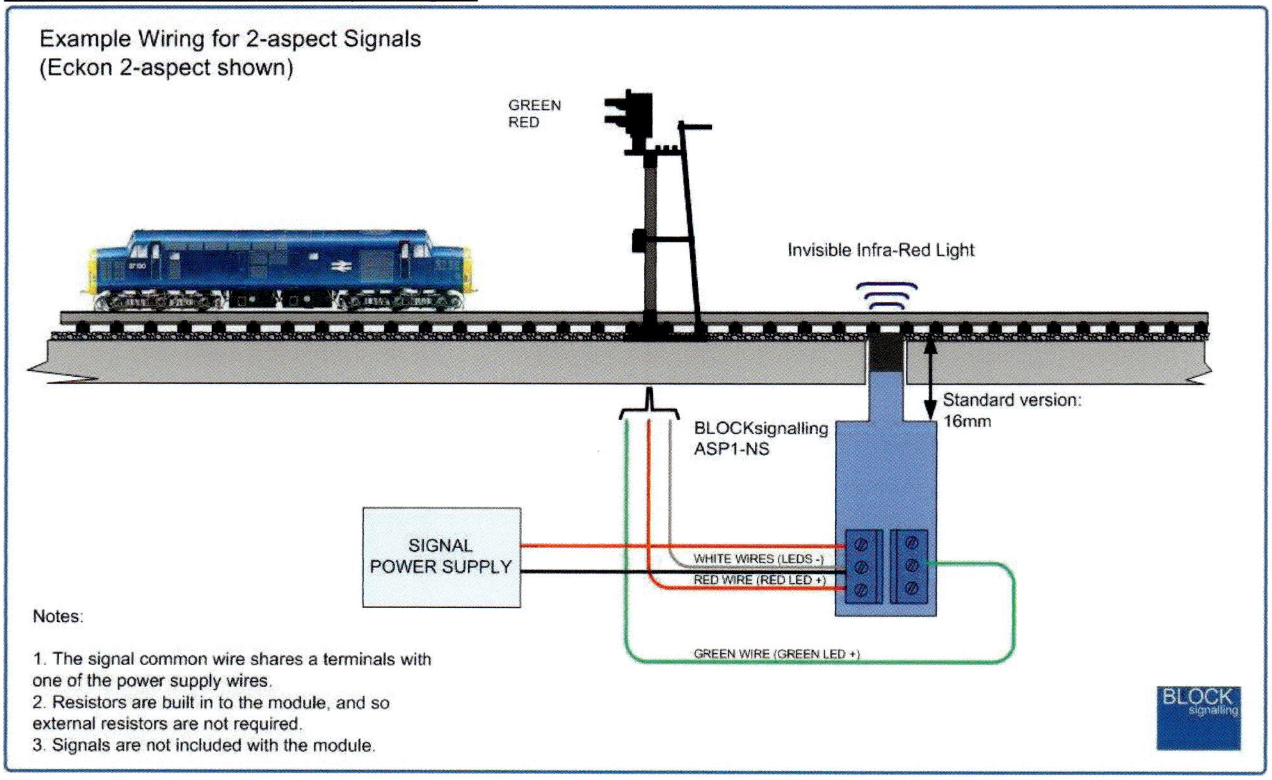

<u>The SRV1-NS controlling a Servo Motor</u>

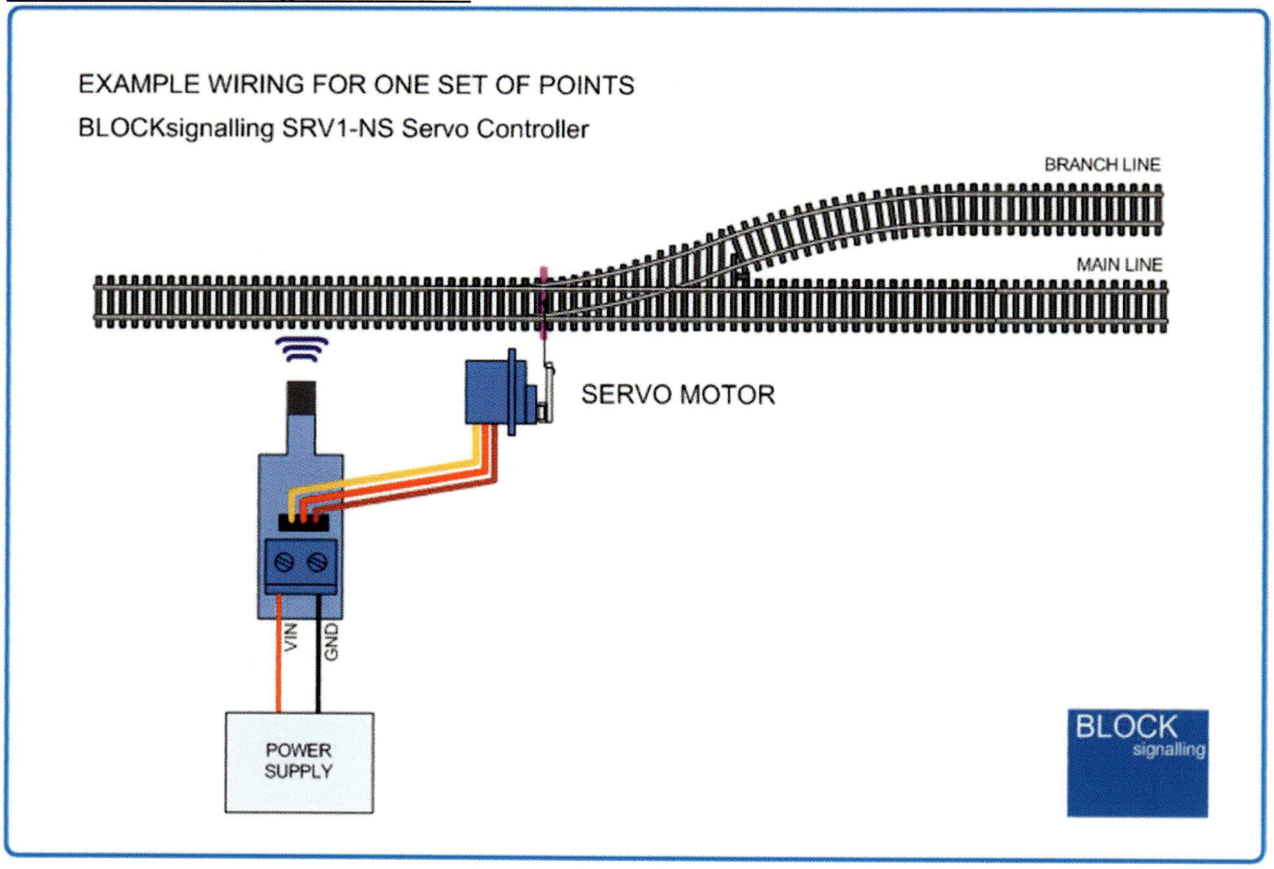

The MR208 can be used with a range of Sensors directly connected to the PCB or on flying leads so that the circuit can be positioned anywhere under the baseboard or near the control panel. It comes with a built in timer which will allow the RED signal to remain on for up to 20 seconds after the train has passed. This same relay can also be used to Isolate the track behind the signal for a period of time.

2 Aspect Signal

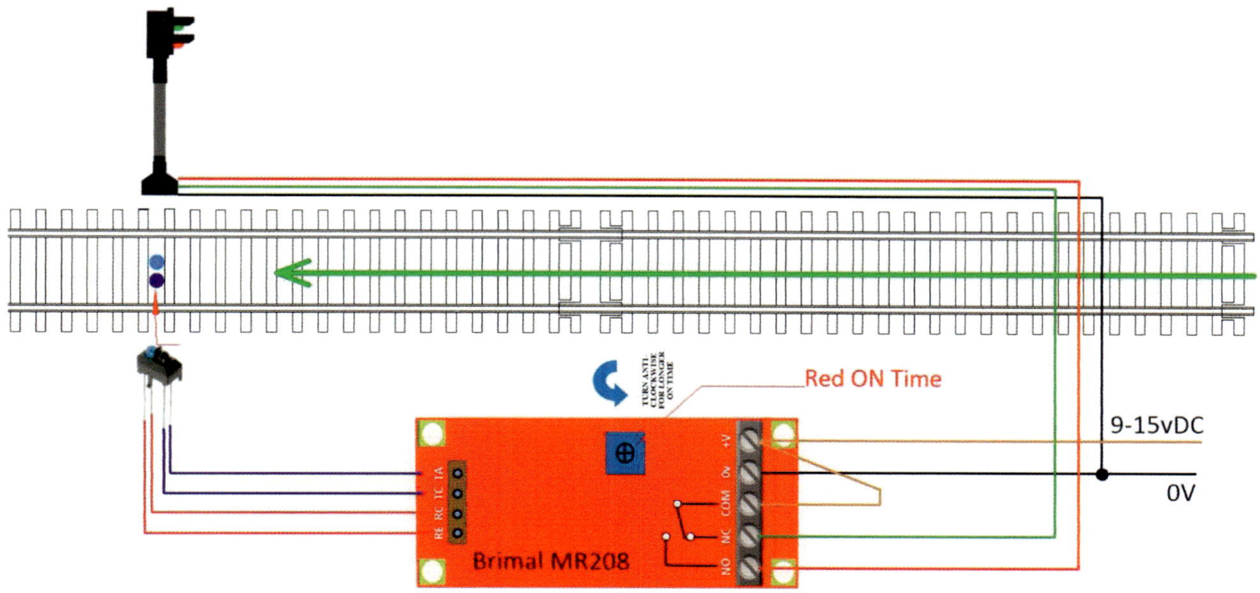

Siding Occupied

Here the Infrared is being used to detect a Train in a siding. As long as the train is over the sensor the relay will be ON and therefor the RED LED will be illuminated. If the timer is set close to '0' then as soon as the Train moves away the relay will switch OFF and the Green LED will be illuminated. You can use two separate LED's here or a 3 pin Bi-colour LED.

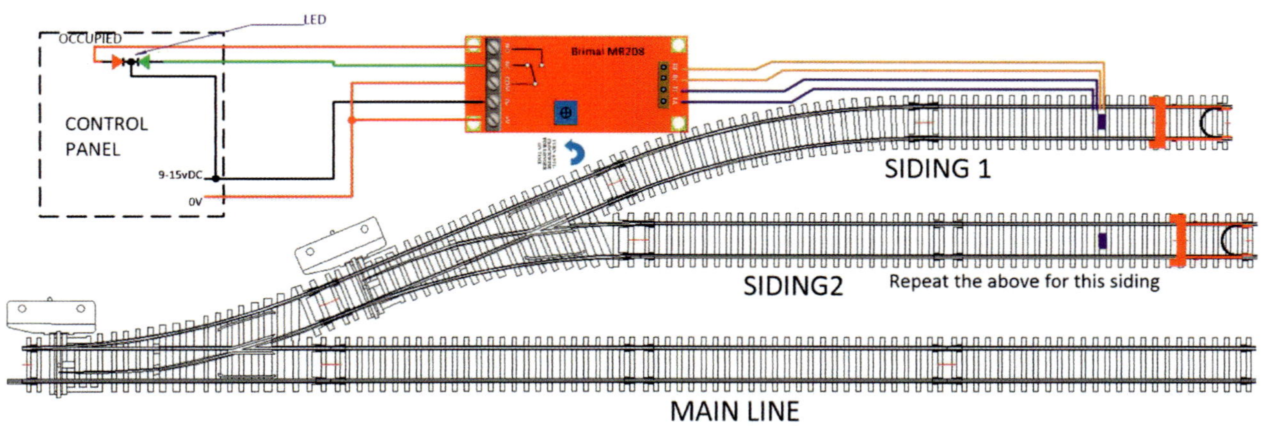

Other uses

Counter / Counting

There may be times when you will want to count how many times a Train goes around a layout, or how many carriages there are in a train length, to see if it will fit into a siding. Lets start with counting the laps of a train.

Counting Laps

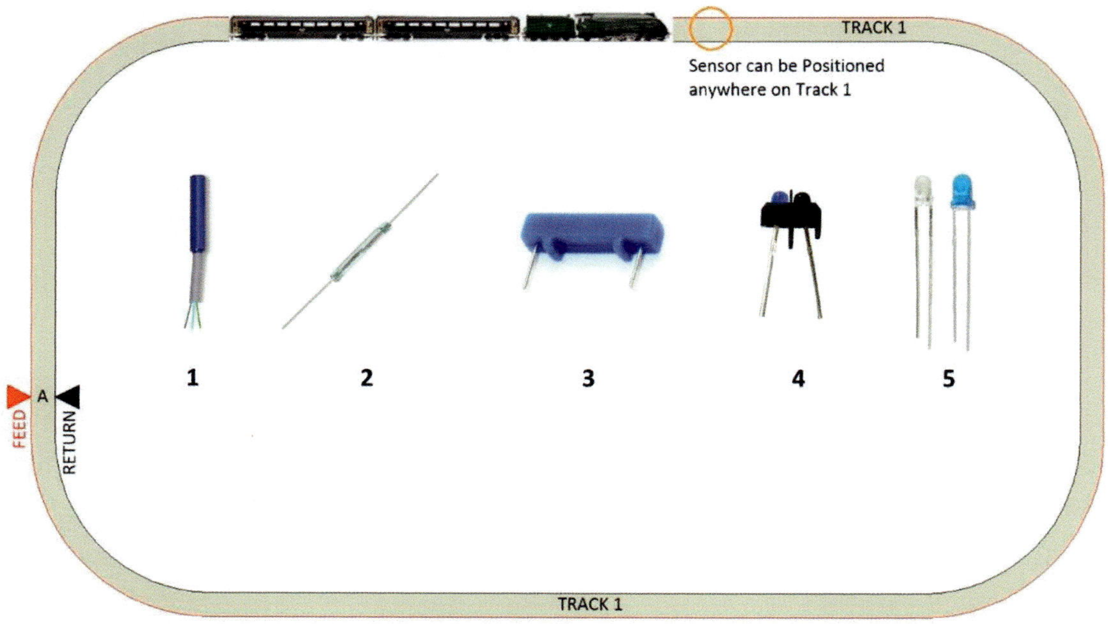

Sensors 1 to 3 are reed switches so require a magnet fitted to the underside of the Locomotive.

Sensor Type 1 SW910

This is by far the easiest to install, but unfortunately the most expensive. I requires a 6mm hole through the base board coming up between the sleepers.

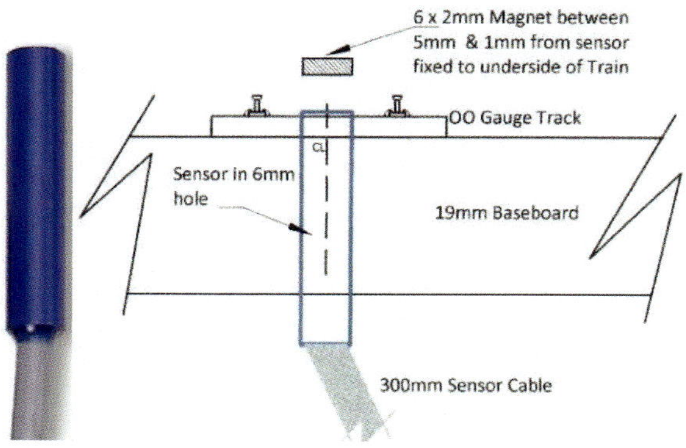

Sensor Type 2 SW925

This is a little more complicated to install as You will first have to cut the sleeper joiners under the rails. Then drill 2 holes 1.5mm approx. 5 mm from the rails to accept the wire from the reed switch. Before installing please add some heatshrink to each pin to insulated them from the rail track

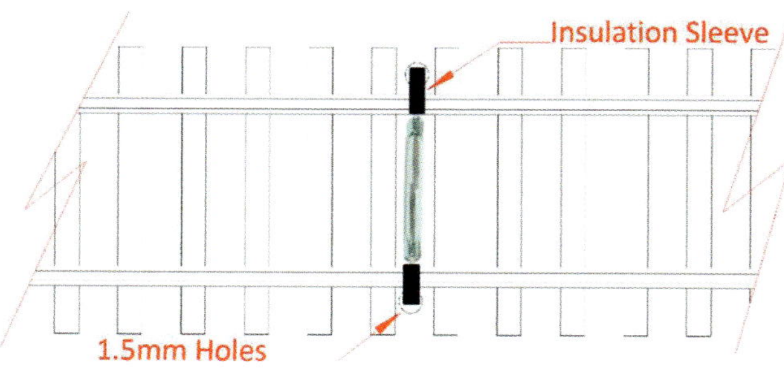

Sensor Type 3 SW923

This sensor fits between the rails on an 00 Gauge layout. It just requires 2 holes 1.5mm diameter drilled through the baseboard for the leads. Again any solder joints should be protected with some Heatshrink.

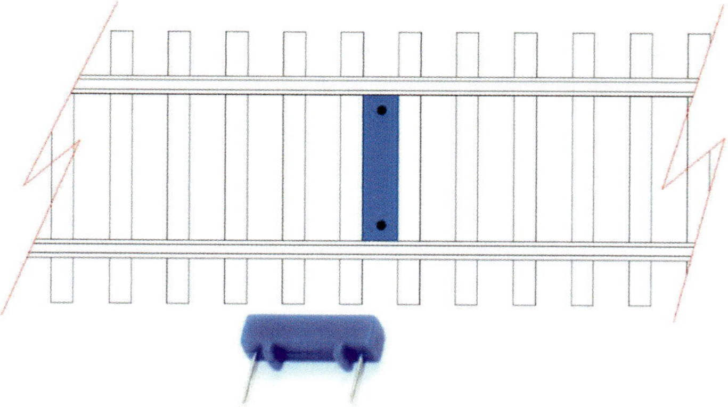

This is an example of the fitting of the magnet to the underside of the Locomotive. In this application we have used 2 magnets to bring the magnet down to within 5mm of the sensor. The same magnet can be used for the infrared reflective surface. This allows both systems to be used on your layout .

All three sensors work the same way, they all have a normally open contact which closes when the magnet is placed near to the reed switch. *So now the counting circuit.*

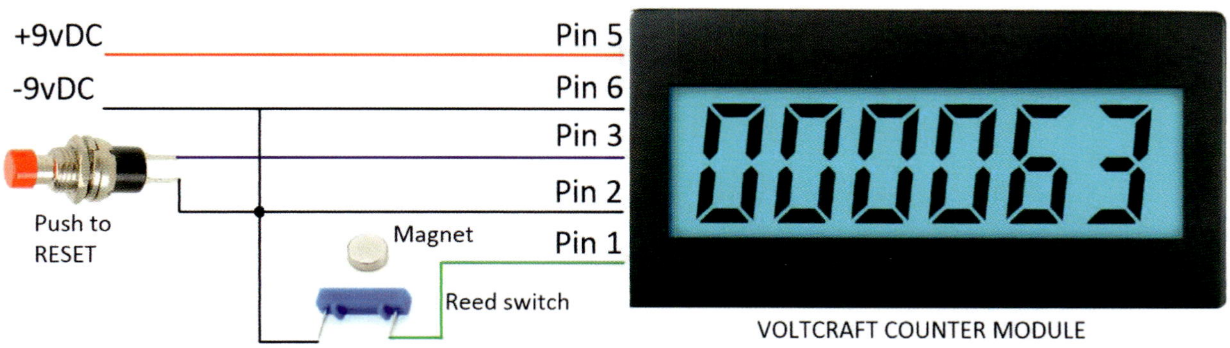

In the diagram above we are showing the SW923, however the circuit will be the same for all three types of Reed switch as long as it has a Normally Open contact (NO). The Reset button is a Normally Open push to make mini push button switch SW551. Please follow the manufacturers instruction on the usage of the Voltcraft Counter DCM220W.

Using Infrared Sensors

There are many types of Infrared sensors, which consist of a Transmitter and a Receiver. All sensors require an electronic circuit to transmit a signal and receive a signal, and act on it. There are a number of manufacturers of Infrared sensor equipment, we will concentrate on the one manufactured by Brimal the MR208.

The important thing to remember is the underside of the train or Locomotive must only have one reflective surface, otherwise it may be triggered more than once. The principle is explained in the following drawing. The Transmitter sends a signal which bounces off the reflective surface and is picked up by the Receiver to trigger the circuit. As it is Infrared it will work in normal daylight and in the darkness (tunnels)

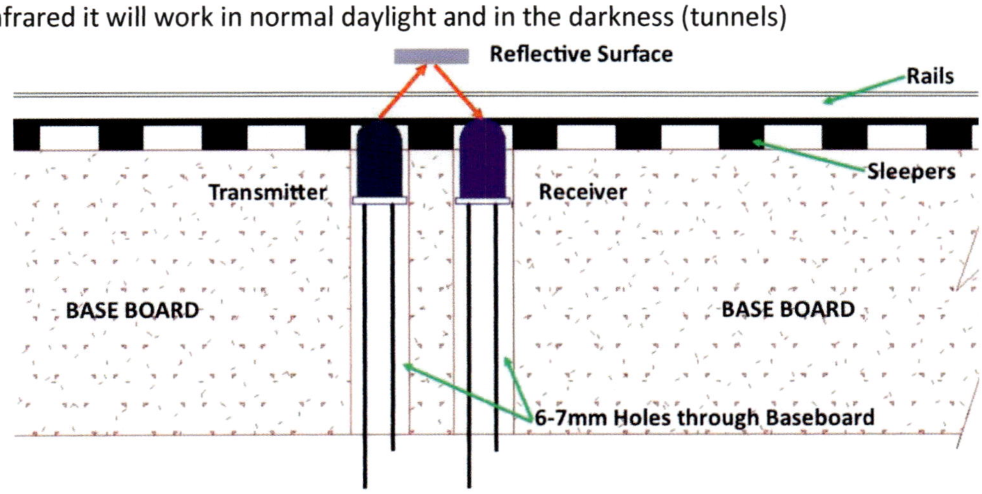

Sensor Type 4 SW700

This sensor will fit on the baseboard, you just need to cut one sleeper out and drill a 4mm hole under the unit for the 4 wires from the sensor.

The circuit for this sensor is as follows.

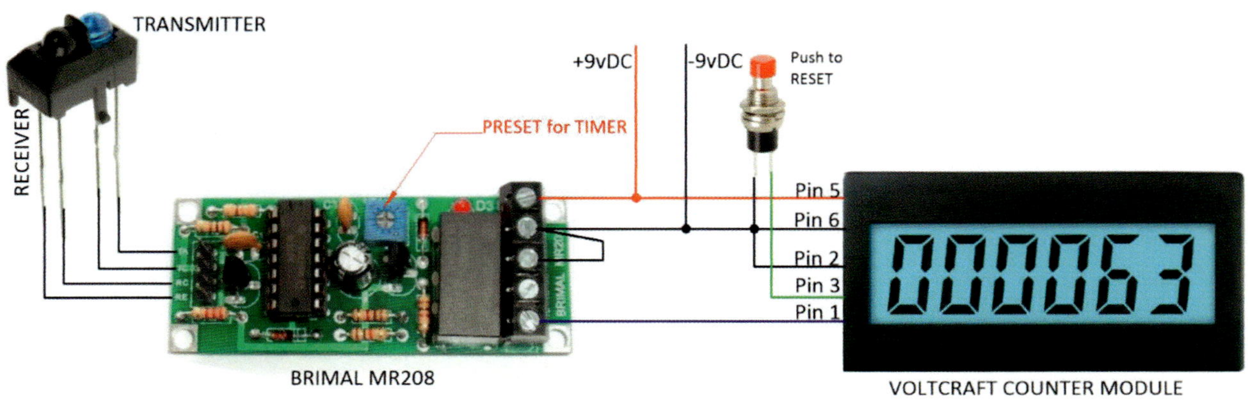

Each time a Locomotive passes over the sensor the relay will switch over for a fraction of a second, the counter will register one more. The PRESET shout be set for the minimum *Full anti-clockwise*. Opposite shows the wiring diagram for the 4 pins on the sensor That correspond with the lettering on the Printed Circuit Board.

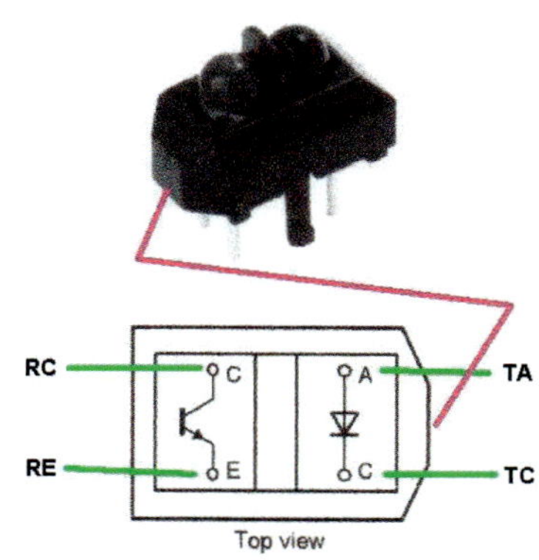

Counting Axles Sensor Type 5 SL710

In this application the sensors are epoxied into a 4mm Aluminium tube as shown below. The tube is fixed so that the Transmitter sees the Receiver just above the rails. This means each time a wheel blocks the signal the counter will register 1, and so on.

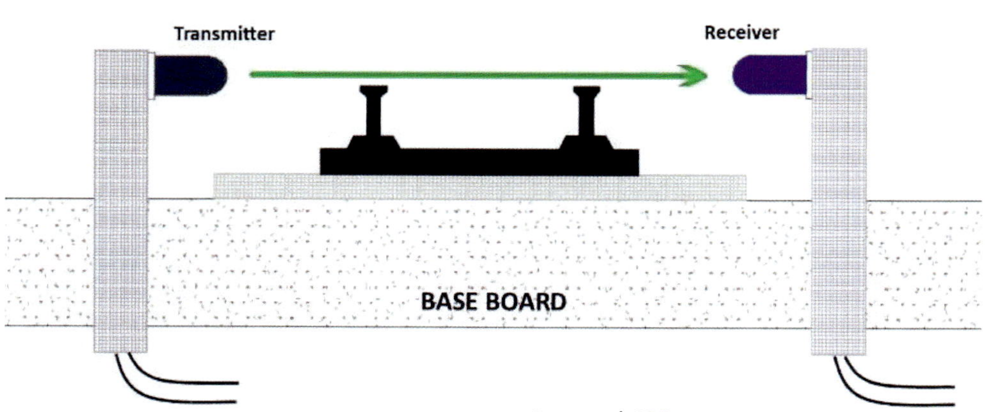

Counting Carriages Sensor Type 5 SL710

In this application the sensors are fixed at body height, lower than windows, but higher than the undercarriage. This means that the counter will register each time it is blocked by a Loco or Carriage.

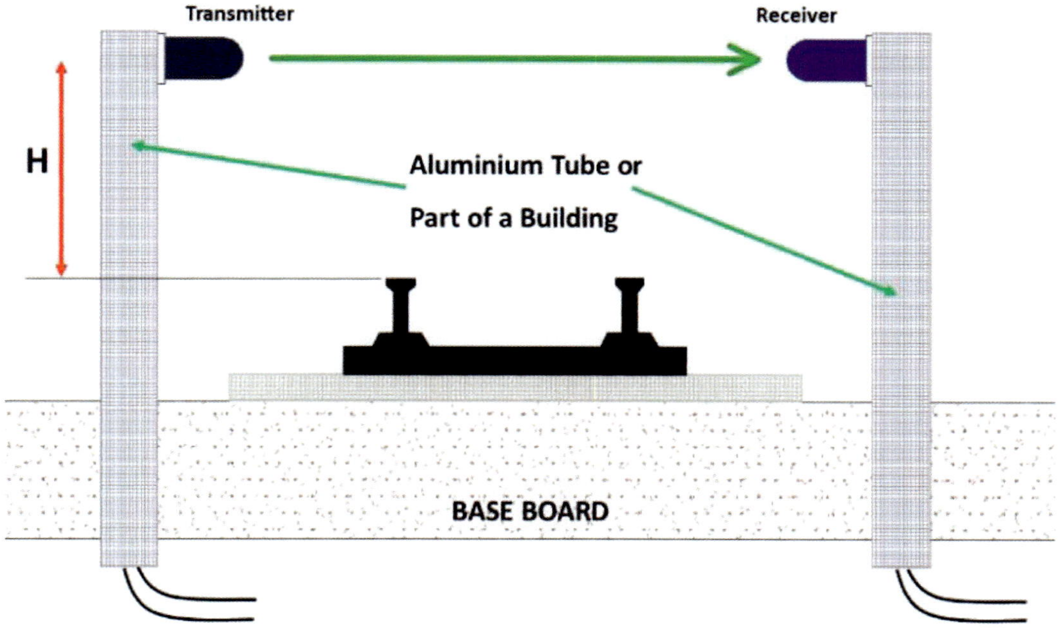

Both Sensors work in the same way
See circuit below.

The relay on the MR208 will be energised when the Receiver is activated, and will de-energise when the Receiver is no longer activated, as long as the Preset is set to 0 that is *fully anti-clockwise*. The trigger wire for the counter comes from the NO (Normally Open) contact. This means nothing is going to the counter until a gap between wheels or carriages is detected.

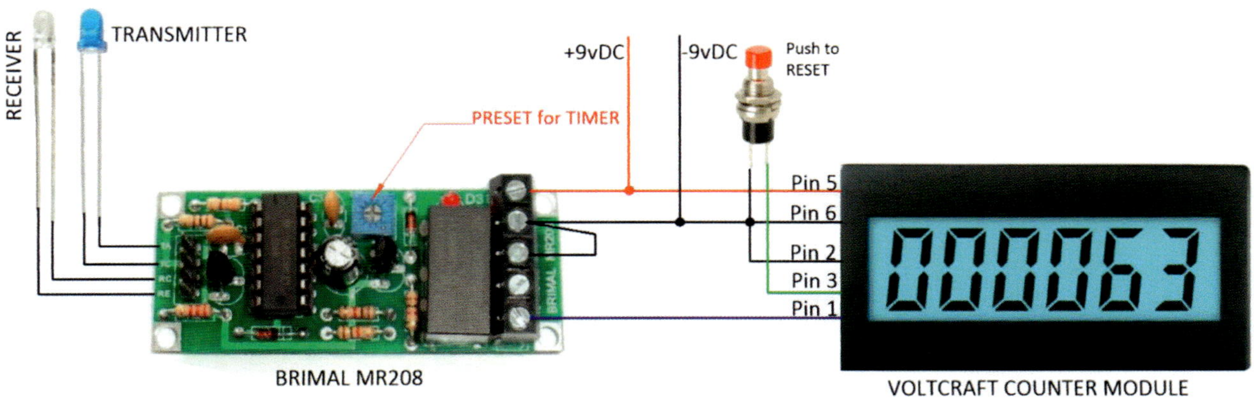

I am sure there are many other uses for counters on a Model Rail Layout. The principle will always be the same as long as you use a Negative pulse to activate the counter.

APPENDIX 1

Graph Paper

SQUARE =5mm X 5mm 5mm = ...

Graph Paper

SQUARE =5mm X 5mm 5mm = ...

Graph Paper

SQUARE =5mm X 5mm   5mm = ...

INDEX

NOTES: